INTERNATIONAL
SALVAGE
LAW

INTERNATIONAL SALVAGE LAW

By
ENRICO VINCENZINI
Advocate
CMI Titulary Member

TRANSLATION FROM THE ITALIAN BY
MARGARET DONALDSON

|L|L|P|
LONDON   NEW YORK   HAMBURG   HONG KONG
LLOYD'S OF LONDON PRESS LTD.
1992

Lloyd's of London Press Ltd.
Legal Publishing and Conferences Division
One Singer Street, London EC2A 4LQ

USA AND CANADA
Lloyd's of London Press Inc.
Suite 308, 611 Broadway
New York, NY 10012 USA

GERMANY
Lloyd's of London Press GmbH
59 Ehrenbergstrasse
2000 Hamburg 50, Germany

SOUTH EAST ASIA
Lloyd's of London Press (Far East) Ltd.
Room 1101, Hollywood Centre
233 Hollywood Road
Hong Kong

© Enrico Vincenzini 1987, 1992

First published in Great Britain
as *International Regulation of Salvage at Sea*, 1987
This edition completely revised and reset, 1992

British Library Cataloguing in Publication Data
A catalogue record for this book
is available from the British Library

ISBN 1–85044–401–3

Text set in 10 on 12pt Linotron 202 Times by
Promenade Graphics, Cheltenham, Glos.
Printed in Great Britain by
WBC Print Ltd.
Bridgend, Mid Glamorgan

*In memory of Tito Neri,
to whom I owe the discovery, many years
ago, of the fascinating world
of salvage at sea*

ACKNOWLEDGEMENTS

I wish to give my affectionate and grateful thanks for the help I was given in preparing this book to Professor Dante Gaeta, who was always more than generous with his suggestions and always ready to take on the burden of reading and commenting on my work.

I also thank my colleague Richard Olsen for sending, in good time, his interesting articles, which supplied me with a precious source of information, and the documents in English that I needed.

Again, my heartfelt thanks to my collaborators: Margaret Donaldson, for her usual accurate translation of the text into English, and Michela Resio and Cristina Bertagni for having accurately typed and corrected the text on the computer, in spite of the very short time I gave them to do so.

Finally, my particular thanks to my wife who, yet again, put up—with great patience—with my dawn arisings and the sacrifice of most of my free time, both of which were necessary in order to write this book without stealing from the time dedicated to my professional life.

ENRICO VINCENZINI

PREFACE

When, in his 1986 review (in *Diritto Marittimo*) of the Italian edition of *International Regulation of Salvage at Sea*, Francesco Berlingieri expressed the hope that I would complete my work once the new Convention of Salvage had seen the light of day. I am sure that even he, President of CMI and leading promoter of the 1981 Montreal Draft Convention, never expected the new Convention's approval to have been so promptly concluded.

So, following his suggestion and that of Richard Olsen (who, when reviewing the English edition of the book in *Lloyd's Maritime and Commercial Law Quarterly* in 1989, wrote, "It is to be hoped that a new edition of this excellent book will be produced in due course, continuing the story up to the 1989 Diplomatic Conference and the resulting Convention, and covering the introduction of the 1990 Edition of Lloyd's Form"), I decided to complete, in this new book, my study of the evolution of the law and of the contracts relating to salvage at sea in an international field.

I hope neither of my two friends will be disappointed.

ENRICO VINCENZINI

CONTENTS

PART TWO—THE MOVEMENT FOR CHANGE IN THE LAW OF SALVAGE AT SEA

Chapter Three—Salvage at sea in international contractual practice (LOF 1980)

Chapter Four—Salvage at sea in the Comité Maritime International Draft international Convention (Montreal 1981)

PART THREE—ACCOMPLISHING THE REFORM OF INTERNATIONAL SALVAGE LAW AND ITS CONSEQUENCES

Chapter Five—The London International Convention on Salvage 1989 and its sphere of application

BIBLIOGRAPHY

Abecassis, *Law and Practice Relating to Oil Pollution from Ships* (London, 1978).

——, "Some topical considerations in the event of a casualty to an oil tanker" in [1979] L.M.C.L.Q. 940.

——, "The Patmos" in [1985] L.M.C.L.Q. 382.

Abraham, *Das Seerecht* (Berlin, 1960).

Albano, "Ricupero, ritrovamento di relitti e occupazione di cose abbandonate in mare" in Riv. Dir. Nav., 1954, II, 88.

Allen, "International Convention on Salvage and LOF 90" in *11th International Tug Convention and International Marine Salvage Symposium* (Halifax, 1990, Surrey, 1991), 127.

Alpa, *La Responsabilità della Impresa per i Danni all'Ambiente ed al Consumatore* (Milan, 1978), 177.

Arena, "Il risultato utile nella assistenza e salvataggio ad opera di una pluralità di soccorritori" in Riv. Dir. Nav., 1963, I, 51.

Arnould, *The Law of Marine Insurance* (London, 1961).

Benfante, *Il salvamento e l'assistenza nel diritto marittimo* (Turin, 1889).

Berlingieri, F., "Dell'assistenza ad opera di navi da guerra" in Dir. Mar., 1948, 423.

——, "Sul debitore del compenso di assistenza e salvataggio" in Dir. Mar, 1954, 425.

——, "Problemi connessi con l'entrata in vigore in Italia della Convenzione di Bruxelles del 29 novembre 1969 sulla responsabilità civile per danni derivanti da inquinamento da idrocarburi" in Dir. Mar., 1979, 307.

——, "La XXXII Conferenza del CMI, Montreal 28–29 Maggio 1981" in Dir. Mar., 1981, 297.

——, "Le projet d'une nouvelle convention sur l'assistance et les sauvatages d'épaves maritime" in Dir. Mar., 1988, 1.

——, "Maritime liens and mortgages and related matters" in *CMI News Letter*, April 1990, 2.

Berlingieri, G., "Assistenza e Salvataggio" in *Nuovo Digesto Italiano*, 996.

——, "Compenso per salvataggio di persone in mare e assicurazione" in Dir. Mar., 1960, 311.

Berlingieri, G., "Revisione dell'art. 14 della Convenzione di Bruxelles del 1910 sull'assistenza e salvataggio delle navi in mare" in Dir. Mar., 1959, 429.

——, "Salvataggio e assistenza marittima in acque interne ed aerea", in Dir. Mar. 1967, 8.

——, *Studi in onore di F. Berlingieri* (Rome, 1983).

Berlingieri, R., "Salvataggio e assistenza, ricupero e ritrovamento di relitti della navigazione" in *Novissimo Digesto Italiano App.*, Vol. VI, 922.

Bessemer Clark, "The role of Lloyd's Open Form" in [1980] L.M.C.L.Q. 293.

Boglione, "Salvataggio, LOF 1980 e misure antinquinamento, deducibilità dei relativi oneri in avaria generale, e loro ripartizione tra assicuratori corpo e merce e P. and I. della nave" in Dir. Mar., 1983, 594.

Boi, "Brevi note sui rimorchiatori adibiti ad operazioni di soccorso" in Dir. Mar., 1974, 587.

Brice, *Maritime Law of Salvage* (London, 1983).

——, "The New Salvage Convention: green seas and grey areas" in [1990] L.M.C.L.Q. 32.

Brocker, *1910 Salvage Convention and Lloyd's Open Form under Pressure* (Rotterdam, 1983).

Brown, "Has the keel been laid for liability salvage in Fifth Circuit?" in 19 *Journal of Maritime Law and Commerce*, 1988, 583.

Bruce, "Treasure Salvage beyond the Territorial Sea" in 20 *Journal of Maritime Law and Commerce*, 1989, 1.

Brunetti, "Il caso dell'Atlantique ed il compenso ai salvatori nel diritto francese e italiano" in *Studi in onore di F. Berlingieri* (Rome, 1933).

Buccisano, *L'invenzione di cose perdute* (Milan, 1963).

Caliendo, "Osservazioni sul progetto di Convenzione IMO in materia di assistenza e salvataggio" in *Trasporti*, 1988, II, 153.

Carbone, *La disciplina giuridica del traffico marittimo internazionale* (Bologna, 1982).

Carbone & D'Angelo, *Cooperazione tra imprese e appalto internazionale* (Milan, 1991).

Carver, Carriage by Sea (London, 1963).

Chaveau, *Traité de droit maritime* (Paris, 1958).

——, "Sauvetage et remorquage devant les tribunaux francaise" in Dir. Mar., 1964, 154.

Chorley & Giles, *Shipping Law* (London, 1963).

Cobianchi, "Sul diritto e compenso degli ufficiali della R. Marina per l'assistenza prestata a navi da guerra" in Dir. Mar., 1939, 557.

Cohen, "Revisions of TOVALOP and CRISTAL: Strong ships for stormy seas" in *Journal of Maritime Law and Commerce*, 1987, 525.

Colinvaux, The Law of Insurance (London, 1984).

Comenale Pinto, "La responsabilità per inquinamento da idrocarburi fuorius-
  citi da navi e il regime di norme di diritto uniforme" in *Diritto dei Trasporti*,
  1990, I, II.
Congoon, *On General Average* (New York, 1952).
Coulthard, "A new cure for salvors? A comparative analysis of the LOF 1980
  and the CMI Draft Salvage Convention" in *Journal of Maritime Law and
  Commerce*, vol. 14, 1983, 47.
Crisafulli Buscemi, *I contratti di utilizzazione della nave: il contratto di rimor-
  chio* (Rome, 1973).
Dani, "In tema di responsabilità del soccorritore" in Dir. Mar., 1972, 435.
——, "In tema di flotilla rule" in Dir. Mar., 1977, 107.
——, *Responsabilità limitata per crediti marittimi* (Milan, 1983).
Darling & Smith, *LOF 90 and the New Salvage Convention* (London, Lloyd's
  of London Press Ltd., 1991).
Dawson, "Negotiorum gestio, the altruistic intermeddler" in *The Harvard
  Law Review*, 1961, No. 5, 817.
De Cupis, "Trovamento dei relitti marittimi e aeronautici" in Riv. Dir. Nav.,
  1955, I, 117.
De Juglart & Villeneau, *Répertoire méthodique et pratique de l'assistance en
  mer* (Paris, 1962).
Diena, *Principi del diritto internazionale privato marittimo* (Milan, 1955).
Dubais, "The liability of a salvor responsible for oil pollution damage" in
  Journal of Maritime Law and Commerce, 1977, 375.
Ferrarini, "Assistenza e salvataggio senza mezzi nautici" in Dir. Mar., 1949,
  395.
——, "In tema di partecipazione dell'armatore della nave soccorritrice alle
  operazioni di salvataggio" in Dir. Mar., 1956, 72.
——, *Il soccorso in mare* (Milan, 1964).
——, "Il salvataggio come avaria comune" in *Trasporti*, 1977, 7.
——, "Il progetto del CMI (1981) di Convenzione Internazionale sul salva-
  taggio" in *Annuali della Facoltà di Giurisprudenza di Genova*, 1980–81,
  401.
——, *Le assicurazioni marittime* (Milan, 1981).
Frankenstein, *Internationales Privatrecht* (Berlin, 1929).
Gaeta, "Nave" in *Enciclopedia del diritto*, XXVII, 601.
——, "Sul diritto dell'equipaggio alla ripartizione del premio da salvataggio"
  in Riv. Dir. Nav., 1941, II, 225.
——, *Le fonti del diritto della navigazione* (Milan, 1960), 206.
——, "Assistenza e rimorchio" in Riv. Dir. Nav., 1967, I, 124.
——, "La modifica dell'art. 14 della Convenzione di Bruxelles del 1910, sul-
  l'assistenza e salvataggio" in Riv. Dir. Nav., 1968, I, 231.
——, "La difesa del mare nel diritto italiano" in Dir. Mar., 1984, 839.
——, "La Convenzione di Londra del 1989 sul soccorso in acqua" in Dir.
  Mar., 1991, 291.

Gasparino, "La nave armata ed equipaggiata per prestare soccorso: un orientamento ormai consolidato" in Dir. Mar., 1989, 453.

Gaskell, "Enactment of the 1989 Salvage Convention in English law: policy issues" in [1990] L.M.C.L.Q. 352.

——, "The Lloyd's Open Form and Contractual Remedies" in [1986] L.M.C.L.Q. 306.

Ghionda, "In tema di assistenza e rimorchio" in Riv. Dir. Nav., 1937, I, 180.

——, "Sull'assistenza prestata da navi da guerra" in Riv. Dir. Nav., 1939, II, 64.

Gilmore & Black, *The Law of Admiralty* (New York, 1975).

Giuliano, "Le nuove norme di diritto privato in tema di navigazione" in Riv. Dir. Nav., 1942, I, 21.

Gold, "Marine salvage, Supertankers and oil pollution: New pressure on ancient law" in *Revue de droit de l'Université de Sheerbrook*, 1981, 127.

——, *Handbook on Marine Pollution* (1985).

——, "No Cure No Pay? . . . No Way? Towards a New International Legal Regime for Marine Salvage" in *Cinquième Congrés Annuel de la Société Quebecoise de Droit International,* Université de Montreal, 1988.

——, "Marine Salvage: Towards a New Regime" in *Journal of Maritime Law and Commerce*, 1989, 407.

——, "A Time for Needed Change, Current Developments in the International Law of Marine Salvage" in K. D. Troup (ed.), Proceedings of the 9th International Tug Convention.

Gouillod, "Les mesures de sauvegarde (de quelques difficultés liées à l'imdemnisation des frais de lutte contre la pollution)" in D.M.F., 1980, 397.

Halfweeg, "State of the Art of Offloading Cargo from a Stricken Vessel" in International Symposium on Marine Salvage, New York, 1979, Washington MTS, 1980, 227.

Hastings, "Non-tidal salvage in the United Kingdom: Goring, Goring, Gone" in *Journal of Maritme Law and Commerce*, 1988, 473.

Hudson, *The York-Antwerp Rules* (London, Lloyd's of London Press, 1991).

Jarrett, "The Life Salvor Problem in Admiralty" in *Yale Law Journal*, 1954, 779.

Kennedy, *Civil Salvage* (London, 1958).

Kerr, "The 1989 Salvage Convention, Expediency or Equity?" in 20 *Journal of Maritime Law and Commerce*, 1989, 506.

——, "The philosopy of 'no cure no pay' " in *11th International Tug Convention and International Marine Salvage Symposium* (Halifax, 1990, Surrey, 1991), 253.

Kovats, *The Law of Tugs and Towage* (Chichester and London, 1990).

——, "Lloyd's Open Form Salvage Agreement Changed" in *Seaways*, 1990, 11.

——, "Lloyd's Open Form: Salvor's Gain" in *Seatrade*, June 1980, 75.

Lacey, "Expansion of the salvage industry to meet modern requirements and the need for substantial rewards to sustain the industry" in *Salvage,* Lloyd's of London Press Conference papers (London, 1990), 11.

Lebrun, "Assistance et sauvetage par navire de guerre" in D.M.F., 1954, 253.

——, *Assistance sauvetage et obligation de service* (1950).

Le Clere, *L'assistance aux navires et le sauvatage des épaves* (Paris, 1954).

——, "Assistance, remorquage et abordage pour les navires d'Etat à la suite du décret du 28 Septembre 1955" in D.M.F., 1961, 707.

Lefebrve D'Ovidio, "Assistenza Salvataggio, ricupero e ritrovamento di relitti" in *Studi per la Codificazione del diritto della navigazione* (Rome, 1941), IV.

Lownders & Rudolf, *The Law of General Average* (London, 1964).

Malintoppi, *Diritto uniforme e diritto internazionale privato* (Milan, 1955).

Manca, *Studi di Diritto della Navigazione* (Milan, 1959).

——, *Commento alle Convenzioni Internazionali Marittime* (Milan, 1974).

Maresca, "L'interruzione delle operazioni di rimorchio in alto mare" in Dir. Mar., 1939, 605.

Matray, "Les Leçons de la Catastrophe de *L'Amoco Cadiz*" in *Environmental Policy and Law,* 1978, 172.

Mensah, "Deficiencies found in the regime under the 1910 Convention" in *Salvage,* Lloyd's of London Press Conference papers (London, 1990), 1.

Miller, "Lloyd's Standard Form of Salvage Agreement—LOF 1980: A commentary" in *Journal of Maritime Law and Commerce,* 1981, 243.

Mirabelli, *L'atto non negoziale nel diritto privato italiano* (Naples, 1955).

Mongrandi, "Modifica della Regola VI delle Regole di York ed Anversa 1974" in Dir. Mar., 1990, 861.

Mustyll & Royd, *Commercial Arbitration* (London, 1982).

Nicolò, "Configurazione giuridica del ricupero marittimo" in Riv. Dir. Nav., 1937, I, 155.

Nielsen, "CMI report to IMO on Draft International Convention on Salvage" in *CMI Newsletter,* September 1984.

——, "International Convention on Salvage, report to CMI" in *CMI Newsletter,* December 1989,

——, "Overview—Improvement and Deficiencies from the Legal View Point" in *Salvage,* Lloyd's of London Press Conference papers (London, 1990), 53.

Noble, "International Salvage—The current dilemma" in *P. & I. International,* April 1991, 10.

Norris, *The Law of Salvage* (Mount Kisco N.Y., 1958).

——, *The Law of Salvage* (New York, 1983).

Olsen, "The 1989 Salvage Convention, some problems solved and some problems exacerbated" in *IBA Conference,* New York, 1990.

——, "The Enhancement of Salvage Awards" in *11th International Tug Convention and International Marine Salvage Symposium* (Halifax, 1990, Surrey, 1991), 141.

O'May, "Lloyd's Form and Montreal Convention" in *Tulane Law Review*, 1983, vol. 67, 1412.

O'Neill, "LOF Salvage arbitrations, publication of awards and appeals" in [1988] L.M.C.L.Q. 454.

Owen, "The Abandoned Shipwreck Act of 1987, Goodbye to Salvage in Territorial waters" in 19 *Journal of Maritime Law and Commerce*, 1988, 499.

Parks, "The 1910 Bruxelles Convention, The United States Salvage Act of 1912 and Arbitration of Salvage Cases in the United States" in *Tulane Law Review*, 1938, 1456.

Peet, "Salvage, Hazardous Cargoes and Environmental Protection" in *Salvage*, Lloyd's of London Press Conference papers (London, 1990), 25.

Pescatore, "Requisizione di nave e compenso di assistenza e salvataggio" in *Foro italiano*, 1955, I, 1084.

Piombino, "Sull'elemento pericolo nell'assistenza, e salvataggio e sulla ripartizione del compenso tra l'equipaggio della nave soccorritrice" in Dir. Mar., 1990, 735.

——, "Solidarietà tra debitori del compenso di assistenza e salvataggio: orientamenti giurisprudenziali e soluzioni adottate nella pratica (LOF 1990)" in Dir. Mar., 1991, 154.

Querci, *Pubblicità marittima e aereonautica* (Milan, 1961).

Rawakrishna, "Environmental Concerns and the New Law of the Sea" in *Journal of Maritime Law and Commerce*, 1985, 1.

Reiningert, "Marine Emergency Services: Towards a New Understanding" in *11th International Tug Convention and International Marine Salvage Symposium*, Halifax, 1990, Surrey, 1991, 169.

Reuter, *Le notion d'assistance en mer* (Fontanay le Comte, 1975).

Riccardelli, "La partecipazione dell'armatore alle operazioni di soccorso della nave in pericolo ed il suo diritto al compenso economico" in Riv. Dir. Nav., 1955, II, 236.

——, *Il contratto di rimorchio* (Rome, 1977).

Righetti, "Salvataggio di persone in mare e assicurazione" in *Assicurazioni*, 1961, I, 291.

——, *Le responsabilità del vettore marittimo sul sistema dei pericoli eccettuati* (Padua, 1966).

——, "Ancora sui diritti dei soccorritori spossessati, licenziati e sostituiti" in Dir. Mar., 1979, 420.

Ripert, *Traité de droit maritime* (Paris, 1953).

Rodière, *Traité general de droit maritime: Envenements de mer* (Paris, 1972).

——, *Précis de droit maritime* (Paris, 1974).

Rose, "Restitution for the rescuers" in [1989] 9 O.J.L.S. 184.

Russel, *On Arbitration* (London, 1982).

Russo, "Per una costruzione unitaria dei rapporti di assistenza, salvataggio, ricupero e ritrovamento di relitti" in Riv. Dir. Nav., 1950, I, 3.

Russo, "Questioni in tema di compenso e assistenza e salvataggio" in Riv. Dir. Nav., 1950, II, 120.

——, "Ancora dell'assistenza e rimorchio" in Riv. Dir. Nav., 1956, II, 51.

——, "Gestione di affari da parte dell'armatore e debitori del compenso di salvataggio" in Riv. Dir. Nav., 1961, II, 312.

Schaps-Abraham, *Das deutsche Seerecht* (Berlin, 1921).

Schlegelberger-Lieseke, *Seehandelrecht* (Berlin, 1959).

Scotti, *La rimozione di cose sommerse* (Milan, 1967).

Selvig, "Rapporto preliminare al Sottocomitato Internazionale" in *Documentation Montreal 1981*, Salvage I, II, 80.

Seward, "The Insurance Arrangements Underpinning the Payment of Salvors' Remuneration and P. & I. Insurance" in *Salvage*, Lloyd's of London Press Conference papers (London, 1990), 115.

Shaw, "The insurance arrangements undersigning the payment of salvor's remuneration" in *Salvage*, Lloyd's of London Press Conference papers (London, 1990), 109.

Sheen, "Convention on Salvage" in *Tulane Law Review*, 1983, vol. 57, 1386.

Siccardi, "Studi sul contratto di rimorchio", in Dir. Mar. 1990, 684.

Smeesters & Winkelmolen, *Droit Maritime et Droit Fluvial* (Brussels, 1938).

Staniland, "Towage or Salvage" in [1988] L.M.C.L.Q. 16.

Summerskill, *Oil Rigs Law and Insurance* (London, 1979).

Sutton, *The Assessing of Salvage Awards* (London, 1949).

Taylor, "Revision of the York and Antwerp Rules 1974" in *CMI Newsletter*, Autumn 1990, January 1991, 1.

Tetley, *Maritime Liens and Claims* (London, 1985).

Thomas, "Lloyd's Standard Form of Salvage Agreement, a description and analytical scrutiny" in [1978] L.M.C.L.Q. 279.

——, "Life Salvage in Anglo-American Law" in *Journal of Maritime Law and Commerce*, 1979, 78.

——, *Maritime Liens and Claims* (London, 1980).

Torrente, *I contratti di lavoro della navigazione* (Milan, 1948).

Udina, *Le disposizioni preliminari del Codice della navigazione* (Trieste, 1942).

Vincenzini, F., "Rassegna di giurisprudenza in tema di assistenza, salvataggio, rimorchio e ricupero" in Riv. Dir. Nav., 1980, II, 148.

——, "Soccorso per ordine dell'autorità o legge regolatrice del rapporto" in Dir. Mar., 1982, 264.

——, "Il soccorso in mare nel diritto marittimo Romano" in *Trasporti*, 1984, 60.

——, "Brevi osservazioni in tema di Liability Salvage" in Dir. Mar., 1983, 221.

——, "Ancora in tema di soccorso in acque portuali e determinazione del compenso" in Dir. Mar., 1983, 381.

——, *Profili internazionali del soccorso in mare* (Milan, 1985).

Vincenzini, E., *International Regulation of Salvage at Sea*, Lloyd's of London Press (London, 1987).

——, "Il soccorso in acque portuali" in Dir. Mar., 1980, 347.

Volli, "In tema di cooperazione personale dell'armatore della nave soccorritrice alle operazioni di soccorso" in Dir. Mar., 1956, 372.

——, *Assistenza e Salvataggio* (Padua, 1957).

——, "Limiti della rappresentatività sostanziale e processuale del comandante della nave in pericolo specialmente nei confronti del carico" in Riv. Dir. Nav., 1963, I, 310.

——, "La responsabilità civile nel trasporto di merci pericolose alla luce delle recenti Convenzioni internazionali" in *Trasporti*, 1981, 75.

Wagner, "The Oil Pollution Act: An Analysis" in *Journal of Maritime Law and Commerce*, 1990, 569.

Wall, "Overview—improvements and deficiencies from a Government viewpoint" in *Salvage*, Lloyd's of London Press Conference papers (London, 1990), 73.

Wildeboer, *The Brussels Salvage Convention* (Leiden, 1964).

Wuestendoerfer, *Neuzeitliches Seehandelrecht* (Tubingen, 1950).

Zammitti, "Il soccorso preparatorio nella assistenza e salvataggio marittimo" in *Trasporti*, 1981, 153.

TABLE OF CASES

TABLE OF LEGISLATION

References in **bold type** are to sections where the text of the legislation is set out.

TABLE OF OTHER MATERIALS

INTRODUCTION

INTRODUCTION

The international law of assistance and salvage or, as it has been better defined by our present doctrine which now dates back to the start of the century, rescue at sea[1] (as with all laws which are subject not only to the wear and tear of time but also to a loss of connection with the technical-juridical realities which they were intended to regulate) has begun to show marked symptoms of inadequacy and gaps which must be filled if we are to have a uniform international doctrine which fully fulfils the purpose for which it was created.

Indeed, from 1910 (the year of the international Convention of Brussels) up to the present, salvage and assistance had undergone considerable and continuous modifications, perhaps more so than any other maritime law, to the technical vehicle—the ship—and to developments in maritime traffic. This is especially so in sectors such as the carriage of oil and chemical products and of what are known as hazardous and noxious substances. It was therefore felt that there was an overall need to make substantial modifications to the international law and to contractual practice within it.

This movement of revision had its beginnings, and the starting-point for its development, in 1978 with the *Amoco Cadiz* disaster on the Brittany coasts (with the consequent pollution of wide stretches of sea and shore) as well as other serious incidents which had already sounded the alarm (e.g. the case of the *Torrey Canyon*). These convinced the international organisation in charge of the study of international maritime law (IMCO) that it should promote a study of the law on salvage at sea in view of the problems which the disasters had grimly brought to light and in relation to which, within the laws of the 1910 Brussels Convention, there appeared to be no legislation, nor any adequate law.

The IMCO Secretary concluded in 1978 the study of "certain legal aspects of intervention, notification and salvage" in respect of incidents like the *Amoco Cadiz*. After having first examined all aspects of the individual national laws in particular and international law in general (none of which were fully regulated) an area of research in which the revision movement of the existing international Convention should be developed was singled out. It

---

1. Ferrarini, *Il soccorso in mare* (Milan, 1964).

3

was emphasised that the principal problem in need of solution was that involving the relationship between the principle of the law, identified as the voluntary act of lending assistance at sea to properties or persons in peril (ships, cargoes, human life), and the problems arising in more recent times. Those relate to the risks of pollution by oil or by "hazardous substances" wherever such risks occur as the result of maritime accidents and when salvage operations are not merely for the salvage of properties at risk during carriage by sea but rather for eliminating, or at least reducing, more serious risks which an accident may cause for the environment and to the coasts of the neighbouring States.[2]

The need for a revision of the international law of salvage now having been acknowledged, IMCO accepted with pleasure the initiative which the Comité Maritime International had already resolved to take, promoting the study of a new draft for an international Convention on assistance and salvage at sea, the draft subsequently being finalised at the 1981 Montreal Conference.[3] The CMI, therefore, received from IMCO's Legal Committee the commission to study the expediency of a revision of the 1910 Brussels Convention. Below is the text of the resolution by which CMI was given this task:

"— The Committee has held a wide-ranging exchange of views on the generous offer of the CMI to assist IMCO particularly in a study of the question of salvage. The Committee expressed its approval and gratitude for the proposal.
— It considered that the CMI should be requested to review the private law principles of salvage, centring its examination of the matter on the 1910 Convention for the Unification of Certain Rules of Law relating to Assistance and Salvage at Sea, with Protocol of 1967. Such a review would not encompass questions of coastal State intervention or the control of salvage operations by public authorities in the context of intervention.
— The Committee would be grateful for all the facilities of co-operative effort which have characterized the collaboration between IMCO and the CMI in the past. It would be desirable for the international sub-committee established by the CMI to be guided entirely by its own expertise, with the understanding that among the purposes of the two Organisations undertaking this study were the need to induce and accelerate effective salvage operations in particular cases and generally to encourage the salvage industry in its beneficial activities."[4]

---

2. In this respect the study carried out by Abecassis, *Law and Practice Relating to Oil Pollution from Ships* (London, 1978), 247, is of particular interest. For the importance attributed to the necessary interdependence of the problems relating to oil pollution and salvage at sea, see also Brice, *Maritime Law of Salvage* (London, 1983), 4; and Sheen, "Convention on Salvage" in the *Tulane Law Review* (1983), vol. 57, 1386. Recently, on the theme of US legislation on oil pollution, see Wagner, "The Oil Pollution Act: An Analysis" in *Journal of Maritime Law and Commerce*, 1990, 569.

3. For a full and penetrating investigation of the codification work carried out by CMI see: Carbone, *La disciplina giuridica del traffico marittimo internazionale* (Bologna, 1982), 35 *et seq.*

4. See on this point F. Berlingieri "La XXXII Conferenza del CMI Montreal 28–29 May 1981", in Dir. Mar. 1981, 297; and O'May, "Lloyd's Form and Montreal Convention", in *Tulane Law Review* (1983), vol. 57, 1412.

The draft approved at the CMI Conference in Montreal affords a clear indication of the problems which a uniform international law had to resolve by means of appropriate regulation, and of the trends of the institute in question for the near future. In fact the new Convention, approved in London in 1989, included the greater part of the regulations proposed in the draft, and also took into consideration that which, after 1981, was defined as "The Montreal Compromise".

Moreover, Anglo-Saxon contractual practice which, on this subject, has always performed an anticipatory and promotory function for the solution of the various problems emerging, especially in insurance, had, as a result of the development of maritime traffic, dealt with the particular aspects of the institute of salvage at sea in 1980. This it did by inserting in the new wording of the Lloyd's Open Form (LOF) the first, embryonic elements of evaluation and of firm remuneration for so-called "liability salvage", even though limited to an intervention by the salvors of a tanker and cargo of oil with the purpose of removing, containing and reducing the risks of pollution damage to the environment. This awareness of the enormous damage which maritime accidents, involving tankers of huge dimensions and oil cargoes, could cause to the coastlines, had already produced in the international field several initiatives. These resulted in a voluntary agreement among owners of tanker vessels, drawn up in 1969 and known as TOVALOP (Tanker Owners Voluntary Agreement concerning Liability for Oil Pollution). In 1981 this gave way to the supplementary agreement named CRISTAL which set up a fund for the compensation of damage from pollution caused by vessels carrying oil products. Both of these agreements were revised in the subsequent editions of 20 February 1987.[5] This agreement, entered into on a voluntary basis by shipowners, was followed by various international Conventions upon the study of which IMCO had opportunely resolved. These are, in chronological order:

(1) The International Convention of Brussels of November 1969 relating to Civil Liability for Oil Pollution Damage, the basis of which is summarised in the initial resolution which reads:

> "The States Parties to the present Convention, conscious of the dangers of pollution posed by the world-wide maritime carriage of oil in bulk, convinced of the need to ensure that adequate compensation is available to persons who suffer damage caused by pollution resulting from the escape or discharge of oil from ships, desiring to adopt uniform international rules and procedures for determining questions of liability and providing adequate compensation is available to persons who suffer damage caused by pollution resulting from the escape or discharge of oil from ships, desiring to adopt uniform international rules and procedures for determining questions of liability and providing adequate compensation in such cases . . . "

5. Abecassis, *op. cit.*, 235; Sheen, *op. cit.*, 1396; Gold, *Handbook on Marine Pollution* (1985), ch. 1; and Cohen "Revisions of TOVALOP and CRISTAL: Strong ships for Stormy Seas" in *Journal of Maritime Law and Commerce*, 1987, 525.

(2) The International Convention of London of 1976 on Civil Liability for Damages caused by Oil Pollution.

(3) The International Convention of Brussels of 1971 and that of 1976 for the setting-up of a fund for the compensation of damage caused by oil pollution.

Various serious accidents which occurred in the 1980s, resulting in extremely serious damage to the environment (the most serious of these accidents being that of the *Exxon Valdez* in Alaskan waters), acted as a driving force in achieving the rapid approval of the new Convention on Salvage at Sea, which saw the light of day in London in April 1989 and which, though not yet in force (the required number of ratifications not having yet been registered), has certainly influenced international contractual practice by way of the approval of the new LOF 1990. This form inserts and incorporates the basic points of the New Convention in its own conditions of contract.[6]

Therefore, the purpose of this work is to examine the results, in the international field, of the studies set in motion for the revision of the 1910 Brussels Convention. This will be by way of perusal of the present international law of salvage and of the rules contained in the legal systems of the individual States, taking into consideration the adaptation of the law, in the light of that revision, in contractual and underwriting practice.[7]

6. Berlingieri, "Le projet d'une nouvelle Convention sur l'assistance et les sauvetages d'epaves maritimes" in Dir. Mar. 1988, 1; and Brice, "The New Salvage Convention; green seas and grey areas" [1990] L.M.C.L.Q. 32.

7. Ferrarini, *Il soccorso in mare*, 127, and *Le assicurazioni marittime* (Milan, 1981), 164; also Gold, "Marine Salvage: Towards a New Regime" in *Journal of Maritime Law and Commerce*, 1989, 487.

PART ONE

CURRENT INTERNATIONAL REGULATIONS ON SALVAGE AT SEA

CHAPTER ONE

THE BRUSSELS INTERNATIONAL CONVENTION 1910 AND ITS SPHERE OF APPLICATION

1. WORK PREPARATORY TO THE CONVENTION AND THE PROBLEMS IT SOUGHT TO SOLVE

The International Convention on Maritime Assistance and Salvage was one of the first international Conventions approved by the diplomatic Conference on Maritime Law and was the outcome of one of the very first studies which the Comité Maritime International undertook, soon after its foundation in 1897.

The necessity for a uniform international system for maritime law was, in fact, immediately recognised by the CMI in relation to cases of assistance, salvage and collisions between ships, in so far as such juridically relevant events usually occur in international waters and, very frequently, between vessels of different nationalities. The fact of the international nature of the environment in which such events tend to occur and the international nature of the parties involved constituted a valid reason for an initial attempt to unify maritime law. This purpose began to be achieved, if not at a faster pace than in the past, at least during the course of this century.[1]

In fact it was necessary initially to cope with several of the law's various and differing concepts, rooted in the past in the legal systems of different States. There were those systems which intended to maintain, with regard to maritime salvage, two different forms of the same law (distinguishing them as assistance and salvage), and systems of States based on the English tradition of "salvage", within which term various aspects of salvage are included, especially salvage of a wreck.[2]

One of the primary tasks which the CMI had proposed in the preparatory work to the Convention was the elimination of the division between "assistance" and "salvage" and the return of the law to a unitary concept of salvage.

1. For a full picture of the increasing "internationalisation" of maritime law and of the increasing importance of the uniform law governing maritime relations, see the recent study by Carbone, *La disciplina giuridica del traffico marittimo internazionale*, (Bologna, 1982), 14, *et seq*.
2. See on this point: Kennedy, *Civil Salvage* (London, 1958), 7, where, among salvage services, he expressly indicates "bringing derelict or wreck into safety"; Brice, *Maritime Law of Salvage* (London, 1983), 114; and Gaskell, "The Lloyd's Open Form and Contractual Remedies" [1987] L.M.C.L.Q. 307.

This was required in order to end the differing juridical qualifications of the law which, on the subject of remuneration, had its origins in two different forms of salvage. In the case of assistance, this was determined on the basis of the circumstances of the event and of the services rendered by the salving vessels. In the case of the salvage of an abandoned vessel, it was determined on the basis of an application of a set ratio to the value of the salved properties.

This conceptual trend derived in part from the elaboration of standards whose source was clearly the Ordonnance de la Marine of 1681 where the structure of salvage was that of *sauvetage d'épaves*, i.e. of the salvage of a wreck or of things or jettison coming from wrecks in relation to which the salvors were entitled to a fixed portion of the saved or rescued value, whilst only the refund of the costs sustained, plus a remuneration proportionate to the services rendered, was due for assistance given to vessels which had been grounded or beached.[3]

In fact, the distinction between assistance and salvage (besides the afore-mentioned differentiation of salvage services qualified according to the presence or absence of the crew on board the distressed or wrecked vessel) found a final justification in those legal systems which had incorporated that distinction into their own positive legislation, in the differing service rendered by the salving party who, in the course of assistance, as distinct from salvage, had the benefit of the collaboration of the salved vessel.[4] The work preparatory to the Convention clearly indicates an intention to eliminate this distinction and, indeed, right from the time of the Convention's *avant-projet*, which was discussed at the International Conference of Brussels in 1905, it was decided that all legislative distinctions between assistance and salvage should be abolished.

This decision, which was definitively adopted in Article 1 of the 1910 Brussels Convention (though the wording was different, the substance was identical), was reached after the CMI had contacted the individual national associations on this point and obtained their prevailing opinions with regard to the abolition of the distinction.

It is worthwhile to recall the positions adopted by some of these associations in relation to this point so that some idea may be formed about what amounted, in effect, to a debate which, in spite of the time now gone by, has lost none of its importance or topical nature with regard to the attainment of an increasing uniformity of the law.

3. Reuter, *La notion d'assistance en mer* (Fonteney le Comte, 1975), 41; Ferrarini, *Il soccorso in mare*, 3; G. Berlingieri, "Salvataggio e assistenza marittima, in acque interne ed aerea", in Dir. Mar., 1967, 8. For the latter, the salvors were entitled to a quota of the saved properties as it was to be considered that the previous owner had, to all effects, lost those properties in the case, for example, of an abandoned ship which could actually be taken over by the salvors.

4. It must be noted that this distinction, as yet without practical effect due to the lack of a corresponding differentiated discipline with regard to the application and regulation of patrimonial relations inherent in the diverse salvage services, would, strangely enough, persist in our 1942 Code of Navigation to the extent that the Code's Report (under section 299) supplies a justification for the persistence of that distinction by identifying the collaboration of the passive subject as the discriminatory criterion between the two forms of salvage.

Even then the Italian Association declared itself in favour of retaining the distinction and this attitude and trend were subsequently reproposed both in Law No. 939 of 14 June 1925 (which, although acknowledging the conventional structure, maintained the distinction) and in the 1942 Code of Navigation in which the distinction was confirmed.[5]

Neither the Belgian nor the French Associations followed suit and both fell into line with the abolitionism which prevailed in the common law countries and to which other countries such as Germany (which had in the past favoured the distinction between the two forms) subsequently adhered during the course of the final discussions on the draft Convention.[6]

The acceptance by the Convention of the concept of salvage should, according to the English concept of "salvage at sea", have divided the doctrine into contrasting positions since, whilst on one hand it was held that the new international law of salvage was not meant to regulate the law of salvage of wrecks (or salvage of wrecked, sunken or abandoned vessels[7]), there was a wish, both in the past[8] and more recently,[9] to include in the scope of the term "salvage at sea" all those services rendered by one party for the property of another party which may be in danger of being lost or which may already be materially lost, in full adherence to the unitary concept of salvage which ties up with the English system of "salvage at sea".

In the English system the term "wreck" is expressly mentioned in section 546 of the Merchant Shipping Act 1894, which reads:

"Where any vessel is wrecked, stranded, or in distress at any place on or near the coasts of the United Kingdom or any tidal water within the limits of the United

5. On this see Ferrarini, *Il soccorso*, 8.
6. For a survey of the individual national laws before the Convention see G. Berlingieri, "Assistenza e Salvataggio" in *Nuovo Digesto Italiano*, 996.
7. G. Berlingieri, in *Studi in onore di F. Berlingieri* (Rome, 1933), 75; and, more recently, G. Berlingieri, "Salvataggio e assistenza marittima", Dir. Mar., 1967, 24; and in Dir. Mar., 1968, 294; Manca, *Studi*, 208.
8. Brunetti, *Studi in onore di F. Berlingieri* (Rome, 1933), 165.
9. Ferrarini, *op. cit.*, 8. Russo had assumed a particular position, "Per una costruzione unitaria dei rapporti di assistenza, salvataggio, ricupero e ritrovamento dei relitti" in Riv. Dir. Nav., 1950, I, according to which not only was the recovery, but also the finding, of a wreck to be included in the unitary construction of salvage. This prospect has been justly criticised by Ferrarini on two considerations: first, that the Convention did not consider the finding of a wreck as an aspect of salvage—as, in effect, neither did the English system which inspired the Convention; second, that the finding of a wreck does not result in a salvage service to which, in particular, Russo himself related his reason for his unitary construction of the law of salvage.
An intermediate position was assumed by Volli, *Assistenza e salvataggio* (Padua, 1957), 14. Though favouring the distinction of the concept between the two laws (as criteria for the distinction he considers that, in salvage, the property to be saved exists as yet in its original form, though in peril, whilst in salvage of a wreck, the element of peril has passed and the property is physically lost) he finds that the conceptual limits of such a distinction are not very clear when, for example, "we are faced with a vessel in a poor condition, abandoned by her crew, hardly afloat and sometimes already submerged". The only precedent relevant in our jurisdiction conformed to this view (see Court of Cassation, 18 September, 1961, No. 2033, in Riv. Dir. Nav., 1961, II, 167).

Kingdom, and services are rendered by any person in assisting that vessel or saving the cargo or apparel of that vessel or any part thereof, and where services are rendered by any person other than a receiver in saving any wreck, there shall be payable to the salvor by the owner of the vessel, cargo, apparel, or wreck, a reasonable amount of salvage to be determined in case of dispute in manner hereinafter mentioned."[10]

It is therefore evident that the English system and also the Convention do not allow that salvage of a wreck represents a law apart and distinct from salvage, just as, on the other hand, the attempt to set up a law distinguished from the salvage of a wreck, in spite of its separate position within the terms of the Italian legal system (Articles 501 *et seq.* of the Navigation Code), would appear to be a purely formal arrangement. In fact, the law applied by the legislator to such cases is, on the whole, not unlike that of assistance and salvage since our Code with regard to the salvage of wrecks no longer provides that the salvor is to be remunerated with a portion of the salvaged goods (as is the case in the remuneration of the finder of a wreck—Article 510 of the Navigation Code) and, even for the finder of a wreck, remuneration is determined on the basis of criteria which the law relates to the rendering of a salvage service in the widest sense of the word.[11]

Moreover, the problem of the inclusion of the salvage of wrecks into the international law of salvage, and of whether, in the course of the Convention's work of revision, it justified a more precise definition of the limits of application of the law to the salvage of a sunken vessel and of a wreck, was solved in the Draft of the new Convention approved by the 1981 CMI Conference of Montreal. Among the more important changes is that of the inclusion within the concept of "salvage" of the salvage of a stranded or sunken vessel, but the exclusion of the removal of wrecks.[12] In effect, according to the Anglo-Saxon concept, the purpose of "removal of wreck" operations is the removal of the obstruction or of the peril which the wreck presents to ship-

---

10. Kennedy, *Civil Salvage*, 385. This author supplies a full explanation of the term "wreck" by means of the jurisprudential evolution of recovery, as a true and proper aspect of salvage, and by means of the differing terminology used by the Admiralty Court in cases adjudged (flotsam, jetsam, ligan, derelict), with regard to the various species of wreck.

11. For a distinction between the different elements of salvage and the finding of wrecks, see Ferrarini, *op. cit.*, 239. In the salvage of wrecks, there is the assumption that the wreck is rendered available as a result of specific activities carried out to that end, i.e. a juridical action in the strictest sense; whilst the finding of a wreck consists of the mere meeting with and sighting of a wreck, which would represent a juridical fact in the strictest sense.

12. In the presentation of the Draft Convention (approved at Montreal, at IMO on 22 September, 1981) by the President of the CMI, the English version of the text reads: "This was done in order to include vessels which are stranded or sunk, but excluding the removal of wreck. Salvage therefore covers all service rendered to a vessel in respect of which there may be a reasonable expectation of avoiding a definitive loss. The concept of danger is thus correspondingly widened, so as to include the situation of a vessel which, after a major accident such as stranding or sinking, may suffer an even greater and more definitive loss." From this it follows that the loss of the vessel in the specific case can already be considered as definitive if the salvors' efforts must have the purpose of preventing an even more definitive loss ("more definitive loss" in the English text, "plus definitive" in the French text).

ping rather than the actual salving of the wreck itself, which therefore sets this law outside even the widest concept of salvage.[13]

It must however be acknowledged that the 1910 Convention, although leaving open and unsolved several problems pertaining to particular and specific aspects of salvage, such as those already mentioned, did carry out well, for over 80 years, its function of unifying the individual national laws by supplying a uniform international law which in its completeness and consistency was highly valid, especially if one considers the time in which it was approved. Concrete evidence of its validity is the great number of ratifications and adherences to this Convention to date, as distinct from other, no less important, maritime Conventions.

2. THE SPHERE OF APPLICATION OF THE RULES OF THE CONVENTION

Article 15 of the Convention specifies the sphere of application of the Convention itself: "The provisions of this Convention shall be applied as regards all persons interested when either the assisting or salving vessel or the vessel assisted or salved belongs to a State of the High Contracting Parties, as well as in any other cases for which the national laws provide."

This Article led to doubts being raised as to the correct delimitation of the Convention's application since it was maintained[14] that the phrase "belongs to one of the States of the High Contracting Parties" could, in effect, mean that the assisted or salved vessel belongs to a subject of the one of the States of the High Contracting Parties. This would thus operate a split between the nationality of the salved vessel and the nationality of the person owning the salved vessel, which could only add useless uncertainty about interpretation in the application of the Convention's uniform provisions.

This interpretation cannot be accepted: in the first place, because the Convention makes no mention whatsoever of the nationality of the person owning the salved vessel, but only of the nationality of the vessel herself; in the second place because, as has been recently and clearly demonstrated,[15] the

13. In effect, in the Italian system, "the removal of wrecks" largely belongs to the public aspects of navigation and in particular to safety of navigation, which falls within the scope of port administration and policing (Art. 73, Cod. Nav.; Arts. 90 *et seq.*, Reg. per la navig. marittima). On this point see Scotti, *La rimozione di cose sommerse* (Milan, 1967), 37 *et seq.* In Anglo-Saxon practice the risk relating to the "costs and expenses of or incidental to the raising, removal, destruction, lighting or marking of the wreck of a ship" is the subject of specific cover by the P. & I. Clubs, quite different from the covering of salvage costs and remuneration which are normally covered by the hull insurance.

14. Wildeboer, *The Brussels Salvage Convention* (Leiden, 1964), 35.

15. Carbone, *op. cit.*, 70 *et seq.* For this author the nationality of the vessel "constitutes the sole, undisregardable supposition in the presence of which international law attributes to the State which has authorised the vessel to fly its flag, the right to exact that other States abstain from material interference on board or with regard to the activities of the vessel, at least while she is in maritime waters which are not subject to the sovereignty of any State whatsoever".

nationality of the vessel has assumed increasing juridical importance as a point of connection with the law applicable to the vessel and her status in so far as she belongs to a specific legal system.[16]

A further, much more serious problem arises when it is necessary to establish the application of the Convention on the basis of the expression "soit le navire assistance ou sauveteur, soit le navire assisté ou sauveé"—i.e. when it is necessary to establish whether, in order to apply the Convention's uniform provisions, both vessels, the salved and the salvor, must belong to Contracting States or whether it is sufficient for one of them to do so.

It is wise to begin by pointing out that though, from a strictly literal point of view, it is true that the conjunction *soit* in French (as is the case for its Italian equivalent *sia*) may have either a disjunctive ("either") or a cumulative ("both") significance,[17] the equivalent expression used in the English text of the Convention would not appear to have any cumulative significance whatsoever in so far as the locution "either-or" demonstrates that this is clearly a disjunctive expression and as such has the sole purpose of rendering the Convention's provision applicable should either one or the other of the vessels, the salved or the salvor, belong to a Contracting State.[18]

Moreover, research into the minutes of the work preparatory to the Convention leads one to conclude, as has already been noted,[19] in favour of the

16. For Ferrarini, *op. cit.*, 15, the nationality of the vessel is decisive to the extent that the individual nationalities of the persons on board, of the crew and of the freight and cargo interests, are totally irrelevant whilst, instead, the nationality of the salvors is relevant in the specific case of salvage services rendered without use being made of nautical craft.

17. On this point see G. Berlingieri, *op. cit.*, 20, who, maintaining that in this case the term *soit* is neutral in the sense that it lends itself equally to both interpretations, concludes for the disjunctive "whether . . . or . . ." interpretation of the term.

18. On this point international doctrine is somewhat divided. The prevailing German doctrine favours the theory that it is not necessary that both vessels, the salved and the salvor, must belong to Contracting States: Frankenstein, *Internationales Privatrecht* (Berlin, 1929), II, 553; Abraham, *Das Seerecht*, (Berlin, 1960), 171; Wuestendoerfer, *Neuzeitliches Seehandelsrecht* (Tubingen, 1950), 410; and, in Italy, Manca, "Commento alle Convenzioni Internazionali marittime", *op. cit.*, 180; G. Berlingieri, *op. cit.*, 20; in favour of the cumulative interpretation of the expression and of the need of the aforementioned vessels belonging to Contracting States are: Diena, *Principi del diritto internazionale privato marittimo* (Rome, 1937), 66; Russo, item "Assistenza e Salvataggio", *cit.*, 34, and Ferrarini, *Il soccorso in mare*, 15. However, what would appear to be the determinant is the different formula adopted in the same diplomatic Conference relating to the International Convention on the Collision of Vessels, which establishes the application of the Convention's law "lorsque tous les navires en cause seront resortissants aux Etats des Hautes Parties Contractantes", indicating differently the various criteria of connection adopted in the two Conventions.

19. G. Berlingieri, *op. cit.*, 20, note; and Manca, *op. cit.*, 181. It must be noted that Italian jurisprudence has frequently assumed a contrasting position with regard to the above-mentioned supposition, categorically declaring that one of the conditions for the application of the 1910 Brussels Convention is that both the salved and the salving vessels are of the nationality of a Contracting State; see Arbitration Award, 28 November, 1965, in Dir. Mar., 1966, 357; Court of Cassation, Section I, 7 May 1976, No. 1596, in Dir. Mar., 1976, 434; Tribunal of Caltanissetta, 21 November 1977, in Dir. Mar., 1978, 483; Naples Court of Appeal, 31 March 1978, in Dir. Mar., 1979, 578. Also to this effect, indirectly, Tribunal of Brindisi, 14 December 1987, in Dir. Mar., 1988, 833 and, *contra*, USDC, Northern District of California, 18 November 1985, in Dir. Mar., 1986, 748.

proposition that the Convention applies even when only one vessel belongs to a Contracting State.

In fact, the dispute which arose during the course of the Conference between the French delegation (which wanted to limit the application of the Convention solely to the Contracting States on the presupposition of the purely contractual nature of international Conventions) and the Belgian and German delegations (which instead opted for the opposite solution) was resolved in favour of the latter as may be seen from the text of the report to the Plenary Assembly of 20 October 1905 where the reasons supporting the proposition were explained:

" . . . mais en matière, il a paru suffisant que, soit le navire assistant ou sauveteur, soit le navire assisté ou sauvé, appartienne a l'un des Etats contractants pour rendre la Convention applicable à tous les intéressés, même en dehors des dispositions spéciales figurantes à cet égard dans les lois nationales. La raison en est qu'il y a toujours lieu d'encourager l'assistance. Il faut d'ailleurs considérer que les services de sauvetage ou d'assistance peuvent être rendus par d'autres personnes que le capitaine d'un et son équipage."

Moreover, indications favouring this interpretation are to be found in Article 15 of the Convention, in its first and third paragraphs, which read:

"1. Qu'à l'égard des intéressés ressortissants d'un Etat non contractant, l'application des dites dispositions pourra être subordonnée par chacun des Etats contractants à la condition de réciprocité."
"3. Que, sans préjudice des dispositions plus étendues des lois nationales, l'article 11 n'est applicable qu'entre navires ressortissants des Etats des Hautes Parties Contractantes."

With regard to the context of the first of these provisions, it may be argued that the right granted to subjects of Contracting States to subordinate the application of the Convention's provisions to subjects of non-Contracting States upon condition of reciprocity proves that the Convention, in principle, is also applicable to the latter when one of the craft involved belongs to a Contracting State. With regard to the second provision it would seem easy to argue that the reference to Article 11 of the Convention indirectly confirms the general principle of the Convention being applicable in other cases of salvage—even of vessels belonging to non-contracting States—in so far as Article 11 is specifically declared to apply only to vessels belonging to Contracting States and is thus intended as an exception to compulsory salvage.

This wide interpretation of the limits of application of international law in relation to these subjects is also positively confirmed in the first paragraph of Article 15, where it is established that the provisions of the Convention will be applied "as well as in any other cases for which the national laws provide". The Convention thus allows the Contracting States to extend independently the sphere of the Convention's application to other facts and legal relationships. In incorporating the uniform international provisions into their own system, they adapt to their own national legislation.[20]

3. THE GEOGRAPHICAL SPHERE OF APPLICATION

A further problem of interpretation arose in relation to the identification and delimitation of the physical sphere of application of the Convention's provisions. Rather than a real problem, it might be said that this was more of an anxiety, from the points of view of jurisprudence and doctrine, to clear the field of application of the uniform international discipline from all and any doubts as to interpretation.

The contents of Article 1 of the Convention would not appear to cause any serious doubts on the point, as it expressly establishes that the Convention itself will apply to assistance and salvage services "sans qu'il y ait à tenir compte des eaux où ils ont été rendus". In spite of this, Italian prevailing doctrine and, on occasion, jurisprudence, have deemed it necessary to stress the irrelevance of the place where the salvage service is rendered. Even more so with regard to those cases involving Italian vessels as either the salved or salving vessel and relating to operations performed in Italian territorial waters in favour of vessels of Contracting States in which some remote perplexity could have arisen about the possibility of the Convention's provisions applying.[21] However, these perplexities would appear to persist, both in doctrine and jurisprudence, when the vessel salved in Italian territorial waters belongs to a non-Contracting State.[22]

Finally, it must be added, about the application of the Convention, that it has extended the application of the provisions on salvage at sea to those cases where salvage has been rendered by or to a craft used on inland waters, so long as one of the craft, the salved or the salvor, is a seagoing vessel,

20. On this point see Malintoppi, *Diritto uniforme e diritto internazionale privato* (Milan, 1955), 48; and Wildeboer, *op. cit.*, 36. For a complete comparison of the Convention and American law see: Parks, "The 1910 Bruxelles Convention, The United States Salvage Act of 1912 and Arbitration of Salvage Cases in the United States", in *Tulane Law Review*, 1983, 1456.

21. In doctrine: Ferrarini, *cit.*, 15; G. Berlingieri, *cit.*, 28; Manca, *cit.*, 184; Wildeboer, *cit.*, 11; in jurisprudence: Arbitration Award, 30 December 1963, in Dir. Mar. 1965, 300; Arbitration Award, 30 January 1979, in Dir. Mar. 1979, 405.

22. See Arbitration Award, 21 July 1966, in Dir. Mar., 1966, 603, for which the assistance supplied by Italian tugs in Italian territorial waters to vessels flying the Liberian flag (a State which did not adhere to the 1910 Brussels Convention) must be disciplined, in accordance with Art. 25, 2nd paragraph of the preliminary dispositions to the Civil Code, by the rules of the relative Code of Navigation. The solution adopted in this Arbitration Award conforms to that upheld by prevailing doctrine because, in cases of salvage services to a foreign vessel belonging to a non-contracting State, rendered by an Italian vessel in its own territorial waters, the provision of Art. 13 of the Code of Navigation (which refers to salvage on the high sea) is not applicable. On this point see Ferrarini, *op. cit.*, 15 *et seq*. It would seem however that one may agree with this theory only where the Italian subject does not regard the Convention's provisions as applying to the foreign subject, due to absence of the requisite reciprocity mentioned under Art. 15, para. 1 of the Convention.

wherever the respective courses of navigation of the two craft intersect, i.e. the fact that the salvage was performed in maritime or inland waters is of no relevance.[23] Furthermore, this application has also been extended to the case where the salvage of a distressed seagoing vessel is effected from the shore, without the use of nautical craft, even though it must be acknowledged that no specific indication is contained in Article 1 of the Convention with regard to this case.

Although, on the one hand, the provision takes into consideration every possible type of salvage at sea rendered to a distressed seagoing vessel, the application of the Convention's provisions to salvage at sea without any use of seagoing craft can be drawn from the context of the provision, for this contains no limit or indication of the equipment which must be used to effect salvage for it to fall within the Convention's law.[24]

4. DELIMITATION OF THE RULES OF THE CONVENTION: CRAFT USED ON INLAND WATERS

Having established that the intention of the Convention was a uniform law:

(1) for assistance to and salvage of seagoing vessels, of things on board, of freight and of persons, even if the salvage is effected without the use of nautical craft;

(2) for assistance and salvage between seagoing vessels and craft used on inland waters;

without our having to take into consideration the waters in which the assistance and salvage are effected, we shall now proceed to examine the limitations

23. It would not seem possible to share Ferrarini's theory, *op. cit.*, 19, as this author appears to wish to tie the phrase in Art. 1 of the Convention (relating to the physical area of its application): "sans qu'il y ait à tenir compte des eaux ou ils ont été rendus" to the sole case of salvage between a seagoing vessel and a vessel of inland navigation whilst, though in such a case the general principle established by the Convention as to the irrelevance of the waters in which salvage services are rendered holds good, yet this principle, as mentioned, also represents a general principle of the Convention's provisions. A fairly recent English judgment is interesting in this respect—*The Goring* [1987] Q.B. 687, C.A., which affirmed the principle of the remunerability of salvage services rendered in inland waters. The House of Lords reversed the decision ([1988] 2 WLR 460), declaring that maritime law could not be extended to internal waters, and therefore the Admiralty Court had no jurisdiction in this respect. See also Hasting, "Non-tidal Salvage in the United Kingdom: Goring, Goring, Gone" in *Journal of Maritime Law and Commerce*, 1988, 473.

24. On this point doctrine is unanimous: Ferrarini, "Assistenza e salvataggio senza mezzi nautici", in Dir. Mar. 1949, 395; Volli, *Assistenza e salvataggio*, 261; De Juglart and Villenau, *Repertoire méthodique et pratique de l'assistance en mer* (Paris, 1962), 104; Kennedy, *Civil Salvage*, *op. cit.*, 7 *et seq.*; G. Berlingieri, "Salvataggio e assistenza", *cit.*, 30; Ferrarini, *Il soccorso in mare*, *cit.*, 21; Wildeboer, *op. cit.*, 11. For a very broad interpretation of salvage without nautical craft being used, there are in jurisprudence the judgments by the Court of Cassation 26 December 1935 in Riv. Dir. Nav. 1936, II, 311, and of the US Court of Appeal (5th Circ.) 24 October 1927, in A.M.C., 1928, 148, which granted remuneration to whoever had provided the vessel with an indication as to the course to be followed, resulting in the removing of the vessel from the situation of peril. With regard to the admission of salvage without the use of seagoing craft, see Tribunal of Brindisi, 14 December 1987, in Dir. Mar., 1988, 833.

imposed by the Convention upon its own provisions, and the specific exclusions which may be drawn from a study of the regulations themselves.

Given that the Convention does not supply a definition of "vessels" but that such a definition may be extracted from the preparatory works[25] (which would appear clearly to exclude from the Convention's provisions all fixed floating objects such as dry docks or pontoons permanently moored inside ports), it is worth noting that the Convention embodies two sets of exclusions: one is implicit and concerns craft used on inland waters (Article 1) and the other is explicit (Articles 13 and 14) and concerns public services of assistance and salvage, ships of war and government ships appropriated to a public service.

We have already had occasion to note that craft used on inland waters may become the active or passive subjects of a salvage operation, thus falling within the Convention's provisions, whether the other vessel or vessels involved (i.e., the salved or the salvors) is or are seagoing vessels. This implicitly excludes from the provisions all those cases where both the active and passive subjects of the salvage are craft used on inland waters, or when the salvage of one of the latter is performed from the shore or from the air without nautical craft being used.[26] It has often been noted in the past, and even more frequently recently, that inland water craft may be widely used (especially in those countries where the existence of large rivers allows the vessel to navigate inland for some distance before reaching the open sea and completing her voyage in a seaport).[27] It must therefore be observed in this respect that the possibility of salvage between inland navigation vessels taking place on the open sea cannot be excluded, in which case it would seem that the argument that the vessel must be qualified according to her regular and prevalent use (rather than to her original and theoretical purpose of inland navigation) must be upheld.[28]

This interpretation could result in problems as it would seem to base its

25. In the Minutes of the 1905 Brussels Conference it is stated that: "Les Dispositions de la Convention seront appliquées à toutes les embarcations de quelque nature qu'elles soient, mais uniquement à des embarcations."

26. Thus Manca, "Commento", 191; Le Clère, *L'assistance aux navires et le sauvetage des épaves* (Paris, 1954), 129; G. Berlingieri, "Salvataggio e assistenza marittima", *op. cit.*, 25; Wildeboer, *op. cit.*, 13.

27. Manca, *op. cit.*, 192. For this author, when the use of the vessel is mixed, the vessel, even if still registered as a vessel of inland navigation, must be considered as seagoing.

28. For Wildeboer, *op. cit.*, 15, the use to which the vessel was originally destined, as may be seen from her structure or from her being entered in a particular register, is a circumstance which can be taken into consideration only subordinately. French doctrine (Reuter, *La notion d'assistance en mer*, *op. cit.*, 102 and Ripert, *Traité de droit maritime* (1950), I, 140), does not consider the administrative criteria of distinction between the two different forms of navigation to be of any relevance. In fact the latter maintains that: "Les limites de l'inscription maritime n'ont pas été fixées arbitrairement. On a tenu compte de l'état physique des lieux et la possibilité de la navigation. Si une partie des fleuves a été soumise au régime de l'inscription maritime, c'est la partie où les conditions physiques et politiques de la navigation sont les mêmes qu'en mer. Le droit maritime est, dès lors, naturellement appelé à s'appliquer à cette navigation."

logical reasoning on the fact that salvage between two inland navigation vessels would qualify as a salvage at sea when performed in maritime waters, thus rendering the uniform international provisions of the Convention applicable to the case. Instead, the Convention expressly excludes salvage from being considered as maritime on the basis of mere geographical criteria such as those relating to the waters where the service is rendered.

A more detailed investigation of this point and a more precise identification of the qualifications for salvage at sea for the purposes of the application of the Convention reveal that, in such a case, salvage is considered to be maritime not so much because it is performed at sea as because the vessels involved in the operation at that time, by use and prevalent appropriation, are real and proper seagoing vessels.[29]

Those cases which, instead, are explicitly excluded from the Convention's application are those indicated in Articles 13 (salvage and assistance services rendered by public authorities) and 14 (ships of war or government ships appropriated to public service).

5. SALVAGE BY PUBLIC SERVICES

It must be noted first that the two provisions, taken together, appear to confirm the prevailing attitude of the Convention not to interfere with the public aspects of the individual national laws of the Contracting States.[30] It has in fact been discussed whether the intention of Article 13 of the Convention was to remove from the Convention's law any case involving assistance or salvage by a public service, or whether the intention was to acknowledge the right of the individual States to govern, with their own laws, the organisation of salvage services without removing from the Convention's law the private relationships which ensue between the parties.[31]

29. Ferrarini, op. cit., 19, would instead seem to opt for the absolute exclusion of salvage between vessels of inland navigation regardless of the waters in which the salvage services are rendered. The extension of maritime law to internal navigation was accepted only to a limited extent, for those cases where maritime navigation and inland navigation intersected. This would explain why the Convention insists that at least one seagoing vessel be the active or the passive subject of the services as, with this criterion, it has been possible to regard as irrelevant the maritime or inland nature of the waters in which the salvage takes place.

30. On this point Wildeboer, op. cit., 33; G. Berlingieri, op. cit., 35.

31. In our jurisprudence an isolated judgment by the Court of First Instance of Naples, 8 January 1969, in Dir. Mar. 1969, 141, correctly acknowledges that the reason for the provision is to be sought in the intention, which transpires from the Convention, of not interfering in situations of public interest which each individual State may best appreciate. This is also the basis of other provisions of the same Convention, such as Art. 12 which leaves to each individual State the choice of the measures to be taken in order to penalise the violation of the duty (established by the previous Art. 11) upon the master to render assistance to whomsoever may be in peril, even should he be an enemy. Art. 14 is another provision under which the Convention is not applicable to vessels of war or to government vessels appropriated exclusively to public service, since the question of the regime to which State-owned properties are generally subject is considered to be an extremely delicate one.

It would, therefore, seem advisable to draw a distinction between the two different cases. In the first, in fact, there exists a proper public salvage service (i.e. in the Italian system salvage performed by craft belonging to the Port Authority). In the second, there is the simple issuing of rules governing and organising the salvage services which every Contracting State is entitled to promulgate within its own system with respect to aspects of public law and port and navigation policing.

It is, therefore, essential to distinguish between salvage services rendered using ships of war of government vessels (covered by the provisions of Article 14 of the Convention) and salvage services governed by the individual State systems as provided by Article 13 of the Convention. Salvage services rendered by the individual State systems would not, therefore, seem to represent a true exclusion of the application of the Convention to particular cases of salvage (public salvage services) but rather a simple delimitation of the law, limited to the organisation and regulation of those services, to prevent the Convention's provisions from interfering with the public aspects of the matter in hand.

The opinion, adumbrated in doctrine, according to which Article 13 of the Convention is interpreted as meaning that, in the absence of any law on public salvage services within the internal rules of the individual Contracting States, such cases fall within the Convention and are to be regulated by it, cannot be shared.[32] In fact if, on the one hand, the Convention does not appear to contain particular rules with regard to the "organisation" of salvage services, neither does it, on the other, by regulating exclusively those relationships of private law, appear to intend in any way to interfere with the strictly public aspects of the law.[33] Moreover, it cannot be denied that the reservation acknowledged by the Convention in favour of public powers of regulation by the individual systems within the international community had been recognised, as long ago as 1910. It was seen as a necessity, on the part of the international system, to grant particular legal situations to coastal States even with regard to certain cases beyond maritime areas which were subject

32. G. Berlingieri, *op. cit.*, 35; Wildeboer, *op. cit.*, 33, who identifies this need as that of regulating public services with particular regard to the removal of wrecks, in view of the fact that many of the legal systems of the individual States participating in the Conference provided in public law for this case. In particular this author, pointing out that Art. 13 speaks of "all" public services of assistance and salvage, expresses the doubt that the intention of those drafting the Convention was that of making it apply to public salvage services in the absence of internal regulations within the individual systems of the Contracting States.

33. From the Minutes of the Conference it can be seen that the *ratio* of Art. 13 is meant to prevent this sort of interference: "Il a été signalé à juste titre à la Conférence, que certains Pays avaient, soit dans leur législation, soit dans le recueil de leurs traités, des règles particulières sur l'organisation des services d'assistance et de sauvetage par les autorités publiques ou sous leur contrôle, et qu'il convenait qu'une clause spéciale vint marquer que le traité n'entendait pas innover dans ce domaine."

to their exclusive sovereignty. As has been recently noted,[34] particular and significant requirements are reposed even today for cases in which unilateral measures must be taken, even against foreign vessels, in areas not subject to the sovereignty of the coastal State, when, for example, serious cases of pollution and heavy damage to the environment are involved.

6. SHIPS OF WAR AND GOVERNMENT VESSELS APPROPRIATED TO PUBLIC SERVICE

The intention of Article 14 which, as we shall see, has undergone perceptible changes as a result of the coming into force of the Protocol amending the Convention (signed at Brussels on 27 May 1969 and which came into force on 15 August 1977, after more than the five instruments of ratification required for validity had been lodged), was to exclude from the uniform international law all ships of war and vessels belonging to States which had appropriated them to a public service.

The motives apparently leading to this exclusion are to be sought in the influence which the system of the common-law[35] countries had always had on salvage. At that time in the United Kingdom the system did not allow the application of the principles of salvage to government vessels before the coming into force of the Crown Proceedings Act 1947 which regulated salvage services performed in favour of or by the Royal Navy in the same way as the relations in *subjecta materia* between private parties are regulated. This conformed with the tendency in those civil law countries which had considered this aspect, especially in cases of salvage services rendered by ships of war, as the performance of a public function—and hence their necessarily gratuitous nature.[36] However, the application of the individual laws did not prevent, salvage services to or by government vessels from being regulated in accordance with the normal legal principles.[37]

It is sufficient to recall, given the amendment to Article 14, that a vast area

---

34. Carbone, *op. cit.*, 106.

35. Kennedy, *Civil Salvage*, 365; Brice, *Maritime Law of Salvage*, 111. The latter notes that the need to modify Art. 24 of the Convention derived not only from the fact that many national legislations contained no analogous principle, but also from the fact that those systems which provided this exclusion were in the process of adapting to the prevailing tendency of excluding State immunity, finding, in the wake of various decisions in jurisprudence (see The *"Philippine Admiral"* [1977] A.C. 373, 402, 403, P.C., and *Trendtex Trading Corporation* v. *Central Bank of Nigeria"* [1977] Q.B. 529, C.A.), that not only the circumstance of the vessel being State-owned should be considered, but also that consideration should be given to the fact that the vessel was used in normal commercial traffic "as a mere trading vessel". This was to prevent immunity being granted when not deserved, for example to ex-Iron Curtain Countries where only government-owned vessels existed.

36. Volli, *Assistenza*, 269.

37. Wildeboer, *The Brussels Salvage Convention*, 28.

of national and international doctrine[38] favoured a radical reform of the provisions in question. This was in view of the ever-increasing number of government-owned vessels at sea (e.g. vessels owned by Communist countries) and in view of the fact that many could see no good reason for excluding government or war vessels from the provisions governing salvage at sea, whether the vessels were the passive or the active[39] subjects of the salvage service. Moreover, consideration was given to the fact that the salvage of a vessel in distress does not always fall within the institutional functions of the States.[40]

A movement against this principle was seen at the 1959 CMI Conference in Fiume, by the Scandinavian delegates and, in particular, by the Finns who pointed out that the services rendered in their sea by ice-breakers could be considered as salvage services whilst, instead, set tariffs were applied as for any public service. However, it was immediately clear that such services were to be considered as included with those the organisation of which is reserved, under Article 13 of the Convention, to the individual internal systems of the Contracting States.[41]

7. AMENDMENTS TO ARTICLE 14 OF THE CONVENTION

Thus the movement for reform of the rule contained in Article 14 of the Convention began with the above-mentioned 1959 CMI Conference at Fiume. Specific proposals were made by the various national delegations to eliminate any doubts as to interpretation with regard to the type of exclusion which the Convention, by this rule, had intended to make to its uniform law.

In fact while it was maintained that the inapplicability of the Convention to ships of war or government ships appropriated to a public service represented a general and absolute impediment to the right of those vessels to remuneration for salvage services, and to the consequent duty to remunerate the salvor for such services, there were some who maintained, more correctly, that the inapplicability of the Convention to salvage in such cases as those men-

---

38. F. Berlingieri, "Dell'assistenza ad opera di navi da guerra", in Dir. Mar. 1948, 423; Volli, *op. cit.*, 269; Ferrarini, *Il soccorso*, 25 and 78; Chauveau, *Traité de droit maritime* (1958), 599; Lebrun, "Assistance et sauvetage par navire de guerre", in D.M.F. 1954, 253; Ripert, *Droit Maritime*, III, 2158; Le Clère, *L'assistance aux navires et le sauvetage des épaves* (Paris, 1954), 132, also "Assistance, remorquage et abordage par les navires d'Etat à la suite du Décret du 28 septembre 1955", in D.M.F. 1961, 707; Wildeboer, *op. cit.*, 28.

39. See on this point Ferrarini, *Il soccorso*, 24; Manca, "Commento", 198.

40. See arbitration award, 20 October 1929 in DOR, XXII, 127, and in doctrine: Ghionda, "Sull'assistenza prestata da navi da guerra", in Riv. Dir. Nav. 1940, II, 170; Russo, "Assistenza ad opera di nave dello Stato", in Riv. Dir. Nav. 1939, II 64; Cobianchi, "Sul diritto a compenso degli ufficiali della R.M. per l'assistenza prestata a navi da guerra", in Dir. Mar. 1939, 557.

41. Wildeboer, *op. cit.*, 31.

tioned by no means prevented the individual States involved from applying their own national law.[42]

In this respect the proposal that the Convention should be envisaged to apply also to salvage services performed by or to government ships and ships of war prevailed; but jurisdiction over resulting actions at law was reserved exclusively to the courts of the State of the salved vessel. The proposed amendment read as follows:

"The Plenary Conference of the Comité Maritime International requests its President to submit to the Belgian Government the resolution of the Comité Maritime International for inviting the Bruxelles Diplomatic Conference for Maritime Law to substitute in an appropriate manner to Art. 14 of the International Convention on Assistance and Salvage the following text:

The provisions of this Convention apply also to services of assistance or salvage rendered to a ship of war or to any other ship owned or operated by a State or any Public Authority.

Claims against a State for assistance or salvage services rendered to ships of war or to ships appropriated exclusively to public non-commercial services shall be brought only before the Courts of such State.

When a ship of war or any other ship owned or operated by a State or Public Authority has rendered assistance or salvage services, such State or Public Authority has liberty to claim remuneration but only pursuant to the provisions of this Convention.

The High Contracting Parties reserve to themselves the right of fixing the conditions in which Art. 11 will apply to masters of ships of war."

Having been included on the agenda of the 1961 Diplomatic Conference of Brussels, the amendment was not discussed further due to lack of time, as the delegates were completely absorbed in discussions on the Convention relating to the Liability of Owners of Nuclear Vessels. The amendment was, therefore, reproposed at the 1967 Diplomatic Conference of Brussels where it was approved in its original wording.

The amendment having come into force in 1977 (after the minimum number of instruments of ratification and adherences had been lodged),[43] it is held by some[44] that the Protocol is destined to regulate relationships only

42. See the publication by the CMI, *Conferenza de Rijeka* (1959), 433; G. Berlingieri, "Revisione dell'art. 14 della Convenzione di Bruxelles del 1910 sull'assistenza e salvataggio delle navi in mare", in Dir. Mar. 1959, 429; Gaeta, "La modifica dell'art. 14 della Convenzione di Bruxelles del 1910 sull'assistenza e salvataggio", in Riv. Dir. Nav., 1968, I, 231.

43. To date the following countries have ratified the Protocol: Austria, Brazil, Belgium, Arab Republic of Egypt, Great Britain and Yugoslavia. The following have adhered: Jersey, Guernsey and the Isle of Man, Papua New Guinea and Syria.

44. G. Berlingieri, "Salvataggio e assistenza", 37. It must be noted that whilst this author considered the application of the Protocol to salvage services in which vessels of Contracting States are both the active and passive subjects as obvious for vessels of war and government vessels, he opted, with regard to the general principle of application of the Convention, for the point of view (see note 18) that it was not necessary for one of the two vessels, the salved or the salvor, to belong to a Contracting State.

between States which have ratified it, and that, in all other cases, the national laws of the various States will come into play.

We wonder whether a solution to the problem (already discussed at the beginning of this chapter) as to whether or not the Convention is applicable to those cases of salvage where, as salvor or salved, there is only one vessel belonging to a Contracting State (i.e. when the salvage services are performed by, or in favour of, a vessel belonging to a non-contracting State—a problem which, as we have seen, would be resolved positively[45]), is that the new law of Article 14 contained in the Protocol must be considered applicable, even should the salvage services performed by or to a government vessel be rendered by or to a vessel belonging to a non-contracting State.

From the text of Article 1 of the Protocol it would seem impossible to arrive at a different solution as both the French text ("rendus par ou") and the corresponding English text ("by or") have the same result of incorporating into the rule both the case of salvage rendered in favour of a government vessel as well as that rendered by a government vessel without, however, there being any indication in the rule to the effect that one or other of the salving or salved vessels must necessarily belong to a Contracting State. We have already noted that other Conventions had made express mention of this point when, as in the case of the Convention on Collisions at Sea (Article 12), it is specified that the Convention is applicable "when all the vessels involved belong to States of the High Contracting Parties".

A new controversy arose with regard to the new wording of Article 1 of the Convention, following from the application of the Protocol, about the interpretation of the term "au service public non-commercial" contained in the second paragraph of Article 1 of the Protocol. This establishes that suits brought against a State for assistance and salvage services rendered to a vessel of war or to any vessel which, at the time of the claim being brought, is appropriated exclusively to a non-commercial public service, must be brought before the courts of the State to which the vessel belongs.

The need to clarify the significance which the Protocol meant to ascribe to the term "non-commercial public service" arises from the necessity of identifying those cases in which salvage services rendered to or by a government vessel, as well as falling within the Convention, are removed from the exclusive jurisdiction of the State to which the vessel belongs. By comparing the Protocol with Article 3 of the Brussels Convention of 10 April 1926 on the Unification of Certain Rules relating to the Immunity of Government Vessels,[46] it can be seen that government vessels appropriated to a "commercial service" are excluded from the concept of government vessels as adopted by

---

45. See on this point notes 18 and 19 and the doctrine and jurisprudence cited therein.

46. We have seen that this possibility had been foreseen by the 1926 Brussels Convention which had explicitly granted that claims relating to assistance and salvage services rendered to a government vessel could be brought before the courts of the State to which the vessel belonged. See on this point Ferrarini, *Il soccorso*, 26 and 28; G. Berlingieri, "Salvataggio e assistenza", 43.

the uniform international law. Also excluded are those expressly indicated as vessels performing a public service, such as State yachts, coastguard craft, hospital ships, auxiliary vessels and all vessels destined exclusively for public service.[47]

Therefore, wherever the government vessel has been used in commercial service she will be considered, for the purposes of the applicable jurisdiction, to be a normal commercial vessel and claims against the State to which she belongs will continue to be governed by the 1910 Convention—although with some limitations with respect to preventive measures for obtaining security and for the conservation of the salvage claim.[48]

A final problem regarding interpretation, which arose in relation to Article 14 of the Convention, concerns the concept introduced by Article 1 of the Protocol whereby vessels "operated or chartered" by a State or public authority are included with ships of war or government vessels.

This expression would seem to lead to that used in the 1934 Protocol on the Immunity of Government Vessels, whereby the protocol was intended to resolve doubts as to the interpretation of the expression "exploités par lui" used in Article 3 of the 1926 Convention. The Protocol (though for purposes quite different from those under discussion) specified that vessels "operated" by a State included any ship on voyage or time charter to a State wherever such a ship was used exclusively for public and not commercial services.

However, these classifications and distinctions have dwindled in importance and have maintained only limited relevance for the purposes of the second paragraph of Article 1 of the 1967 Protocol on Assistance and Salvage at Sea since, as has correctly been pointed out by several parties,[49] for the purpose of its first paragraph, all vessels, without exception, be they private or State-owned, be they the active or the passive participants in the salvage operations, fall within the Convention's sphere of application.

47. The general concept of "government trading vessel" is similarly indicated in Art. 9 of the Geneva Convention of 29 April 1958 on the Regime of the High Seas, and in Art. 10, subpara. 3, of the Brussels Convention of 25 May 1952 on the Liability of Operators of Nuclear Vessels. On this point: Gaeta, *op. cit.*, 246; Manca, "Commento", 280.

48. Ferrarini, *Il soccorso*, 26; Kennedy, *Civil Salvage*, 366. Art. 3 of the 1926 Convention on the Immunity of Government Vessels textually establishes that such vessels: "shall not be subject to seizure, arrest or detention by any legal process nor to any proceedings *in rem*".

49. Gaeta, *op. cit.*, 43; Manca, *op. cit.*, 276.

CHAPTER TWO

THE LAW OF SALVAGE AT SEA UNDER THE RULES OF THE 1910 CONVENTION

8. THE MATERIAL SUBJECTS OF SALVAGE

After having indicated the application of the Convention by pointing out the particular cases which it intended to exclude from the international rules governing salvage, it is necessary, within that sphere of application, to identify the material subjects and the active and passive subjects of salvage to which the Convention's rules fully apply.

As possible material subjects of salvage the Convention indicates, in Article 1, seagoing vessels, things which are found on board them, the freight and price of passage, and also craft used on inland waters which, as we have seen, may come within the international law of salvage when salvage has been rendered by a seagoing vessel.

Human lives come into consideration as possible objects of salvage within the Convention's rules (although not specifically indicated in Article 1), in the context of Article 9. That, as a general principle, excludes the right to remuneration for saving human lives at sea, but indicates these as possible material subjects of salvage. It brings the case within the application of the Convention when it establishes the right of the savers of human life to participate only in an equitable share of the remuneration granted to the salvors of the ship, the cargo and her accessories, on all occasions when, in a complex salvage operation with several salvors involved, some of them have devoted themselves exclusively to the saving of human life. The aim is to avoid unfair discrimination against those who, in salvage, have fulfilled the moral obligation of lending assistance to those whose personal safety is at risk.

Although excluding the right to a separate remuneration for the saving of human life alone, it should be noted that the Convention indicates among the qualifying elements of salvage the fact that the salvors, in salving the ship and its cargo, have also saved human life, for Article 8 of the Convention includes, among the elements of remuneration, and as a primary consideration, the danger incurred by the passengers and crew of the salved vessel.

It is therefore evident that the remuneration will be increased when, at the

27

same time as salving the ship in peril, human lives in material danger of being lost have been saved.[50]

Concerning the tendency in the past for such a case to be excluded from any right to remuneration,[51] the Convention introduces two significant changes in the subject of the saving of human life at sea, without prejudice to the traditional moral principle that such services should be free of charge. So it acknowledges that the saver of human life, who had rendered his assistance on the occasion of the salvage of a ship performed by others, should share in the compensation due for this, and introduces the element of saving human lives in peril on board the salved ship as a specific qualifying element of the services in order to determine the compensation due to the salvor.[52]

It should be noted that both in the case of effectively sharing in the apportionment of the remuneration (Article 9, paragraph 2) and in the case where the determination is influenced by the contemporaneous salvage of ship, cargo and human life (Article 9, paragraph 1), the individual persons saved do not have to pay remuneration as do the owners of the things salved (ship, cargo, freight).[53]

50. Kennedy, *Civil Salvage*, 98; Gilmore and Black, *The Law of Admiralty* (New York, 1975), 532; G. Berlingieri, *Salvataggio ed assistenza*, 468; Ferrarini, *Il soccorso*, 22; Manca, *Commento*, 202; Reuter, *La notion d'assistance*, 162 *et seq.* Wildeboer, *The Brussels Convention*, 243 *et seq.*; this author provides a wide view of the discussions which arose between the delegations of the various Contracting States regarding the method of applying a uniform law to the saving of human life at sea, and ends by recognising that the differences which emerged in the discussions between the various delegates, were the reason why the Convention left the Contracting States free to incorporate the rule deriving from the Convention into their own national laws. Rather than leaving the party States free to adopt the provisions of Art. 9 in their own national legislations, the Convention seems to have wished to lay down that its own rules on the subject of saving human life cannot introduce modifications to what is provided on the subject by the individual national laws ("but nothing in this article shall affect the provisions of the national law on this subject").

51. Kennedy, *op. cit.*, 377 *et seq.*; and recently Brice, *op. cit.*, 83 *et seq.* and English jurisprudence quoted therein, through which the author provides an outline of the progressive adaptation which has been made in the law of saving human life at sea through court decisions, until it approaches the law established in the 1910 Convention, which had already been accepted in England in section 544 of the Merchant Shipping Act 1984.

52. Our jurisprudence has pronounced a series of substantially similar judgments on the point: cf. Arbitration Award, 30 December 1963, in Dir. Mar. 1965, 300; Arbitration Award, 28 November 1965, in Dir. Mar. 1966, 357; Trib. Napoli, 8 January 1969, in Dir. Mar. 1969, 141; and App. Napoli, 13 August 1970, in Dir. Mar. 1970, 407; these decisions are however incorrect where they rule that, according to Art. 9 of the Brussels Convention 1910 on Assistance and Salvage, the reference to the national law for the saving of persons is allowed only when this is carried out in relation to persons and is therefore disassociated from the salvage of things, because the phrase "nothing in this article shall affect" refers to the whole text of Art. 9 of the Convention and thus also to the second paragraph of that Article.

53. Italian jurisprudence has accepted (App. Trieste, 10 August 1962, in Dir. Mar. 1963, 106, and in Riv. Dir. Nav. 1963, II, 193) that the shipowner who has paid the reward requested by the salvor of the crew of a shipwrecked vessel, is entitled to seek a refund from the National Institute of Insurance for the Prevention of Industrial Accidents, classing this form of insurance as an insurance against damage. In agreement: Cass. 19 July 1966, No. 1948, in Dir. Mar. 1966, 479. However the solution to the problem lies in the Code of Navigation (Art. 493). *Contra*, G. Berlingieri, "Compenso per salvataggio di persone in mare e assicurazione", in Dir. Mar. 1960, 321, and Righetti, "Salvataggio di persone in mare e assicurazione" (Arts. 493 and 985 Nav.

It may be concluded that, under the Convention, human lives are considered as possible objects of salvage, but the international rules have imposed certain limitations with respect to this particular object of salvage:

(a) that no remuneration is due for the saving of persons;

(b) that the salvor of human lives may share in the remuneration of the salvor of the ship, cargo and freight, only when the assistance rendered by the latter has achieved a useful even though partial result[54];

(c) that the saver of human life who has at the same time or even at successive different times also salved things (the ship or part of it, the cargo or part of it) has the right also to be remunerated for the saving of persons; the latter is included as an element in determining the remuneration.[55]

The main object of salvage, according to the Convention, is the vessel. In effect the salvage operations have, in most cases, the specific purpose of salving the seagoing vessel, because all other cases of salvage (salvage of only the cargo of a ship in peril, salvage of the cargo and freight, salvage of a part of the cargo, of accessories or parts of the salvaged ship), form particular aspects of salvage. We have already seen that the Convention does not provide a definition of a vessel, and it is necessary to refer to the preparatory work[56] to find that the Convention applies to all vessels of any nature, but solely to *vessels*

Code), in *Assicurazioni* 1961, I, 291. Of interest is the case-book of English jurisprudence on the point, quoted by Ferrarini, *Il soccorso*, 154, or more recently by Brice: *op. cit.*, 83. Typical is the case of *The cargo ex Sarpedon* quoted by Ferrarini, *Il soccorso*, 154, where the request of the salvors of the crew of the ship, which subsequently sank, who had also salved part of the cargo, was rejected because it was put forward against the shipowner who had not had anything salved.

54. On the subject of salvage of freight it is interesting to mention the case of *The Medina*, 1 P.D. 272 in Chorley & Giles, *Shipping Law* (London, 1963), 257, in which it was recognised that the saving of the passengers of a shipwrecked vessel, who had paid the shipowner for their passage, constituted salvage of freight because the salvors had salved something more than human life. In Italian law, see Tribunal of Brindisi, 14 April 1986, in Dir. Mar. 1987, 115, which established that the salving crew members of a ship in peril are entitled to payment of the remuneration acknowledged as owing to them by the owner of that vessel, wherever that owner, having been summonsed before the court, fails to summons the crew's Seamen's Fund.

55. Regarding the fact that salvage of human life and of property need not necessarily be contemporaneous, see the reports of the preparatory work of the Convention (Reports, 1909, 141), which recognise the unitary nature of the salvage services rendered by a ship at two different times; the first, to remove the persons and crew of the salved ship from danger; the second operation, resumed even after some time, to bring the ship and her cargo to safety. *Contra*, but without a convincing reason, Reuter, *La notion d'assistance*, 167, who writes, with reference to Art. 17–1 of the French law of 1967 which reproduces almost exactly the French text of Art. 9 of the Convention: "Un navire rencontre en mer des personnes en danger, soit qu'elles soient à bord d'un batiment en péril, soit qu'elles l'aient déjà quitté. L'assistant ne peut ou ne veut s'occuper du navire et se borne a recueillir les personnes. Il ne reçoit pour cet acte ni remboursement des frais ni rémuneration; l'article 17–1, est formel: 'Il n'est dû aucune rémuneration pour les personnes sauvées.' Peu importe que le navire abandonné se soit par la suite perdu, ou ait été sauvé par d'autres assistants ou, à la limite, par ceux-la mêmes qui ont secouru les personnes et qui, apres les avoir mises en sécurité, seraient revenus sur les lieux assister le navire."

56. Cf. Brussels Conference 1905, Reports, 174, 175.

(the concept of a vessel is applicable to all vessels which are used for navigation, maritime traffic and, in certain cases, as we have seen, for internal navigation) designed to go by sea for the purpose of carriage, even if for other specific activities (towing, fishing, sport, scientific purposes). Within the meaning of the Convention, certain fixed objects are not vessels, although intended for port services, such as dry docks stably moored in a port and pontoons stably anchored to the bottom, while some mobile objects should be considered as such, for example floating objects capable of moving under their own propulsion or under tow.[57] The same conclusions may be reached by comparing the Convention rule with Article 136 of the Italian Code of Navigation which in paragraph 3 reads: "The provisions concerning vessels also apply, unless otherwise specified, to mobile floating objects used for any service in connection with navigation or traffic in maritime or internal waters".

The definition of a maritime or seagoing vessel which emerges from the text of the Convention appears to be full and similar to that which emerges from the almost contemporaneous Convention on Collision; identical elements of qualifying the vessel can be found in the preparatory works on them.[58]

It has been questioned whether a vessel removed from the Register or a vessel under construction can form the subject of salvage[59] because the former has ceased to be a vessel and the latter has not yet become one. The solution to be adopted in these borderline cases seems to be to accept both the vessels, the one deleted from the Register and the one not yet entered, as vessels within the meaning of the Convention and, as such, capable of becoming objects of a salvage operation.

In the former case if, at the time of deletion (which is a purely administrative procedure having a declaratory effect) it is agreed that, from a merely physical point of view, the ship should be considered as lost, salvage law will apply by virtue of the reintroduction of salvage of wreck in the concept of salvage coming within the Convention.[60] In the latter case, although the ship lacks the formal legal seaworthiness to undertake navigation conferred on her only by entry in the Registry admitting her to navigation, it may in certain

57. *Contra*, Leclère (in note to App. Rennes, 23 March 1960, in D.M.F. 1960, 413), which endows the convoy (the towing craft and the craft under tow) with a unitary concept, reconnecting the combined whole to the concept of a ship, if the convoy or part of it is salved. Italian jurisprudence has decided that the law of salvage applies to a dredger lost by the tug which was towing it and subsequently salved by the same tug, taking it that the concept of a ship is to be extended to this mobile craft. Cf. Arbitration Award of 4 May 1963, in Dir. Mar. 1965, 276. For a clear explanation of the concept of a ship on the basis of Italian legislation, cf. Gaeta, item *Nave* (dir. nav.) in *Encyclopedia del dir.*, 601 *et seq*.

58. At the meeting of 4 October 1909 delegate Frank stated in this regard that: "Il est bien d'ajouter que le mot navire s'entend dans le sense le plus large, englobant toutes les variétés de bâtiments qui se déplacent sur l'eau servant au transport des personnes ou des choses ou se livrant a des opérations commerciales, scientifiques, techniques ou sportives."

59. G. Berlingieri, *Salvataggio ed assistenza*, 24.

60. Ferrarini, *op. loc. cit.*, 28.

cases be considered that, since it is a mobile floating construction suitable for navigation, it is a real and proper vessel for the purposes of salvage.[61] There is also, for example, the case of a ship which has been built in a shipyard of another Contracting State and finds herself after or during her launching in a situation of peril and has to be salved by the tugs of the latter. In this case it appears clear that salvage law will be fully applicable and the Convention's rules will come into play, due to the subjective international nature of the matter. No importance would be attached to the location of the port where the salvage has taken place[62] in view of the specific affirmation contained in Article 1 of the Convention "without having to take account of the waters where the services were rendered" ("sans qu'il y ait à tenir compte des eaux où ils ont été rendus" in the French text).

In effect, as the Convention admits that its own law also applies to vessels engaged in internal navigation, they may become objects of salvage in particular circumstances, that is to say, when the salvage involves at least one seagoing vessel, regardless of the location where the salvage operation takes place. This means that, in order to come within the application of the Convention, the seagoing vessel is categorised on the basis of the material subjects of salvage, not on the basis of the type of navigation in which it is engaged at the time when the salvage is performed.[63]

One of the objects of salvage, on the basis of the Convention, is represented by the "cargo" of the ship in peril, that is, the entire totality of things, whether goods, baggage or effects of the crew, and including the ship's stores. All fall within the full meaning of the term used in Article 1 of the Convention where it says that the object of salvage consists of the things which are on board at the time of the salvage itself. It has been questioned whether "things which are found on board" is intended to mean also the appurtenances of the ship and not only the parts which can be separated from them as *res connexae* because, while some authors opted for their inclusion,[64] others more correctly

61. This point is amply covered by Querci, *Pubblicita marittima ed aeronautica* (Milan, 1961), 83 *et seq*.

62. Regarding this see E. Vincenzini, "Il soccorso in acque portuali", in Dir. Mar. 1980, 347. On the subject of salvage in port waters, see also Arbitration Award of 22 March 1989, in Dir. Mar. 1990, 416. Reuter, *La notion d'assistance*, 101, does not consider correct the definition of a maritime ship for the purposes of the application of the law of salvage to a ship under construction. For a necessary presence of the property salved on the water and not on shore, see Gilmore and Black, *The Law of Admiralty*, 538 and American jurisprudence quoted there.

63. Wildeboer, *The Brussels Convention*, 18, provides a full comparative examination between the notion of a *navire* as it is indicated in the text of the Convention, and the same notion indicated from the legislation of the various Contracting States.

64. Wildeboer, *op, cit*., 21; G. Berlingieri, *Salvataggio ed assistenza*, 25; on the legal nature of the appurtenances and on the distinction between the constituent parts of the ship and the appurtenances, see Gaeta, *Nave*, 648 *et seq*., who notes that the non-material connection may determine or otherwise the loss of the autonomy of the part with regard to the ship, giving rise to the formation of constituent parts or of appurtenances, depending on whether the thing connected is used for the *perfectio* of the whole or is intended for its service and adornment.

rejected the idea that the appurtenances could come within the concept of "things loaded", in view of their close connection with the ship to whose service they are bound.[65]

Given the legal nature of appurtenances, it does not seem possible that they can form a separate object of the salvage, as they form an integral part of the ship as a whole, and in this context come under the law as set up by the Convention. It should not be overlooked, however, that appurtenances can form a separate object of salvage. In that case, since they lack the material connection to the main object (the ship), the salvage of the appurtenances will come within the partial salvage of the goods of the passive subject, which is different and distinct both from the ship and from her cargo.

A final discussion would seem to be appropriate on the subject of things loaded or things which are to be found on board the salved ship. It is clear that the goods, baggage, gear, effects, and stores take relevance from the facts that they were loaded on board the ship in peril[66] and that they were on board the ship at the time when the peril occurred. The salvage operation must necessarily begin after the danger, even if only presumed, has occurred, and, therefore, the things salved during the salvage operation need not necessarily be found on board the ship at risk, when the services of the salving vessel begin. Let us take, for example, the case of cargo jettisoned by a ship in peril which has sent out a signal calling for help, and where part or all of the cargo jettisoned has been saved or recovered by the salvors. In this case the operation should be regarded as a single salvage operation, shared over a number of different services between the ship and the jettisoned cargo, no importance being attached to the fact that the things salved (goods, effects, etc.) are not on board at the time of the salvage; nor can the recovery of the jettisoned cargo be qualified as the finding of a wreck.[67]

It would seem difficult to subscribe to a theory in doctrine which seeks to equate the things transported by a ship to the things being transferred under tow, whether a floating dock, a lighter full of logs or a floating container used

65. For the exclusion of the appurtenances from the concept of *chose se trouvant à bord*, Ferrarini, *Il soccorso*, 27, for whom even the ship's provisions are to be excluded; and Manca, *Commento*, 204.

66. Thus correctly Ferrarini, *op. loc. cit.*; the problem had also been mentioned by De Juglart and Villeneau, *Repertoire methodique*, 96, and debated in the preliminary draft at the Conference of 1905, where in the first instance there had been talk of assistance to *un navire en peril ou à sa cargaison*; but at the session of the Conference in September 1909 the text was changed to the present text, the Commission having standardised the wording with that used for the International Convention on Collision of Ships. While, in collision, the things damaged must necessarily be on board the ship which has entered into collision, in salvage this necessary presence does not have the same importance.

67. Cf. G. Berlingieri, *Salvataggio ed assistenza*, 26, who opts for classifying the two different operations as salvage of ship and recovery of cargo, noting the limited difference in practice, seeing that the position of the recoverer, so far as determining the remuneration is concerned, is very similar to that of the salvor.

for transporting liquids.[68] This theory, correctly formulated with regard to the cargoes contained in mobile craft transported under tow, does not appear to hold good when it is sought to extend the concept of cargo also to the object being towed, which (as it must necessarily be a floating object and if towed a mobile floating object) has to be considered, for the purpose of the Convention rules, as a vessel, because it is capable of moving over the sea, and that *a fortiori* in a case where it is used for the purpose of carrying goods.

If one were to adhere to the latter concept it would be possible, in particular cases, to arrive at abnormal solutions on the question of the correct application of the principles of salvage, as laid down by the Convention.

Consider the case of a tug which is towing a floating lighter loaded with liquids, and which, as a result of a gale, loses it. After requesting help, the lighter is recovered and salved by another seagoing vessel which has intervened for the purpose. Were the lighter and its cargo to be considered as a single cargo of the towing ship (this not being in peril and the salvage not being performed for the ship and cargo within the meaning of the same salvage operation), the law of the Convention would not apply to such a case, because salvage of cargo is admitted only in the case where the assisted ship has been lost, i.e. when the salvage of the cargo or part of it assumes the character of a partially useful result within the context of a single service for the benefit of the whole venture at risk.[69]

Freight and price of passage are indicated in Article 1 of the Convention as a possible material subject of salvage. It would have been more appropriate to have included these, with the saving of human life, not so much with the specific objects of the law being studied, but rather among the components of evaluation and the fixing of remuneration indicated in Article 8 of the Convention.[70] The reason for this lies in the principle, already established in the saving of human life at sea, that the fixing of the compensation due to the salvor, in the case of the salvage of a ship and cargo, can be influenced by the fact that freight has also been saved (although this obviously cannot in itself form an object of salvage capable of allowing the salvor to receive a separate remuneration). There cannot be a salvage of freight unless another part of the

68. On this subject Ferrarini, *op. cit.*, 27, who examines the circumstances in the light of Italian national law (Art. 136 Nav. Code).

69. Of interest on this point are the decisions quoted by Brice, *Maritime Law of Salvage*, 107, in the case of *The Gas Float Whitton (No. 2)* [1895] P. 301; [1896] P. 42; [1897] A.C. 337, where the tug and lighter under tow were considered as a single nautical unit, because the salvage had involved both the vessels, and thus in *The Rilland* [1979] 1 Lloyd's Rep. 455. In the case of *The J. P. Donaldson*, in 1897 167 U.S. 599, the convoy was considered as forming two separate units, the tug and the lighter both being regarded as *separate vessels* and as such subject to a separate salvage, because, being considered as two separate nautical vessels, one cannot be considered as *the cargo of the other*. *Contra* we have seen Ferrarini, *Il soccorso*. For the concept of convoy see Dani, "In tema di 'flottilla rule' ", in Dir. Mar., 1977, 107 *et seq*.

70. Thus Manca, *Commento*, 20; G. Berlingieri, *Salvataggio ed assistenza*, 28; Wildeboer, *The Brussels Convention*, 21, who considers that the inclusion of the *freight* amongst the objects of the salvage mentioned by Art. 1 of the Convention represents an error by its authors.

material subject of the venture (ship, cargo or passenger) to which the freight strictly relates[71] has been salved wholly or in part.

A distinction should also be made between freight relating to the carriage of goods to destination and hire for the use of the ship. This distinction determines whether or not this element is to be included in the factors fixing the compensation. The time charter hire or the freights for the bareboat charter, even if at risk for the ship itself, are not considered as forming an element for appraising the compensation itself,[72] since consideration has to be given to the freights effectively at risk for the seagoing vessel ("freight at risk") at the time of the salvage.

The term "freight" applicable to the case is that which is conditioned (in so far as due to the carrier) by the redelivery of the goods at destination, i.e. that which is connected with the carriage of the goods and to the accomplishment of the voyage; it is also that which, being "prepaid and earned in any event", is considered to be acquired by the carrier even if the ship or cargo are lost ("not returnable even in the event of the ship or cargo being lost"). The freight, however, assumes relevance in determining the value of the goods, because it is by its nature an element in that evaluation, distinguished (in this sense) from the freight at risk which may in fact constitute *a separate subject of salvage*. It has been observed that, although it does not constitute a maritime property but only a simple transfer of money, the freight may nevertheless, in certain cases, form a monetary element of considerable interest to the extent that it would make the owner of the ship, if salved, liable to remunerate the salvor of the cargo or lives to which the freight refers.[73]

9. THE ACTIVE SUBJECTS OF SALVAGE

So far as concerns the active and passive subjects of salvage, it must first be noted that the Convention's rules do not contain provisions which either

71. According to Ferrarini, *op. cit.*, 31, freight answers to the general concept existing in other maritime laws, such as general average and marine insurance, by which freight forms an element of the venture and as such may be salved.

72. Thus Brice, *Maritime Law*, 108, for whom: "Freight is a term frequently used in practice to cover two concepts namely the remuneration payable for the carriage of goods in a ship on the one hand, on the other the sum payable for the use of the ship. Salvage is concerned with the use of the term in the first sense. In the second sense it is useful to refer to that type of payment as 'hire'. Hire is not subject to salvage"; and Ferrarini, *Il soccorso*, 31. It should be noted that in the most recent Anglo-Saxon arbitration practice, time charter hire, particularly if of some duration, instead of being considered as an element for evaluating remuneration, has been considered as an element for determining the value of the salved ship.

73. Brice, *op. cit.*, 139, Kennedy, *Civil Salvage*, 384, who refers to the case of *The Medina*, 1 P.D. 272, 2.P.O.5, which was lost on a shoal in the Red Sea and from which 550 pilgrims who were on their way to Jeddah, were transshipped. The price of the passage was considered together with the persons as a salved property, and the ship which had completed the voyage was granted reward determined on the basis of the passage price earned by the owner of the *Medina*.

specify these two categories of subjects, or provide regulations in respect of them.

As has been correctly noted,[74] in the text of the Convention only certain indications can be found regarding the identification of the active and passive subjects of the salvage, but this identification is derived not so much from an actual list of such subjects as from the co-ordination and interpretation of certain rules not expressly intended for the purpose.

On reading the statements and records of the Conference, the impression is given that the delegates did not pay much attention to the identification of the subjects of salvage.[75] Only in the preparatory works of the Conference can elements of a certain debate on the problem of identifying such subjects be found,[76] although, at the end of it, we find no valid and explicit grounds on the basis of which any particular instruction in this respect was proposed in the draft Convention.

It has been noted in this regard[77] that the text of the Convention gives the impression that, at the end of the discussion, the intention of the delegates was to avoid regulating in any way, either with lists of subjects or with rules governing the relations between them, the problems relating to persons who may find themselves on the one hand creditors, or on the other debtors, of salvage remuneration, for it was decided during the Brussels Conference to leave it to the national laws of the individual Contracting States to regulate these particular aspects of salvage.

Although, therefore, the Convention qualifies salvage on the basis of the material subjects, in view of the fact that salvage is rendered to the ship-cargo-freight, the term *navire* (ship) used in the Convention generically identifies all the active and passive interests which are brought into play and, consequently, the persons with whom these interests are associated.

74. Wildeboer, *op. cit.*, 66 *et seq.*
75. Cf. Reports: I, 38–39; II, 195–196; III, 92–215–222; IV, 45–46–54–100–101.
76. Bulletin VIII, II, IX, 146 *et seq.*
77. Wildeboer, *op. cit.*, 67; this author notes that in the reports of the preparatory work of the two almost contemporaneous Conventions, that on collision and that on assistance and salvage, the principle was stated, for both the Conventions, that they would have to govern uniformly the relations concerning salvage of one ship by another ship and collision between two or more ships, leaving it to the national laws to regulate the relations between the various persons and between the parties involved in the salvage operations or in the collision, and reports two significant passages from these reports: "Le mot 'navire' personnifie tous les intérêts en cause, activement et passivement. Activement, il désigne, et ceux qui conduisent le navire, capitaine, pilote, officiers, et tous les préposés divers qui peuvent engager la responsabilité du propriétaire. Sur cette responsabilité, sur les diverses personnes qui peuvent en avoir la charge—propriétaire, armateur, affréteur, etc.—le texte n'entre dans aucun détail. Le navire représente tous les intérêts corps . . . Passivement, pour le dommage subi, la même terme désigne tous ceux qui ont le droit de réclamer du chef du navire. Les lois nationales conservent sous ce double rapport leur plein empire. C'est à elles, par exemple, de déterminer quelles sont les personnes qui peuvent être considérées comme les préposés du propriétaire. Cette manière de procéder ne paraît devoir soulever aucun inconvénient, car il n'est sur ces points que des divergences de détail et la solution qui y est donnée dépend souvent de l'ensemble des principes juridiques formants la base des législations nationales. Les résoudre dans la convention serait une enterprise extrêmement malaisée."

This doctrinal theory seems to imply that (following the historical evolution of the law, which at the start showed a distinct emphasis on the personal element of salvage without nautical craft instead of on the economic element, salvage with nautical craft, but which later, on the introduction of steam propulsion, underwent an inversion in order of importance of these elements) this has made economic participation in the operation of greater importance, for the purpose of identifying the salvor, than the active subject of the relationship.[78]

Thus not only does the owner of the ship performing the salvage represent the subject of salvage, but this status also belongs to the master and crew of the salving ship, and in particular cases to subjects outside this category: passengers, pilots, mooring crew, etc. It seems, then, that the correct doctrinal tendency is that which, for the purpose of identifying the active subjects, benefits the organised complex relating to the ship, i.e. to the shipping company and consequently to the persons forming part of that organisation.[79]

For a correct formulation of the problem to enable it to be solved, it is necessary to seek, within the Convention's rules, such indications as, although in an informal way, identify the active subjects of the salvage as adopted by the Convention itself.

The only rule which helps for this purpose is Article 6, paragraph 3, of the Convention which, in the French text and the English text respectively, reads as follows:

"La répartition entre le propriétaire, le capitaine et les autres personnes au service de chacun des navires sauveteurs sera reglée par la loi nationale du navire".

"The apportionment of the remuneration amongst the owner, master and other persons in the service of each salving vessel shall be determined by the law of the vessel's flag."

Establishing, by a reference to national law, how the remuneration is to be apportioned between the active subjects of the salvage, this Article identifies these subjects as the "owner" of the vessel and the "other persons in the service of the salving vessels".

The article with its imperfect wording, hardly improved by the existence of a bilingual text, (for example, *propriétaire*—owner; *loi nationale* —law of flag), does not appear to solve fully the problem of finding a correct identification of the active subjects of the salvage within the uniform rules of the Convention.[80]

78. Ferrarini, *Il soccorso*, 58 *et seq.*
79. Ferrarini, *op. loc. cit.*
80. Cf. Wildeboer, *op. cit.*, 68. This author, while maintaining that the incorrect translation in the English text of *loi nationale du navire* could signify that no account should be taken of the law of the flag when the ship flies a flag of convenience but rather of the law associated with the nationality of the owner, concludes by acknowledging that the law of the state to which the owner of the salving ship belongs does not apply if the nationality of the ship is different on the basis of the law of the flag. On the problem of the existence or otherwise of a *genuine link* between the ship and the state whose nationality is possessed by the ship, see Carbone *op. cit.*, 72 *et seq.*

In the first place, the French term *propriétaire*, which corresponds to the term "shipowner", can cause confusion if related to terms which do not correspond in the other national laws, with consequent difficulties of identifying the most relevant active subject within the scope of salvage.[81]

It has been noted that the French term *propriétaire* is the source of doubts of interpretation because, by virtue of the reference made by Article 6, paragraph 3, of the Convention to the national laws of the individual salvors, these laws, containing terms which do not correspond to the French term, could hinder the application of the Convention's rules to the operators, charterers and other associated subjects, because the Convention makes no mention whatsoever of any possible right of these others to remuneration.[82]

This idea does not seem to hold good. In fact, although the English term "owner" is ambivalent because it identifies both the owner and the operator of the ship,[83] according to the commonly accepted meaning of these terms (for example, in Italian legislation) it is clear that the Convention did not intend to identify the active subject of the salvage with the bare ownership of the ship, but with the operative phase.

Existing Italian and international doctrine has come out in favour of the identification of the most important active subject of the salvage as the "operator" (whether the owner of the ship or not), this latter being understood as a subject primarily associated with the shipping company and the "operation" of the ship, but not excluding from the list of such possible subjects, even those people who, by virtue of a contract with the bare owner (time charterers, bareboat charterers, demise charterers, etc.) are given, either wholly or in part, the right to claim or to share in the apportionment of a salvage reward.[84]

In addition to the operator, Article 6, paragraph 3, of the Convention includes among those entitled to salvage remuneration the master of the ship and the other persons who are in her service.

There is no doubt that in the meaning of this last term must be included the members of the crew of the salving ship, which—as we shall see later—does not mean that members of the crew of the salved ship are excluded in particular cases, but it is open to question whether the pilot can be considered, within the meaning of the Convention, to be in the service of the salving ship.

81. Ferrarini, *Il soccorso*, 58; Volli, *Assistenza*, 91.

82. Wildeboer, *op. cit.*, 68 *et seq.* Think for example of the Italian Code of Navigation in which the term *proprietario* does not mean the same as *armatore*, while in German law the *Reeder* is always the owner of the ship.

83. Cf. Kennedy, *Civil Salvage*, 124, where, when listing the categories of the active subjects of the salvage, he places them in four categories: "(1) owners of a salving vessel; or (2) demise-charterers who are, or, it seems charterers who by the express terms of the charterparty in relation to salvage become *pro hac vice* owners of the salving vessel; or (3) master or crew of a salving vessel; or (4) persons who have personally engaged in the service in respect of which they claim reward, whether or not they also fall within any of the above three classes".

84. Cf. Ferrarini, *Il soccorso*, 58; Volli, *Assistenza*, 91; G. Berlingieri, *Salvataggio ed assistenza*, 321; Wildeboer, *op. cit.*, 68 *et seq.*; Kennedy, *op. cit.*, 124.

Italian doctrine was, in the past, divided on the qualification of the crew as an active subject of the salvage. A certain doctrinal opinion tended to exclude the members of the crew from being active subjects of a salvage, maintaining that, as the entitlement of the crew to act depends on the operator's failure to take the action involved, this showed that the crew is the sole true party entitled to take such action. This confused a purely procedural reservation in Italian law in favour of the operator with the actual existence, of an effectively overriding right for the crew to receive remuneration for assistance rendered.[85] More convincing is the contrasting theory of a more recent current of doctrinal opinion, which attributes the status of subject of salvage to the crew of the salving ship also that is to be found in the text of the Convention, based on the following particular considerations: that the operator has the exclusive right to the entire remuneration when the assistance is rendered by a vessel especially operated and equipped for that specific purpose; that the right of the crew lies outside the employment contract and as such is directly related to the salved ship; and that, in the case of assistance rendered by a "sister-ship", it is clear that the right which can be claimed is predominantly that of the crew of the salving ship because the operator, in this particular case, finds himself in the double position of active and passive subject of the salvage.[86]

By its laconic nature the text of the Convention appears to exclude, from the right to share in the remuneration, and consequently from the category of the active subjects of the salvage, the crew of the salved ship, referring solely to all "the other persons in the service of each of the salving ships" ("les autres personnes au service de chacun des navires sauveteurs"), but this exclusion should be regarded as operative only when the services rendered by the crew of a ship in peril are duties arising from the employment contract.[87] When the crew of the assisted ship, after having abandoned her by order of the master due to her being in serious danger or on the point of sinking, performs salvage work (for example, by returning or remaining on board the ship), it should be said that the Convention did not intend to exclude the crew from the active subjects of the salvage because, during the time that the Convention has been in force, a substantial number of decisions has recognised

85. Cf. in this sense G. Berlingieri, *Salvataggio ed assistenza*, 317 *et seq.*; Pescatore, *Requisizione di nave e compenso di assistenza e salvataggio*, 1084; Russo, "Questioni in tema di compenso di assistenza e salvataggio", in Riv. Dir. Nav. 1950, II, 120; Id., "Assistenza e salvataggio", in *Encyclopedia del dir.*, 841; Volli, *Assistenza*, 101.

86. Torrente, *I contratti di lavoro della navigazione* (Milan, 1948), 75 *et seq.*; Ferrarini, "Profilo dell'assistenza e salvataggio nel codice della navigazione" in Riv. trim. dir. e proc. civ., 66 *et seq.* See also the decision by the Court of Cassation of 9 February 1988, n. 1373, in Dir. Mar., 1989, 457, where this criterion of exclusion of the crew of a ship equipped for salvage from sharing in the remuneration is confirmed, and the note by Gasparino, "La nave armata ed equipaggiata per prestare soccorso; un orientamento ormai consolidato". Recently, see also the Arbitration Award of 12 April 1989, in Dir. Mar., 1990, 735, with note by Piombino, "Sull'elemento pericolo nella assistenza e salvataggio e sulla ripartizione del compenso fra l'equipaggio della nave soccoritrice".

87. Cf. Manca, *Commento*, 193.

that the crew has the status of salvor in the technical sense, and is hence granted special remuneration for assistance rendered.[88]

It should be mentioned here that the problem of an express attribution to the master and members of the crew of the salvaged ship of the status of salvors was discussed in the work preparatory to the Convention, and one of the preliminary drafts of the Convention contained a rule on the matter which read: "Le pilote et l'équipage du navire en péril n'ont droit a aucune rémuneration, même pour services extraordinaires comme rentrant dans les limites de leurs services respectifs".[89]

This rule, which moreover did not specify whether these extraordinary services rendered by the crew were to be considered as falling within a continuing contractual relationship with the shipowner, and not after the relationship had been ended, was not included in the final text of the Convention. It had been decided to leave the national laws of the individual States to deal with this particular point.

The other active subject of salvage, expressly mentioned by Article 6, paragraph 3, of the Convention, is the master of the salving ship. As he is the holder of a right to separate compensation, no particular questions seem to have arisen either in doctrine or in jurisprudence about this. It should be noted that Article 11 of the Convention, binding the master to render assistance to persons whose personal safety is in peril, implicitly grants him the status of an active subject of salvage if this rule is read with Article 9 of the Convention, where the right to compensation for saving human lives is acknowledged when this has occurred on a salvage operation in which the vessel and her cargo have also been saved.

The discussion, which has provoked much debate in both Italian and international doctrine, is more than anything concerned with the powers of agency of the master vis-à-vis his own owners, both in the case of mandatory salvage and in that of optional salvage, and more precisely whenever he concludes a salvage contract with the vessel to be salved.

The problem does not lie in the question of the identification of the master as an active subject of the salvage because, as has been categorically stated,[90] he intervenes in the salvage in a dual capacity, on his own behalf and in the capacity of owners' agent. It is in the former instance that he assumes the

88. Cf. Ferrarini, *Il soccorso*, 75 and Italian and foreign jurisprudence quoted there. Manca, *Commento*, 193. Both these authors consider it necessary that the employment contract of the individual crew members with the owner should be terminated, as a precondition for the crew to be granted the status of voluntary salvor in the same respect as any other parties not bound by any contract with the shipowner. In this regard, see Tribunal of Brindisi of 4 April 1986, in Dir. Mar., 1987, 115, and with respect to English jurisprudence on the same subject, *The Neptune* 1 Hagg. Adm. 236 and *The Florence* 16 S.U.R. 572.

89. Cf. Reports I, 21 and IV, 101.

90. Ferrarini, *Il soccorso*, 64; Manca, *Studi*, 220 *et seq.*; Volli, *Assistenza*, 90 *et seq.*; Id. "Limiti della rappresentanza sostanziale e processuale del comandante della nave in pericolo, specialmente nei confronti del carico", in Riv. Dir. Nav. 1963, I. 310; G. Berlingieri, *Salvataggio e assistenza*, 316; Carver, *Carriage by Sea* (London, 1963), 836; Kennedy, *op. cit.*, 331.

status of salvor in a technical sense, becoming the holder of a right to compensation distinct from the right to compensation pertaining to the shipowner whose agent he is and whose ship he has used in the salvage operations.

The limits of this agency, although not fixed by the uniform international rules laid down by the Convention, need mention here, in the order which has been elaborated by doctrine, considering the fact that the master's capacity as owners' agent, in the case of salvage at sea, assumes a necessary character, due to the concurrent salvage, which very often does not allow the owner to take his own decisions, nor the master to obtain the necessary instructions from the owner.

These limits have been correctly indicated as follows:

(1) the necessity for prior requests, where possible, for instructions on the part of the master of the salving ship from his own owner;

(2) the impossibility for the master, who has not been able to obtain such instructions, to agree upon compensation with the representatives of the properties salved, although he is allowed to insert an arbitration clause into the text of the salvage agreement[91];

(3) the impossibility for the master to conclude the agreement after the salvage operation has been completed.[92]

We have seen that the Convention does not mention, among the possible active subjects of the salvage, other persons who are outside the group of those included in the employment contract, that is to say the owner, the master, and the crew of the salving ship.

Nevertheless, the doctrine remains[93] that some of these persons, by virtue of the reference rule contained in Article 6, paragraph 3, of the Convention, come within the category of active subjects of the salvage (passengers of the salving ship, pilot, personnel attached to port services) while others (owners of the cargo of the salving ship, passengers of the salved ship) cannot assume the capacity of salvors, either because of the existence of a contract which hinders any such assumption and/or due to the existence of a specific interest in the salvage.

Regarding the right to compensation of those passengers of the salving ship, as took an active part in the salvage operations, even incurring personal risks, there is no difference of opinion in doctrine or in jurisprudence. Compensation is to be determined on the basis of the services actually rendered and the risks incurred, and not on the basis of a calculation of loss to the pas-

---

91. To the contrary, but isolated, is the theory of Smeesters and Winkelmolen in Droit maritime, III, No. 1224. A single English decision, *The City of Calcutta*, quoted by Kennedy, *op. cit.*, 328, note 18, had raised the problem but left the question undecided.

92. Ferrarini, *Il soccorso*, 65 *et seq.*; Kennedy, *op. cit.*, 331.

93. Cf. Wildeboer, *op. cit.*, 70 *et seq.*; Ferrarini, *Il soccorso*, 68 *et seq.*; G. Berlingieri, *Salvataggio ed assistenza*, 323 *et seq.*; Kennedy, *op. cit.*, 29. Carver, *op. cit.*, 811; Norris, *The Law of Salvage* (Mount Kisco, N.Y., 1958), paras. 53 and 77; Brice, *Maritime Law of Salvage*, 31. See also, Cass, 18 November 1987, n. 8456, in Dir. Mar., 1989, 935.

sengers as a result of the delay caused to them by the deviation from her course of the salving ship and her use in the salvage operations.[94]

As regards awards to the pilot and personnel engaged in port services (mooring crew, stevedores, crane operators, lightermen, etc.) doctrine is divided, but most opinion has come out in favour of admission within the category of active subjects of the salvage of the pilot and also, in special cases, of personnel engaged in port services, subordinating their right to remuneration or to any share in the overall reward due to the salvors as a whole, to the requirement that their services should be exceptional and extraordinary, not rendered within the scope of their contractual obligations or legal duties, but whilst accomplishing or fulfilling them.[95]

It has been maintained that the pilot's inclusion with the crew of the ship, although by virtue of a right (the pilotage contract) which is different from the employment contract, confers upon him, when he renders extraordinary services for salving a ship, the right to remuneration; but in this specific case also it should be understood that its sharing out should be made not so much within the rules governing the right of the crew to remuneration, as within the principles governing its apportionment among co-salvors.[96]

It is appreciated that the rules of the Convention do not mention the pilot, while in the draft Convention the subject was mentioned in an Article relating to pilotage services rendered to a ship in peril. This Article was removed at the start of the Brussels Conference. This led to the impression that the delegates' intention, lacking the grounds mentioned in the reports, was to avoid

94. G. Berlingieri, *Salvataggio ed assistenza*, 322; Norris, *op. cit.*, paras. 53 and 56. Opposed to acceptance of a passenger of the salving vessel among the active subjects of salvage is Riccardelli, "La partecipazione dell'armatore alle operazioni di soccorso di nave in pericolo ed il suo diritto al compenso economico", in Riv. Dir. Nav. 1955, II, 236. This acceptance is nevertheless recognised in jurisprudence by the Court of Trapani, 4 December 1954, *ibidem* and in Dir. Mar. 1956, 372 with a critical note by Volli, "In tema di cooperazione personale dell'armatore della nave soccorritrice alle operazioni di soccorso"; in Dir. Mar. 1956, 372 with a critical note by Volli, "In tema di cooperazione personale dell'armatore della nave soccorritrice alle operazioni di soccorso", and in Dir. Mar. 1956, 72 with a note by Ferrarini, "In tema di partecipazione dell'armatore della nave soccorritrice alle operazioni di salvataggio" which attributes to a passenger who is an active subject of the salvage the status of co-salvor, excluding any possibility of his sharing in the apportionment of the remuneration on the terms and in the proportions laid down for crew members.

95. Opposed to granting the status of salvor to the pilot are: Volli, *Assistenza*, 178, and a large part of French doctrine: cf. Le Clère, *L'assistance aux navires*, 145; Ripert, *Droit maritime*, III, 2160 b. In favour: G. Berlingieri, *Salvataggio*, 326, Ferrarini, *Il soccorso*, 72; Manca, *Commento*, 194; Kennedy, *op. cit.*, 47 and 51; the latter even admits that the pilot on board the salving ship may assume the status of an active subject of the salvage when he "has performed pilotage service which could not be considered to be within the scope of his contract as pilot"; Reuter, *La notion d'assistance*, 236. English jurisprudence has recently confirmed its trend in favour of allowing pilots to be granted the status of salvors in *The Helenus and The Motaqua*, in Dir. Mar. 1983, 381 and [1982] 2 Lloyd's Rep. 261. Italian jurisprudence (Trib. Brindisi, 14 December 1986, in Dir. Mar., 1988, 833) awarded this status to port pilots who, if called upon by the Master of a ship in peril, perform services which go beyond the scope of the contractual limits of their duties, and who are therefore entitled to remuneration.

96. G. Berlingieri, *Salvataggio*, 326 *et seq.*

the possibility of the pilot being tempted to persuade the master of the ship that the situation was much more dangerous than it really was, with a view to receiving extraordinary remuneration for any eventual services rendered to overcome this unreal situation of peril. Consequently, it was imagined, the delegates wished to prevent the pilot being given the capacity of a salvor no matter what the circumstances might be in which his services were rendered. These conclusions do not seem to be fair, and it seems to us preferable, and in keeping with the prevailing trend of jurisprudence internationally, to acknowledge that a correct solution of the problem should be sought in the reference rule contained in Article 6, paragraph 3, of the Convention. That, although not regulating this particular case, left the task of covering this lacuna to the individual national legislations of the party States, especially bearing in mind that all their regulations did not contain an identical principle rendering it legitimate for the pilot to claim a salvage reward.[97]

The status of active subject of salvage may be assumed in occasional cases even by those who are engaged in port services, such as stevedores, crane operators, mooring crews, boatmen, etc., provided that they render services which, in the presence of an actual serious situation of peril, are not comparable to those normally offered by them during the work for which they are licenced or for which they are employed. The typical case is that of the fire-fighting services provided by the fire brigade.[98]

On the other hand, it was intended to deny those passengers of the salved ship, who rendered assistance in salving her, the status of salvors in a technical sense and the consequent right to remuneration, on the fairly straightforward ground that the passengers of the salved ship, who, like the ship, are in a situation of peril, have a particular independent but concurrent interest in the salvage.[99]

However, doctrine tends to allow a passenger who has had the choice between seeking his own immediate safety, by abandoning the ship, and co-

97. Wildeboer, *op. cit.*, 72. It should be noted that in France a law of 28 March 1928, modified by Decree No. 69, 515 of 19 May 1969, "on the regime of pilotage in maritime waters", obliges the pilot to render his assistance when he is on board a ship in peril, allowing him special remuneration and thus excluding his right to any real and proper reward to be fixed according to the principles governing the law of salvage. The English courts have usually acknowledged the pilot's right to salvage reward, placing on him the *onus probandi* that the services rendered are salvage services and not pilotage services. Cf. Brice, *op. cit.*, 29, which reports the reasons for the judgment of *The Aldora* [1975] 1 Lloyd's Rep. 617 *et seq.* which states as follows: "The general principle governing claims for salvage by a pilot engaged to pilot a ship, or by tugs engaged to render towage service to her, is that they are only entitled to claim salvage if, first, the ship is in danger by reason of circumstances which could not reasonably have been contemplated by the parties when the engagement to pilot or tow was made, and, secondly, risks are run, or responsibilities undertaken or duties performed, which could not reasonably be regarded as being within the scope of such engagement."

98. G. Berlingieri, *Salvataggio*, 328; Ferrarini, *Il soccorso*, 74; Norris *op. cit.*, para. 82 and case studies reported there: Gilmore and Black, *The Law of Admiralty*, 543 *et seq.* Cf. Trib. Brindisi, 16 December 1987, in Dir. Mar., 1988, 833.

99. Wildeboer, *op. cit.*, 71; G. Berlingieri, *Salvataggio*, 325; Ferrarini, *Il soccorso*, 76; Norris, *op. cit.*, para. 77; Kennedy, *op. cit.*, 74. See also note 93 on the subject.

operating in the salvage operations, and who remains on board the ship in peril in order to render aid, the status of co-salvor.[100]

An unusual stance has been adopted in doctrine regarding the position (assumed in the case of salvage of a ship) of the owner of cargo carried on board the salvaging ship who, although not actively participating in the salvage operations as an active subject, sustains a loss as a passive subject, normally due to delay, because the ship carrying his cargo deviates from her course to render assistance and incurs, with the cargo carried, the risks inherent to the salvage operation.

The delegates at the Brussels Conference concerned themselves with the problem, following a position taken by the French delegation who insisted on the insertion, amongst the subjects indicated in Article 6, paragraph 3, of the owner of the cargo of the salving ship. This request met marked opposition from delegates of all the other participating States, specifically on the ground that Article 8, paragraph 1, of the Convention, which mentions the risk of responsibility encountered by the salvors as an element in fixing compensation, envisages that the damage sustained by the cargo transported by the salving ship should be settled between the owner of the ship and the owner of the cargo in the same way as regulated by the carriage contract. But the problem seems to be easily overcome within the rules of the Convention, because Article 8 includes among the expenses and damages those liabilities towards third parties on the part of the owner of the salving ship, when he uses his ship in a salvage operation, for the loss to the cargo carried is clearly included among these responsibilities.[101]

In contrast, the Convention mentions expressly among the active subjects of the salvage the tug (*rectius*, the owner of the tug) which renders, within a towage contract, exceptional services for the towed craft, but those services cannot be regarded as fulfilling particular contractual obligations. It is sufficient at this point to mention the existence, in the Convention rules, of this active subject of salvage, and to refer to Section 20 of this chapter where the

---

100. Carver, *Carriage*, 821 writes on this: "But a passenger is not bound to remain by the ship; he may take the first opportunity of escaping and saving his own life. If then, instead of doing so, he remains on board for the purpose of rendering assistance in saving vessel, he may be entitled to salvage."

101. See Reports IV, 45 and IV, 100–101. In favour of excluding the owner of the ship salved from the category of active subjects of the salvage are: Wildeboer, *op. cit.*, 20; Ferrarini, *Il soccorso*, 59 *et seq.*; Kennedy, *op. cit.*, 217; Norris, *op. cit.*, para. 55; while those in favour of recognising the right of the cargo owner to a certain compensation are Gilmore and Black, *op. cit.*, 569, on the basis of the fact that the laws on the carriage-by-sea contract exonerate the carrier from compensating the damage sustained by the cargo as a result of deviations made to render assistance, stating as follows: "The carrier is not liable for damage to cargo resulting from salvage deviations. Since cargo, if damaged, now has no remedy under the contract of affreightment it is placed at risk to exactly the same extent as the salving ship. Conceptually, therefore, it has as much right as the owner to share in the award." A decision by the Italian courts (Trib. Brindisi, 14 April 1986, in Dir. Mar., 1987, 115) declared the master and chief engineer entitled to remuneration. The ship had been abandoned by all her crew members following a fire, but the

regulations in the rules of the Convention governing the relations between a towage contract and salvage will be examined.

10. THE PASSIVE SUBJECTS OF SALVAGE

Turning to the passive subjects of salvage, i.e. the identification of those subjects who are the debtors of the remuneration, it should first be noted that the Convention does not indicate expressly these subjects, but contains a rule (Article 9) which, albeit from a negative point of view, faces the problem of identifying the passive subjects of the salvage, excluding as a matter of principle the human lives saved. We can find no debate in the records of the Conference regarding this problem.[102] The records relating to the discussions on Article 1 of the Convention clarify the delegates' intention not to lay down specific rules regarding such persons as creditors of the salvage reward. Instead, reliance is to be placed on the principle of the interest in assisted and salvaged properties, as being the moment of connection between the material subjects of the salvage and the passive subjects of it.[103]

This conclusion was reached by an authoritative doctrine which, in this way, superseded a doctrinal trend which had been increasingly affirmed in legislation before the Italian Code of Navigation, and was consolidated under its provisions. This line of thought had put forward the theory that the passive subject of the salvage operation was identifiable as the salved ship and consequently as her owner, because the duties assumed by the master in the event of salvage should be understood as being assumed in the interest of the ship and of the venture.[104]

master and chief engineer, together with certain other members of the crew, had returned on board and brought the ship into port.

102. Cf. in this regard Wildeboer, op. cit., 72.

103. Wildeboer, op. et loc. cit. Worthy of note in Italian jurisprudence is the decision by the Court of Cassation of 1 August 1987, n. 6715, in Dir. Mar., 1988, 1120, by which the passive subject of the salvage is identified as the owner, the latter being entitled to commence an action for recovery against the owner of the properties whose loss was prevented.

104. Ferrarini, Il soccorso, 181; Volli, op. cit., 106 et seq.; the contrary theory put forward before the entry into force of the Code of Navigation by Benfante, Il salvamento e l'assistenza nel diritto marittimo (Turin, 1889), 65, was included in the meaning of "management" of the salved ship by Pescatore, "Requisizione di nave e compenso di assistenza e salvataggio", in Foro It., 1955, I, 1084; by Russo, "Gestione di affari da parte dell'armatore e debitori del compenso di salvataggio", in Riv. Dir. Nav. 1961, II, 312, and in jurisprudence by the Court of Cassation decision of 20 October 1953, in Dir. Mar. 1954, with a note by F. Berlingieri, "Sul debitore del compenso di assistenza e salvataggio". In foreign doctrine the theory found supporters in Gilmore and Black, op. cit., 574, where it is stated that: Usually the owner of the salved ship settles with the salvors in full and then requires cargo owners to reimburse him for their proportionate share. As between the shipowners and the cargo owners, salvage is a general average expense; the shipowner, who has a lien against the cargo for such expenses, is in a position to protect himself by holding or by requiring that a bond be posted for its release. The rateable contributions of ship, freight and cargo will be worked out in a general average adjustment. Moreover, the draft of the new Convention of CMI states expressly in Art. 1–4–2, that the obligations assumed by the master of the ship are assumed as agent of necessity and not as the agent of the shipowner. On this point see The Choko Star [1990] 2 Lloyd's Rep. 516 (C.A.), which clearly

This problem is tied up with the problem of the capacity that the master of the ship assumes when the salvage agreement is signed (in the case of contractual salvage) or in the act of salvage in the case of non-contractual salvage.

It is clear that in these circumstances it does not matter that the master is also the agent of the owner. Rather, it is significant that the master is the head of the venture and to him are given the power and the duty of asking for assistance at any time when this relationship is in danger of being lost. The result is that the duties assumed by the master, as such, are linked with the owners of the various interests involved (ship, cargo, freight), but without forming any legal connections between them for payment of remuneration.[105]

Moreover, this principle is fully confirmed and approved in the standard contracts which, in Anglo-Saxon practice, have been prepared by Lloyd's with its famous Lloyd's Open Form Contract. In the last two editions (clause 13 in the previous edition, and clause 17 in the 1980 edition) that reads: "The Master or other person signing this Agreement on behalf of the property to be salved enters into this Agreement as Agent for the vessel, her cargo, freight, bunkers and stores and the respective owners thereof and binds each (but not the one for the other or himself personally) to the due performance thereof ".

From this it may be observed that the master who signs the contract signs it as the representative of the ship, the cargo and the freight, and consequently of the respective persons having interests in them, thus binding them, without legal connection between them, to fulfil the duties arising out of the contract.

11. OBLIGATORY SALVAGE

As regards mandatory salvage, whether imposed by law or by order of authority, the Brussels Convention does not lay down any particular rules. It confines itself, in Articles 9 and 11, to the determination of the legal duty to save human life, and admits in Article 13 that such assistance can be made mandatory by order of a public authority of a Contracting State. In that case it is left

established as follows: "If the master decided that salvage services were necessary and if that decision was justified by the circumstances, he could not be prevented from engaging salvors on reasonable terms by the cargo-owners; if the terms were regarded as unreasonable, then the shipowners would be liable for the whole of the agreed sum and could only recover from the cargo-owners whatever it was fair and just they should pay as their proportion of a fair salvage award."

Opposed on this point in Italian jurisprudence cf. Cass, 19 July 1966, No. 1948 in Dir. Mar. 1966, 479; Trib. Messina, 21 November 1961, *ibidem*, 1962, 376; Trib. Brindisi, 1 December 1962, *ibidem* 1965, 185; Trib. Latina, 22 February 1961, in Riv. Dir. Nav. 1961, II, 312, quoted by Ferrarini, "Il salvataggio come avaria comune", in *Trasporti*, 1977, 7.

105. Ferrarini, *Il soccorso*, 83; Kennedy, *op. cit.*, 273. The latter, providing a relative case-study in jurisprudence, states that "in the absence of a salvage agreement by which the shipowner is bound to pay all the salvage, the interests in ship and cargo are only severally liable each for its proportionate share of the salvage remuneration". Thus *The M. Vatan* [1990] 1 Lloyd's Rep. 336, and Trib. Brindisi, 14 December 1987, in Dir. Mar., 1988, 883. Recently, and erroneously, the opposite principle was affirmed in Italian jurisprudence; see *The Patmos*, Trib. Messina, 11 September 1988, in Dir. Mar., 1989, 1114.

to the individual national laws to perform the task of regulating the organisation of the salvage services *as ordered* by authority.

The Convention, therefore, provides that assistance is mandatory by law only
for the purpose of saving human life. Consequently, if the salvage of things is not
strictly connected with the need to bring persons to safety, and they can be
assisted independently of the simultaneous salvage of things, the assistance rendered to persons would no longer come within mandatory salvage, but would
represent non-contractual salvage.[106] In the same way, mandatory salvage by
order of public authority should also be considered as accepted by the Convention's rules, because, were it not so, it would not have been necessary to state, in
international law (Article 13) that this leaves to the national legislations of the
individual Contracting States the task of dictating the rules governing the *organisation* of the public assistance services, and the salvage of fishing vessels, which
are thus placed outside the Convention's rules of salvage at sea.

The fact that salvage by order of public authority may be governed by the
Convention's rules is a problem which has divided Italian jurisprudence,[107]
but it seems possible to resolve it in the light of the following considerations:

(1) In matters concerning assistance by order of authority and public
    assistance services, the Convention refers to the national laws inso-
    far as the regulation of the organisation of this type of salvage is con-
    cerned, not excluding the possibility that the Convention's rules
    contemplate this type of mandatory assistance;

(2) the rules of the individual national laws, (as, for example, in the case of
    Italy, Article 70 of our Code of Navigation) cannot prevail over the
    Convention's rules in any of those cases where, by virtue of Article 15,
    the Convention fully applies, due to the fact that the Convention, to be
    applicable, does not require that the individual national laws should
    embody express rules of reference in this respect[108];

(3) the fact that the Convention (Article 13) recognises the exclusivity
    of national laws or international treaties with regard to salvage by
    order of authority when the salvage concerns fishing vessels, acts as
    a proof *a contrariis* in favour of the thesis that the Convention
    applies to all other cases of salvage of ships, expressly excluding fish-
    ing vessels when the salvage has been ordered by a public authority.

A particular case of mandatory salvage is that relating to the obligation to

106. Ferrarini, *Il soccorso*, 137 *et seq.*; Wildeboer, *op. cit.*, 251 *et seq.*

107. The following exclude the possibility that salvage made by order of authority can be governed by the Convention's rules: Arbitration Award of 18 December 1972, in Dir. Mar. 1972,
655, and Arbitration Award of 24 February 1981, *ibidem* 1982, 264, with a critical note by E. Vincenzini, "Soccorso per ordine dell'autorità e legge regolatrice del rapporto". In favour of the
opposing theory: Arbitration Award of 9 May 1981, *ibidem*, 1982, 704.

108. Cf. regarding this E. Vincenzini, *Soccorso per ordine dell'autorità*, 266. The Arbitration
Award of 18 December 1972, *loc. cit.*, maintained that, as Art. 70 of the Italian Nav. Code contained an express reference to Art. 491 of that same Code, this reference must be considered to
preclude the application of the 1910 Brussels Convention to the case.

assist imposed by Article 8 of the Brussels Convention of 1910 on the collision of ships as a reciprocal obligation for ships which have come into collision. This mandatory salvage, although not expressly mentioned by the Convention on assistance and salvage, should be understood as equally accepted by the Convention's rules and regulated by them when, on the basis of Article 1, the act of salvage has had a useful result. Indeed, Article 2 refers indiscriminately to all acts of salvage, quite apart from the fact that the act itself was spontaneously brought into being by the salvor; it depends on a contractual duty freely assumed by him, or on a legal obligation, as in the case of collision, deriving from the above uniform international rule to the extent to which it applies.[109]

12. CONTRACTUAL SALVAGE

Just as it regulates mandatory salvage, even if only with regard to the legal obligation to assist, with the limitations imposed by the combined Articles 9 and 11, so the Convention regulates both contractual salvage and spontaneous or non-contractual salvage.[110]

However, Article 1 of the Convention, although not mentioning any specific type of salvage, is conducive to the view that the international rules are intended to regulate all those circumstances open to discussion in which the law develops, despite the fact that Articles 3 and 4 are undoubtedly associated with a non-contractual supposition of salvage, and Articles 6 and 7 with a contractual form of it.[111]

On the subject of contractual salvage, the Convention not only accepts that the parties, by agreement, introduce this into typical salvage circumstances, that is, circumstances regulated by law (with the effect of regulating the right of the salvor to interfere with the interests of the persons who own the things in peril, preventing them from forbidding him to perform the salvage[112]), but expressly admits (Article 6) that, in fundamental elements of the law, which

109. Art. 8, para. 1 of the 1910 Brussels Convention on Collision reads: "Après un abordage, le capitaine de chacun des navires entrés en collision est tenu, autant qu'il peut le faire sans danger sérieux pour son navire, son équipage et ses passagers, de prêter assistance à l'autre bâtiment, à son équipage et à ses passagers". A pointed explanation is provided in this respect by Ferrarini, *Il soccorso*, 38 and 141, to the effect that the duty of reciprocal assistance in event of collision is based on private purposes, quite different from the duty to save persons, this duty being embodied in the duty of a person who has caused damage to take steps to reduce its results.

110. Mandatory salvage does not exclude the possibility that an agreement may be entered into between the salving vessel and the salved vessel for the purpose of regulating the method of proceeding to salvage and the fixing of the remuneration. In this sense Volli, *Assistenza*, 87; Ferrarini, *Il soccorso*, 138. Opposed: Russo, *Assistenza*, 812.

111. In this sense Manca, *Commento*, 185, and Id, *Studi*, Vol. II, 194; Ferrarini, *Il soccorso*, 130; G. Berlingieri, *Salvataggio*, 50; *contra*: Udina, *Le disposizioni preliminari del codice della navigazione* (Trieste, 1942), 65 and Giuliano, "Le nuove norme di diritto privato in tema di navigazione", in Riv. Dir. Nav. 1942, I, 21.

112. Thus Ferrarini, *Il soccorso*, 111.

cannot be varied by agreement between the parties, they are to fix the amount of remuneration, in their salvage agreement.

In fact, the first paragraph of Article 6 of the Convention reads: "The amount of the remuneration is fixed by agreement between the parties and, failing agreement, by the court". That clearly indicates that recourse to judicial authority is additional, laid down by the Convention's rules only where agreement between the parties is not reached, not only in relation to the obligation to perform salvage but also with regard to the salvage remuneration.

Although it must be acknowledged that this possibility of a binding preliminary agreement on the fixing of remuneration meets with difficulties of application in practice,[113] and is immediately mitigated in Article 7 of the Convention (clearly indicating the limits within which an agreement on remuneration can be considered as validly made), it should also be recognised that these Convention rules are innovatory in comparison with the previously consolidated legislation (which in the past forbade any prior agreement on salvage remuneration between the parties).[114]

It would appear, from a systematic perusal of the Convention's text, that the intention is to indicate that contractual salvage is the normal and most frequent case of salvage, seeing that Article 6 is the first rule of uniform international law which speaks of determining the amount of remuneration and which associates it with the possible existence of a salvage agreement made between the parties. The court is given the task of this determination only where there is no specific agreement with regard to it, or where the remuneration has been agreed (Article 7) under the pressure of the particular situation of peril, and one of the parties asks the court to cancel the agreement.

The second paragraph of Article 6 refers to agreement between the parties and, failing that, to the intervention of the court, for the apportionment between the various salvors of the overall remuneration due to them for the salvage work carried out. This again confirms the Convention's tendency to favour contractual salvage as prevailing over the other various remedies which salvage gives.[115]

---

113. Brice correctly maintains in *Maritime Law of Salvage*, 187 *et seq.*, that a certain change in contractual practice occurred from the beginning of the century, and in fact many if not almost all salvage contracts entered into at present do not specify a predetermined sum for the remuneration of a salvage operation governed by the Convention's rules, but refers its determination not so much to judicial authority as to arbitration, with an appropriate arbitration clause inserted in the contract. Similarly De Juglart et Villeneau, *Repertoire metodique*, 37 *et seq.*

114. Thus, the medieval maritime laws, and the Italian Code for the Merchant Marine, mentioned by Ferrarini, *Il soccorso*, 130, and doctrine before the Code of Navigation mentioned there. The possibility of fixing the remuneration beforehand in the salvage agreement is admitted by Le Clère, *L'assistance aux navires*, 209, provided that it respects the other necessary condition that a reward is due for the assistance rendered; thus also Kennedy, *op. cit.*, 291.

115. Also for Ferrarini, *Il soccorso*, 112 *et seq.*, the system of contractual salvage has in practice existed for a long time. It is the custom to enter into an agreement not only in the case of voluntary salvage, but also when the salvage is mandatory.

The definition of the concept of a "salvage agreement" or "convention d'assistance et sauvetage", (depending on whether the English or French text of the Brussels Convention is used) and of the nature of the obligations assumed by the parties under the contract, has engaged the attention of both Italian and international doctrine.

In Italy, various theories have been put forward concerning contractual salvage: some writers have seen in contract law a complex instance of consequential build-up[116]; others have viewed it as negotiations capable of producing both preliminary results such as the obligation to render assistance, and final results such as a right to remuneration, conditional upon there being a useful result,[117] and finally the prevalent current of doctrinal opinion which has put the case in the *locatio operis* characterising this contract with a rather strong, even if normal, element of chance.[118]

Present international doctrine has given the salvage agreement a fairly clear, although somewhat meagre, definition, as follows:

"A salvage agreement, properly so called, is an agreement which fixes the amount to be paid to the salvor for his assistance or provides for its assessment by arbitration, but still leaves the right to any payment contingent upon the preservation of some part at least of the property in peril. Such an agreement does not alter the character of the service or of the reward. An agreement may provide, however, for remuneration on alternative bases without losing its character as a salvage agreement. It may provide for salvage remuneration for an amount agreed or to be fixed by arbitration, in the event of the services proving successful or beneficial, and for payment of expenses, loss or damage incurred if the services are not successful or beneficial. Such a provision does not prevent the agreement as a whole from being regarded as a salvage agreement. But if no property is ultimately in some way preserved the remuneration payable will not be salvage remuneration"[119];

and it has stated that two types of salvage contract exist, which must be kept quite distinct from each other: one which concerns the contract made by the master of a ship in peril, under the pressure of circumstances (*in extremis*); another which provides that the salvage agreement shall be made by the shipowner with a professional salvor, after the immediate peril has passed, with a view to raising or to refloating a ship which is aground or stranded, or to salving her cargo.[120]

With regard to the form of contract most commonly used in practice, we

116. Volli, *Assistenza*, 143 *et seq.*

117. Nicolo', "Configurazione giuridica del recupero marittimo", in Riv. Dir. Nav., 1937, I, 155 *et seq.*

118. Ferrarini, *Profilo*, 664 *et seq.* and *Il soccorso*, 116 and previous doctrine quoted there.

119. Kennedy, *op. cit.*, 291. In this regard see also Wildeboer, *op. cit.*, 49 *et seq.*, who admits that the salvage agreement may even be made in anticipation of future danger and not only when the danger exists, thus denying that the salvage contract constitutes a *locatio operis faciendi*, and adhering to the theory that the contract does not oblige the salvor to achieve a final useful result in all events, but rather to exert certain efforts likely to achieve this.

120. In this sense Brice, *op. cit.*, 578 *et seq.*

refer to what is said later (Chapter 3, Section 24) where we shall deal specifically with the forms prepared by Lloyd's, with the well-known, Lloyd's Open Form (LOF), also called Lloyd's Standard Form of Salvage Agreement—No Cure No Pay.

Returning again to the uniform rules of the Convention, and in particular to Article 7, which is expressly associated with contractual salvage, it is to be noted that it is accepted that the court may cancel or modify such terms of the contract as one of the contracting parties may consider to have been concluded under the influence of the peril in which the property to be salved was found; or where the consent of one of the parties was vitiated by fraud or non-disclosure; or lastly because the terms of the contract are disproportionate to the services rendered, whether in excess or in deficiency.[121]

First, it must be noted that Article 7 of the Convention contains a clear distinction. The first paragraph provides for the case where the salvage contract may be cancelled or modified when, due to the emergency caused by the situation of peril, it contains terms which are unfair to either of the contracting parties. The second paragraph formulates a general hypothesis (*dans tous les cas* in French, "and in all cases" in English) which, apart from the influence of the peril on the decisions of one of the contracting parties, accepts that the salvage agreement can be cancelled or modified, due to vitiation by fraud or non-disclosure of one of the parties, or because there is a disproportion between the services rendered and the remuneration agreed.[122]

This principle, which is accepted in almost all the national regulations of the Contracting States, with only slight differences,[123] was introduced into the

121. On the possibility that not only the salved subject but also the salving subject may call for the cancellation or modification of the salvage agreement, see: Kennedy, *op. cit.*, 316, who reports the case of *The Phantom*; App. Poitiers of 31 March 1954 in D.M.F. 1954, 408, and Wildeboer, *op. cit.*, 171.

122. In this sense Wildeboer, *op. cit.*, 166 *et seq.*, for whom the first paragraph of Art. 7 refers to any contractual term which may be considered unfair by one of the parties. Thus also Ferrarini, *Il soccorso*, 131, while the second paragraph would seem to refer only to cases of disproportion between services and remuneration, and to bad faith on the part of subjects. While in the first instance only unfair contract terms would be required, in the second an *extraordinary disproportion* between the duties of the two contracting parties would be required.

123. Cf. Wildeboer, *op. cit.*, 176 *et seq.* and rules for the acceptance and adaptation of the national laws indicated therein. Brice, *op. cit.*, 218, who recalls that in English legislation the salvage contract may be subject to the provisions of the Unfair Contract Terms Act 1977 which requires, in section 11, that for any contract "to satisfy the 'requirement of reasonableness' the term shall have been a fair and reasonable one to be included having regard to the circumstances which were, or ought reasonably to have been, known to or in the contemplation of the parties when the contract was made". However the principle has not been accepted in our legislation. The Report on the Code of Navigation (No. 306) states: "With regard to the determination to be made by the court, it has not seemed appropriate to reproduce the rule laid down in the Brussels Convention 1910 by which the judge may reduce or take away the right to remuneration if it appears that the salvors have, by their fault, rendered the salvage or assistance necessary, and in the case of thefts or fraudulent acts having been committed during the salvage operation". This rule partly derives from principle and is partly contradictory to principle. It derives from principle where it excludes indemnity and reward in the case of a blameworthy creation of the situation

Convention's rules following the agreement reached by the delegates during the preparatory work for the 1909 Brussels Conference.[124] This principle has been confirmed in some court judgments, so providing cases for interpretation and to which reference can be made, indicating instances of cancellation of salvage agreements due to fraud, or non-disclosure, "mis-statement or non-disclosure of a material fact", and for disproportion between the remuneration and the services.[125]

With regard to this disproportion, it must be noted that the second paragraph of Article 7 of the Convention refers to the disproportion either to the harm of the property saved or to the harm of the salvors, with a distinction in the two cases regarding the determination of the moment when the disproportion occurs: in the former case, only the situation when the salvage contract is made is relevant; in the latter case, the situation at the time or during a period after that can also apply.

Mere increases in the risk to the salvor which come under the particular kind of the contract, characterised by a high normal risk, cannot be considered as unfair disproportions. In fact, the cancellation or modification of the contract must be allowed when, due to a substantial change in the circumstances, not attributable to the salvor, the salvage operation undergoes a radical change with regard to the contract originally envisaged by the parties.[126]

On the subject of contractual salvage, the systems which existed under the laws of the individual Contracting States, before the Convention came into force, were very different, and it cannot be denied that the Convention represented an important step forward towards the achievement of a uniform law

which made the assistance or salvage necessary, and in the case of fraudulent acts committed during the salvage operation. But in a case where the Convention provides for a reduction in the reward, according to Italian principles only two solutions are admissible: either the conditions are met for excluding the reward, which comes under the first case, or these conditions are not met, when the reward must be allocated according to the criteria laid down".

124. See Reports on the preparatory work of the 1909 Brussels Conference, 115 *et seq.*, where it states that the first paragraph of Art. 7 of the Convention concerns cases where the salvage agreement has been made by the master of the salved ship under the influence of the peril; the second paragraph concerns the instance of a salvage contract entered into on shore by the owners of the ship to be salved, without the pressing influence of peril.

125. The precedents available are scarce and rather old; see the cases quoted by Ferrarini, *Il soccorso*, 155 and by Kennedy, *op. cit.*, 304 *et seq.* The most recent is a case quoted by Brice, *op. cit.*, 288, *The Unique Mariner* [1978] 1 Lloyd's Rep. 438, in which it is recognised that the Admiralty Court has always exercised an equitable jurisdiction in declaring invalid, so as to deny effect to, salvage contracts if they are considered seriously unfair to one or other of the parties. It was ruled that a Lloyd's form salvage contract which had been made by the master of the ship in peril with a salvor other than the one sent by the owners of the ship herself, could be cancelled. It was stated in the judgment: "There was nothing in the circumstances which should have made the captain realise that the master was expecting another tug which had been arranged to be sent to him; there was nothing unusual in the master accepting the services of *Salvaliant* on the terms of the Lloyd's form without first seeking to communicate with his owners and agents and there was no good reason why the captain should have asked him whether he had done so." For further information, see Gaskell, "The Lloyd's Open Form and Contractual Remedies", *op. cit.*, 306.

126. See on this Ferrarini, *Il soccorso*, 133; Kennedy, *op. cit.*, 305 *et seq.*; Brice *op. cit.*, 232 *et seq.*; Volli, *Assistenza*, 150.

on this rather delicate aspect of the law. There is no doubt that the adoption of the Convention's rules in the various national laws, with different and, at times, contrasting rules of adaptation, forms a real obstacle to the perfect achievement of such a uniformity, with the result that, as we shall see later on (Chapter 4), both the contents of the rule and its text will need some revision when a revision of the Convention's law is undertaken in the future.[127]

13. NON-CONTRACTUAL OR VOLUNTARY SALVAGE

As we have seen, the Convention refers to non-contractual or spontaneous salvage in Articles 3 and 4, although these references are concerned with particular cases from which it is inferred, *a contrariis*, that the Convention's rules govern spontaneous salvage as a typical case coming within the general scope of the uniform law of the Convention itself.

In fact, Article 3, by providing that those who have rendered assistance despite the express and reasonable prohibition by the master or the owner of the ship to which the salvage services have been rendered, have no right to any remuneration, tacitly accepts that those who voluntarily, in the absence of any such prohibition, have rendered assistance to a ship or property in peril, have a right to remuneration.

Similarly, Article 4, by accepting that a tug which renders assistance, in exceptional circumstances, to a craft under tow and by virtue of a regular towage contract, is entitled to remuneration for the services rendered when such services cannot be regarded as coming within the terms of the contract, confirms that the Convention governs, among the various instances in which salvage arises, this non-contractual or spontaneous salvage as well.

It has also been held that Article 5 of the Convention implicitly admits non-contractual or spontaneous salvage, given that the existence of a contract would be inconceivable in salvage rendered by a ship belonging to the same operator or owner as the salved ship, for a contract is an agreement between two or more parties and cannot be unilateral.[128]

It should be mentioned, however, with regard to Article 3, that the effect of recognising the possibility of spontaneous salvage, and the fact that it is subject to the Convention's rules, are purely circumstantial. The rule finds its *ratio* in the delegates' wish to discourage coercive forms of salvage. That had often occurred in the past in coastal areas of the world where the local populations had frequently compelled ships in difficulty to accept their own salvage services, which were not professional.[129]

---

127. In this sense: Wildeboer, *op. cit.*, 192.
128. Thus Manca, *Commento*, 185 *et seq*. On the subject of voluntary salvage carried out by the pilot and crew of the salved ship while awaiting the respective contracts with the shipowner, see Ferrarini, *Il soccorso*, 92 and Kennedy, *op. cit.*, 25 *et seq*.
129. Wildeboer, *op. cit.*, 126, and documentation quoted there regarding the preparatory work of the Convention, Reports, II, 99, 130, 132 *et seq*. and III, 92.

Characteristic of this typical example of salvage is "voluntariness", that is to say, the voluntary initiative taken by the salvor in rendering assistance to a ship in peril, without any agreement having been concluded between the active and passive subjects of the salvage. This initiative is linked to the moral obligation on which this law has been based ever since the earliest forms of sea navigation and the earliest known maritime laws existed.[130]

Neither in national nor in international doctrine do there seem to have been any doubts or considerable disagreement in the past about the attempt to insert non-contractual or spontaneous salvage into the legal concept of *negotiorum gestio*. This was on the premise that spontaneous salvage is reflected in legal salvage, despite there being notable differences between the particular law and the general law especially concerning the usefulness of spontaneous salvage. In salvage, or the management of others' affairs, the usefulness must exist and have effect from the outset.[131]

Existing Italian doctrine has come to the conclusion that the comparision between *negotiorum gestio* and spontaneous salvage does not go beyond some relevant points of contact, both because of the different historical backgrounds of the two laws, and because spontaneous salvage is a typical example of special law, governed by a system which is of a particular character and which is internationally uniform.[132]

Internationally, although there have been some adherents to the theory of spontaneous salvage as a management of other parties' affairs, the conclusion has been reached that spontaneous or non-contractual salvage is only a particular form of *negotiorum gestio* which arises whenever there is no one on board the ship in peril who represents the owners or the persons interested either in the ship or in her cargo.[133]

This comment must be examined, within the purview of spontaneous

---

130. Kennedy, *op. cit.*, 28. See also, E. Vincenzini, "Il soccorso in mare nel diritto marittimo romano" in *Trasporti*, 1984, 60.

131. Thus Ferrarini, *Il soccorso*, 92; Id, *Profilo*, 665 *et seq.*; Volli, *Assistenza*, 155; Russo, *Assistenza*, (1953), 142; Smeester and Winkelmolen, *Droit maritime et droit fluviale*, 389. Although the individual national laws of the civil law countries such as France, Belgium, Germany, Italy and Holland contain specific rules concerning the *negotiorum gestio*, no rule exists on the subject in the common law countries such as England and the United States. Cf. Dawson. "*Negotiorum gestio*, the altruistic intermeddler", in *The Harvard Law Review*, 1961, No. 5, 817 and No. 1073. In US law changes have been made to federal law in respect of the recovery of so-called "historical wrecks"; see, Owen, "The Abandoned Shipwreck Act of 1987, Goodbye to Salvage in Territorial Sea" in 19 *Journal of Maritime Law and Commerce*, 1988, 499.

132. Ferrarini, *Il soccorso*, 93, and *Profilo*, 665; Volli, *Assistenza*, 162. For Ferrarini voluntary salvage assumes the guise of a non-contractual legal act, understood to be an act to which the law attributes particular effects in consideration of the fact that it concerns a voluntary act which includes the intention that such an event occur.

133. Thus Wildeboer, *op. cit.*, 41 *et seq.* He seeks to qualify voluntary salvage as *negotiorum gestio* and to overcome the objections raised in doctrine by Ripert, *op. cit.*, 142 *et seq.*, who found that we can speak of *negotiorum gestio* only insofar as the management of someone else's affairs concerns a legal subject who is absent or inactive, while in salvage the owner of the ship in peril is represented by a subject who is present (the master) who actually co-operates with the salvors.

salvage, in relation to the salvage of wrecks spontaneously undertaken by the salvor, an operation which, as was seen in Section 1, the Convention's rules are intended to govern in the same way as assistance and salvage, by refusing to recognise that such an operation can be subject to a law different from salvage and, as such, be governed by another set of rules.[134]

Having established that the express and reasonable refusal of the assisted ship (*du navire secouru*) forms, for Article 3 of the Convention, an insuperable barrier to the possibility of spontaneous and non-contractual salvage, it is necessary to ascertain how such a refusal is to be shown, and on what assumptions the *reasonableness* should be based in order to produce its excluding effect, following a valid spontaneous salvage which could come within the general principles of Article 2 of the Convention.

By establishing that the refusal must be "express", the Convention indicates that the refusal cannot be signified in an equivocal manner. Otherwise, acts or behaviour might mislead the potential salvor. The expression in the French text, *du navire secouru*, clearly indicates that the parties entitled to give such a refusal are the master of the ship, her operator or her owner,[135] and that, in order to prevent the salvage operations, this refusal must be notified before the start of the operations, because any express refusal after the operations have begun represents, instead, a dismissal or a dispossession of the salvor.

The requirement of "reasonableness", a typically English condition and one which has been widely acknowledged in Anglo-Saxon jurisprudence, is to be assessed in each case, bearing in mind what decision would have been taken by an expert and prudent master, and also giving due consideration to the very wide limits recognised by Anglo-Saxon jurisprudence to decisions taken by owners or operators as well as by their masters. This applies especially in possible or supposed situations of peril, or when the maximum damage which can be assumed as a result of the peril for the ship and her

---

134. It has been affirmed that voluntary salvage of wreck, instead of being included in management of affairs, must be included in the law of finding lost things: thus De Cupis, "Trovamento dei relitti marittimi ed aeronautici" in Riv. Dir. Nav. 1955, I, 117; Albano, "Ricupero, ritrovamento di relitti e occupazione di cose abbandonate in mare", *id*. 1954, II, 88, and lastly, Buccisano, *L'invenzione di cose perdute* (Milan, 1963), 30 *et seq.*, but this theory seems to be easily disproved by the simple statement that finding things lost occurs *absente domino*, while the voluntary salvage of a wreck usually takes place in the presence of the master or owner of the wrecked vessel. Prevalent practice today is to include voluntary salvage in the category of non-contractual legal acts. Thus Mirabelli, *L'atto non negoziale nel diritto privato italiano* (Naples, 1955), 254 and Ferrarini, *Il soccorso*, 93.

135. The idea had been put forward in doctrine (see: Schlegelberger-Liesecke, *Seehandelsrecht* (Berlin, 1959), 202), that the refusal of the master could be cancelled by a subsequent consent of the shipowner, who in any case is entitled to make the final decision, the master acting merely as his agent, but this theory has been correctly refuted by Ferrarini, *Il soccorso*, 98, in view of the consideration that, in arranging for salvage, the master is acting as the head of the venture, that is to say on the basis of powers conferred on him by law, and not by the relationship of agency between him and the shipowner.

cargo has already occurred, and there is no longer any pressing need to take hasty decisions, so that the situation can be assessed in a calmer frame of mind. This is to identify the best solution to be adopted in the interests of the ship and cargo, and does in fact happen in almost all instances of wreck salvage.[136]

There is no doubt, where those interested in the properties in peril (whether ship or cargo) have lost possession of them, that those persons cannot object to the assistance which the salvor intends to render or has already begun, unless they intervene directly and personally, or replace the salvor in the assistance which has been started. In this case, the spontaneous salvor will be entitled not only to remuneration for the operations he has carried out until the interruption and for the results achieved, even if only partial; but also to compensation for the possibility which the salvor would have had, without the enforced interruption, of bringing about a useful final result.[137]

In spontaneous salvage, therefore, a special importance attaches, within Article 3 of the Convention (the scope or relevance of Article 4 will be discussed in Section 20), to the owner of the ship being salvaged forbidding the salvor to carry out or to continue his assistance to the property in peril, under the double aspect of the implicit general acceptance, already mentioned, that spontaneous salvage is included within the rules of the Convention, and of the particular point of the replacement of the salvor and the problems which arise on the subject of the eventual apportionment of remuneration between the dispossessed salvor and the one replacing him.

Although the Convention's rules do not contain any provision about this, the British theory of "dispossession" is fully applicable under the Convention itself because—as has been recently stated[138]—"as there is no duty on the spontaneous salvors to continue and complete the work of salvage they have begun, nor is there any obligation on the owners of the salved goods to guarantee their employ, the rights of the spontaneous salvors arise and are limited in relation to the principles, intended to safeguard the public interest, of maritime common law, according to which they are entitled to a payment for the

---

136. English jurisprudence attributes predominant importance to the rights of the shipowner and operator. See Kennedy, *op. cit.*, 9 *et seq.*, United States Jurisprudence, and Norris, *op. cit.*, 114 *et seq.* However, the latter notes (*op. cit.*, 199) that if there are persons on board the ship in peril, prohibition to salvage the ship would involve a prohibition to save persons, and this could be deemed unreasonable.

137. In this sense *The Unique Mariner No. 2* [1979] 1 Lloyd's Rep. 37, and in Dir. Mar. 1979, 420 with a note by Righetti, "Ancora sui diritti dei soccorritori, spossessati, licenziati e sostituiti". Also see Righetti, "La teoria della 'dispossession' in assistenza e salvataggio" in Dir. Mar. 1960, 223 as a note to the Arbitration Award of 28 March 1960, and Wildeboer, *op. cit.*, 136 for whom the displaced salvor "has a right to the sum he would have earned as salvage award if he had been permitted to execute those salvage activities which, given the circumstances, he might reasonably have expected to be allowed to undertake".

138. Brice, *Maritime Law of Salvage*, 100, and jurisprudence quoted there.

work actually effected over and above a certain amount for the work which they were ready to carry out later if they had not been dismissed".[139]

14. THE BASIC ELEMENT CONSTITUTING SALVAGE: THE PERIL OF BEING LOST

There are two elements fundamental to salvage according to the uniform rules of the Convention: the danger in which the property to be salved finds itself, and the useful result achieved by the salvor. This is deduced not only from the placing of these elements in the opening articles of the Convention's rules (Articles 1 and 2), that is, in the rules which define salvage as accepted by the Convention, indicating its essential elements and the scope and their limits of application; but also because all the other elements which might be considered as co-existent in salvage, together with these two, are listed in Article 8, which gives the elements for evaluating reward on the basis of which remuneration for the operation is to be fixed. This placing therefore clearly makes the elements of salvage essential fundamental elements (the peril; the useful result) and also essential evaluative elements (the efforts and risks of the salvors; the time spent by them in the salvage operations; the expenses incurred and damage sustained; the values of the property salved and of the salvor's property exposed to risk) among those relating only to the fixing of remuneration.

It should be noted that, while peril is looked upon as an essential initial element for salvage (considering that salvage is intended to remedy a situation of peril), the useful result is looked upon as an essential final element if the activity of the salvor (the usefulness of which constitutes finality) is to be considered as having produced that end, giving rise to the salvor's right to remuneration.[140]

It has been noted that the fact that peril was not mentioned in the preliminary draft of the Convention, but was inserted only later after some dis-

139. Thus the text of the above decision *The Unique Mariner (No. 2)* [1979] 1 Lloyd's Rep. 37. In doctrine: Brice, *op. cit.*, 92 *et seq.* and Ferrarini, *Il soccorso*, 107. The latter affirms that as there is no duty on the voluntary salvor to perform the salvage, there can be no liability on his part for non-fulfilment as a result of an interruption of the salvage operations. Finally see on this subject: Righetti, "Ancora sui diritti dei soccorritori spossessati, licenziati e sostituiti", 424, and Gaskell, *op. cit.*, 328 *et seq.*

140. Thus Ferrarini, *Il soccorso*, 44 and 115 *et seq.*, who denies that the peril constitutes not an element of the law, but a presupposition of it, because the peril, or more precisely its removal, forms the purpose of the salvage. We cannot share the theory put forward by Volli, *Assistenza*, 25 *et seq.*, where he tries to include in the essential elements of salvage the extraneousness or voluntariness of the salvor, that is to say, the need that the person rendering assistance shall not be required to undertake the operations for any other reason, and reasonable refusal, because the elements mentioned concern only voluntary salvage, of which those elements form a definition or at least the simple conditions for the existence of the salvage itself.

cussion, shows clearly that, in the intentions of the drafters of the Convention, peril itself constituted a natural condition of salvage rather than an essential element of it.[141]

Although the Convention mentions peril as an essential element of salvage (Article 1) and as a fundamental factor in the determination of remuneration (Article 8), it does not define it. During the preparatory works the German Association had proposed to formulate a definition of "peril" in the text, but this proposal was not accepted.[142]

Thus, to limit peril for the purposes of the Convention (rather than according to the rules of the Convention) it is necessary to refer to the definitions which Italian and international jurisprudence have given to it, and on the basis of which salvage at sea is limited.

However, it seems to us to be significant that, although in Article 1 the Convention speaks of peril run by the salved property, yet in Article 11 where it regulates assistance to persons and the saving of human life at sea, it adds the words "of being lost" to the dangers run by them (*de se perdre* in the French text). That, on the one hand, would seem to restrict this essential element to risk of actual loss of human life; on the other hand, it may lead to acceptance that the type of peril which the Convention indicates as an essential element of services rendered to ship and cargo is a danger, not so much of being lost, as of sustaining substantial damage, or a loss worse than what, when it occurred, was the reason for the request for salvage.[143]

---

141. Manca, *Commento*, 208 and Wildeboer, *op. cit.*, 76.

142. The text of the proposed definition was as follows: "Il y a danger de mer, ou bien lorsq'il y a pour le navire ou pour sa cargaison un danger immédiat insurmontable, ou bien lorsqu'une prévision raisonée fait naître une crainte justifiée qu'à la suite de certaines nouvelles circonstances un tel danger puisse se produire, et qu'en outre ce danger ne puisse être écarté par l'unique action des moyens de secours dont dispose le navire lui-même."

143. Ferrarini, *Il soccorso*, 47 *et seq.*; Manca, *Commento*, 209; Reuter, *La notion d'assistance*, 176; Kennedy, *op. cit.*, 14; Norris, *op. cit.*, 97; Wildeboer, *op. cit.*, 95; Brice, *op. cit.*, 13. This author admits that the peril may be formed by a *financial danger* which exists with regard to the physical danger run by the salved goods, and mentions a series of decisions where this element has been taken into consideration, noting in particular that: "The courts have long recognised as a type of danger the financial consequences to the owners of having a disabled vessel, and have awarded salvage in respect of services by salvors which have protected the owners from such financial consequences even when the casualty was in little, if any, physical danger. Very often in practice physical danger and consequential financial losses go hand in hand; for a vessel which is seriously damaged and in need of assistance will cease to be a profit-earning asset for the owners until preserved and later repaired. Further, there may be circumstances where a vessel or her cargo pose a threat to others such as the owners of an adjacent port or coastline or other vessels (leading to the prospect of a claim by such owners against the owners of the casualty)." Thus in our jurisprudence in favour of the principle: App. Lecce, 12 April 1985, in Dir. Mar., 1986, 906; App. Naples, 29 June 1985, in Dir. Mar., 1986, 912; Trib. Genoa, 11 October 1985, in Dir. Mar., 1985, 955; Arbitration Award of 21 February 1987, in Dir. Mar., 1988, 517; Trib. Brindisi, 14 December 1987, in Dir. Mar., 1988, 833; Arbitration Award of 11 August 1989, in Dir. Mar., 1990, 182; Arbitration Award of 22 March 1989, in Dir. Mar., 1990, 416; Arbitration Award of 12 April 1989, in Dir. Mar., 1990, 755. Cf., the following decisions: Trib. Massa, 20 August 1985, in Dir. Mar., 1986, 443; App. Genoa, 20 June 1987, in Dir. Mar., 1988, 437; Trib. Brindisi, 10 February 1988, in Dir. Mar., 1989, 818.

Our more recent jurisprudence[144] has provided a fairly adequate study of cases according to the Convention's rules on the requirement of peril, sufficient to enable the reader to reach a correct definition of that element.

It has been recognised that peril may constitute a real objective risk of the ship being lost, when, for example, driven by the wind and sea against the breakwater of a port, she is unable to move away from it under her own power[145]; similarly it should also be considered that peril exists for the salved ship when she finds herself at sea in a difficulty which could cause damage, and possibly even the loss of the ship, without being able to escape under her own power, or to escape only at the cost of considerable sacrifices.[146]

Finally, a very recent decision has made an important new contribution to the Convention's definition of peril by pointing out that peril should be interpreted as formed by a risk of financial loss to the owner of the ship, depending not only on physical damage to her, but also on any liability of the owner resulting from the loss, introducing into the rules of the Convention the concept of "liability salvage", which had been categorically rejected in the past by prevailing jurisprudence and doctrine.[147]

International jurisprudence provides an equally wide view, giving a definition of peril which is correct and not restricted only to the risk of total loss of ship and cargo.[148] Some of the more recent court judgments are significant.

144. For a view of Italian national jurisprudence before 1960, cf. E. Vincenzini, "Rassegna di giurisprudenza in tema di assistenza salvataggio, rimorchio e ricupero", in Riv. Dir. Nav. 1960, II, 148.

145. Cf. Arbitration Award of 30 December 1963, in Dir. Mar. 1965, 300.

146. Cf. Arbitration Award of 24 May 1968, in Dir. Mar. 1968, 221; in the same sense Trib. Caltanissetta 21 November 1977, in Dir. Mar. 1978, 493; Arbitration Award of 31 January 1979, in Dir. Mar. 1979, 405.

147. Cf. Arbitration Award of 26 November 1982, in Dir. Mar. 1983, 580 et seq., with note by E. Vincenzini, "Brevi osservazioni in tema di Liability salvage". In agreement, in an equally novel sense, in British jurisprudence, The Helenus and Motaqua [1982]2 Lloyd's Rep. 261 and in Dir. Mar. 1983, 381 with note by E. Vincenzini, "Ancora in tema di soccorso in acque portuali e determiniazione del compenso". Thus also Brice, Maritime Law, 8, who states: "That the salved property has been preserved from danger is an essential element if a claim for salvage is to succeed. It is necessary to consider what is meant by danger in this context and then to approach the topic under two broad headings: first, the risk of physical danger to or destruction of some or all of the salved property and secondly the risk of some financial harm to the owners of the salved property arising out of the circumstances of the casualty." Contra on this point Ferrarini, Il soccorso, 159; Volli, Assistenza, 187; and Arbitration Award of 24 February 1981, in Dir. Mar. 1981, 264. The last decision was issued on the basis of Italian law but the arbitrators, on the specific point of liability salvage, had excluded the possibility that the solution could have been different from that reached if the case had been decided according to the Convention. In our recent jurisprudence also, see Arbitration Award of 22 March 1989, in Dir. Mar., 1990, 416. Recently, rejecting liability salvage in US jurisprudence, U.S.D.C. Northern District of California, 16 November 1985, in Dir. Mar., 1986, 748, which declared that for the purposes of determining remuneration under Art. 8 of the 1910 Convention, the liability of the owner of the salved property towards third parties cannot be included in the value of such salved properties. See also, in the opposite sense on this point, E. Vincenzini, "Liability salvage e limitazione di responsabilità dell'armatore della nave soccorsa in una recente sentenza statunitense", in Dir. Mar., 1990, 209.

148. For a wide view of international jurisprudence up to 1964, cf. Wildeboer, op. cit., 82 et seq.

They have, with regard to the continuance of a peril capable of making the operations for a ship and its cargo come into the category of salvage operations, attached importance to the fact that the ship, in the absence of such operations, would have remained long immobilised, with considerable economic loss to her owner. In this way we may affirm the existence of the so-called "financial danger", which may co-exist with the physical danger run by the salved property and actually assume an overriding importance in respect of it.[149]

Having thus defined the element of peril, it is possible to summarise the possible result under the Convention, even given the laconic nature of its text,[150] as follows:

(1) peril must have that character not only because of the risk of ship and cargo being lost, but also because they may sustain substantial damage or greater losses than those which gave rise to the salvage operation, not excluding the economic losses ("financial danger") which may arise from these losses for the parties interested in the venture;

(2) peril consists of a particularly hazardous situation which has occurred at sea, and in relation to which the intervention of a third party is required to escape[151];

149. *The Oceanic Grandeur* [1972] 2 Lloyd's Rep. 396; this decision includes among the qualifying elements of *danger* assessed by the judges for the purpose of fixing remuneration, the fact that the vessel would have remained immobilised and that there would have been a loss to her owners; in this sense: *The Troilus* [1951] 1 Lloyd's Rep. 467; *The Cythera* [1965] 2 Lloyd's Rep. 454; *The Orelia* [1958] 1 Lloyd's Rep. 441. In this respect see Brown, "Allseas Maritime S.A. v The Mimosa, Has the Keel been Laid for Liability Salvage in Fifth Circuit?" in *Journal of Maritime Law and Commerce*, 1988, 583 and the US jurisprudence cited in note 11. Commenting on the decision, the author quotes the following, rather significative paragraph: "There is a considerable merit, nevertheless, in the position that the salvors should be compensated for liability avoided. Whether the salvors protect a shipowner's vessel or his other assets the economic benefits are equally valuable."

150. After examining the peril element on the basis of the Convention and its unifying effects in Holland, France, Belgium, Germany and England, Wildeboer, *op. cit.*, 52, concludes that: "it cannot be said that the Convention has had a significant unifying effect as regards the requirement of danger. Although it is true that the deviations mentioned in the preceding paragraphs now occur less frequently, it is questionable whether this is due to the Convention only, The text of Art. 1 contains only the words 'en danger' and, therefore, leaves the question discussed in this chapter unanswered. A rather distinct difference between English law on the one hand and the law of the other four countries on the other was, and still is the fact that in England a ship and/or her cargo are more readily considered to be in danger, so that in English law a right to salvage remuneration is more easily obtained."

151. On the point regarding the necessary localisation of the danger, with reference to the sea and navigation, see Manca, *Commento*, 210 *et seq.*; Ferrarini, *Il soccorso*, 47 *et seq.*, who notes that the German expression used to classify the danger is significant, in that the term *Seenot* means literally a situation of necessity at sea. Similarly Wildeboer, *op. cit.*, 80, where it is admitted that the danger may also come from the shore, but must be to a ship which is in port, in the ship lanes, or a short distance from the coast, when, for example, the danger comes, as in wartime, from a bombardment from coastal batteries of a belligerent State. The decision rendered by the Arbitration Award of 11 August 1989, in Dir. Mar., 1990, 183, is innovative where it establishes that a judgment as to the possibility of a real and serious risk, even if not imminent, to the

(3) the peril must exist objectively, i.e. it must be *material and percept-ible* although not necessarily imminent, and not merely supposed or quite imaginary, the subjective valuation of the peril at the begin-ning of the salvage operation[152] being significant subject to full con-firmation of its correctness being established during a later evaluation;

(4) the causes producing the situation of peril are not important, whether they consist of natural causes or depend on human actions, including such actions as constitute acts of war.[153]

15. THE USEFUL RESULT

The useful result is an essential element, with peril, for the existence of sal-vage. In fact, in the absence of a useful result, although salvage was rendered to a ship in peril and the salvor incurred expenses and sustained loss as a result of the efforts made, the services rendered will not be considered as sal-vage and the salvor will not, so far as the Convention is concerned, have any right to be remunerated for them.

As a preliminary it is necessary to mention that, while the French text of Article 2, in its first and second paragraphs, speaks of the *resultat utile*, the English text distinguishes this element by two different definitions: "useful result" in the first paragraph and "beneficial result" in the second.

Although the Convention does not adopt explicitly the term "no cure no pay", it looks upon this principle as a basis of salvage, so that neither remuneration nor reimbursement of expenses or losses are due to the salvor unless some salvage is effected or unless the salvor at least contributes to it. Thus the English version of the text should be understood as more correct and more in keeping with the spirit of the Convention's rules, for it brings out not only the conditions deemed by the Convention to be necessary in effecting salvage: the "success" (or "useful result") and the "beneficial result" (or "beneficial service"), the final useful result, but also the fact that the salvor's services which have usefully contributed to the salvage, are related to it as cause to effect.[154]

safety of the ship, must be formulated *ex ante* based on the circumstances and on the master's evaluation of the same.

152. Ferrarini, *Il soccorso*, 51; Kennedy, *op. cit.*, 14 and 21; Brice, *op. cit.*, 8; Wildeboer, *op. cit.*, 87. Norris, *op. cit.*, 101; and case histories quoted there, regarding the decisions which excluded the presence of a danger as an essential element of the salvage, where the danger is unreal or imaginary; Schaps-Abraham, *Seerecht*, II, 1120; Reuter, *La notion*, 184. For this author the fact that the Convention takes no account of the unreasonable refusal of the salved subject, confirms the thesis of irrelevance of subjective appraisal of danger on the part of the latter.

153. Manca, *Commento*, 212; Ferrarini, *Il soccorso*, 50; Wildeboer, *op. cit.*, 80.

154. Thus Ferrarini, *Il soccorso*, 53; Brice, *Maritime Law of Salvage*, 36; Chorley and Giles, *Shipping Law*, 265; Kennedy, *op. cit.*, 107; Norris, *op. cit.*, 88; Reuter, *Notion*, 73; Manca, *Commento*, 213. The latter states that the Convention's rules exclude from salvage operations in the legal sense, such operations as have not achieved a useful result, recognising nevertheless that

Within the Convention, if it is necessary to achieve a useful final result to have a right to remuneration, it is also unnecessary for salvage to consist of a total salvage of the property in peril. It is sufficient for the property to be partly salved and for what is salved to have some economic value. However, the operations by the salvor must have contributed in an effective and decisive way to the securing of the useful result. No importance attaches to the making of noteworthy efforts and the rendering of meritorious services if no benefit for the salved property resulted.[155]

The result may be partial where the salvage of the ship only or of the cargo only is effected, or where it concerns part of them, when the salvage operation may be considered as a partial contribution to a final useful result; or, finally, where the operation itself has improved the original situation of peril, so that salvage will be possible at some future time, although by others.[156]

Since within the Convention the unitary concept of "salvage" (which is understood to include the salvage of wrecks and the principle of "no cure no pay", both of clear English derivation) is accepted, the salvor, although meritorious, is not entitled to any separate remuneration for loss sustained or expenses incurred when no useful result, or only a partial result, has been

they represent operations in the technical sense, and it is not possible to remove such operations from existing merely because they have not achieved a success. In this respect Wildeboer, *op. cit.*, 104, asks whether: "the fact that there are two interrelated but independent conditions to be fulfilled, before a right to salvage remuneration exists, gives rise to the question of what is, in fact, meant by the adage 'no cure no pay'. Does it refer to the provision of Art. 2 sect. 2 or to that of Art. 2 sect. 3? Does it mean 'no beneficial result no pay' or 'nothing saved no pay'? From a linguistic point of view both opinions can be defended. It is notworthy that this question cannot be answered. In practice 'no cure no pay' is sometimes interpreted in the one sense, and at other times in the other sense, without apparent disadvantages". See also in our jurisprudence, Cass, 5 August 1987, n. 6715, in Dir. Mar., 1988, 1120, which acknowledged that, with the fulfilment of the legal obligation of salvage, following the total or partial elimination of the risk there arises the obligation to pay the salvor his remuneration.

155. Kennedy, *op. cit.*, 107 *et seq.*, after stating that "services, however meritorious, which do not contribute to the ultimate success, do not give a title to salvage reward", provides a full case study in British jurisprudence, on the basis of which he considers it possible to summarise the principles in relation to *success* as follows: "Success is necessary for salvage reward. Contributions to that success, or as it is sometimes expressed, meritorious contributions to that success give a title to salvage reward. Services, however meritorious, which do not contribute to the ultimate success, do not give a title to salvage reward. Services which rescue a vessel from one danger but end by leaving her in a position of as great or nearly as great a danger, although of another kind, are held not to contribute to the ultimate success and not to entitle to salvage reward. If a salvor is employed to do anything and does it, and the property is ultimately saved, he may claim a salvage award, though the thing which he does, in the events which happen, produces no good effect. If a salvor is employed to complete a salvage and does not, but, without any misconduct on his part, fails after he has performed a beneficial service, he is entitled also to a salvage award. If a salvor is employed to do a thing and does not do it, and no doubt uses strenuous exertions and makes sacrifices but does no good at all then it seems to me he is not entitled to salvage."

156. We cannot share the opinion expressed by Volli, *Assistenza*, 27, when he states that although useful result is included among the essential elements of salvage, it does not form an indispensable precondition of it, because this theory, although valid in relation to some particular national laws, is not so for the Convention, under which there can be no right to any refund or remuneration unless at least a partial result has been achieved.

achieved.[157] The damage and expenses in fact combine to form, on the basis of Article 8 of the Convention, with the other elements indicated in it, the standard for determining the total remuneration. It is allowed that this will not only take account of the risk of not achieving anything if there is no "beneficial result", but also of the fact that any useful result achieved by the salvor, especially if he is a professional, should reward him for all those cases where he has not succeeded in obtaining any reward and where he has vainly incurred risks and expenses which are normally those of a salvage company.[158]

16. "ENGAGED SERVICES" OR "SERVICES AT REQUEST"

A final point to be examined, within the essential element of salvage formed by the useful result, is the so-called "engaged services" or "services on request", because such services, not being expressly mentioned by the Convention, would seem to form an exception to the general provisions contained in Article 8, section 2.

Doubts have been expressed by several people as to whether such services, rendered at the express request of a ship in peril, can be considered to fall within the international law of salvage. By their very nature, they are not services to achieve success, even if they may contribute to allowing the salved ship or third parties to achieve it, when no salvage contract or agreement has been made.[159]

There is no doubt that engaged services form a special kind of service rendered at the request of the ship in peril. In some cases, and apart from the lack of any express provision in the Convention, it cannot be denied that they may constitute real and proper salvage services, co-existent with others in achieving the final success or, at any rate, services which have enabled success to be achieved. So they could be deemed, in the context of the overall salvage operation, to be one of the means by which the original peril has been removed.

It must be said that the Convention's rules did not need any specific men-

157. G. Berlingieri, *Salvataggio e assistenza*, 369; Wildeboer, *op. cit.*, 105.

158. Contra: Wildeboer, *op. cit.*, 96 and 104. For this author *no cure no pay* would be harder for occasional salvors than for professional salvors who, simply because they have adequate equipment and crew for salvage at sea, incur less risks than those who occasionally, with inadequate equipment, perform the task of salving a ship. In agreement in Italian jurisprudence: Trib. Naples 8 January 1969 in Dir. Mar. 1969, 141; Trib. Genoa 13 May 1970, in Dir. Mar. 1970, 203.

159. In favour of the idea which supports that "engaged services" have the character of salvage in the real sense are: Kennedy, *op. cit.*, 112; Brice, *op. cit.*, 39; Manca, *Commento*, 214 *et seq.*; Righetti, *La teoria del dispossession*, 237. Opposed to this are: G. Berlingieri, *Salvataggio ed assistenza*, 371 *et seq.*; Wildeboer, *op. cit.*, 115 *et seq.*; Reuter, *La notion*, 279 *et seq.*; F. Berlingieri, "Sulla nozione di engaged services" in Dir. Mar., 1970, 204. *Contra* in our jurisprudence, Trib. Brindisi, 14 April 1986, in Dir. Mar., 1987, 115.

tion of "engaged services" and their particular introduction into the scheme of salvage, even if only as an exceptional extension to such services, because the uniform international rules govern all those cases where the services rendered according to Article 2, paragraph 2, of the Convention have "led", wholly or partially, on their own or in conjunction with others, to a "beneficial result".[160]

In fact the Convention contains the necessary and sufficient elements to qualify all those "engaged services" which have helped in the production of a result which is useful in any way, either as a modest contribution to the complex of salvage operations, or as a simple partial salvage activity, or finally as a simple peace-making function, providing greater safety for whoever is attempting to complete this operation, as real and proper acts of salvage in the technical sense or at least as services rendered in connection with salvage, for the rules speak precisely of "every act of assistance" and of "services rendered".[161]

---

160. We cannot share the definition of *services at request or engaged services* given by a recent Italian decision (Trib. Genoa, 13 May 1970, in Dir. Mar.; 1970, 204) which identifies service at request as a mere *locatio operis*, and as such subject to remuneration for it would concern activities preliminary to salvage. When salvage services are carried out at a later stage, in this case, the extinguishing of a fire on board, then the service at request would be absorbed by the real and proper salvage operation, and account would be taken of this service when determining the global reward.

With regard to the preparatory work of the Brussels Convention and the discussions regarding *engaged services*, cf. Manca, *Commento*, 217 *et seq.*, Smeesters and Winkelmolen, *op. cit.*, 1212; Wildeboer, *op. cit.*, 115 *et seq.*; G. Berlingieri, *Salvataggio*, 371 *et seq.* They seem to support the conclusions of Brice, *op. cit.*, 41, where this author affirms: "to conclude, if either the would-be salvor does what he is engaged to do, confers no direct benefit, but the vessel is brought to safety by other means or if the salvor does confer a benefit without completing the salvage and the vessel is ultimately brought to safety then a salvage reward is due; if however, the would-be salvor does not do that which he is specifically engaged to do, or if in any event the property is lost, he receives no reward". In jurisprudence cf. Corte di Cassazione 16 November 1967, No. 2755, in Riv. Dir. Nav. 1968, II, 256, by which the non-material assistance would give the owner of the salving ship a right to reward only when there is a causal connection between the services of that ship and the escape by the salved ship from the danger.

161. Thus also Manca, *Commento*, 220. Although during the preparatory work of the Convention the English proposal for an express provision "to remunerate particular services which have been specially and expressly ordered", was rejected even should these services achieve a "beneficial result", a specific provision would not appear to be necessary in the international rules. In this regard, international jurisprudential precedents are extremely useful; in particular for Italy cf. Trib. Genoa 7 June 1933, in Dir. Mar. 1933, 394; Trib. Catania 27 May 1936, in Dir. Mar. 1936, 383; App. Genoa 13 March 1934, in Riv. Dir. Nav. 1935, II, 35; Arbitration Award 28 March 1960, in Dir. Mar. 1960, 237; Trib. Genoa 13 May 1970, in Dir. Mar. 1970, 203. For the international view of jurisprudence; cf. in France: Arbitration Award of 11 July 1925, in DOR suppl. 8, 842; Arbitration Award of 21 November 1929, in DOR suppl. 8, 14; Arbitration Award of 25 April 1961 in D.M.F. 1962, 176; Trib. Comm. Nantes 16 June 1949, in D.M.F. 1950, 244; in Germany: *The G.V. Seeschiadsge* 23 September 1937, in H.G.Z. 1937, B, 387; *The Klora Ratkun*, Hans O.L.G. 22 December 1937, H.G.Z. 1938; B. 43; in England: *The Melpomene* (1873) L.R. 4 A & E 129; *The Undaunted* (1860) *Lush* 90; *The Renpor* (1883) 8 P.D. 115; *The Helvetia* (1894) 8 Asp. M.L.C. 264; *The Dart* (1889) 8 Asp. M.L.C. 481; *The Tower Bridge* (1935) 53 Ll.L.Rep. 171; *The Africa Occidental* [1951] 2 Lloyd's Rep. 107; *The Orelia* [1958] 1 Lloyd's Rep. 441; *The Hassel* [1959] 2 Lloyd's Rep. 82.

17. REMUNERATION OF SALVAGE AND ITS CALCULATION

The Convention, which states in Article 6 that the amount of remuneration "est fixée par la convention des parties et, à defaut, par le juge", leaves the parties free to proceed also under the Convention to estimate the total amount due to the salvor for remuneration, refund of expenses and compensation for loss. This sum may, in certain cases, exceed the value of the salved property,[162] but, if so, the Convention provides for the court to fix the remuneration.

Thus the Convention, on this very important point, has not only carried out a good piece of work in unifying the international law of salvage; it has also introduced an innovation of substance following the "common law" countries, and especially English and North American law, which had always allowed the court wide discretionary powers to fix the remuneration.[163]

We have already seen that Article 2, paragraph 1, of the Convention contains the general principle that a salvor who has achieved a useful result is entitled to remuneration, but, in order to find the bases on which the remuneration itself should be fixed, it is necessary to refer to Article 8, paragraph 1, which contains a description of the criteria.

It has been correctly stated that it can be clearly inferred from the preparatory works of the Convention that the legislators' intention was to provide a certain number of directives for the courts, but without embodying them in mandatory predetermined schemes. In fact the text of the Convention specifies that these criteria should be taken as a basis for fixing remuneration, not excluding other circumstances and elements which may come into consideration, and contribute as a whole to the assessment of the reward.[164]

This opinion would seem to be perfectly correct, especially in the light of some recent precedents in international jurisprudence which have begun to undertake, even though *de jure condito*, the task of finding a more modern

---

162. Thus *The Inna* (1938) 60 Ll.L.Rep. 414 and *The Lyrma (No. 2)* [1978] 2 Lloyd's Rep. 30 whereby: "a Court assessing a salvage award after the event will never make an award amounting to the whole value of the salved property at the time and place of the termination of the services. There are cases, however, where remuneration for salvage services is not left to be assessed by the Court after the event, but is fixed in advance by agreement between the parties concerned. In such a case it may turn out that the remuneration so agreed in advance equals, or even exceeds substantially, the value of the salved property at the time and place of termination of the services. Yet, unless the agreement can be impugned on some equitable or other grounds the salvors are entitled to proceed against the salved property in respect of the services and to obtain a judgment for the full agreed amount of remuneration against it; and the result of that will inevitably be that the salvors' judgment, if given priority, will absorb the whole of the value of the salved property, leaving nothing for other claimants of whatever category whose lines attached before the salvage services were rendered." However, the principle regarding appeals for unfairness of remuneration specified in Art. 7 of the Convention holds good. In agreement Kennedy, *op. cit.*, 316 *et seq.*; Ferrarini, *Il soccorso*, 164; in opposition Manca, *Commento*, 237.

163. Kennedy, *op. cit.*, 174; Norris, *op. cit.*, 238; Brice, *op. cit.*, 63; Sutton, *The Assessing of Salvage Awards* (London, 1949), 3 *et seq.*; Gilmore and Black, *op. cit.*, 562 *et seq.*

164. Thus Wildeboer, *op. cit.*, 195 and Bolletino CMI, IX, 146.

interpretation of the present international law, adapting it to historical realities which could certainly not have been taken into account by the legislators as far back as 1910.[165]

The criteria indicated in Article 8, paragraph 1, are divided into two groups:

"(a) firstly, the measure of success obtained, the efforts and deserts of the salvors, the danger run by the salved vessel, by her passengers, crew and cargo, by the salvors, and by the salving vessel; the time expended, the expenses incurred and losses suffered, and the risks of liability and other risks run by the salvors, as well as the value of the property exposed to such risks, due regard being had to the special appropriation (if any) of the salvors' vessel for salvage purposes; (b) secondly, the value of the property salved."

There can be no doubt as to the underlying reason for this division, considering that the expressions "firstly" and "secondly" clearly signify, not so much that it was wanted to attach greater importance to the first category in the fixing of remuneration, but rather that it was wanted to remove any over-emphasis on the value of the salved property in contract and in jurisprudence, which adopted standards for determination which were often, and almost exclusively, linked to a percentage proportion of the remuneration, and depended on the economic benefit obtained by the salved property.[166]

This means that we do not have to think that the standard, following an original and compulsory order adopted by the Convention (especially in view of the complexity and variety of the circumstances in which a salvage operation may take place), causes sometimes one, but sometimes another element to assume greater importance when it is assessed in relation to the case to be judged.[167]

165. English jurisprudence with *The Helenus and Motaqua* [1982] 2 Lloyd's Rep. 261 and in Dir. Mar. 1983, 381 and Italian jurisprudence with the Arbitration Award, 26 November 1982, in Dir. Mar. 1983, 380, with a note by E. Vincenzini, "Brevi osservazioni in tema di 'Liability Salvage' ". have taken into consideration, both the criteria detailed in Art. 8 of the Convention, and also the liability risks of the salved subjects as an additional and not irrelevant element for the purposes of fixing remuneration.

166. Reuter, *La notion*, 81, notes that the hostility to this line of thought during the preparatory work of the Convention was general, and quotes the opinions expressed in this regard by the various national associations Thus Wildeboer, *op. cit.*, 198 who also concludes on the subject: "As regard Art. 8 Sect. 1 it should be remarked that, in the Convention, that system has not been followed whereby salvage remuneration has to be determined as a certain percentage of the value salved. This used to be customary in some countries. It does not follow from the Convention that the court would be in error if it determined the salvage remuneration at a certain percentage of the value salved. The court is free in its judgment, as long as it attempts to assess a salvage remuneration which is equitable with regard to the circumstances", Also see the aforementioned US decision *The Mimosa* (1987) A.M.C. 2523, the question being hypothetical in that case, as the *liability salvage* was conditioned by the existence of the owner's right to limit his liability.

167. In this sense Ferrarini, *Il soccorso*, 176, who maintains that the significance of the provision contained in Art. 8 of the Convention is to give a warning about the need to evaluate the salvage operation in its structural components before considering the value of the property salved. Thus also Brice, *op. cit.*, 65, for whom: "It is not possible to lay down any particular fixed order of precedence as to the importance of one element in a salvage case as compared to another. Each depends upon its own facts. For example, in one case the dangers may be very high

Having said so much, let us now examine the above elements, following the order in which they appear in the Convention's rules, and dividing them into elements relating to the salvor and elements relating to the assisted ship.

The elements concerning the salvor are: (a) the success obtained; (b) the efforts and merits of the salvor and the time spent; (c) the expenses, loss and liability risks of the salvor, and the value of the equipment used; (d) his qualifications as a professional salvor.

(a) The success obtained

This element, which appears to be a mere repetition of one of the two essential elements of salvage, i.e. the useful result, is in fact somewhat different, because there is an element of comparison of the result actually achieved with that which, theoretically, could have been achieved. A typical case is a partial salvage which has prevented greater loss to ship and cargo than had already occurred in the accident.[168]

The assessment of remuneration, on the basis of the above standard, should be made after a balancing of the success achieved, although only partial, with the services rendered by the salvor, as well as the other elements which the Convention indicates as elements contributing to the fixing of the reward.

(b) The efforts and deserts of the salvor and the time taken for salvage operations

The fact that the Convention, unlike some national laws,[169] indicates that the efforts of the salvor must be deserving, strengthens the opinion that the various standards for fixing remuneration must be taken into consideration in

but the services short; in another the services may be prolonged and expensive but the danger low; in either of the last two mentioned situations the fund may be a large or small one, the salvors may be professional or non-professional and may or may not have themselves been in danger. Obviously an imminent and high degree of danger, promptness and great skill by the salvor and serious but necessary risks run by him in performance of the service are considerations which go to enhance the award". *Contra* Cass. Sez. I, 7 May 1976 No. 1596, in Dir. Mar. 1977, 433, by which the principles of the discretion exercised by the judge of the duty to take account of each individual criterion, and of the lack of relationship among the individual criteria indicated, would not be of value for the Convention, while they would carry weight in Italian law, on the basis of Art. 491 of the Code of Navigation.

168. Thus Ferrarini, *Il soccorso*, 177; Wildeboer, *op. cit.*, 197; Kennedy, *op. cit.*, 174; Reuter, *La notion*, 75. In jurisprudence see Arbitration Award of 30 December 1963, in Dir. Mar. 1965, 300, which recognised that the requirement of a useful result is met when the tugs try, even without success, to bring the ship away from the rocks, because their pulling has the effect of reducing impacts on the ship, and thus preventing her from capsizing or sinking. An isolated decision should be noted in this regard: Trib. Caltanissetta 21 November 1977, in Dir. Mar. 1978, 483, which identifies the success obtained by the salvors as the "value" of the damage avoided, i.e. in practice the cost of the repairs and other expenses avoided by the intervention of the salvor.

169. Thus for example Italian Code of Navigation, Art. 491; Norwegian maritime law, Art. 221 and Swedish maritime law, Art. 224(b), which mention only the efforts, not the merits.

close association with each other and on the basis of the final result which, although partial, must be regarded as a condition for any entitlement to remuneration.

The competence of the salvor, and his ability to use equipment which is adequate and sufficient for the purpose, will form an important element in all those cases where the salvor's efforts assume a more deserving character; when, for example, they have made it possible in a short time to end a dangerous grounding which would certainly have deteriorated, with the most extreme results, either through a worsening of the weather conditions, or due to an increase in the ship's list in a case of shifting cargo, with consequent danger of capsizing or sinking.

It is most evident that, in such or similar circumstances, the quick and timely intervention of the salvor, with the use of adequate equipment (although it may at times seem disproportionate to the task at hand), must be carefully evaluated in relation to the shortening of the time spent over the operation.[170]

It is evident, in fact, that faced with a useful result achieved with courage, diligence and adequate equipment, the shorter the time, the more it contributes to confirming that the salvor's efforts have been particularly deserving, since a greater delay in cases of particular emergency and imminent peril might indirectly give the impression that the salvor was not so able and competent and that the use of salvage equipment was inadequate.

On the other hand, time spent in the salvage operation assumes importance in the opposite sense, of lasting longer, when time is not needed to remove the state of peril, but is considered merely as a factor in the measuring of a part of the salvage operations, for example, the towage of a damaged ship under adverse weather conditions, or the lightening of a ship aground, so that she can be raised and refloated, when the more time is spent, the more it is evident that the salvage operation was increasingly difficult, and the same applies to the *quantum meruit* of the salvor.[171]

---

170. See G. Berlingieri, *Salvataggio*, 386; Ferrarini, *Il soccorso*, 178, and the jurisprudence quoted there; Volli, *op. cit.*, 192; Kennedy, *op. cit.*, 204; Sutton, *op. cit.*, 7; Gilmore and Black, *op. cit.*, 562; a contrary opinion is that of Manca, *Commento*, 353, which cannot be shared, by which a salvage lasting for a prolonged period would deserve a higher remuneration than a salvage completed in a few hours. This line of thought seems to be followed by Wildeboer, *op. cit.*, 200, who does not seem to be concerned by the fact that the time element, according to the circumstances with which it is associated, may have varying importance, with completely contrasting results when evaluating this element for the purposes of remuneration.

171. In Italian jurisprudence some importance attaches to the conclusions reached, although in a case not governed by the Convention, by the Arbitration Award, 30 July 1963, in Riv. Dir. Nav., 1964, II, 92, by which the time spent by the salving ship in the salvage operations should be taken into consideration both from the viewpoint of the criteria on which the reward is fixed, as an indication of the extent of effort exerted, and also, with greater relevance, for fixing the damages and expenses, because the compensation for loss of profits is payable on the basis of the average net profit of the salving ship in proportion to the time spent in the salvage. A decision by the Tribunal of Brindisi of 14 December 1987, in Dir. Mar., 1988, 833, confirms that Art. 8 of the

(c) The expense, loss and liability risks of the salvor, and the value of the equipment used

This element for determining remuneration distinguishes the Convention from Italian law which (unlike the laws or regulations of other Contracting States, which have accepted the Convention completely even on the subject of the fixing of remuneration) makes a clear distinction between the refund of expenses and damage, and reward for the salvage services rendered.[172]

The Convention bears in mind, for purposes of fixing remuneration, that the salvor often claims a certain amount for expenses and loss which have been caused by the salvage operations with which they are in fact connected by an "aetiological" link.[173] The salvor may, firstly, have incurred expenses which he would never have encountered if it had not been for the fact that he gave the salvage services; secondly and especially in the case of a non-professional salvor, he may have lost his normal commercial profits, having left his normal service; or thirdly, a professional salvor may have incurred expenses which, although not connected with a particular case of salvage, are general expenses associated with the maintenance of his own salvage ships and their equipment, as well as the specially trained crews, whose use is solely connected with the possibility of rendering assistance at sea.[174]

As has already been mentioned, in order to be taken into account for assessment of reward, the expenses and loss must have been due to the operations carried out for the purpose of rendering assistance, and this causal relationship must be determined on the standard of "adequate causality" (*causalita adeguata*), according to which the concept of adequacy prevails over that of a direct relationship between the salvage operations, expenses and loss.[175]

This raises the problem of determining what loss and expenses should be

Convention differs from our national law, in so far as it does not include, among the elements used in determining remuneration, the salvors' general expenses.

172. The principle of the Convention on the subject of expenses and damage has been accepted not as a separate right to credit for the salvor, but rather as an element for assessing the remuneration due by the maritime laws of Norway, Sweden, Denmark, Greece, West Germany, France and Spain and, although Panama did not ratify the 1910 Brussels Convention, by Panamanian law.

173. Ferrarini, *Il soccorso*, 165.

174. Thus Brice, *op. cit.*, 211 states that: "The amounts of expense, damage or loss ought not, under ordinary circumstances, to be taken as 'moneys numbered' to be added to the amount of the reward for actual salvage services. If the court gives the amount of the damage, loss or expense specifically, it will take care not to give the amount twice over by again considering them when it comes to fix the amount due for salvage remuneration proper, that is, the remuneration for risk, etc . . . , in the service." This interpretation regarding the "money numbered" originates in English jurisprudence, cf. *The St. Melante* (1947) 80 Ll.L.Rep. 588, and has recently been confirmed by another decision, *The Ben Gairn* [1979] 1 Lloyd's Rep. 410.

175. Thus literally Ferrarini, *Il soccorso*, 168; English jurisprudence quoted by Kennedy, *op. cit.*, 212 *et seq.* and by Brice, *op. cit.*, 71 *et seq.*, is more closely linked to the criterion of the *causa proxima*, that is to say, a direct relationship of causality between salvage and damage.

taken into account as contributing to the composition of the reward. That is to say, whether only the loss and expenses of an extraordinary nature in comparison with the normal use of the salving vessel should be admissible for this purpose, or whether consideration should also be given to all those expenses and losses (such, for example, as ordinary consumption, engine stresses, wear and tear on towing cables, etc.) which, it seems, would be considered ordinary in cases where assistance is rendered. The Convention seems to lean towards the expense and loss being of an extraordinary nature even if, in establishing these, the court must proceed, in each case, to verify not only the extraordinary nature of the expense and loss but also the need for them in relation to the salvage.[176]

As well as the expenses and loss, consideration should also be given to the liability risks of the salvor, in addition to the other risks incurred by him in carrying out the salvage operations, and to the value *du materiel exposé par eux*, as stated in the Convention.[177]

These risks have been identified, by current doctrine, as those liability risks which might be incurred by the owner of the salving ship in relation to his own insurers or in relation to the persons or goods transported, in respect of his failure to finish (the contract of carriage) or the interruption of it.[178]

Insurance policies in fact cover risks relating to incidents which arose from a deviation of the ship to render assistance to other ships or to persons in peril.[179]

With regard to liability towards the cargo, it has been observed that such

176. Ferrarini, *Il soccorso*, 169 *et seq.*; Kennedy, *op. cit.*, 218; Brice, *op. cit.*, 75. The latter authors consider that there is a simple presupposition in favour of this relationship of necessity between the salvage operation and the expenses or damage. In this regard see also Wildeboer, *op. cit.*, 209, for whom "the category 'costs incurred and losses suffered' comprises a large number of ways in which the salvor can suffer capital depreciation which can be estimated in money. For example, it includes damage suffered by the ship and the salvage material, the consumption of coal, the wear of cables and anchors, the rent of salvage material, the wages of persons specially engaged, and the depreciation of machines. It also includes damage suffered, for instance that caused the ship not to arrive in time; missed profits, such as bonuses for the punctual arrival of the ship; and missed profits such as missed fishing opportunities, frequently mentioned in the decisions dealing with salvage effected by fishing boats. Especially as regards the latter group, it is necessary to bear in mind that only such profits are concerned as have been missed as a direct consequence of the assistance." Obviously the loss of profits does not only come into play with fishing boats and vessels. See on this the case studies quoted by Kennedy, *op. cit.*, 76.

177. This requirement has been removed from Italian Law; Art. 491 of the Italian Navigation Code mentions only the risks run by the salvor. The Report on the Code (No. 340) explains the reasons for this removal by the fact that this value "either becomes a loss suffered when the equipment is lost or deteriorated or, on the contrary, is included in the risks run by the ship which has rendered the service".

178. Ferrarini, *Il soccorso*, 174, and in *Le Assicurazioni marittime*, 167 *et seq.*; Wildeboer, *op. cit.*, 201; G. Berlingieri, *Salvataggio*, 383 *et seq.*; Kennedy, *op. cit.*, 207 *et seq.*; Norris, *op. cit.*, 55; Righetti, *Le responsabilita del vettore marittimo nel sistema dei pericoli eccettuati* (Padua, 1960), 125.

179. For the saving of persons see *The South Sea* [1932] Lloyd's Rep. 374, where the liability risk was assessed much higher by the judge because the salving ship was a passenger ship. See also Carver's, *Carriage of Goods*, (1963), 601 *et seq.*

damage as may be sustained by the owner of the carried goods is an expected peril for the Brussels Convention on Bills of Lading considers acts of or attempts at salvage and assistance, or deviation of a voyage for that purpose, and states expressly, in Article 4, paragraph 4, that a deviation for the purpose of salving property or of saving human life shall not be considered a breach of contract, nor shall any other deviation which has been brought about by a reasonable cause.[180]

Further, the Hamburg Convention of 31 May 1978 (United Nations Convention on the Carriage of Goods by Sea) states in Article 5, paragraph 6, that: "the carrier is not liable, except in general average, where loss, damage or delay in delivery resulted from measures to save life or from reasonable measures to save property at sea".

While the Convention was being prepared, there was debate on the problem of inserting into it a right of the cargo owner to a certain remuneration for the risks incurred by him, *vis-à-vis* the salved ship and the party owing the remuneration, but this proposal was rejected after a full discussion.[181]

As we have seen, the Convention adds to the elements fixing the remuneration the liability risks of the salvor, and also, as a contributing factor, although not a determinant one, the value of the equipment used on the occasion and which was exposed to these risks in the salvage operation.[182]

The point must not be overlooked that the value of the salving ship may, or may not, assume any particular importance in a higher evaluation of the salvage services, and of the consequent remuneration, because, in certain circumstances, the salvage, although performed by a vessel of insubstantial or at most of modest economic value, can achieve a useful result, despite the dis-

---

180. G. Berlingieri, *Salvataggio e assistenza*, 383 *et seq.*, Norris, *op. cit.*, 55; Kennedy, *op. cit.*, 207 *et seq.*; Wildeboer, *op. cit.*, 201 and 213; Ferrarini, *Il soccorso*, 175; Righetti, *op. cit.*, 135 *et seq*. According to this author the principle of reasonable deviation also applies to a case of salvage, because acts of assistance and salvage at sea, even when voluntary, may form the precondition for invoking excepted peril, provided that they have not represented the extremes of an unjustified deviation.

181. Cf. Reports on the session of 19 November 1910, 100 and 101; Manca, *Commento*, 254; Wildeboer, *op. cit.*, 71. Also US doctrine has aligned itself with the above line of thought, so that Gilmore and Black, *op. cit.*, 560 note that: "If, as the American writers suggest, cargo is never entitled to share in the award then (if from the salvor's point of view there is no risk) there is no reason to include it."

182. For Manca, *Commento*, 254, on the contrary also, the value of the property represents a determining factor for calculating the remuneration, although he does not offer any valid grounds in support of this theory. Account should also be taken of the value of the salving ship, as she also is exposed to the risks of a salvage operation according to English jurisprudence. See *The City of Chester* (1884) 51 L.T. 485. On this subject Sutton, *op. cit.*, 7, states that: "Risk to the salving property is caused in much the same way as is risk to the salving personnel. There is the same general run of usual and expected risks to salving vessels associated with the various physical circumstances, whereby overall importance is again increased without separate assessment. This is an abstract conception of risk, the importance of which has to be borne in mind in any separate variation according to the value of the salving vessel. Adjustment can be made when it is clear that the general level of risk associated as usual with a particular condition has been exceeded or has not been attained in any particular instance."

proportion between the value of the salving vessel and that of the salved property.

The fact that the value of the salving equipment, unlike that of the salved property, does not set any limit either to the entitlement to reward or to the fixing of its amount, is confirmed not only by Article 8 of the Convention, but also by a single arbitration award.[183]

(d) Special qualifications as a professional salvor

The last of the elements indicated by the Convention to fix remuneration, and which relates to the party providing the salvage services, is the qualification of the latter as a professional salvor, *rectius*, the fact of the ship being especially appropriated for salvage, i.e. that she has been fitted out and equipped for the specific, if not exclusive, purpose of rendering assistance at sea.

It is clear from the Convention's rules that, in considering the qualification of the active *subject* of the salvage, i.e., subjective capacity as a salvage company, no importance attaches, for the purposes of the Convention, to the existence of a salvage company to which the salving vessel must necessarily belong.[184]

Since, the Convention does not require that the salving ship should belong to a salvage company, that is to say a professional salvor, the theory may be accepted by which "salvage vessels" fall into two distinct categories: (a) ships exclusively appropriated to salvage at sea, which are kept near so-called "salvage stations", without engaging in any other activity; and (b) ships which, fitted out and equipped for the purposes of rendering assistance, are used in other activities (port towing, deep sea towing), although they are ready and available to intervene, where necessary, and assist ships in peril.[185]

For the first of these categories, there is no question but that the compensation due to the salvor should be increased, in consideration of the capital investment placed by him at the service of ships in peril and not used for long periods, while in the second category account should be taken only of the fact that the ships possess special gear and equipment. The initial purchase cost of

183. Cf. Arbitration Award Manzitti/Ripert 1958, *M/c Mare Nostrum*, unpublished but quoted by Ferrarini, *Il soccorso*, 182, in which a small fishing boat which had assisted a large tanker was awarded a reward exceeding the value of the fishing vessel itself. In this regard we think it worthwhile to mention the clear explanation of Kennedy, *op. cit.*, 203, where he clearly indicates what part should be played by the value of the salving vessels in determining the reward, of which it neither can nor should form either a limit or a factor in devaluing the salvage service.

184. Thus also Ferrarini, *Il soccorso*, 183 *et seq.*; G. Berlingieri, *Salvataggio e assistenza*, 387 *et seq.*; Volli, *Assistenza*, 192; and Italian jurisprudence: Cass. 19 February 1957, in Dir. Mar. 1957, 145; App. Genoa 21 March 1961, in Temi gen. 1962, 143; Arbitration Award 24 May 1968 in Dir. Mar. 1968 in Dir. Mar. 1968, 221; Trib. Trieste 20 September 1973, in Dir. Mar. 1974, 587, with note by Boi, "Brevi note sui rimorchiatori adibiti and operazioni di soccorso", App. Naples 31 March 1978, in Dir. Mar. 1979, 578; App. Venice 6 March 1980, in Dir. Mar. 1980, 249.

185. Thus Ferrarini, *Il soccorso*, 84; G. Berlingieri, *Salvataggio e assistenza*, 392.

that is normally considerable, but the general expenses of the company for the use of these ships is almost completely amortised by the carrying out of her other activities.[186]

There are two elements in determining remuneration which concern the persons saved and property salved: (a) the peril run by the persons and property salved; (b) the value of the property salved.

(a) The peril run by the persons saved and the goods salved

We have already discussed this element (Section 14), because it performs a dual function. The principal function is essential for salvage at sea joined with the other contributory element, the useful result; the secondary function concerns the evaluation of remuneration of salvage services.

We will here deal with the second of these two functions, noting that, for the purposes of fixing remuneration, this element is more important than the others, seeing that it supplies, as has been correctly stated, the degree of usefulness of the service rendered.[187]

We have already established that, although the Convention excluded the possibility that the saving of human lives gives the salvor a right to remuneration, it still includes the saving of lives at the same time, or at least on the same occasion as the salvage of property, among the elements for evaluation of the work done by the salvor and of his *quantum meruit*, for the purposes of fixing remuneration.[188]

Also, with regard to the concept of peril, which has already been examined, the peril should be a real, if not an imminent, one. In evaluating it, for the purposes of fixing remuneration, due account should be taken of the wide

---

186. Cf. Wildeboer, *op. cit.*, 203 and the vast array of European jurisprudence quoted. Present English doctrine and jurisprudence are in the same sense. See Brice, *op. cit.*, 152 *et seq.*; Kennedy, *op. cit.*, 168 *et seq.*, and the wide range of case law quoted by these authors. The position of French doctrine and jurisprudence is special, tending to allow a certain reward to salvage ships stationed in the Mediterranean, considering the reduced possibility of intervention in that sea as compared to more dangerous seas, and the consequent reduced possibility of recovering the expenses of company management; cf. De Juglart and Villeneau, *Repertoire*, 273, and French arbitration decisions of 1 August 1949 in D.M.F. 1950, 235; 27 April 1956 in D.M.F. 1957, 40 and 25 February 1957 in D.M.F. 1957, 500.

187. Thus Ferrarini, *Il soccorso*, 185; G. Berlingieri, *op. cit.*, 460.

188. On this point cf. Italian jurisprudence: Arbitration Award 30 December 1963, in Dir. Mar. 1965, 300; Arbitration Award of 28 November 1965, in Dir. Mar. 1966, 357; App. Naples 13 August 1970, in Dir. Mar. 1970, 407; French jurisprudence: Arbitration Award 13 March 1951, in D.M.F. 1951, 340; English jurisprudence quoted by Sutton, *op. cit.*, 5 and 572 *et seq.*, and by Brice, *op. cit.*, 83; and finally US jurisprudence quoted by Gilmore and Black, *op. cit.*, 570 *et seq.* It is evident that the saving of persons assumes greater importance when the assistance is rendered to a passenger ship as in the case, already mentioned, of *The Southsea* [1932] 44 Lloyd's Rep. 373.

range of cases where various degrees of peril appear, and of the possibility that the property at risk might, in such a situation, escape the peril.[189]

The various degrees in peril may, instead, relate to the ship and her cargo, just as the ship and the cargo may, in special circumstances, incur perils of a different nature.

With regard to these cases, it has been pointed out that it is an open question whether the different degree of danger run by the goods at risk and the different nature of the peril itself allow the payment of separate amounts of remuneration to the salvor, to be fixed in proportion to the two different degrees of peril, or simply to the two different perils, for which payment is due separately from the owners of the ship and of the cargo respectively.[190]

In the first case, that is to say, the case of perils of a different degree, the operation should be considered as a single one although, for example, the cargo had been easily salved by discharging or lightening. Further, the salving is regarded as a way leading to the subsequent salving of the ship, as a working out of one phase of the complex salvage operation which is considered as a single unit.[191]

---

189. Thus Wildeboer, *op. cit.*, 199, who suggests that the method of assessment which should be applied by courts in determining the "danger" element should be as follows: "When determining the danger run by the ship salved, her passengers, crew and cargo and by the salvors and the salving vessel, the court will pay special attention to the diverse elements which determine how great the possibility was that the goods and people in danger would be damaged or injured, or would perish completely. At this point, therefore, consideration is given to the weather conditions, the position of the vessel and the condition of her crew, the spot where the salvage services had to be rendered, etc". For our jurisprudence on the subject of assessing the "danger" element up to 1959, see E. Vincenzini, "Rassegna di giurisprudenza in tema di assistenza salvataggio, rimorchio e ricupero", 147; and later Trib. Naples 25 February 1961 in Riv. Dir. Nav. 1962, II, 306; Arbitration Award 28 March 1960, in Dir. Mar. 1960, 223; Arbitration Award 30 December 1963, in Dir. Mar. 1965, 300; Arbitration Award 24 May 1968, in Dir. Mar. 1968, 221; Arbitration Award 21 July 1966, in Dir. Mar. 1966, 603; Arbitration Award 28 November 1965 in Dir. Mar. 1966, 357; App. Naples 13 August 1970, in Dir. Mar. 1971, 407; Trib. La Spezia 21 November 1970, in Dir. Mar. 1971, 213; Trib. Livorno 2 February 1971, in Dir. Mar. 1971, 222; Arbitration Award 18 December 1972, in Dir. Mar. 1972, 655; Trib. Caltanissetta 21 November 1977, in Dir. Mar. 1978, 483; Arbitration Award 31 January 1979, in Dir. Mar. 1979, 405; Arbitration Award 9 May 1981, in Dir. Mar. 1982, 704; Trib. Massa, 20 August 1985, in Dir. Mar., 1986, 443; App. Leece, 12 April 1985, in Dir. Mar., 1986, 906; App. Naples, 29 June 1985, in Dir. Mar, 1986, 912; Trib. Genoa, 11 October 1985, in Dir. Mar., 1986, 955; App. Genoa, 20 June 1987, in Dir. Mar., 1988, 437; Arbitration Award 21 February 1987, in Dir. Mar., 1988, 517; Trib. Brindisi, 14 December 1987, in Dir. Mar., 1988, 833; Trib. Brindisi, 10 February 1988, in Dir. Mar., 1989, 818; Arbitration Award 9 September 1988, in Dir. Mar., 1990, 182; Arbitration Award 22 March 1989, in Dir. Mar., 1990, 416; Trib. Genoa, 27 December 1989, in Dir. Mar., 1990, 406; Arbitration Award 12 April 1989, in Dir. Mar., 1990, 755. On the subject of different degrees of risk see Kennedy, *op. cit.*, 266 *et seq.* and English jurisprudence amply quoted for the different types of danger, Brice, *op. cit.*, 148 *et seq.*

190. Ferrarini, *Il soccorso*, 187 and English and US jurisprudence quoted there.

191. This is the sense of the opinion of English and US doctrine on the point; see Kennedy, *op. cit.*, 266; Carver's *op. cit.*, 695; Brice, *op. cit.*, 148; Congdon, *On General Average* (New York, 1952), 108; and on the subject of general average see Lowndes & Rudolf, *The Law of General Average* (London, 1964), 137 *et seq.* and the theory of the sharing the expenses of a complex salvage operation. Lastly see Ferrarini, "Il salvataggio come avaria comune", 5.

(b) The value of the property salved

In the order set up by the Convention, this element is to be considered last and separately from the other elements for the fixing of remuneration, because the Convention's rules attribute less importance to it when compared with all the other elements just examined. The Convention lays down that those should be considered firstly (*en premier lieu*).[192]

However, it would appear that today, and despite the dislike shown by present doctrine to the trend, the salvor's reward is fixed, after evaluating the elements which should be examined firstly (*en premier lieu*), on the basis of a simple percentage calculation on the value of the property salved.[193]

There can be no doubt that, even were this standard to be adopted, it cannot be separated from comparison with other much more influential determinant elements, such as the peril of being lost and the useful result. Due account should, however, be taken of the fact that, although calculating remuneration on the basis of a percentage of the value salved eases the court's task in practice, it ignores some of the fundamental principles of salvage at sea, which require that the special difficulty of the operation and the deserving nature of salvage services should be given an almost overriding importance.

The approach, now almost universally adopted by jurisprudence when fixing remuneration on the basis of a percentage of the value salved, must also

192. Since the discussion of the preliminary draft of the Convention in 1905, the secondary ranking of the value of the property salved as an element for the fixing of remuneration was stated in the reports which read: "The value of the property salved is a less important element than the bases of assessment listed in the first place."

193. In favour of calculating remuneration as a percentage of the value of the property salved in our home jurisprudence are: Trib. Naples, 8 June 1963, in Dir. Mar. 1965, 221; Trib. Messina 23 January 1969, in Dir. Mar. 1969, 437; Trib. Livorno 2 February 1971, in Dir. Mar. 1971, 222; and lastly Cass. 7 May 1976, in Dir. Mar. 1976, 434; App. Naples, 29 June 1985, in Dir. Mar., 1986, 912; Arbitration Award 21 February 1987, in Dir. Mar., 1988, 517; Trib. Brindisi, 19 December 1987, in Dir. Mar., 1988, 833; Trib. Bari, 9 March 1988, in Dir. Mar., 1989; Trib. Livorno, 21 December 1988, in Dir. Mar., 1989, 1127; in opposition, as well as present doctrine: Ferrarini, *Il soccorso*, 189; G. Berlingieri, *Salvataggio*, 462; Norris, *op. cit.*, 380, are the following decisions of Italian jurisprudence: Arbitration Award 13 June 1952, in Dir. Mar. 1953, 119; Arbitration Award 24 June 1955, in Dir. Mar. 1956; 101; Trib. Messina 7 October 1961, in Giur. si. 1962, 701; Arbitration Award 25 July 1963, in Dir. Mar. 1965, 295. More recently, see Arbitration Award 11 August 1989, in Dir. Mar., 1990, 182, in which it is established that for the purposes of calculating remuneration, the element of the value of the ship salved, even if high, is of no direct relevance once the likelihood of her total loss has been excluded. French jurisprudence, although adopting the calculation of a percentage of the value salved, applies the principle according to which the higher the values salved, the lower the percentage: cf. Arbitration Award, 6 July 1956, in D.M.F. 1957, 47; Arbitration Award 5 March 1958, in D.M.F. 1958, 297; Arbitration Award 4 July 1960, in D.M.F. 1961, 105. French doctrine, on the other hand, seems to incline towards the application of the principle which fixes the remuneration of the salvor in any event as a percentage of the value of the property salved. See on this subject Rodière, *Traité général de droit maritime*, 182, and Id, *Précis de droit maritime* (Paris, 1974), 465, which states plainly that: "the salvor is given a sum which represents a fraction of the value of the property salved". In English jurisprudence see *The Queen Elizabeth* (1949) 82 Ll.L.Rep. 803.

be recognised as equally correct, by which the percentage is reduced as the values salved are higher.[194]

The value of the property salved (*les choses sauvées*) which, according to the Convention, has to be taken into account to fix remuneration for salvage, is not difficult to discover. Excluding any attribution of a monetary value to human lives, which are obviously neither things nor properties, such property is identified as the ship, the cargo and the freight.

The value of these properties must of course be established as at the time and place of salvage, that is to say, at the end of the operations, taking into account the state and condition of the properties when the operations are finally completed.[195]

In determining the value of the property salved, therefore, no importance attaches to possible loss sustained after the end of the salvage operations, fluctuations in the market price either of the ship or of the goods, and any expenses not causally connected with the accident. It is not possible, for example, to allow as a deductible expense from the value of the salved property the cost of bringing the salved ship into the salvage port, when this task has been assigned to port tugs after completion of the salvage operations; but it is permissible for the expense of transferring the wreck from a salvage port to a breakers' yard to be deducted from the value salved, when the salved ship cannot be repaired and must be considered a total constructive loss.[196]

In cases where the salved ship can be repaired, it is normal to adopt the market value of the ship, after deducting the cost of the repairs and the damage sustained by her before the end of the salvage operations.[197]

194. Thus Russo, *Salvataggio ed assistenza*, 810; Ferrarini, *Il soccorso*, 189; G. Berlingieri, *Salvataggio e assistenza*, 462; Volli, *op. cit.*, 194 *et seq*. A particular position seems to be that of Sutton, *op. cit.*, 39 *et seq*. who attempts to construct a comparative scale of rewards to be fixed on the basis of a percentage of the value salved and assisted, exaggerating this criterion in an unacceptable way, because the other criteria for fixing payment, which are much more important, seem to lose all their relevance.

195. In this regard Wildeboer, *op. cit.*, 204 writes: "The value of the goods salved constitutes the fund which serves for the remuneration and indemnification of the salvors. The consequence of this concept is that the value of the goods salved must be determined as the value they have at the moment and at the place of salvage. This means, *inter alia*, that the value in damaged condition is concerned; moreover, it means that the objective value is concerned and not the (subjective) value which the ship and the cargo salved represent for the owners". On the point of the fixing of the final moment of the salvage operations, see in Italian jurisprudence the recent Arbitration Award of 26 November 1982, in Dir. Mar. 1983, 580, which recognised that the refloating of the ship and her tow into port after the entire cargo had been lightened, constitutes a phase, (the last) of a complex salvage operation and not a distinct service.

196. Cf. *The Germania* (1904) 9 Asp. M.L.C. 358, and *The Ningpo* [1923] Lloyd's Rep. 16, 392 quoted by Brice, *op. cit.*, 126. It seems relevant to mention the Arbitration Award of July 1963, in Dir. Mar. 1965, 282, which states that when the value of the ship in a damaged state corresponds to the demolition price, account must be taken, as a component of this value, of the State subsidy for demolition as well. The same opinion is held by G. Berlingieri, *Salvataggio*, 465.

197. Thus Ferrarini, *Il soccorso*, 190; Norris, *The Law of Salvage* (New York, 1983), paras. 262, 263. In Italian jurisprudence the above Arbitration Award of 4 July 1963, in Dir. Mar. 1965, 282 agrees with this line of thought; a special decision, for which there are no precedents, is that of the Court of Cassation, Sez. I, 7 May 1976, No. 1596, in Dir. Mar. 1976, 434, which fixed the

While present doctrine agrees in regarding as incorrect the valuation of the salved ship based on the price of construction, reduced according to her age and state of wear, a certain difference of opinion has arisen regarding the use of the insured value, that is to say, the estimated value agreed for insurance purposes. Although it is affirmed that this value cannot be considered for this particular purpose because it forms a *res inter alios acta* insofar as it is an agreement between insured and insurer which cannot bind any third parties, and is not strictly linked to fluctuations in market prices; nevertheless it was wished to attach decisive importance to the insured value for the purpose of valuing the property salved.[198]

One authoritative doctrine maintains that the problem of valuing a ship is stated in the same way as when it is a question of compensation for her loss under her insurance cover. In particular, here also the question would arise whether, for valuation purposes, account can be taken of the value which the ship has for her owner; that value can truly be more or less than her market value.[199]

This theory does not seem to hold good. It may be acknowledged that the subjective valuation is irrelevant, so that it can be taken into account only in exceptional circumstances[200]; but it cannot be denied that, whether in the event of total loss or of salvage, the insured value, for an estimated policy, corresponds to the value which the ship has in the first instance for the insured who, if he loses her, is entitled to receive compensation corresponding to that value and not to any other[201]; while, secondly, this value corresponds to the

value of the salved ship by taking the mean between the market price of the ship and the price of building a new one.

198. Ripert, *Droit maritime*, II, 150; French Arbitration Award of 27 April 1956, in D.M.F. 1957, 40. An intermediate position is taken by Norris, *op. cit.*, (ed. 1983), para. 263, which with regard to the insured value maintains: "In the absence of evidence of market value, the amount for which the ship has been insured, or the insurance companies' appraisal of value for insurance purposes, may be received in evidence as a factor or circumstance which may be considered in estimating value. It is not, however, regarded as conclusive evidence of value nor does it have much weight in that respect".

199. Thus Ferrarini, *Il soccorso*, 191. However, the Arbitration Award of 24 June 1955, in Dir. Mar. 1956, 101 seems too rigid, and even inexact, where it maintains that, for consistent jurisprudence in matters of salvage, no relevance attaches to insured value in fixing the value of the property salved.

200. Cf. *The Castor* [1932] Lloyd's Rep. 43, 261, which took account of a long-term charter-party. *Contra*, in Italian jurisprudence Trib. Lecce 16 April 1973, in Dir. Mar. 1965, 14.

201. Ferrarini, *Le assicurazioni marittime*, 236 *et seq*. With regard to the vagueness of the estimate the author clearly explains the reasons underlying this principle: "With the estimate, the value of the ship is disassociated from the frequent and often relevant fluctuations in the freight market, and hence in the price of ships, and a constant evaluation is maintained over a period of time, which is necessary for both parties to the insurance. In fact, the insured undertakes an investment spread over a certain period of time, and cannot run the risk of receiving, in the event of the loss of the ship, an indemnity lower than the value which the ship has in the balance sheet of his company. On his side, the insurer has many reasons for maintaining the value of the insured ship constant, because it has a bearing not only on total loss but also, and far more frequently, in cases of particular average, on compensation, which is not influenced by fluctuations in the market for ships." See more recently on this point, Arbitration Award 11 August 1989, in Dir. Mar., 1990, 184, which pointed out that in matters of salvage, the amount indicated in the

sum which the insurer has at risk and in which he will have to indemnify his insured should the salvage operations fail.

In this case the value of the salved property represents, for the insurer, as regards the insured value, a saving in comparison with what he would have had to pay had there been a total loss of the ship. It is thus difficult to understand why the salvor, who has brought about this particular success, should see it, and the following compensation, evaluated on the bases of different standards.

Similarly, the value of the cargo to be assumed in fixing remuneration is what it has at the place where it is at the end of the salvage operations. If the goods have to continue on to their final destination, the loss sustained before the end of the salvage operations and the expenses incurred for continuing the voyage must be deducted.[202]

Finally, freight should be evaluated, bearing in mind whether there is risk for the goods, i.e. whether it is a case of freight earned in any event ("ship lost or not lost") or whether there is risk for the vessel.

In the first case, since the shipowner is no longer concerned with the vicissitudes of the voyage and its fulfilment, the value of the freight is relevant only for the cargo owners. To the cargo value, the freight must be added if the cargo arrives at destination, while the freight must be considered lost like the cargo if the latter is lost.

If, on the other hand, the freight is at risk for the ship, a distinction must be made where the salvage service is ended at the port of destination, when the freight salved is the amount due for the entire voyage. If the salvage service ends at a port of refuge, a further distinction has to be made because, if the goods do not continue on their way, the freight to be assumed is that shown in the carriage contract. If they are to continue to their final destination, the freight to be assumed is that collected, less the expenses incurred in reaching that destination.[203]

Closely connected with the problem of fixing the value of the property salved, there are three particular aspects of such evaluation relevant in fixing later the remuneration due to the salvor: (a) the calculation of such taxes as

hull and machinery insurance policy is not to be considered as estimated, nor is the insured value to be considered as binding in calculating the remuneration.

202. We share the assertions made by G. Berlingieri, *Salvage*, 466, for whom damage sustained by the goods during the course of resumed carriage to final destination would be deductible from their value, because the salvor must not bear the risk of the goods being damaged after he has salved them. In Italian jurisprudence an isolated decision (App. Ancona 28 November 1974, in Dir. Mar. 1975, 64) has identified the criterion for determining the value of the cargo as being its cif price, in compliance with current international practice, with no importance attaching to the profit of the importer as an element in making up this criterion. In agreement on this point Brice, *op. cit.*, 138, and English jurisprudence quoted there.

203. Thus Ferrarini, *Il soccorso*, 192; G. Berlingieri, *Salvataggio*, 466; Kennedy, *op. cit.*, 282 *et seq*. Note the remark of this author to the effect that in the case of the "salvage" of a wreck, there can be no salving of freight. Norris, *The Law of Salvage* (ed. 1983), para. 261; Brice, *op. cit.*, 140 *et seq.*; Wildeboer, *op. cit.*, 206.

the salvor has to pay on the amount received, so reducing his remuneration; (b) the definition of the remuneration as a debt of value or as a debt of currency, and the identification of the currency in which the payment must be made; (c) the determination of the interest due to the salvor.

With regard to the first point, we can agree with English jurisprudence, which quite recently rejected the notion that taxes, particularly directly imposed taxes, should be deducted from the payment due to the salvor, because the payment of tax is the taxpayer's responsibility and not that of third parties.[204]

With regard to the credit in salvage rewards, subject or not to revaluation, Italian jurisprudence used to solve this problem by finding that the credit for the reward for assistance and salvage was subject to revaluation only when the creditor could prove greater loss as a result of default by the debtor. This jurisprudence has been followed here by very authoritative doctrine,[205] although confirmation that credit is not subject to revaluation has meant some revaluation on the basis of the straightforward consideration that, if the salvor had been in possession of the sum due as remuneration for the salvage operations, he would have used it to good purpose for his company's business. That would have removed the ruinous effects of inflation, and established the principle that such a revaluation does not need proof of loss, but may be based on mere presumption (*presumptio hominis*).[206]

Of particular interest to international jurisprudence are some recent decisions which have gone against these trends and have specifically awarded revaluation of remuneration, although one North American decision has maintained that the judge is allowed to take account of the devaluation of the local currency during the period of time between the completion of the salvage operations and the time of the fixing of the reward relating to them.[207]

As regards the currency in which the reward is to be paid, it cannot be other than that of the country to which the salving ship belongs. The parties are, however, entitled to agree upon a different currency.[208]

---

204. Cf. *The Makedonia* [1957] 2 Lloyd's Rep. 575, and *The Frisia* [1960] 1 Lloyd's Rep. 90, which amended a previous decision in favour of deducting taxes from the salvage payment, *The Telemachus* [1956] 2 Lloyd's Rep. 490. The same opinion is held by Brice, *op. cit.*, 81, who notes that in the United Kingdom the Finance Act 1972 provides that salvage and towage services are not subject to V.A.T.

205. Ferrarini, *Il soccorso*, 194, and Cass. (US) 8 July 1955, No. 2128, in Dir. Mar. 1956, 177, which confirmed a jurisprudence which had already been consolidated by the decisions of Cass. 20 October 1953, in Dir. Mar. 1954, 425 and App. Bari 12 February 1977, in Dir. Mar. 1978, 66, and, more recently, Arbitration Award 9 September 1988, in Dir. Mar., 1990, 172.

206. Arbitration Award of 24 February 1981, in Dir. Mar. 1981, 274, and Trib. Massa 31 December 1982, in Dir. Mar. 1983, 569. Recently, on this point, Trib. Brindisi, 14 December 1987, in Dir. Mar., 1988, 833, which excluded revaluation of remuneration in favour of pilots and mooring men taking part in a salvage.

207. Cf. *The Teh Hu* [1969] 2 Lloyd's Rep. 365; *The Folias* [1978] 1 Lloyd's Rep. 535, and *The Fairisle* (1949) A.M.C. 408.

208. Ferrarini, *Il soccorso*, 195; Schaps-Abraham, *Seerecht*, II, 1153; and *The Teh Hu*, already mentioned.

Finally, with regard to assessing interest on the reward due to the salvor, the Convention's rules provide that the reward also includes expenses and loss, but the Convention does not contain any specific rule on the particular point. Thus, the fixing of interest should be left to the courts and arbitrators of the country where the case is heard. In practice, and especially in arbitration cases, it is normal to award the salvor sums inclusive of interest up to the date of the decision. This determines a time for the debtor to pay the sum due, with statutory interest accruing only after this time has expired.[209]

18. APPORTIONMENT OF THE REMUNERATION

In the Brussels Convention of 1910, the important rules about the apportionment of remuneration as regards the active subjects of the salvage (apportionment between co-salvors and apportionment between owner and crew), are Articles 6, paragraphs 2 and 3, and Article 8, paragraph 2. The Convention does not contain a rule specifying the basis for apportionment among the passive subjects of the salvage. Instead, there is Rule No. 6 of the York and Antwerp Rules 1974 which reads: "Salvage remuneration. Expenditure incurred by the parties to the adventure on account of salvage, whether under contract or otherwise, shall be allowed in general average to the extent that the salvage operations were undertaken for the purpose of preserving from peril the property involved in the common maritime adventure."

As regards apportionment among co-salvors, (except for the possibility of an apportionment where successive and different services are rendered by various parties[210]) Article 6, paragraph 2, of the Convention states that the method of calculation is governed by the terms of the contract entered into by the parties or, in the absence of any such terms, by the court.

There may be either a single salvage operation completed by several salvors when Article 8, paragraph 2, of the Convention comes into play, and refers us to the provisions of Article 6, paragraph 2. That refers us on to the standard laid down by the Convention for fixing remuneration.[211] Alternatively, there

---

209. Thus Ferrarini, *Il soccorso*, 194, and Brice, *op. cit.*, 81 *et seq.* and jurisprudence quoted there: *The Aldora* [1975] 1 Lloyd's Rep. 617; *The Ben Gairn* [1979] 1 Lloyd's Rep. 410; *The Rilland* [1979] 1 Lloyd's Rep. 455; *The Ilo* [1982] 1 Lloyd's Rep. 39, *The Helenus and Motagua* [1982] 1 Lloyd's Rep. 261.

210. In this case it is clear that it is a question of two distinct and separate operations for which separate remuneration must be given, to be fixed on the basis of the usefulness of the former intervention and the success to the latter. Thus App. Montpellier 24 May 1950, in D.M.F., 544, and in doctrine De Juglart and Villenau, *Repertoire*, 327. In Italian jurisprudence, see Trib. Messina, 12 September 1988, in Dir. Mar., 1989, 1114, and, in US jurisprudence, U.S.C.A., 5th Circuit, 25 June 1987, in Dir. Mar., 1989, 283.

211. Cf. Ferrarini, *Il soccorso*, 198, and French and English jurisprudence quoted there; French Arbitration Award of 1 July 1952, in D.M.F. 1952, 547. For G. Berlingieri, *Salvataggio*, 490, in this case there would not be a division of the payment, but an entry, in the expenses of the salvor entitled to receive them, of the amount paid by him to the co-salvor employed in the salvage. A special position, the idea underlying which we cannot accept, is that adopted in Italian

may be a salvage consisting of two distinct operations because the service is given by several salvors, who have not necessarily entered into a contract between themselves. In that case, the rewards due to them will be fixed separately for each salvor unless the various active subjects agree to ask for a single reward.

Since it is unnecessary for the separate amounts of remuneration to be fixed in the same court or arbitration tribunal, but the total of the amounts paid is not to exceed the limits imposed by the Convention in Article 2, paragraph 3, where this limit is exceeded, it is necessary to reduce the separate amounts proportionately.

A court or an arbitrator may not necessarily be aware of the amount of reward granted in another court or arbitration to a co-salvor. Consequently, when assessing the various amounts, there could be some difficulty in taking account of another decision, without bearing in mind that, in an out-of-court settlement of the co-salvor's remuneration, it might be not only difficult but downright impossible for the judge or arbitrator to obtain this information and so evaluate the overall reward due. It must, however, be accepted that notification to the judge or arbitrator of the amount paid should form a duty on the part of the owners of the salved property.[212]

It must be recognised that the sum representing the values of the property salved forms a maximum for the court or the arbitrators whose duty it may be, even if separately, to fix the remuneration due to the co-salvors. It cannot be agreed that, on the basis of the Convention, the court or arbitrators should arrive at a remuneration which, in its total, exceeds an obligatory maximum imposed by the Convention. Similarly, it is hard to reconcile recent Italian

doctrine by Arena, "Il resultato utile nella assistenza e salvataggio ad opera di una pluralita di soccorritori", in Riv. Dir. Nav., 1963, I, 51, who distinguishes between "multiple salvage" in which there would be as many operations as there are salvors, with a plurality of salvages, the last of which would be successful, and "collective salvage" which would consist of only one operation in which the co-salvors would take part, contributing different lengths of time. As well as being artificial and not very clear, this construction leaves wide areas of the law uncovered and especially leaves out the more frequent case of salvage performed by several salvors at successive times. Similarly the concept of "preparatory salvage" recently proposed in doctrine as an independent case of salvage is unacceptable, particularly if it is realised that it is intended to regard this type of salvage as not being contrary to the Convention, although it does not achieve a useful result. See in this regard Zammitti, "Il soccorso preparatorio nell'assistenza e salvataggio marittimi", in Trasporti, 1981, 23, 153.

212. An old English precedent is quoted by Brice, op. cit., 70, and an equally old North American one by Norris, op. cit., (ed. 1983), paras. 229 and 230. Italian jurisprudence has recently established, by a decision of the Corte di Cass. Sez. I, 7 May 1976 No. 1596, in Dir. Mar. 1976, 434, that when the reward due to one of the salvors is fixed independently of that due to the other salvors, the judge is not bound to consider the reward laid down in another place for the latter, nor is he influenced by it. The decision does not seem to us to be correct, and the solution adopted in the same case (M/V Lykayon) seems to us to be more correct, namely that of the Arbitration Award 1972, in Dir. Mar. 1972, 655, which recognised that: if several salvors have taken part in a salvage operation, the arbitrator called upon to fix the remuneration due to only one of these parties must consider the service within the framework of the whole operation and give it a coherent appraisal. This has been confirmed in a subsequent Arbitration Award of 24 February 1981, in Dir. Mar. 1981, 264.

jurisprudence which, making an exception to the basis on which, under the Convention, disbursements and loss must be included in the total compensation, has accepted, for many co-salvors, the need to arrange a separate settlement of these disbursements and losses, holding that apportionment according to the merits of each of them affects only remuneration.[213]

With regard to apportionment of remuneration between the owner and crew of the salving ship, the Convention simply refers the matter to the law of the ship's flag (Article 6, paragraph 3), stating that: "the apportionment of the remuneration amongst the owner, master and other persons in the service of each salving vessel shall be determined by the law of the vessel's flag".

However, if a party who has contributed to the salvage does not form part of the crew in even the broadest sense, (e.g. a passenger), he is entitled to share in the remuneration as a co-salvor, and not as a person in the ship's service.

It may be asked whether the Convention's aim was to give the law of the flag the further task of limiting the meaning of "crew", seeing that some problems may arise in identifying those belonging to it, and bearing in mind that there are often persons on board who are simply helpers of the crew and of the master, such as the pilot, mooring gangs and personnel employed by the owner but who do not form part of the crew in the strict sense,[214] or whether the Convention has limited this reference simply to the apportionment of remuneration as provided by the law of the flag of the salving ship.

The second solution seems to us to be more acceptable, if it is considered that there is a clear indication in the final paragraph of Article 6, of the broadening effect of the wording adopted by this provision of the Convention. It omits the use of the term "crew" (although it does at the same time use the terms "shipowner" and "master"), and adopts a completely general term "persons in the service of the ship". In the widely accepted meaning of that term, many persons extraneous to the crew in the strict sense can be included.

Having referred the matter to the national law, *rectius*, that is, to the law of the flag of the salving ship,[215] it remains at this point only to note that the laws

213. Cf. Arbitration Award of 9 May 1981, in Dir. Mar. 1982, 704. For a wide view of English precedents on division of reward amongst co-salvors, see Sutton, *op. cit.*, 638 *et seq.*

214. The reason why the Convention opted for the term "les autres personnes au service de chacun des navires sauveteurs" was to avoid including, in the text of the Convention, a concept of "crew" in the strict sense. See the Reports of the Brussels Conference 1910, 100. If a subject who has intervened in salvage does not form part of the crew even in the wider sense either (for example a passenger), he has a right to a share in remuneration just as a person in the service of the ship. Thus in doctrine Ferrarini, *Il soccorso*, 201, and in jurisprudence Trib. Trapani 9 December 1954, in Dir. Mar. 1956, 72. Of interest is the English case *The Southern Venturer* [1953] 1 Lloyd's Rep. 428, which establishes four categories of persons who were on board at the time of the salvage, determining which of them could be included in the crew in the broad sense and which had to be excluded from it.

215. A recent current of Italian doctrine has underlined the risks which the system of referring to the "law of the flag" involve for the legal operator in the international context, due to the distortion caused by the States of the so-called "open registries" (Panama, Liberia, Cyprus, etc.) where there is an effective and objective lack of "genuine link" between the law of the nation to

of most countries specify that the apportionment between the shipowner, the master and the crew is to be by agreement between the parties or by the court, for only a limited number of laws on the matter lay down instead standards for the sharing of remuneration, already laid down as predetermined percentages.[216]

With regard to the division of remuneration between the crew members, the Convention refers to the separate national laws of the salving ships. At this point it is useful to recall that the jurisprudence of various States has adopted a fairly uniform standard, using a division in proportion to the wages received by the separate crew members and in relation to the deserving service carried out by them in the salvage operation.[217]

On the subject of the apportionment of remuneration, it remains to examine apportionment among the passive subjects of the salvage, although this is not expressly specified by the Convention.

The legal basis of this apportionment comes within the so-called "maritime venture" considered as a whole complex of properties at risk. In relation to them, a calculation is made *a posteriori* with respect to the overall fixing of the reward, proportionate to the values of the separate properties, and the consequent apportionment of the reward itself.

Save in exceptional cases,[218] the reward is in fact normally made with direct reference to the "voyage" and to the property which it may place at risk,

which the owner belongs and the law of the flag. See at length: Carbone, *La disciplina giuridica del traffico marittimo internazionale*, 69 *et seq*.

216. In doctrine see Gaeta, "Sul diritto dell'equipaggio alla ripartizione del premio di salvataggio", in Riv. Dir. Nav. 1941, II, 225. Apart from our Code of Navigation which states in Art. 496 that one third of the reward is payable to the owner and two thirds to the crew, strangely mitigating the criterion and establishing in the second paragraph of this rule that the remuneration due to the crew may not in any case be less than a half, the respective proportions of the payments are predetermined as fixed percentages, for example, by the law of Federal Germany (H.G.B. para. 749); Swiss Law (Law of 23 September 1953, Art. 75); the Bulgarian Maritime Code of Navigation (Art. 328); the Greek Maritime Code (Art. 251); Swedish Maritime Law (Art. 229); Norwegian Maritime Law (Art. 229); and Danish Maritime Law (Art. 228). Special in every respect is the criterion laid down by the Soviet Mercantile Marine Code 1968, Art. 272, of which states: "La rémuneration due à un sauveteur déterminé est repartie entre l'armateur, les membres de l'equipage et les personnes conformément aux instructions adoptées par les ministères et administrations centrales de l'U.R.S.S. intéressées avec l'accord des comités centraux des syndicats concernés".

217. Cf. English jurisprudence quoted by Ferrarini, *Il soccorso*, 202, and North American jurisprudence quoted by Norris, *op. cit.*, (ed. 1983), para. 284, who states: "The first person generally considered is the master of the salving vessel. Since he bears the responsibility of the success or failure of the venture as well as the safety of the lives and property in his care, he is usually favoured with the largest portion of the crew's share. As to the apportionment among the crew, the method most generally followed, and one which I regard as singularly just and appropriate, is that of sharing in proportion to the wages each man earns". A fairly recent Australian decision, *The Oceanic Grandeur* [1972] 2 Lloyd's Rep. 397, divided the payment in a particular way on the basis of merit, awarding the master, the first and second officers, a fairly large proportion of the reward as compared with the total amount awarded to the rest of the crew consisting of 51 persons.

218. Such are *The Velox* 10 Asp. M.L.C. 277; *The Lista* (1946) 79 Ll.L. 401; *The Longford* (1889) 14 P.D. 34.

without taking into account the fact that the salvors' efforts have been different in quantity and quality with regard to the separate interests, and that the perils run by them have also been different in quality and gravity.[219]

The apportionment must therefore be made on the basis of the separate values of the properties and on the basis of a proportionate calculation which takes into account the values which the salved properties have at the end of the salvage operation.

As has been correctly noted, the right to the salvage reward thus starts by being already apportioned between the passive subjects of the salvage unless, by virtue of a special agreement, the shipowner has assumed the entire duty to pay it.[220]

Some clarification is still needed about the relationship which exists between contractual salvage and general average. For every contractual salvage which involves several properties at risk (ship, cargo) there must be a corresponding act of general average. That act is the decision of the master or shipowner to take measures for the maritime venture to be salved. From those measures there arises a loss or expense to be shared by contributions proportionate to the values salved. This complies with the provisions of Rule No. 6 of the York and Antwerp Rules 1974. However, this does not always happen because, even in contractual salvage (see, for example, the old edition of the LOF and the new 1980 LOF), the debt for remuneration is already apportioned from the outset, and there is no mutual dependence between the various parties interested in the venture. They are consequently liable *pro quota* for the remuneration itself.[221]

---

219. In this sense Brice, *op. cit.*, 148. For example it has been considered irrelevant that the goods are salved before the ship, this separation in time of the salvage operations not creating any distinction within the complex composing the "venture". Cf. *The Emma* (1844) 2 W. Rob. 315, also quoted by Brice, *op. cit.*, 149. In our more recent jurisprudence, see Arbitration Award of 12 April 1989, in Dir. Mar., 1990, 756, where an extra share of remuneration was awarded to those members of the crew whose efforts were particularly meritorious, the total of these extra rewards being deducted from the share due to the rest of the crew.

220. Ferrarini, *Il soccorso*, 204. In jurisprudence see Trib. Messina 15 July 1964, in Dir. Mar. 1965, 603.

221. Thus Ferrarini, *Le assicurazioni marittime*, (1981), 172, who firmly maintains: "However, it must be borne in mind that, if it is true that, in the general run of cases, the salvage expense may be likened to a general average expense, the requirements for such an assimilation do not always exist. I will limit myself to quoting two cases: (a) in the case of voluntary salvage, that is to say performed without the request of the master or owner, or reasonably refused, the debt in relation to the salvor originates already divided pro-quota among those who have benefited from the salvage; (b) in the case of contractual salvage, made with the form known as Lloyd's Salvage Agreement (LOF 1980) the debt vis-à-vis the salvor originates divided, because the form excludes any solidarity among those taking part in the venture (Art. 17)." In agreement Volli, *Assistenza*, 237; Carver, *op. cit.*, 840. *Contra* in jurisprudence: Cass. 19 July 1966 No. 1948, in Dir. Mar. 1966, 479; Trib. Messina 21 November 1961, *ibidem*, 1962, 376; Trib. Latina 22 February 1961, in Riv. Dir. Nav. 1961, II, 312, and Trib. Brindisi 1 December 1962, in Dir. Mar. 1965, 185, which had established that although the request for assistance or salvage, being included in the measures which the master must take as head of the maritime venture, cannot be referred to the owner as such, the owner is nevertheless the passive subject of the right to payment, subject to any counterclaim action against the parties interested in the venture; and more recently in this

There is a difference between salvage and general average. In salvage the values considered are, as we have seen, fixed on the basis of the value of the properties salved at the time and place where the salvage operations are completed. In general average, the goods must be valued at the end of the venture, after deducting the loss sustained and expenses incurred for the completion of the voyage. There are different standards in calculating the loss resulting to goods voluntarily sacrificed by the act of general average as contributing to the entire debt, unlike the properties sacrificed, damaged or lost in the salvage operation which, on the contrary, are not taken into consideration for the purposes of fixing the reward.[222]

19. REDUCTION AND EXCLUSION OF THE RIGHT TO REMUNERATION

Finally, the Convention must be studied to see how it applies to those cases where, due to fault or fraud on the part of the salvors, the remuneration which may be due to them for having brought about a useful result should be greatly reduced, if not completely denied. The relevant rule is Article 8, paragraph 3, which reads:

"The court may deprive the salvors of all remuneration, or may award a reduced remuneration, if it appears that the salvors have by their fault rendered the salvage or assistance necessary or have been guilty of theft, fraudulent concealment, or other acts of fraud."

The text of this Rule describes two kinds of conduct on the part of salvors: faulty conduct, where blame attaches to the salvor insofar as he has made the salvage necessary; and particular fraudulent acts, such as theft, fraudulent concealment and other fraudulent acts indicated in a general way.

The wording of the provision does not seem to be particularly fortunate, and it leaves wide areas of uncertainty about the correct identification of such conduct as international law has tried to indicate, to enable the judge, in relation to such conduct, to reduce remuneration or to exclude it.[223]

It has been noted that, bearing in mind the dangerous nature of the oper-

---

respect (and erroneously), *The Patmos*, Trib. Messina, 12 September 1989, in Dir. Mar., 1989, 1114; and in doctrine G. Berlingieri, *Salvataggio*, 1968, 12. Opposed to the above line of jurisprudence and doctrine is Ferrarini, *Il salvataggio come avaria comune*, 3, who rightly points out that that jurisprudence falls into the error of considering that the request for assistance made by the master would make the shipowner liabile for the entire payment in that the master is his agent, overlooking the fact that the measures for the safety of the venture are taken by the master as its head (Art. 302 Cod. Nav.) and not as the agent of the shipowner.

222. Thus clearly: Ferrarini, *Il soccorso*, 207; Id, *Le assicurazioni marittime*, 172; and Lowndes and Rudolf, *General Average*, 242 *et seq. Contra*: G. Berlingieri, *Salvataggio*, 1968, 15 *et seq.*, and in English jurisprudence: *Anderson Tritton & Co.* v. *The Ocean Steamship Co.* (1884) 10 App. Cas. 107, H.L. and *Australian Coastal Shipping Commission* v. *Green* [1971] 1 Q.B. 456 quoted also by Brice, *op. cit.*, 205.

223. Thus Wildeboer, *op. cit.*, 222 *et seq.*

ations carried out by the salvor and the considerable risk of damage to property which these operations often necessarily involve, it is incorrect to speak
of degrees of fault of the salvor, but rather of the different standards of care
which the salvor himself has exercised in the course of his own activity, taking
account of the circumstances, his position as a voluntary or as a professional
salvor, and the other elements going to make up the complex operation.[224]

Other authoritative contributions have been made about this doctrinal
theory. In international doctrine, they have tended to confirm the opinion in
favour of the salvor, with the reservation that, in cases of serious misconduct,
he might be made to suffer a reduction or even the loss of the right to receive
remuneration for the assistance given.[225]

The last paragraph of Article 8 of the Convention allows for two specific
suppositions. The first concerns the fact that the judge may reduce or cancel
the remuneration whenever it appears that the salvor has made the salvage
necessary through his fault; the second covers all fraudulent and deceitful acts
which may be performed by the salvor.

The difference, where there are several salvors or where the conduct of the
individual members of the crew of the salving ship is concerned, lies in the
fact that, in the first instance, the fault is regarded as referring to the abstract
entity constituted by the ship jointly. So the fault is a single one and, as such,
affects all those who make up the whole company of salvors. In the second
instance, the misconduct of individual salvors should be considered separately, as individuals *uti singuli*. Therefore, the fraudulent act of one cannot
affect the right of the other to compensation, when he is found innocent of the
relevant act.[226]

Finally, a recent English decision has provided an important precedent on
the subject of loss caused by the salvor to the salved ship. A reduction was not
made in the remuneration nor was it cancelled as provided by the Convention. Instead, the owners of the salved properties were granted a right to compensation for the loss sustained due to the salvor's fault. This was so even in a
case where his efforts had achieved a useful result, but the amount of the

224. Ferrarini, *Il soccorso*, 180.
225. There are some American and English decisions in this sense: *The Esso Greensboro*
(1953) A.M.C. 1541; *The Alenquer* and *The Rene* [1955] 1 Lloyd's Rep. 101, from which it
appears that *ordinary negligence* is not sufficient, it being necessary, if the remuneration due to
the salvor is to be reduced, to find *gross negligence* or *wilful misconduct*. Thus also Kennedy, *op.
cit*, 127; Brice, *cit.*, 68, and the ample case law quoted by Norris, *op. cit.*, (ed. 1983), para. 98 *et
seq*. See also, more recently, Siccardi, "Studi sul contratto di rimorchio" in *Dir Mar.*, 1990, 684.
226. Schlegelberger-Liesecke, *Seehandelsrecht*, 209; Ferrarini, *Il soccorso*, 180; and in jurisprudence see *The Kenora* (1921) 5 Ll.L.Rep. 115. For Brice, *op. cit.*, 68, Art. 8 of the Convention does not cover all the cases where the judge can reduce or refuse remuneration, because the
guidance provided by the Convention's rule of international law seems too restrictive with regard
to the wide range of circumstances which may occur in practice. For an exhaustive list of the various kinds of deceitful and fraudulent acts of a salvor, see Norris, *op. cit.*, (ed. 1983), para. 102 *et
seq*. According to Wildeboer, *op. cit.*, 239, the penalty of reducing or refusing the reward would
be of a penal nature and would correspond to a fine imposed on the salvor.

damages payable were not limited to the sum to which he was entitled as remuneration for the services rendered.[227]

20. CONTRACTS OF TOWAGE AND SALVAGE

Article 4 of the Convention governs the legal position of a tug which renders exceptional service to the towed ship and her cargo, stating that: "A tug has no right to remuneration for assistance to or salvage of the vessel she is towing or of the vessel's cargo, except where she has rendered exceptional services which cannot be considered as rendered in fulfilment of the contract of towage."

The relationship between a pre-existing towage contract and the salvage assistance after it, has given rise to some debate in doctrine, and has been the occasion and cause of a fairly large number of decisions in jurisprudence.

The exceptional nature of the service caused by a perilous situation in which the craft towed have found themselves, during the normal course of the towage, whether the service can be described as a towage for transportation or for port manoeuvre, creates a change in the position originally envisaged by the two contracting parties. As has been correctly noted, this presents an absolutely unforeseen impossibility of performance of contract, with consequent release of the party which has promised its service.[228]

The termination of the contract between the towed craft and the tug, on account of the danger in which the craft found herself, necessitates a correct identification of the amount when this termination happens. Although it does not seem to comply with a certain view of doctrine by which at that precise moment there would be a *conversion* of the towage contract into a salvage contract,[229] there is no doubt that the moment assumes particular importance for determining, on the one hand, the cessation, *rectius*, that is, the possible interruption of the duties of the contracting parties, and, on the other hand, the coming into being of an independent salvage relationship undertaken by the tug voluntarily or contractually, as the case may be.[230]

227. *The Tojo Maru*, in Dir. Mar. 1972, with note by Dani, "In tema di responsabilita del soccorritore" and [1971] 1 Lloyd's Rep. 341. The decision has been fully commented on by Brice, *op. cit.*, 280, in the light of the existing ample English jurisprudential case law, but it is rather old if we exclude *The Cythera* [1965] 2 Lloyd's Rep. 454; *The Belize* [1966] 2 Lloyd's Rep. 277, and *The St Blanc* [1974] 1 Lloyd's Rep. 557. Also on the argument cf. Dani, *Responsabilita limitata per crediti marittimi* (Milan, 1983), 82 *et seq*. Further on this point, though with limited references to LOF 1990 or to English jurisprudence (*The Unique Mariner (No. 1)* [1978] 1 Lloyd's Rep. 439; *The Unique Mariner (No. 2)* [1979] 1 Lloyd's Rep. 37), see Gaskell, *op. cit.*, 306.

228. Thus Ferrarini, *Profilo*, 662, and Id, *Il soccorso*, 69 *et seq*.

229. See Manca, *Commento*, 226, who provides, for the purposes of this conversion, a correct identification of the four presuppositions on the basis of which this conversion would occur.

230. It does not seem possible to accept the opinion expressed by Ferrarini, *Il soccorso*, 70, where he apparently wishes to limit to voluntary or spontaneous salvage, the assumption of the salvage operations on the part of the tug, since one cannot exclude the making of a salvage contract by the parties interested in the pre-existing, but now cancelled, towage contract. We can

On a careful reading of Article 4 of the Convention, it seems that its main purpose was to establish a rule of a general nature aimed at preventing a tug from claiming a salvage reward, in addition to the agreed towage price, for every salvage service it has to render during the performance of the towage contract. Equally, it does not seem that we can accept a theory, put forward in doctrine, which seeks to maintain that the Convention's rule intended to include in the sum agreed for the towage contract any reward for salvage services rendered every time the craft under tow finds itself in a situation of peril and the tug saves her.[231] In fact, even if it is true that the parties can make a towage contract to remove a ship from a situation of peril, agreeing on a price for towing which to some extent takes account of the peril which has been averted, it is not possible to accept the theory by which every time the towed craft finds herself in peril and the tug salves her, the service should be considered as coming within "the scope of the contract".

Regard must be had to the moment when the peril actually arises. If it arises before the towage contract, and the contract is entered into with the purpose of removing that peril, then this theory can be accepted, even if it can be maintained that a salvage contract (improperly called a towage contract) has been made, fixing in advance the remuneration for it by contract. For the entire duration of the peril originally foreseen, the towage services cannot be regarded as exceptional. If situations of peril other than those originally foreseen and later occurring arise during the performance of the towage contract,

accept without reservation the thesis acutely put forward by Gaeta, *Assistenza e rimorchio*, in Riv. Dir. Nav. 1967, I, 124 *et seq.*, by which the rendering of salvage as an exceptional and independent service is included in the towage contract, not cancelling it, but allowing it to exist without reducing its efficacy, although to some extent suspending its effects, which may be resumed when the salvage is completed and there is a normal resumption of the contract originally made. The occurrence of a dangerous situation would not necessarily make it impossible to provide the service and therefore cancel the towage agreement. Thus also G. Berlingieri, *Salvataggio*, 327 *et seq.* Contrary to the conversion of the towage contract into a salvage contract in the absence of a real and concrete peril, see App. Genoa, 23 November 1987, in Dir. Mar., 1988, 801; Cass 27 May 1989, n. 2571, in Dir. Mar., 1990, 62; and Trib. Genoa, 27 December 1989, in Dir. Mar., 1990, 406.

    231. Thus Wildeboer, *op. cit.*, 144 *et seq.*, who maintains: "It is clear that a tug under a towage contract is likely to be called upon to render services in the nature of salvage to the ship in tow. It is equally clear that the parties to a towage contract do not intend to grant the tug a separate claim to a salvage award each time the tow is in a position of danger and the tug saves her. The sum agreed upon in the towage contract already is a reward for the salvage services the parties may expect from a normal performance of the agreement, and, therefore, partly bears the character of a salvage award." In our doctrine see Spasiano, "Questioni, varie in tema di assistenza ad aeromobili", in Riv. Dir. Nav. 1937, II, 151, who "after noting that Art. 4 of the Brussels Convention of 23 September 1910 was written in anticipation of the case where assistance is rendered during the execution of a towage contract, concluded before the danger", considered that its scope could not be limited to the sole idea which had inspired the formulation of the rule because, although it presupposed a towage contract in progress, it did not require that such a towage contract should have been concluded before the danger occurred. The logical reason for the provision was "the existence of a towage contract, not its pre-existence before a situation of danger". The Draft Convention of the CMI (Montreal 1981), as we shall see later (Chapter 4) will clear the field of any doubt in interpretation with the phrase contained in Art. 3–6 "can be reasonably considered as due performance of a contract entered into before the danger arose".

then the remuneration fixed in the contract cannot take on, in part, the nature of a salvage reward already agreed by the parties to cover the eventuality of a salvage operation made necessary during the subsistence of the contract.[232]

In this regard, we can agree wholeheartedly with that part of doctrine which has thought it necessary to make a careful check, for the purpose of correctly determining the law, on the services given by the tug, i.e. whether they were reasonably specified in the original agreement and could have exceeded what could equally reasonably be considered as having been the intention of the contracting parties.[233]

Undoubtedly, apart from the possibility already mentioned, that the removal of a peril is initially assumed as being the reason for a towage contract, it is in the relationship between the peril and the exceptional nature of the tug's service that that moment must be sought, that is, not when the towage contract ends and the salvage relationship begins, whether spontaneous or contractual, but when the services contractually foreseen between the parties are suspended.[234]

When the peril occurs and the following salvage operation is undertaken by

232. On the subject of qualifying a towage contract arranged for the purpose of removing a situation of danger, see Gaeta, *Assistenza e rimorchio*, 131 and Italian and foreign doctrine quoted there. A special theory is that of Volli, *Assistenza*, 282 who, while affirming that the possibility of laying down exceptions from the law governing the relationship between assistance and salvage, gives the parties the free option of reaching the same purpose by another agreement which would exclude the law of salvage, accepts the use of a contract (towage contract) for aims which fall under another contract (assistance and salvage). In jurisprudence see Trib. Naples 8 June 1963, in Dir. Mar. 1965, 221.

233. Thus Gaeta, *Assistenza e rimorchio*, 130. According to this author particular consideration should be given to the fact that "if it were possible to down-grade the contract made in the presence of danger to a towage contract, there would be an alteration in the legal reason for the agreement, which is an objective element not subject to the changeable will of the parties, who cannot lay down a regulation of interests which deviates from the economic-social function which the law recognises as worthy of protection", and Brice: *op. cit.*, 31, who in this regard quotes the *UK Standard Conditions for Towage and Other Services* (1974) which state in Art. 6: "nothing contained in these conditions shall limit, prejudice or preclude in any way any legal rights which the Tugowner may have against the Hirer including, but not limited to, any rights which the Tugowner or his servants or agents have to claim salvage remuneration or special compensation for any extraordinary services rendered to vessels or anything aboard the vessels by any tug or tender". For a wide review of English jurisprudence on the relations between towage and salvage, see also Kovats, *The Law of Tugs and Towage* (Chichester and London, 1980), 134 *et seq*.

234. Thus Norris, *op. cit.* (ed. 1983), para. 185, who states that for there to be a case of salvage during the towage contract, there has to be the presence of "some degree of danger and some need of extraordinary assistance". See also *The Athenian* (1877) 3F.248 (D. Mich.). In agreement *The Homewood* (1928) 31 Ll.L. Rep. 336; and of interest is the recent case *The North Goodwin No. 16* [1980] 1 Lloyd's Rep. 71, where it was denied that the service rendered by the tugs was different from the normal service of a towage contract, the tugs having faced up to foreseeable risks. See, in South African jurisprudence, the case of *The Manchester* [1988] L.M.C.L.Q. 16, and Staniland, "Towage or Salvage?" [1988] L.M.C.L.Q. 16 who, criticising the aforementioned decision, concluded as follows: "So, the question can be posed: is it fair and just that the tug, having gone out to perform services for a guaranteed and profitable towage rate and having performed neither more not less than was contemplated by the parties, should be allowed to claim, in addition to towage, an enhanced salvage award? Surely not. To sum up, the court adopted a construction of the agreement which is neither in accordance with the test for salvage, nor is it in the public interest, nor fair and just."

the tug, whether a proper tug in the technical sense, or a conventional ship used for the towing operation,[235] while the tug will suspend the towage contract originally made so as to devote itself to the operations made necessary by the peril, the towed vessel will suspend the payment of the price agreed for such towage. Both these parties will resume their normal services from a legal and technical point of view once the tug, having removed the peril and completed the salvage operation, can re-activate the towage contract and perform that particular contractual duty by completing the towage.[236]

The occurrence of a peril while the towage contract is being performed is therefore regarded as a necessary condition, but not sufficient in itself, for the ordinary towage service to be suspended and the salvage service to begin. If the law is to be correct both from the strictly technical and from the legal point of view, the salvage services of the tug must be considered as exceptional with regard to the normal services agreed under the contract. This exceptional character must be established in relation to the service agreed upon between the parties, bearing in mind the characteristics of the towed craft and of the tug, and the condition of the towed craft. So a comparison has to be made between the circumstances and the supervening risks, and the services and efforts made in order to overcome them.[237]

In the absence of peril, a possible exceptional service by the tug cannot change the contractual relationship which is in existence. Consequently, in some cases, the parting of the tow rope in weather conditions which are not particularly dangerous for the towed craft, has not been regarded as a condition sufficient for the necessary services rendered for the resumption of the towage to be termed a salvage operation.[238]

235. On the possibility that the towage contract may be carried out even by a conventional ship, Italian doctrine is in agreement: cf. Ferrarini, *Il soccorso*, 71; Gaeta, *Assistenza*, 154 and jurisprudence quoted there; Manca, *Commento*, 227; Crisafulli Buscemi, *I contratti di utilizzazione della nave: Il contratto di rimorchio* (Rome, 1973), 22; Riccardelli, "Il contratto di rimorchio", in Riv. Dir. Nav. 1956, II, 51, for whom the distinction between a tug and an ordinary ship would lie in the fact that the towing service rendered by a ship not normally designed for towing is of itself exceptional. In international doctrine the following agree on this point: Lebrun, *Assistance sauvetage et obligation de service* (Auch., 1950), 55; Schaps-Abraham, *Das deutsche Seerecht* (Berlin, 1921), I, 852.

236. Thus also Gaeta, *Assistenza*, 150, who warns of the risk of confusing suspension of contract with suspension of the carrying out of the service. *Contra* Brice, *op. cit.*, 207, who commenting on the case of *The Leon Blum* [1915] P. 290 C. A. holds that "during the time that salvage services were being so rendered the towage contract is suspended".

237. Thus Ferrarini, *Il soccorso*, 71. For Riccardelli, *Il contratto di rimorchio*, 107 *et seq.*: "The concept of operation over and above the towage service is arrived at on the basis of a causal criterion, in the sense that the exceptional nature consists in any service which does not come under the heading of performance of the towage contract which also presupposes the existence of a normal environment".

238. Wildeboer, *op. cit.*, 147 and ample international jurisprudence quoted there. In agreement Ferrarini, *Il soccorso*, 73; Manca, *Commento*, 230; G. Berlingieri, *Salvataggio*, 343; *Contra* Le Clère, *op. cit.*, 157, for whom the breakage of the rope would represent in all cases, for the tug, an ending of the contract with consequent non-existence of any duty to intervene. Contrary to this last mentioned theory is the decision of the Trib. Comm. of St. Nazaire of 17 December 1958, in D.M.F. 1959, 555.

It seems appropriate, at this point, to mention, referring yet again to the rule of international law contained in Article 4 of the Convention, that it was formulated differently from, for example, the text of Article 106 of the Italian Code of Navigation. The Convention Rule seems to allow the possibility of making a towage contract for the particular purpose of removing a peril (which may even be a supposed one) in which the vessel to be towed finds herself.

. . . "A tug", so reads the Convention, "has no right to remuneration for assistance to or salvage of the vessel she is towing or of the vessel's cargo except where . . . etc". By this the Convention seems to admit the possibility of assistance and salvage services being foreseen in a towage contract, and of assistance and salvage services which, due to their "exceptional character", cannot be regarded as included in the services foreseen by the contract. There is nothing in the Convention's rules to prevent a ship which, say, due to an engine breakdown, finds herself unable to move in calm weather conditions (i.e. in a situation of supposed peril) from concluding a towage contract to be brought to a safe port, and agreeing a price for the towage with the tug. That price cannot be subject to any change, whatever may be *nomen juris* which it is intended to give such a contractual agreement. On the other hand, the approach of Italian law in these circumstances is different. Article 106, by stating: "A tug which, for the purpose of assisting or salving the towed vessel, performs work exceeding that normally performed in towage, is entitled to the indemnity and reward specified in Article 491", does not hint or assume that the normal work of towage was agreed to remove a peril. The Convention has, however, express provision, both in the French text, with the sentence: "n'a droit à une remuneration pour l'assistance ou le sauvetage du navire par lui remorqué que s'il a rendu des services exceptionnels . . . "; and in the English text: "has no right to remuneration for assistance to or salvage of the vessel she is towing except where she has rendered exceptional services". This allows, and in a certain sense assumes that, by making a towage agreement, the intention was to prevent the tug from being able to claim, in any event, for any salvage service which she may have had to render during the performance of the service foreseen by the contract, a salvage reward in addition to the price agreed for the towage.[239]

239. Thus Wildeboer, *op. cit.*, 144, who moreover notes that this type of agreement can always be cancelled in accordance with the principles laid down in Art. 7 of the Convention, that is to say if "les conditions convenues ne sont pas équitables". In agreement Ferrarini, *Il soccorso*, 114, who points out the not infrequent case of tugs which flatly refuse the salvage contract, preferring to offer their services against payment of a daily hire, that is to say a hire payable in any event, because it is independent of the result of the operation. It here seems appropriate, in order to clarify the differences between the Convention's rule and Italian law, to point out that, at the time when Italian navigation law was being codified, "a contradiction in terms was noted, because it implicity presupposes salvage operations which may come within the scope of performing the towage contract, while it is evident that if salvage conditions are present, towage conditions cannot be present, and *vice versa*". Thus Lefebvre D'Ovidio, "Assistenza, salvataggio,

It would seem therefore that, in the light of Article 4 of the Convention, it is unnecessary to check whether the *nomen juris* given by the parties to the contract corresponds in the technical sense to a service either of simple towage or of salvage, but rather to check whether the salvage services rendered by the tug during the towage contract assumed the character of exceptional services with respect to those agreed *ab initio*.[240]

It remains to examine the validity, with respect to the Convention's rules, of those clauses, often encountered in international practice of deep sea towage, which expressly exclude the possibility of regarding the tug's services as exceptional, even if they are to save the towed vessel.

These clauses, variously called "no salvage", "no salvage to towing tug", "no salvage charges" and such like are quite different from the "no cure no pay" clause.[241] They are, if examined in the light of Article 4 of the Convention, exceptions to the Convention, because they remove any possibility of the tug being allowed remuneration for salvage if it performs exceptional services. The problem, therefore, is whether or not Article 4 of the Convention is open to exceptions.

A certain current trend of Italian doctrine, although referring in some cases to Article 106 of the Italian Code of Navigation, has upheld the validity of these clauses in that their sole purpose and effect is to establish what are the normal services which the tug is obliged to render.[242] On the other hand, other authors, for different reasons, have held that such clauses are null and void. Some maintain that the tug would be obliged by the clauses to render salvage services without remuneration, with the result that the contractual duties would be invalid, for these had been agreed beforehand with the aim of obtaining unremunerated services.[243] Others, by a more convincing logical

ricupero e ritrovamento di relitti", in *Studi per la codificazione del diritto della navigazione*, IV, Rome, 1941, 1172.

240. See G. Berlingieri, *Salvataggio*, 347. In Italian jurisprudence the following are in favour of appraising the danger as an element qualifying the service as salvage instead of towage: Trib. Naples, 25 February 1961, in Riv. Dir. Nav. 1962, II, 306; Trib. Naples, 8 June 1963, in Dir. Mar. 1965, 221; Trib. Messina 15 July 1964, in Dir. Mar. 1965, 603; Arbitration Award of 21 July 1966, in Dir. Mar. 1966, 603; App. Venice 28 April 1967, in Dir. Mar. 1967, 197; whilst the following attach greater importance to the exceptional service: Trib. Naples, 21 January 1963, in Dir. Mar. 1965, 211; Corte di Cass. 16 November 1967, No. 2755, in Dir. Mar. 1968, 95; Arbitration Award 31 January 1982, in Dir. Mar. 1983, 569. See also for jurisprudence from 1942 to 1960: E. Vincenzini, *Rassegna di giurisprudenza*, 152. For French jurisprudence consult the full case histories quoted by Chauveau, "Sauvetage et remorquage devant les tribunaux Français", in Dir. Mar. 1964, 154 *et seq.* and by Reuter, *La notion*, 226 *et seq.* For English jurisprudence Kennedy, *op. cit.*, 63 *et seq.* and more recently Brice, *op. cit.*, 206; for US jurisprudence Norris: *op. cit.*, (ed. 1983), para. 185 *et seq.* and updating of paras. 185 and 103 of the supplement.

241. We cannot share the theory of G. Berlingieri, *Salvataggio*, 341, who includes the above clauses in a single category, overlooking the fact that the "no cure no pay" clause derogates from the method of fixing remuneration, while the others derogate from the law of salvage, completely excluding relative remuneration. *Contra* Manca, *Commento*, 234. See also Siccardi, *op. cit.*, 682.

242. Thus Ferrarini, *Il soccorso*, 72; U. Maresca, "L'interruzione delle operazioni di rimorchio in alto mare", in Dir. Mar. 1939, 608; Ghionda, "In tema di assistenza e rimorchio", in Riv. Dir. Nav. 1937, I, 180; G. Berlingieri, *Salvataggio*, 341.

243. Manca, *Commento*, 234.

process, uphold the mandatory nature of all those rules whose purpose is to encourage salvage services for ships in peril. Such a purpose would be nullified by preventive agreement which, in practice, denies or refuses to acknowledge the right to salvage remuneration.[244]

Considering that the Convention is already changing the law by admitting assistance operations which might come within the duties of a towage contract, one could share the opinion that these clauses are invalid whenever they concern the occasional services which the Convention expressly regards as deserving remuneration as being real and proper salvage services. This is because it cannot be denied that the rule which has the aim of providing for the immediate giving of help when the towage contract is no longer operative, is statutory.[245]

21. SALVAGE AND FINDING OF WRECKS

We have already mentioned (Section 1) that, although the Convention does not contain any specific provision about the salvage of a sunken ship or part of her ("wreck"), its intention is to govern the salvage of a wreck, for it includes that within the notion of salvage, and excludes from the Convention's rules only the finding of wrecks.

It should be noted that while, in international doctrine and jurisprudence, and especially the Anglo-Saxon, the problem is not even raised, because in common law countries the recovery of a sunken vessel is clearly included within the law of salvage, nevertheless in Italy there has been a doctrinal dispute, with individual authors taking up completely opposing positions, and

---

244. Gaeta, *Assistenza e rimorchio*, 132. In English doctrine a special position is that of Kennedy, *op. cit.*, 64 who, although he seems to admit the validity of the clause, subjects it to challenge by the crew of the tug because "the tugowners have no authority to bind the master and crew of the tug by an agreement depriving them of salvage remuneration, and their rights in such case include a claim against the ship and freight as well as against the cargo."

245. Wildeboer, *op. cit.*, 17, who maintains that "the question must be answered whether it is important to know when a vessel that has been shipwrecked has become an object which cannot be called a vessel any more. This would be important if the Convention were not applicable in these cases. In my opinion the Convention is applicable, no matter what state the imperilled vessel has been reduced to. If a vessel needs help, this means in many cases that she has suffered damage. This damage may be very serious. The more serious it is the more necessary it is that aid be rendered with the greatest speed. Every statutory provision for salvage services has the purpose of stimulating the immediate giving of help. The same is true of the provisions of the Convention". Kennedy, *op. cit.*, 386 *et seq.* and jurisprudence quoted there; Brice, *op. cit.*, 114 and jurisprudence quoted there; Norris, *op. cit.* (ed. 1983), para. 113 *et seq.* and jurisprudence quoted there. The position of France is special in regard to the salvage of wrecks (*épaves maritimes*) because the special law of 24 November 1961, No. 61–1262, and the decree of 4 February 1965 govern the matter, including in it both the *sauvetage des épaves* (salvage of wrecks) and the *découverte des épaves* (finding of wrecks). See Reuter, *La notion*, 129. Le Clère, *cit.*, 62 *et seq.* notes the incongruity of French legislation which maintains the distinction between *assistance au navire* and *sauvetage des épaves*.

with several solutions being put forward, some of which are hardly convincing.

A part of doctrine, keeping to the unitary concept of salvage (accepted not only in the development of the law made by Anglo-Saxon jurisprudence but also by English legislation[246] adopts the view that the Convention governs both the salvage of a sunken ship and of a wrecked part of her. The Convention, by abolishing any distinction between assistance and salvage, has not only removed a problem of wording but has also made a substantial change in the law of salvage by uniting the two previously existing concepts of *assistance des navires* and of *sauvetage d'épaves* (that is to say, assistance to a ship and salvage of a wreck) within the single Anglo-Saxon concept of "salvage". This abolishes the method of remunerating the salvor with a share in money or in kind of the property salved. That method had indicated the division between the law of salvage and the law of salvage of a wreck.[247]

The contrary theory bases its reasoning on the fact that, in the work preparatory to the Convention, no discussion is to be found about the inclusion in salvage of the salvage of a wreck. The overriding idea was to consider the ships in danger, that is, salvage was understood as assistance in averting the ship's loss, not her salvage after loss has already occurred.[248]

As we have already mentioned, salvage of wreck is one thing, (that is to say, *ricupero* in the accepted meaning of the term in Italian legislation: "salvage of wreck" in English), but it is another to consider the "removal of wreck", which comes under public law. The intention there is to remove the obstacle and peril which the wreck may represent for navigation or fishing, or for port operations and manoeuvres if the wreck is in a port.[249]

The division between the salvage of a wreck and the finding of a wreck is shown, firstly, by the fact that there never exists *l'animus derelinquendi* of the owner. His existence is to some extent foreseen in the Convention, and salvors have to be in contact with him for the salvage operations. In *finding*, which has in common with salvage of wreck the material object formed by the latter, the *animus derelinquendi* may still exist but, if it does not exist, there is some abandonment of possession by the owner (*res vacuae possessionis*) or

---

246. See the Merchant Shipping Act 1984, section 546, which expressly includes a *wreck* among the property subject to salvage at sea.

247. Thus Ferrarini, *Il soccorso*, 9. Note the particular positions taken up by Russo, *Per una costruzione unitaria*, 3 et seq., and by Volli, *Assistenza*, 14 et seq. In the past a view was expressed in favour of again including salvage of wreck within the concept of salvage by Brunetti, *Il caso dell' "Atlantique" ed il compenso ai salvatori nel diritto francese e Italiano*, in *Studi in onore di Francesco Berlingieri*, (1933), 159.

248. G. Berlingieri, *Salvataggio*, (1968), 294, and in jurisprudence; Cass. 18 September 1961, No. 2033 in Riv. Dir. Nav. 1962, II, 167.

249. As we have seen (note 12) the new wording adopted by the draft Convention of the CMI (Montreal 1981) is decisive where the *removal of wreck* has been expressly excluded from the new law of salvage, while at the same time the salvage of a *sunk* ship has been expressly included in the concept of *salvage*.

dispossession, unlike the salvage of wreck, and the activity is not organised for the purpose of salving it.[250]

Furthermore, if the finding is to be regarded as being of a wreck, for the purposes of its possible salvage or recovery, and so as to fall within the Convention as a real and proper object of a salvage operation as accepted by international law, it is necessary for it, as a salved object, to have been, before the peril or accident occurred, a real and proper ship. No importance attaches, for the purposes of the Convention and its application to the difference, in the physical sense, which exists between a "ship" and a "wreck", unless the latter is in a situation where there is no danger of its losing its remaining physical existence and some value, and it does not require a special and immediate intervention for its recovery or salvage.[251]

250. Wildeboer, *op. cit.*, 17, who states: "In the first place, the vessel, or whatever remains of her, must not have been derelinquished by the owner. The Convention assumes the existence of an owner with whom the salvor enters into a certain relation. It does not apply to derelicts and, in particular, it does not touch the question who owns these objects if they are salved"; Ferrarini, *Il soccorso*, 239 *et seq*. This opinion appears to be opposed by Norris, *cit.*, (ed. 1983), para. 133, who defines a wreck as follows: "wreck is a vessel, which has been abandoned without hope or expectation of return".

251. Thus Wildeboer, *op. cit.*, 18, for whom: "for the question whether the Convention is applicable, it is necessary only to inquire whether the object salved was a vessel before the danger appeared. The difference between ship and wreck is of no importance. However, sometimes wrecks do not need immediate help, and therefore are not in peril, so that in certain circumstances the Convention is not applicable for that reason. The same holds good for parts of vessels. In those cases the damage or loss has already been suffered".

PART TWO

THE MOVEMENT FOR CHANGE IN THE LAW OF SALVAGE AT SEA

CHAPTER THREE

SALVAGE AT SEA IN INTERNATIONAL CONTRACTUAL PRACTICE (LOF 1980)

22. THE PROBLEMS LEFT UNSOLVED BY THE 1910 CONVENTION AND SUBSEQUENT PROBLEMS

If we think of the time when the Brussels Convention was approved, and if we also recall that it formed the starting-point of studies for the compilation of the rules of salvage at sea, which had been begun by the CMI (studies which could not fail to take into account the environment of the period and the technology of ships which still depended on steam and sail for their propulsion), it cannot be denied that the work of the 1910 delegates was almost complete, for it did not leave any serious problems unsolved, and it represented for many years a valid source of private international law on salvage at sea.

It seems to us that the only criticisms which we can make on the work of the 1910 legislators are:

(1) They did not clearly specify in the Convention that a ship which was sunk or abandoned by her crew was to be regarded as a salved ship, thus creating the problem, frequently debated in doctrine and jurisprudence in the so-called "civil law countries", of whether or not salvage of wrecks should be included in the law of salvage at sea in the broad sense. This would be more understandable for the "common law countries". For them, as we have seen, the unitary concept of salvage was a fact in the development of legal doctrine and jurisprudence, and had been so almost from the start.

(2) They did not in any way touch on the problem of the limitation of liability of the owner of the salved ship, not even by a rule referring it to the separate national laws, although, at the time, there were no agreed rules of international law about it.[252]

252. The first Convention on the Limitation of the Liability of the Shipowner is dated 1924, the second, 1957. However, Italy did not ratify these Conventions. For the problems in the limitation of liability in cases of marine pollution connected with salvage operations, see: Abecassis, *Oil pollution from ships*, 251: Sheen *op. cit.*, 1403. Lastly see the decision of the District Court of the United States, 18 April 1984, *The Amoco Cadiz* [1984] 2 Lloyd's Rep. 303, by which the liability of the salvors was excluded in the absence of evidence of the "causative gross negligence or wilful misconduct of salvors," while the shipowner was denied that possibility of limiting his own liability in the presence of a similar negligence on his part.

(3) They did not take into account, in listing the elements for evaluating the salvage operation in order to fix remuneration, the liability risks which the ship in peril had avoided by the salvage ("liability salvage").[253]

As has already been mentioned, during the somewhat lengthy existence of the 1910 Convention, technological development increased to such an extent as to make the Convention's rules inadequate. This left new and important aspects of the law of salvage which were not dealt with at all.

The change from steam to motor propulsion had already brought about a considerable revolution in the techniques of ship-building. Ships now had to carry oil in special tanks which, in the event of an accident, could break open and spill their contents, leading to pollution of the sea and coasts.

But it was not only the presence on board the ships of quantities of "bunker" fuel which began to pose problems which could not be solved by the 1910 Convention. The ever-growing consumption of oil products and chemical products by industry throughout the world, and the need to transport them by sea, had led to the construction of tankers, which were merely floating tanks, whose measurements continued to increase with the passage of time, as did the risks of pollution and damage to the environment.

The Convention's rules had for some while shown their inadequacy. The presence of serious gaps concerning such risks in salvage brought in evaluations different from those previously made, and tending to some extent to supersede the traditional aims of salvage, i.e. the salving of the ship and her cargo, and the saving of the human lives on board the ship in peril. With these new aims of salvage, the useful result achieved by the salvor was put on almost the same level as a subject (party) extraneous to the relationship of salvor to property salved in the strict sense, that is, a new party came into existence, which was interested in the salvage operation as a potential victim of pollution.[254]

There can be no doubt, therefore, that the problems which had arisen since the approval of the Convention (1910) had made it necessary to undertake a thorough re-examination of the law. They started a movement towards its

253. Regarding the admissibility of the concept of liability salvage in English jurisprudence see *The Buffalo* (1937) 58 Ll.L.Rep. 302; *The Whippingham* (1934) 48 Ll.L.Rep. 49 and *The Gregerso* [1973] 1 Q.B. 274, quoted by Sheen, *op. cit.*, 145 *et seq.*, and E. Vincenzini, *Brevi osservazioni in tema di liability salvage*, 589 *et seq.*, as a note of Arbitration Award 26 November 1982, and *The Helenus and Motaqua* [1982] 2 Lloyd's Rep. 261.

254. Thus Abecassis, *Oil pollution*, 255, and in jurisprudence: *The Amoco Cadiz*, already mentioned, which acknowledged the right of the coastal State and of the parties sustaining loss from pollution to claim damages from those responsible for it. In the case in point the decision becomes particularly important where it finds that there was liability by the yard which built the ship for fault and negligence in designing it vis-à-vis the shipowner, who, in his turn, incurred liability for pollution as a result of the stranding of the ship. See also Abecassis, "Some typical considerations in the event of a casualty to an oil tanker" [1979] L.M.C.L.Q. 440; and Gold, "Marine salvage, supertankers and oil pollution: new pressure on ancient law" in *Revue de Droit de l'Université de Sheerbrook*, 1981, 127.

change, so as to make the international law of salvage at sea more satisfactory, integrating and co-ordinating it with the considerable number of Conventions and treaties which had been approved in the meantime to prevent marine pollution in general and to protect the environment from such risks.[255]

The reform movement was to begin urged on by technological evolution and a radical change in marine transport which did not admit of any further delays. There were, in addition, political events and happenings which were sometimes placed in a causal relationship with the evolution and the changes, and they formed the background for a reconsideration of salvage law.

There were, for instance, the frequent crises in the Middle East. The closure of the Suez Canal created a need for the building of ever bigger tankers to carry increasing quantities of oil products on a voyage which was considerably lengthened by the circumnavigation of the coast of Africa. There are the risks which the numerous conflicts among oil-producing States created and still create for ships which undertake dangerous and difficult navigation in mined waters or which are subject to air attacks or to missiles launched by the belligerents. There have been cases recently of ships being attacked during the conflict between Iran and Iraq. It has to be concluded that the movement to change the law of salvage, which had started with the new edition of the LOF (1980) and with the Draft of the new Convention prepared by the CMI (Montreal 1981), was certainly necessary. International law could not fail to take account of certain matters which, in this political situation and in a changed technical and legal context, had arisen more recently.[256]

23. THE BEGINNINGS OF REFORM IN SALVAGE AT SEA

The movement to reform the law of salvage at sea began in an awakening awareness, on an international level, of the serious and irreparable damage

255. This complex matter is governed by the Tanker Owners' Voluntary Agreement concerning Liability for Oil Pollution, of 7 January 1969 (TOVALOP); the International Convention on Civil Liability for Oil Pollution Damages, Brussels 29 November 1969; the Contract regarding an interim supplement to tanker liability for oil pollution, of 1 April 1971 (CRISTAL); the International Convention relating to Intervention on the High Seas in case of Oil Pollution Casualties, Brussels 29 November 1969; and the International Convention on the Establishment of an International Fund for Compensation for Oil Pollution Damage, of 18 December 1971. For a wide view on the agreements on international co-operation for anti-pollution measures, see Abecassis, op. cit., 93 et seq. and F Berlingieri, "Problemi connessi con l'entrata in vigore per l'Italia della Convenzione di Bruxelles del 29 novembre 1960 sulla responsabilità civile per danni detivanti da inquinamento da idrocarburi," in Dir. Mar. 1979, 307. See also: Volli, "La responsabilità civile nel trasporto di merci pericolose alla luce delle vigenti Convenzioni internazionali," in Trasporti, 1981, 24, 75. Lastly, see Gold, "Marine Salvage: Towards a New Regime" in 20 Journal of Maritime Law and Commerce, 1989, 487.

256. Sheen, op. cit., 1390, identifies these technico-legal changes as: "(1) The replacement of sailing vessels by power-driven vessels. (2) The invention of power-driven pumps. (3) The invention of wireless telegraphy. (4) The introduction of limited liability companies. (5) The carriage of crude oil, coupled with the recent dramatic increase in the size of ships."

which marine pollution by oil products may cause to the environment, and of the importance which the intervention of salvors takes on in respect of tankers in danger and of their polluting cargoes. These salvors accept the task not only of salving the ships and their cargoes, but also of preventing and avoiding, so far as possible, the possibility of those products spreading in the sea and causing serious pollution and damage to the environment.

In the aftermath of the famous case of the wrecking of the *Amoco Cadiz* in 1978 off the French coast of Brittany, and after other well known cases such as that of the *Torrey Canyon*, wrecked in 1967 with its cargo off the coast of Cornwall, a series of government actions were set in motion (the Civil Liability Convention of 1969 and the voluntary agreements between ship-owners, TOVALOP and CRISTAL) whose aim was to protect those who had suffered damage or loss from oil pollution or who had incurred expense in preventing it. Shipowners had to be signatories to the agreement for giving compensation for the damage and reimbursing the expenses on a mutual basis. The insurance market also began to react under the pressure of these disasters. For a long time, neither the hull underwriters nor the P & I. Clubs had been able to provide adequate cover for salvors who might incur risks of pollution and environmental damage when giving assistance to a tanker in danger of being lost. In some cases this led to a certain understandable reluctance by salvors to intervene. This meant that irreparable delays might occur between the accident, which called for immediate and urgent assistance, and the assistance itself, because, very often, the negotiations for the salvage contract were hindered by the lack of adequate cover against the risks of *oil pollution*.[257]

The first step towards covering the risks was taken in 1972, when agreement was reached between the biggest salvage companies in the world and the P. & I. Clubs, known by the name of the "P. & I. Oil Pollution Indemnity Clause" (PIOPIC). By this the P. & I. Clubs undertook to cover certain pollution risks in certain particular conditions, by inserting a special clause in the salvage and towage contracts.[258]

---

257. Thus Abecassis, *op. cit.*, 250.

258. The above clause reads: "The Owners shall be responsible for and shall indemnify the Contractor, unless guilty of personal wilful misconduct, in respect of all claims for oil pollution damage, including preventative measures, howsoever arising (including contractual liabilities to subcontractors) out of the service performed hereunder provided always that the Owners' total liability arising under this indemnity shall in no circumstance exceed (a) US $15 million less the aggregate amount of all liabilities, costs and expenses for or in respect of oil pollution damage, including preventive measures (otherwise than under this indemnity or similar indemnities given to other persons performing salvage operations in connection with the vessel) incurred or to be incurred by the Owners arising out of or in connection with the casualty to the vessel or the consequence thereof or (b) US $10 million, whichever is the greater; Provided always that if the Owners' total liability arising under this and other similar indemnities given or to be given to other persons performing salvage operations in connection with the vessel exceeds the amount of the applicable limit of liability referred to above such amount shall be distributed rateably among the Contractor and such other persons and the Owners' liability hereunder shall be reduced accordingly. This Clause shall be construed in accordance with English Law."

24. THE NEW LLOYD'S OPEN FORM (LOF 1980)

This first reaction by the insurers was to be followed in international contract (dominated as always by the use of the standard text of the salvage contract known as "Lloyd's Standard Form of Salvage Agreement") by a second, and much more important, step towards the adaption and reform of the law of salvage at sea. This was the putting into definite form of the new Lloyd's Standard Form of Contract of 1980 (known as LOF 1980, i.e. Lloyd's Open Form). In it an initial, and a not insignificant, effort (even if neither quite complete nor entirely satisfactory) was made to take into account, in the new salvage contract, the changed technical and environmental conditions and the need to produce some consequential legal adjustments of substance.[259]

The general principle expressed in Lloyd's Standard Form, up to and including the 1972 edition (which remained substantially the same as the previous editions) was the so-called "no cure no pay" principle. In other words, when making the salvage contract, the salvor undertook to use his best endeavours to salve the ship and her cargo, and also agreed to be remunerated according to the normal principles of the law of salvage only if the endeavours brought about at least a partial useful result. He would have no right to any remuneration or reimbursement of expenses if no useful result were achieved, notwithstanding the attempts made, the expenses incurred and the possible damage sustained during the salvage operations.

This principle, as we have seen, had fulfilled in the past, a special function in giving an incentive to salvage, in so far as the greater the risks incurred by the salvor, the greater the compensation would be when it came to fixing the amount, the increase being proportionate to the serious risk which the salvor ran of being deprived not only of remuneration but also of the reimbursement of expenses incurred.[260] This same principle had now become irreconcilable with the need to introduce, into international contractual rules of salvage, elements which were unknown or at least not regulated in the past either by

259. The Lloyd's Standard Form of Contract has always been the one most used in international practice ever since its first edition in 1882, so that an author can state (cf. O'May, *Lloyd's Form and Montreal Convention*, 1412) that "because of its world-wide use in major salvage cases Lloyd's Form may fairly be said to have a quasi-convention status." The contract has undergone continuous modifications and revisions up to 1972. This edition, although issued after the *Torrey Canyon* disaster, did not contain any substantial modification of the previous wording and no important innovation concerning oil pollution risks. For an analysis of the editions previous to 1972 cf. Thomas, "Lloyd's Standard Form of Salvage Agreement—a descriptive and analytical scrutiny," in [1978] L.M.C.L.Q. 279. More recently, with regard to the LOF 1980, see: Bessemer Clark, "The role of Lloyd's Open Form", in [1980] L.M.C.L.Q. 297. See also Kovats, "Lloyd's Open Form Salvage Agreement Changed" in *Seaways*, 1990, 11.

260. See Brice, *op. cit.*, 174, who maintains that: "in a case where the contractor has incurred substantial expenditure in using his best endeavours to salve ship and cargo but both were lost, the contractor could receive no remuneration in any form even though he might have conferred a benefit upon those underwriters responsible for claims in respect of pollution damage and have benefited a coastal state and landowners and the like by preventing or reducing pollution damage"; and Bessemer Clark, *cit.*, 297.

contract or by law. An example is a reward for the particular efforts of the salvor and a reimbursement of expenses incurred by him, in preventing, removing or at least containing a serious risk of pollution or damage to the environment, especially when his efforts had in any case achieved a useful result, if only by avoiding liability of the salved property vis-à-vis third parties or persons outside the salvage contract ("liability salvage"). Apart from these innovations, one of the problems left unsolved by the Convention has been specifically dealt with in clause 21 of the LOF 1980, where it is stated that the salvor "shall be entitled to limit any liability to the owners of the subject vessel and/or her cargo bunkers and stores which he and/or his Servants and/or Agents may incur in and about the services in the manner and to the extent provided by English law and as if the provisions of the Convention on Limitation of Liability for Maritime Claims 1976 were of the law of England". This was to avoid the possibility that the salvor might (as in the case of the *Tojo Maru*) run the risk of being considered liable without limitation for damage caused to third parties, and consequently also for damage by pollution caused be negligence of persons in the salvor's own employment when, as in the above case, they are not on board the salving ship or the tug, or at any rate are not *in the management of the salving tug* at the time when the act of negligence occurs.[261]

Clause 1(a) of the new LOF 1980 is an almost completely new clause as compared with the wording of previous editions. It contains the most substantial changes made in the law of salvage. In fact, all the other clauses, except clause 21 and those included in the "General Provisions", contain almost entirely provisions relating to procedure in arbitrations as anticipated in the arbitration clause in the contract, the kinds and terms of issue of the guarantee, rules of conduct for the arbitrators in performing their duty, and any appeal for the payment of the amounts indicated in the award (clauses 1(b) to 15). These are of only marginal interest for the present discussion, because they are not relevant to the movement for change in the law of salvage at sea.[262]

Finally, it should be noted that clause 1(a) contains the direction that, apart

---

261. In the case of the *Tojo Maru* [1971] 1 Lloyd's Rep. 341, the court denied the salvor the right to limit his own liability for damage caused by a diver in his employ, who was neither "on board nor in the management of the salving tug." The problem is now resolved by the LOF 1980 which, referring expressly to the 1976 Convention on Limitation of Liability, incorporates the provision of its Art. 13 which defines the salvor "as any person rendering service in direct connection with salvage operations" and Art. 64 which lays down a special calculation base for determining the limitation where the salvor gives assistance, working, not with ships or nautical craft, but with different means. Thus Abecassis, *op. cit.*, 252; Bessemer Clark, *op. cit.*, 303; Coulthard, "A new cure for salvors? A comparative analysis of the LOF 1980, and the CMI Draft Salvage Convention," in *Journal of Maritime Law and Commerce*, vol. 14, 1983, 47 and Dubais, "The Liability of a salvor responsible for oil pollution damage," in *Journal of Maritime Law and Commerce*, vol. 8, 1977, 375 and 381. See also Gold, "Marine Salvage: Towards a New Regime", *op. cit.* 495.

262. For an analytical examination of the clauses of the LOF 1980 from a strictly procedural point of view see Brice *op. cit.*, 252 *et seq.* and Bessemer Clark, *op. cit.*, 302 *et seq.*

from the ship and her cargo, the "bunkers" contained in the salved ship and her "stores" must also be considered as material objects of salvage. This improves the contract's wording and foresees the special risks that the removal of the bunkers may cause in pollution and damage to the environment. It accepts that the mere removal of the bunkers may be a useful result for the purposes of fixing remuneration and expenses, allowing for the fact that the duty to salve and to use best endeavours to prevent the escape of oil from the ship, as laid down in the contract, does not distinguish between oil products carried as cargo and oil products transported as bunker fuel.[263]

25. CHANGES INTRODUCED INTO THE NEW CONTRACT'S WORDING

Clause 1(a) contains the most important changes, as follows:

"The Contractor undertakes to use his best endeavours to prevent the spillage of oil from the assisted ship whilst he carries out the operations for the salvage of the same, of her cargo, of the bunker and of the stores. The operations shall be effected and accepted as salvage services on the basis of the 'No cure No pay' principle except where the property salved is a tanker laden or partly laden with a cargo of oil, if the salvage operations have not secured a useful result or only partially useful or the Contractor was prevented from completing the salvage without this being due to negligence or blame on the part of the Contractor, his Servants and/or Agents."

The new contract distinguishes between the salvage of a "dry" or "general cargo" ship or her cargo (among which must be included container and Ro/Ro ships) and the salvage of tankers loaded or partly loaded with oil products.[264]

---

263. Brice, *op. cit.*, 176; Abecassis, *op. cit.*, 254; Gold, "Marine Salvage: Towards a New Regime", *op. cit.*, 495. Gold correctly points out that only MARPOL 73/78 makes specific reference to polluting substances which may be other than oil products.

264. It seems appropriate to note that the formulation of the rule does not appear to be entirely satisfactory, for it does not define that concept of *oil*, which appears too restrictive if referred only to oil products as in both the LOF 1980 and the International Convention on Intervention on the High Seas in case of Disaster from Oil Pollution, approved in Brussels on 29 November 1969 which, in Art. 2, also makes clear that "oil means crude oil, fuel oil, diesel oil and lubricating oil", since ships may transport chemical products which are equally dangerous and pollutant. The case of the *Cavtat* sunk in the Adriatic with a cargo of highly toxic chemical products may be recalled. It should be noted that proposals have already been put forward to make further modifications to clause 1(a). Recently a clause was formulated to resolve the problem as follows. "Unless otherwise specifically indicated herein by appropriate written amendment signed by both parties, the Contractor's services shall be rendered to the Owners and accepted by them upon the principle of 'No Cure—No Pay' except that where the property being salved is a tanker laden or partly laden with a cargo of oil or is a tanker or any other vessel laden or partly laden with any other form of volatile, poisonous, noxious or potentially dangerous cargo such as liquid gas, acids, chemical products, wastes or other similar commodities capable of causing pollution of the atmosphere, water or land and/or of bringing about death or injury to flora, fauna or to human beings to any substantial degree and without negligence on the part of the Contractor and/or his Servants and/or Agents (1) the services are not successful or (2) are only partially successful or (3) the Contractor is prevented from completing the services."

First, the contract confirms that the "no cure no pay" principle applies so that neither remuneration nor reimbursement of expenses is due to the salvor in the absence of a useful or at least a partly useful result ("without success in the form of tangible property salved: no cure, the salvor receives no remuneration: no pay").

Secondly, the change introduced consists in the removal of the "no cure no pay" principle and the allowance of some refund of expenses to the salvor who, even in the absence of a useful result in the salving of the ship and her cargo, has nevertheless, by using his best endeavours, prevented the cargo of the tanker from escaping and causing damage by pollution.

Before going on to examine the procedure, laid down by the contract for fixing these expenses, it must be noted that, although the relevant clause introduced a change of substance into the terms of the contract in contrast with previous editions, by letting the parties depart from the principles of the Brussels Convention of 1910, it does not seem to have completely determined the law for the purpose of identifying correctly the conditions necessary and sufficient to accept the new terms of the contract as law.

Clause 1(a) seems to limit the salvor's duty to preventing the escape of oil products from the salved ship, but it says nothing about the case where the salvor not only prevents such an escape but also removes or contains the pollution caused by cargo which has escaped from the ship before the salvage operations began.[265]

Indeed, nothing is laid down as to a possible appraisal of the merits of a salvor who not only fulfils the duty of preventing the escape of products from the ship, but actually removes some marine pollution, which was already taking place and which had started before his intervention at the time of the accident.

The exception to the "no cure no pay" principle was, as we have seen, introduced into the new LOF 1980 with regard to assistance rendered to a tanker loaded or partly loaded with a cargo of oil. This exception has effect only if one of three particular circumstances exists as specified by the con-

A similar criticism was made of the contract by Coulthard *cit.*, 55 *et seq.*, who remarked that that text of LOF contains "some severe limitations. Firstly, despite the fact that it applies to all vessels, including oil tankers, it applies only to 'oil,' in plain disregard of the fact that the cargoes of LNG, LPG, and chemical carriers are capable of presenting a far greater threat. Secondly, it applies only to 'prevent the escape of oil,' inferring that there is no duty with respect to oil which has already left the vessel. Both of these restrictions seem to reflect the commercial side of the salvage industry, and the evident unwillingness of commercial interests to adopt the concept of 'liability salvage'." On this point see also: Halfweeg, "State of the Art of Offloading Cargo from a Stricken Vessel", in International Symposium on Marine Salvage, New York, 1979, Washington MTS, 1980, 227; Kovats, "Lloyd's Open Form Salvage Agreement Changed", in *Seaways*, 1990, 11; Kovats, "Lloyd's Open Form: Salvor's Gain", in *Seatrade*, June 1980, 75; and, finally, Gold, "Marine Salvage: Towards a New Regime", 495.

265. Brice, *op. cit.*, 176. This author maintains with regard to the above that: "the prevention of the 'escape' of oil from the vessel does not impose upon the contractor an obligation in regard to oil which has already escaped (which may for example be floating on the water or have reached the neighbouring coast)." Thus also Coulthard, *op. cit.*, 55.

tract, and they must be present without having been caused by the negligence or fault of the salvors, their employees or agents. These circumstances are:

(1) *The services are not successful.* This means that the salvor has failed in his attempt to salve the entire ship or part of her, her cargo, bunkers and provisions. In this connection it has been maintained that the salvage operations are to be considered unsuccessful even if the salvor succeeds in salving something in the purely physical sense, but that is later proved to be of no economic value.

(2) *The services are only partially successful.* The concept of partial success was already contained in clause 16 of the 1972 edition of the LOF, and has been repeated in clause 16 of the LOF 1980. This partial success allows the salvor, apart from the question of expenses incurred in preventing *the escape of oil*, a reasonable remuneration in proportion to the useful result, although it is only partial.

(3) *The salvor is prevented from completing the services.* The clause does not specify by whom the salvage operations may be prevented, nor does it place any restriction on the methods and terms by which the prevention may occur. It has been remarked that this clause appears to apply to all those cases where the salvor gives assistance by order of authority. An authority can always order the suspension of salvage operations, even if a useful result, although a partial one, would have been likely.[266]

It is obvious that the real and correct exception to the "no cure no pay" principle lies only in paragraph (1) of clause 1(a) of the new contract, for paragraph (2), by providing for a partially useful result, would, on normal principles governing the grant of a reward to the salvor (as admitted in the previous 1972 contract), allow the "no cure no pay" principle to be applied to the circumstances, seeing that the major condition of not having salved anything, no cure, would not have been fulfilled.[267]

The condition of paragraph (3) cannot be regarded as a case of the total absence of useful result because, although it is true that no success, even a partial one, has been achieved, it is equally true that a result could have been achieved, if some hindrance to the achieving of it had not occurred, and this hindrance could not be attributed to the conduct or wish of the salvor.

Here also, as we have seen, on the basis of the general principles governing the law of salvage, the salvor would have been entitled to obtain, even if only

266. Thus Brice, *op. cit.*, 176 *et seq*. This author notes that the clause could also apply to salvage operations prevented by the owner of the salved vessel *in breach of the salvage agreement*, which would give the salvor the right to claim damages for the loss of the expected or foreseeable remuneration, on the basis of the principles governing non-fulfilment of contract. It should be noted that a departure from the "no cure no pay" principle applied also by the 1910 Brussels Convention, already exists in Italian legislation (Art. 491 Cod. Nav.) which lessens the rigorous principle of "no cure no pay" by also allowing the salvor the right to reimbursement of expenses and compensation for loss when the property salved is salved independently and outside the work done by the salvor himself. Thus Ferrarini, *Il soccorso*, 54.

267. For O'May, *op. cit.*, 1419, in this case there would be a *partial cure*.

as compensation for loss, what would have been due to him as remuneration.[268]

The principle of "no cure no pay" therefore appears to be effectively lessened by the existence of the two conditions in clause 1(a) of the new LOF 1980, that is to say, by the fact that the assistance was rendered to a tanker laden or partly laden with oil products and that the salvage did not bring about any useful result, even partial, for the property salved (vessel, cargo bunkers and stores).[269]

Another feature of the changed contract is that it established that the exception to the "no cure no pay" principle just mentioned gives the salvor the right to obtain payment of the sums indicated in clause 1(a) in his capacity as a passive subject, from the tanker owner alone. This goes against the ordinary principles of salvage law which regard all the owners of the salved properties (ship, freight, cargo) as passive subjects owing the final remuneration which is due.

The reason for this limiting of the passive subject of this contractual duty must be sought in insurance requirements. It must not be overlooked that, in addition to representatives of tanker owners and professional salvors, representatives of hull underwriters and of the P. & I. Clubs also took part in drawing up the revised text of the contract.

Indeed, since, on the basis of the risks covered, it is the P. & I. Clubs who have to assume responsibility for paying what is due to the salvor for services rendered to the salved tanker ship and to her cargo for the efforts and results achieved in preventing the escape of oil, the debtor for the services would be, automatically, one party only (the owner of the vessel). He would be entitled to the insurance cover by any P. & I. Club, the cargo being completely separate from this type of insurance relationship.[270]

---

268. Cf. in this regard on the subject of *dispossession* Righetti, *La teoria della dispossession nell'assistenza e salvataggio*, 235 *et seq*.

269. Brice, *op. cit.*, 184 notes that: "in the case contemplated of the salvor having to tow the ship and cargo out to sea so that it could be sunk or otherwise destroyed as opposed to being salved by the salvor, the salvor might be able to claim compensation for the lost salvage remuneration he would otherwise have earned." Thus also Gold, "Marine Salvage: Towards a New Regime", 494, who further points out that the new container-carriers carry up to 16,000 tons of bunker oil, this quantity being even larger than those in the well-known cases of *MV Argo Merchant* and *MV Arrow*.

270. Thus Brice, *op. cit.*, 177 and 185, and O'May, *op. cit.*, 1419; Bessemer Clark, *op. cit.*, 299. The problem had already been met in jurisprudence in the case of a sharing between hull insurers and P. & I. Clubs of the remuneration due for the salvage of ship and cargo respectively, on the one hand, and the saving of persons on the other hand. See *Nourse* v. *Liverpool Sailing Ship Owner's Mutual Protection and Indemnity Association* [1896] 2 Q.B. 16, and *Grand Union Shipping Ltd.* v. *London Steamship Owners' Mutual Insurance Association, The Bosworth* [1962] 1 Lloyd's Rep. 483. More recently see the case decided in Italy by the Arbitration Award of 26 November 1982, frequently quoted, with a note by Boglione: "Salvataggio, LOF 1980 e misure antinquinamento, deducibilita dei relativi oneri in avaria generale e loro ripartizione tra assicurazioni corpo e merce e P. & I. della nave." For this author the onus of paying for the expenses incurred in preventing pollution must fall on the P. & I. Clubs which are, under the "Funding

From a strictly legal point of view, this abnormal principle of legal entitlement to the payment of expenses being restricted to only one of the passive subjects of the salvage, seems to be justified by the so-called "liability salvage". It is inherent not so much in the properties salved, their physical entity and intrinsic market value, as in the risks of the carrier of oil products because of the damage which those products may cause to third parties. This is a relationship which goes beyond the bilateral relationship between the salvor and the owners of the salved properties as governed by the general principles of salvage at sea.

26. ENVIRONMENTAL DAMAGE COSTS AND THEIR LEGAL QUALIFICATION

The changes made by the new Lloyd's standard contract, although limited to the case of salvage of a "tanker laden or partly laden with a cargo of oil" and to the principles governing the salvor's obtaining of remuneration and its calculation, were in practice restricted to a recognition of extraordinary expenses (called in practice a "safety net") for a salvor who has used his best endeavours to prevent oil pollution. Those expenses had already been fixed as a percentage by the contract (15 per cent of the expenses actually incurred) which is regarded as a maximum *increment* in the remuneration obtainable in this particular instance.

Clause 1(a) of the LOF 1980 reads as follows: "the Contractor shall nevertheless be awarded solely against the Owners of such tanker his reasonably incurred expenses and an increment not exceeding 15 per cent of such expenses but only if and to the extent that such expenses together with the increment are greater than any amount otherwise recoverable under this Agreement." As can be seen, it is not a question of an *enhancement of the award* due to the salvor as a recognition of his successful efforts to prevent the escape of oil from the salved ship. It is rather the fixed payment of a minimum sum earned in any event. That can be absorbed only by a higher remuneration owed to the salvor on the normal standards for fixing it and only "to such extent as such expenses, together with the increment, are greater than any amount otherwise recoverable under this Agreement".[271]

The change made to the principles which previously governed the fixing of remuneration and to international contract, does not seem to have effected any substantial reform of the principles which governed and still govern the salvage of a ship and her cargo. Those remain unchanged in the LOF 1980

Agreement" made by them with Lloyd's Underwriters Association and with the Institute of London Underwriters, the "shipowners' liability pollution underwriters par excellence."

271. In the "safety net" not only have the actual expenses paid out to be considered, but also an equitable payment for the use of the equipment and crew of the nautical craft: see also Arbitration Award 26 November 1982, already mentioned many times: O'May, *op. cit.*, 1419; Bessemer Clark, *op. cit.*, 300; and Coulthard, *op. cit.*, 57.

both as regards the essential elements of salvage (the danger and the useful result) and also as regards the active and passive subjects of the salvage itself. The sole exception is the laden or partly laden tanker. For that the new clause, as we have seen, introduces a change by creating, not so much a new form of salvage ("liability salvage") and a method of appraising a useful result different, for remuneration purposes, from that traditionally accepted ("prevention of liability risks of the owners of the salved property"), but rather a special case. That is not a replacing of salvage in the strict sense, but concerns an incidental and collateral activity of the salvor. This results only in a higher grant of expenses than those actually incurred, by way of a special but restricted reward for that collateral activity, and a different identification of the passive subject owing it, limited to the owner of the salved tanker.[272]

It must be acknowledged that with the new contract there has been a movement in the right direction. In modern times, the law of salvage at sea could not be tied down to its original purpose of assistance to property of a marine venture which was in danger. Different and internationally important requirements had arisen, such as the protection of the marine and coastal environment, as well as the interest of the owners of the salved goods in preventing, with the salvage of the ship and cargo, not only the intrinsic damage which these goods could suffer, but also the risks towards third parties, resulting from the casualty. The latter were understood as risks of lessening value for the owners of the properties themselves.[273]

It must be remarked , however, that, bearing in mind a "fair rate for all

---

272. As already mentioned, this interpretation is based more on reasons of a practical insurance nature than on legal considerations. However, it is recognised by O'May, *op. cit.*, 1420, that: "This important aspect is, nevertheless, underpinned by the agreement reached under which London Underwriters accept that salvage awards are recoverable from ship, cargo and freight under existing forms of policies covering those interests, notwithstanding that such awards may have been enhanced to take account of measures taken to prevent the escape of oil from the ship. So the interested paying parties, the Underwriters and the P. & I. Clubs, have agreed among themselves the distribution of the liability for pollution avoidance, and for enhanced awards." Thus also Bessemer Clark, *op. cit.*, 301; and Coulthard, *op. cit.*, 58.

273. Precisely to the point here is the only decision which, in Italian jurisprudence, has had occasion to deal with the problem, that is, the frequently quoted Arbitration Award of 26 November 1982, *loc. cit.*, 586 *et seq*. which, among other things, notes: that "maritime insurance on hulls and machinery has embraced additional forms of covering the civil liabilities of the shipowner towards third parties, such as exposure for salvage compensation, contribution in general average, damage from collision (Running down cl. 3/4 or 4/4), from colliding with objects, etc., showing itself to be sensitive to the evolution of the theory of third party liability towards more modern forms, such as liability for company risk." The problem had already been noted by Abecassis, *op. cit.*, 252, before the LOF 1980, who, in relation to the limit to remuneration formed by the value of the salved property, noted: "These limits could lead in practice to a reluctance on the part of a professional salvor to undertake the salvage of a tanker, which, together with the freight at risk and the cargo, is worth less money than may be needed in order to salve her successfully. The fact that oil cargoes are now very often worth more than the ship (this likelihood increases with the deadweight capacity of the ship), due to the high price of oil and the currently low market values of oil tankers, does not in fact relieve this situation, for if the cargo is lost or partly lost in the salvage process, the salvor will be unable to benefit to the extent of the lost cargo. Reward is based upon the value of the property actually saved."

tugs, craft and personnel and other equipment used", the fixed limit for the increase in expenses incurred by the salvor in the attempt to prevent the escape of oil from the salved ship is not limited to a simple increment in the expenses actually incurred in the salvage operation. It represents, although indirectly, the grant of a company profit, especially for the professional salvor. The fact that none of these increased expenses is charged to the owners of the cargo or to their insurers clearly shows (if necessary) that this particular remuneration, as laid down by the LOF 1980, cannot be regarded as being either a reward or a refund of the losses and costs incurred in the salvage. Those sums are normally payable by all the owners of the salved things in proportion to the respective values of the salved properties.[274] So the head difference between the concept of liability salvage and the LOF 1980 contract as regards the rewards of a salvor who has avoided liability risks, lies in the facts that, first, those liable for the reward, on the fixing of which the liability salvage has had some influence, are all the owners of the salved properties without distinction, and secondly, only the owner of the salved tanker is liable, without any proportionate sharing with the other parties involved in the venture.

27. OTHER INNOVATIONS IN THE NEW CONTRACT'S WORDING

Apart from the principal innovations just mentioned, the new LOF 1980 follows the outline of the rules in the old text (the last edition dates back to 1972), both as regards the identification of the contracting parties and their respective duties, and as regards the issue of the guarantees and the

---

274. Thus O'May, *op. cit.*, 1420, note (33), who remarks that, as neither the owners of the cargo nor its insurers are answerable for any contribution to the "safety net," the increase in the expenses must be considered as a "special compensation" which is therefore distinguished from the "normal salvage" remuneration. A criticism of the limited scope of the "safety net" has also been expressed by the French Maritime Law Association at its General Meeting on 12 May 1980 when it maintained: "Par contre, le problème devient difficile, si l'action de l'intervenant n'a pas empeché le dépôt du fonds de limitation, et si les dommages absorbent la totalité du fonds, ou au moins, ne laissent disponible qu'une somme inférieure aux dépenses de l'intervenant. A l'occasion d'un projet de réforme de la Lloyd's Form, la difficulté a été ressentie, et resolue par un accord sur un 'safety net', pris en charge par les P & I. Clubs. Le système est ingénieux, mais il est limité aux cas où une Lloyd's intervient, ainsi qu'aux interessés à l'accord intervenu. Comme l'ont souligné les sauveteurs, qui acceptent cette reforme de la Lloyd's Form à titre interimaire, il faut trouver une solution qui puisse trouver sa place dans une convention internationale."

With regard to the inadequacy of the safety net to reward the efforts of the salvors in particularly serious cases, we can agree with Coulthard, *op. cit.*, 57, where he maintains: "Despite the evident intention of the 'safety net' provision to ameliorate the difficulties of tanker salvage, it is clear that there are a number of deficiencies in the proposal. The first is its restricted application to tankers, in disregard of the environmental threat posed by vessels carrying hazardous cargoes other than oil, or carrying large quantities in bunker. The second is the limitation to 'laden or partly laden tankers.' which means that a VLCC in ballast, which may be carrying up to 1,000 tons of oil in an oil-water mixture, will not come under the exception."

procedural rules for arbitration proceedings, as laid down by the arbitration clause in the contract.[275]

The new contract also contains some minor changes in the previous wording. They are intended to provide greater protection for the interests of the salvors, and deserve to be pointed out because they complete the range of modifications made to the rules of salvage by this initial, although timid, step towards reform.

The most significant of these changes are the following:

(1) The contract expressly indicates as parties to it, and liable to contribute to remuneration, the owners of the bunker fuel and ship stores when they are not the shipowners. This provision adds to the number of those interested in the marine venture, traditionally identified as those interested in the ship on the one hand and in the cargo on the other.

(2) On the foundation of the new rules, the salvor may now redeliver the salved ship at any place where she may lie in safety ("place of safety"). There is no longer any duty on the parties to the contract to agree beforehand on the place of safety. On the other hand, there is a duty for the shipowner to co-operate with the salvors to secure the entry of the convoy into a place of safety. The reasoning behind this term it that, faced with holed tankers and with the risk of the escape of oil, it was difficult for the salvors to take them to a safe port or way, due to opposition from governments and coastal authorities who feared damage to the environment.[276]

275. For an analysis of the previous text (1972) cf. Kennedy, *op. cit.*, 299 *et seq.*; De Juglart and Villeneau, *op. cit.*, 191 *et seq.* and Thomas, *Lloyd's standard form of salvage agreement*, 279. The average number of cases referred to arbitration by Lloyd's on the basis of Lloyd's Open Form amounts to about 250 per annum since the first edition of the standard contract text. In 1981, the first year after the publication of the new LOF, according to statistics compiled by Lloyd's Committee, 265 cases were brought to arbitration. Of these 127 were decided, and 43 awards were appealed. Unfortunately it is impossible to know the results of this enormous number of cases, as the awards are restricted to only the parties, and publication or divulgence is prohibited. On the problem of the future necessity of supplying a wider knowledge of awards by their publication, even if on a "no-names" basis, see O'Neill, "LOF Salvage Arbitrations, Publication of Awards and Appeals", [1988] L.M.C.L.Q. 454: "The LOF arbitration is the most universal forum for determining salvage awards. For consistency of results and to give parties a fairer opportunity to settle cases, the results of the arbitrations need to be more widely known. They could be if Lloyd's published them on a 'no names' basis."

276. See Bessemer Clark, *op. cit.*, 302, who writes: "The problem of redelivery has been a serious one for salvors, as Governments are increasingly reluctant to take the so-called 'international leper.' Frequently stringent conditions are imposed on salvors as well as the owners before a vessel is allowed into port." Also for Coulthard, *op. cit.*, 54, the problem of the so-called "maritime leprosy," that is, the fact that the damaged ship will not be allowed into ports or ship lanes with its pollutant cargo, can only be resolved by full collaboration between the salvors and the owners of the salved property with a view to obtaining the co-operation of the coastal State. See also Bessemer Clark, *op. cit.*, 301; and Miller, "Lloyd's Standard Form of Salvage Agreement—LOF 1980: A commentary," in *Journal of Maritime Law and Commerce* 1981, 243.

A particular case of "place of safety" on the basis of the LOF 1980 is that decided by *China Pacific S.A.* v. *Food Corporation of India*, *The Winson* [1980] 2 Lloyd's Rep. 213, by which it was

(3) The shipowners, their agents and employees, must use their best endeavours to ensure that the cargo owners issue a guarantee to the salvors before the cargo is redelivered to them.

One of the major problems encountered by salvors is the obtaining of a guarantee for the cargo, especially when, because it is a general cargo or is, say, containerised, this is split up under numerous bills of lading, and belongs to many owners who cannot easily be identified quickly.

When this new clause was discussed, the salvors' representatives tried unsuccessfully to obtain acceptance, if not quite for the principle of joint liability between ship and cargo for remuneration, of at least a more stringent clause which would impose on the owners a real and proper duty to ensure that the salvors obtained a suitable guarantee from the cargo interests, with an adequate penalty if this duty were not fulfilled.

The change represents a compromise between the old text and the salvors' wishes, although, in practice the change does not seem to be very great because it is merely a promise to help the salvors and not a duty to ensure that the required guarantee is issued to them.[277]

(4) Arbitrators have the option of issuing an interim award, which is a kind of provisional payment for the salvors, to protect their interests and to enable them to obtain a substantial reimbursement of the expenses incurred in the salvage operation while arbitration proceedings are in progress and the final award is awaited. That may take years in some cases which are difficult to solve. The change seems to be fully justified within the outlook of the new LOF 1980 towards the salvage of tankers and the prevention of damage to the environment. In those cases, the salvors' expenses may become unbearable.[278]

established that the "place of safety" need not necessarily be the same for all the property salved. In the case the ship's cargo of grain was discharged in six separate quantities and at successive times.

277. See Bessemer Clark, op. cit., 302; and Brice, op. cit., 255. For the latter, if the shipowner does not use his best endeavours to help the salvors to obtain a guarantee for the cargo, they may take action to obtain compensation for the damage or loss against the shipowners, maintaining that they are in breach of contract on the basis of normal principles: "If the owners of the vessel were in breach of this clause, did not use their best endeavours and as a result the contractors suffered loss, then the owners of the vessel ought, in accordance with the ordinary principles of contract, to be liable to the contractors in damages for breach of that contractual obligation." We can agree with the opinion of O'May, op. cit., 1415, where he maintains that "this obligation is not absolute, but it is more than merely exhortatory. In practice, it appears to have had a beneficial effect by assisting salvors in obtaining security before cargo is released or dispersed." With regard to the problem of the joint liability of those interested in the ship and cargo, it should be noted that "the master, and any other person who signs the agreement for the property salved, makes the contract as agent of the ship, her cargo and freight and the respective owners, and binds the latter (but not one for the other, or himself personally) to fulfil the contract": Ferrarini, Il soccorso, 130.

278. Brice, op. cit., 274 et seq., remarks that the interim award cannot and must not determine, even provisionally, the remuneration for the salvage operation on the basis of insufficient presumptions or evidence, because to do so would be to infringe "the principles of natural justice", and he quotes The Kostas Melas [1981] 1 Lloyd's Rep. 18 and 26, which indicated the rules

Apart from those changes, the new text of the contract seems to follow that of the previous edition with a different layout.

Some of the principles of the previous edition are confirmed, such as that the contract can be applied retrospectively where it is made between the parties during salvage operations which have already begun, or have even been completed; the agency for the owners of the properties salved of the master of the ship in peril, who can, on their behalf, sign the contract binding them—as we have seen—separately and not jointly, each of them being responsible for a part of the remuneration in proportion to the property which he has at risk; the possibility for the salvor to make reasonable use of the engine, auxiliaries and anchors of the salved ship to complete the salvage operation successfully, with the duty to avoid unnecessary damage, sacrifices or losses of the equipment; the existence of a right over the property salved, that is to say, a maritime lien in favour of the salvor and the consequent duty on the owners of the property salved not to remove it until the guarantee has been issued; the issue of this guarantee; and the arbitration procedure to decide the case, and the fixing of the remuneration.[279]

28. RULES FOR THE BRINGING OF ARBITRATION PROCEEDINGS

Clauses 6 to 14 of the LOF 1980 contain the procedure and provision for the arbitration procedure before the Committee of Lloyd's, laid down by the arbitration clause inserted in the standard contract (clause 1(b)). One of the advantages of using this contract is that the Committee of Lloyd's usually provides a fairly rapid kind of arbitration procedure, free from rigidly formal restrictions, and one which may be completed in a reasonable time to satisfy the expectations of the creditors of salvage remuneration. It is usually based on documentary evidence alone.

One of the problems which may arise in connection with arbitration procedure, which may of course involve parties of different nationalities, is that of the jurisdiction of the arbitrators and the applicable law, but clause 1(d) of LOF 1980 states that the contract "shall be governed by and arbitration thereunder shall be in accordance with English law".

to be followed by arbitrators in issuing an *interim award* "Arbitrators are fully entitled to make an interim award, provided that in so doing they observe the ordinary principles applicable to such awards and furthermore that they do not, in disposing of the matter with such expedition, infringe the general principle that they must act fairly."

279. For a full examination of the new contractual rules regarding the right of the salvor "to take steps to enforce his lien", and also to guarantee that the decisions of the arbitration award will be respected, see Brice, *op. cit.*, 257 *et seq. The Tesaba* [1982] 1 Lloyd's Rep. 397 denied that the salvor who had received a guarantee from the shipowner and not from the cargo, and consequently tried to take action *in rem* against the ship because she had been made unavailable to him with the cargo, has no right to this type of action, but only the possibility of prosecuting the owners of the cargo, *in personam*.

While there is no doubt that because the arbitration takes place in London, before the Committee of Lloyd's, English law is the law applicable to the arbitration procedure (which therefore has to be carried out under the Arbitration Act 1950 and the subsequent Act of 1979), and while there is also no doubt that the contract is governed by English law because the clause referring to it, it is not equally clear that that clause may be a departure from the Brussels Convention of 1910, whenever this has to be applied to the case referred to arbitration, on account of the presence in the case of subjective and objective elements which make the Convention automatically applicable by virtue of Article 15.

We wonder whether, where the salvage of a ship and cargo is clearly governed by the Brussels Convention and the parties, owners of the salved property and salvors, have entered into a LOF 1980, they intended, by virtue of clause 1(d), to remove the case from the Convention and to refer it to arbitrators who are to judge it according to English law, or whether the rules of the Brussels Convention, if and in so far as they apply, cannot be overridden by the parties, except for those provisions where an exception is allowed.

The solution would appear to be this latter. In fact, if it is correct that Article 15 of the Convention makes the Convention prevail over separate national laws, it is even more correct to say that the Convention may not be departed from by mere agreement between the parties contained in the Lloyd's contract referring the matter to a particular national law, English law. It seems to us that, with regard to the question which law the arbitrators must apply to cases brought for their consideration and decision, we can conclude that it need not necessarily be English law as appears to be laid down by the above clause of the LOF 1980. On the contrary, because there are parties of different nationalities, giving a relationship which seems to have an international element, they must first establish whether the case should not be decided in accordance with the law of the Brussels Convention. As has been correctly noted about matters not laid down in LOF 1980, the main purpose of a salvage agreement, which is usually little more than an outline, is to provide that the services contracted for are salvage services, leaving it to the arbitrators to determine the reward for them.

Here is the limited freedom allowed by the law to the parties, who may alter the legal rules by exceptions especially, as we have seen, concerning the principle of "no cure no pay", according to the concept of English doctrine and jurisprudence. Those regard the salvage contract as, basically, an agreement related to and limited to the fixing of remuneration ("an agreement concerning the amount to be paid for the salvage services").[280] This is on the

---

280. Ferrarini, *Il soccorso*, 127; Kennedy, *op. cit.*, 291. With regard to the relationship between arbitration procedure and English law, see Brice, *op. cit.*, 270 *et seq.*, and from a general point of view *Russel, on arbitration* (London 1982); Mustill and Boyd, *Commercial Arbitration* (London, 1982). It is significant that in the new draft Convention prepared by the CMI (Montreal 1981), it is expressly specified in Art. 1 ("scope of application") that the Convention is applied

clear understanding that the arbitration procedure and the interpretation of the contract in the form as prepared by Lloyd's will nevertheless be governed by English law as laid down in the contract.[281]

Another problem concerning the jurisdiction of the arbitrators arises where the parties who own interests in the cargo maintain that the person who signed the contract for them could not be regarded as their agent of necessity, despite the fact that the Lloyd's Open Form, so signed, is binding upon them. In this situation, arbitrators usually have to decide first whether or not the cargo owners are bound by the contract.[282]

The arbitration procedure begins with the issue of the guarantees to the Committee of Lloyd's by the owners of the property salved and with the immediate and automatic appointment of the arbitrator by the Committee itself. If the guarantee has not been issued, the arbitrator may still be appointed at the written request of one of the interested parties, as provided by clause 8 of the LOF 1980. Obviously, the appointment of the arbitrator does not prevent the parties from reaching an amicable agreement and settling the case before the arbitration hearing.

It should be noted that about half of all cases referred to the Committee of Lloyd's are settled amicably between the parties before the arbitration begins.[283] The Committee of Lloyd's *usually* appoints the arbitrator by choosing him from the Queen's Counsel Panel, and from those who have the greatest experience in legal practice of Admiralty law.

The arbitration procedure does not follow excessively rigid formal rules. The parties, represented by their own lawyers, lodge all the necessary docu-

---

"whenever judicial or arbitral proceedings relating to matters dealt with in this Convention are brought in a contracting State". See also: Coulthard, *op. cit.*, 62.

281. In Italian jurisprudence the Arbitration Award of 26 November 1982, mentioned many times, in Dir Mar. 1983, 580 *et seq.*, did not allow the claim that two Italian subjects, by the sole fact of having referred to the LOF 1980 in only four articles of their contract, had intended to submit the contract wholly to English law. They had merely wished to depart in their agreement from the relevant law in the limited matters governed by the above clauses of the LOF 1980.

282. See in jurisprudence: *Luanda Exportadora* v. *Wahbe Tamari and Sons* [1967] 2 Lloyd's Rep. 353, 364 and in doctrine: Brice, *op. cit.*, 265. See further on this point: Brice, "The New Salvage Convention: green Seas and grey areas", 33, and international jurisprudence and doctrine cited therein. In particular, see Rose, "Restitution for the rescuers" [1989] O.J.L.S. 184, and, in English jurisprudence *The Choko Star* [1989] 2 Lloyd's Rep. 47, a decision which acknowledged that the master of the ship was entitled to stipulate a reasonable salvage contract even for the cargo, and without contacting the cargo owners. Critical on this point is Brice, *op. cit.*, 38, who writes: "However, even under the *The Choko Star* test, I believe there may still be circumstances when the court would say that it was not reasonable for the master to enter into a particular salvage contract without consulting cargo owners. Take, for example, a case where a laden tanker is aground close to an oil terminal operated by the cargo owners (with considerable knowledge of local salvage facilities). Assume she is in sheltered waters and in no real physical danger. She needs to be refloated but there is not urgency. The cargo owners are readily available for consultation. In such a case the court might say the master or shipowners acted unreasonably if they went ahead and signed a Lloyd's Form without considering other options with the cargo owners."

283. Brice, *op. cit.*, 266, remarks that: "the mere fact that an arbitrator is appointed would not, of course, cause him to make any award; there would have to be a hearing before an award could be made and published."

ments. Those comprise the reports of the masters of the ships, of the crews and of the surveyors; the meteorological certificates concerning the area of the incident; and the appraisal of the salved properties, and of the craft and equipment used in the salvage operations. All the documents produced must be exchanged between the parties.

The parties are identified by clause 8 of LOF 1980. The following are therefore qualified to take part in the arbitration procedure:

(1) The Owners of the ship.
(2) The Owners of the cargo or any part thereof.
(3) The Owners of any freight separately at risk or any part thereof.
(4) The Contractor.
(5) The Owners of the bunkers and/or stores.
(6) Any other person who is a party to this Agreement.

According to the Lloyd's contract, the insurers of the parties are not entitled to intervene in the arbitration procedure, as they are not normally parties to the contract.[284] It often happens that in arbitration procedures brought before the Committee of Lloyd's, some of the parties listed above intervene while others do not. This happens especially when the cargo of the salved ship consists of general cargo, and many of the owners of the individual lots making up the general cargo do not take part in the arbitration procedure either because they do not wish to do so or because they cannot be traced from the evidence contained in the documents. (Sometimes bills of lading do not indicate the actual shippers or consignees of the goods, but instead the forwarding agents.)

To protect the effectiveness of the arbitration award in relation to all the interested parties, the contract provides that failure to take part in the arbitration means for the parties who are not represented a renunciation of their rights to be heard and to produce documents in evidence. Because the award takes effect against the unrepresented parties, it must be proved that due notice was given to them, in good time, of the place and date of the arbitration.

Normally the arbitration relies on documents, but this does not prevent the arbitrators from asking, in special cases, to hear the parties or their witnesses at the hearing.

Apart from issuing the award which fixes the amount of the salvage remuneration due to the salvors, or of the safety net where this particular type of remuneration applies, the arbitrators can normally adjudicate on the excessiveness of the guarantee required by the salvors, should there have been a formal protest from those interested in the property salved; on the interest and expenses due from the parties who must pay, and of proportionate

---

284. Thus also Brice, *op. loc. cit.* There is no doubt that they can be parties to the contract when they have signed it, as they can be included in the category of subjects indicated in clause 6(b) of LOF 1980.

sharing of the remuneration between the salvors (whether co-salvors, or between the owner, master and crew of the salved ship); and on monetary devaluation and fluctuation in the exchange rates of the various foreign currencies in which the amount of the salvage remuneration may be fixed.[285]

The arbitrators' award may be challenged before an appeal arbitrator, who will judge the case on the documents and evidence provided for the first instance arbitration procedure. The introduction of new evidence is allowed on appeal in exceptional cases only. The appeal arbitrator does not have the power to modify the original award with regard to any parties who have not appealed against the award.

For example, if the owner of the salved ship appeals and the cargo owners do not, the award may be modified only in respect of the part which concerns the relations between the salvor and the shipowner, while the part relating to the cargo interests will not be modified.[286] The conditions and practice for lodging an appeal are given in clause 13 of LOF 1980, but the ordinary courts have the power, in particular cases, to extend the time limits for its presentation.[287]

Finally, clause 15 of the contract lays down the practice and conditions for the payment of the remuneration determined by the award, once the award has become final because there has been no appeal or if the appeal stipulates that, should the parties required to pay the remuneration to the salvor not pay within fourteen consecutive days from the award's publication, then the salvor (the contractor) may exercise his rights on the guarantee lodged with the Committee of Lloyd's.

---

285. Brice, *op. cit.*, 174; and for the acceptance of monetary devaluation in jurisprudence see *The Teh Hu* [1969] 2 Lloyd's Rep. 365, and *Birkett* v. *Hayes* [1982] 2 All E.R. 70, C.A. by which it is acknowledged as equitable "to put the contractor in the position in which he would have been, had the remuneration been paid promptly."

286. *The Geestland* [1980] 1 Lloyd's Rep. 628.

287. In jurisprudence, *The American Sioux* [1980] 2 Lloyd's Rep. 224, C.A., and *Consolidated Investment and Contracting Co.* v. *Saponaria Shipping Co.*, *The Virgo* [1978] 2 Lloyd's Rep. 167, C.A.

CHAPTER FOUR

SALVAGE AT SEA IN THE COMITÉ MARITIME INTERNATIONAL DRAFT INTERNATIONAL CONVENTION (MONTREAL 1981)

29. THE DEVELOPMENT OF THE MOVEMENT OF CHANGE IN THE LAW OF SALVAGE AT SEA

The movement of change in the law of salvage at sea which, as we have seen, had begun with the revision of the standard contract (better known as "Lloyd's Open Form") was to be developed further in the Comité Maritime International (CMI) after the Legal Committee of IMCO (now IMO—International Maritime Organisation) had appointed the Comité to study the timing of a revision of the 1910 Brussels Convention on Assistance and Salvage and, if need be, to prepare a Draft of a new Convention.

After the working group, led by Professor Selvig of the Danish Association of Maritime Law, had been formed, the first preliminary Report in the discussions was sent to CMI. It ended as follows:

"The Salvage Convention, 1910 needs revision in light of subsequent experience and practice. The need for revision is particularly relevant with respect to cases where a marine accident creates risk of damages to third party interests. In such cases the salvage operations must be considered as a whole since it is difficult to distinguish between the salvage of the ship and cargo and the salvage of the third party interests. A comprehensive and coherent regulation of these cases is required. The alternatives seem to be:

(I) To leave the cases where only ship and cargo are in danger to be governed by the 1910 Convention and to draft a separate new convention for cases where the ship, cargo and third party interests are in danger and,

(II) to draft a new comprehensive convention on salvage, while recognising that the need for law revision varies with the particular salvage situations."[288]

In effect the new terms of LOF 1980, restricted as they were to pollution

---

288. See CMI *Documentation Montreal*, 1981: Selvig, *Preliminary Report on the Revision of the Law of Salvage, Salvage*, 1, II, 80, 18. On the preceding events which led to the French government's proposal to revise the law on salvage at sea being brought before IMO, see: Abecassis, *op. cit.*, 255 *et seq.*, Martray, "Les leçons de la catastrophe de l'Amoco Cadiz," in 4, *Environmental Policy and Law*, 1978, 172. Recently, Ferrarini, "Il progetto del CMI (1981) di Convenzione internazionale sul salvataggio," in *Annali della Facoltà di giurisprudenza di Genova*, 1980–81, 1–2, 401 *et seq.* See also F. Brocker, "The 1910 Salvage Convention and Lloyd's Open Form under pressure" (Rotterdam, 1983) and F. Berlingieri, "Le projet d'une nouvelle convention", *op. cit.*, 1.

risks and to environmental damage resulting from the salvage of a loaded or a partially loaded oil tanker, and further restricted in the remuneration for the efforts made and the results obtained in lessening these risks, to the modest acknowledgment of a percentage calculated on the basis of the costs sustained (safety net), had not satisfied the salvage associations. Those were pressing for a more substantial reform of the law and for the concept of liability salvage to be included in the accepted meaning of salvage, i.e. the prevention of damage to third parties in general, a damage not limited to the one case of salvage of oil tankers. The salvage associations were also pressing for an increased emphasis on the risks, efforts and results achieved by the salvors within the meaning of liability salvage for the purposes of fixing their remuneration.[289]

The International Commission, under the chairmanship of Professor Selvig, concluded that the second alternative was more appropriate to a modern international law of salvage at sea, and prepared a Draft for a new Convention which, after study by all the national associations of maritime law, was discussed at Montreal in 1981. It went, first, before the Commission and later to the Plenary Conference where, after a series of amendments, it was approved, with 31 votes in favour and one abstention, by all the associations taking part in the Conference.[290]

30. THE PROBLEMS WHICH THE CMI DRAFT ATTEMPTED TO SOLVE

The intention of the movement for change in the law, strengthened by the approval of the new Draft Convention, was to have due note taken of the altered technical-juridical and environment situations on which salvage law must be based, and of the altered requirements of the international community. That was more concerned that salvors should prevent heavy damage

---

289. One of the major obstacles to the inclusion of the concept of "liability salvage" in the rules of salvage at sea is (as correctly pointed out by Bessemer Clark, *op. cit.*, 301) the difficulty, not to say impossibility, of identifying exactly who has benefited from the salvor's services and of establishing "the potential liability which the salvor has avoided." The opinions of O'May, *op. cit.*, 1424 (who adds to the difficulties that of identifying which party must issue the guarantee in favour of the salvors covering the remuneration relating to "liability salvage") and of Sheen, *op. cit.*, 1407, concur.

290. The CMI Conference in Montreal was attended by 32 of the 38 national associations of maritime law, members of CMI, as well as by observers delegated by IMO, by the International Group of P. & I. Associations, by the International Chamber of Shipping, by the International Oil Pollution Compensation Fund, by the Association Internationale Des Dispacheurs Européens, by the International Union of Marine Insurance, by the Oil Companies International Marine Forum, by the International Salvage Union and by the American Institute of Merchant Shipping. See as to this F. Berlingieri, *The XXXI Conference of the Comité Maritime International*, 297 *et seq.*

following marine accidents rather than with the traditional salvage of vessel and cargo. It is obvious that the international community was not only concerned that an efficient and adequate organisation for maritime salvage should exist, but also that international laws encouraging the efficient maintenance of this organisation should exist, and that these laws should not act as a brake (in the case of accidents involving high risks to the environment and to third party interests) on salvors, who could consider their efforts and the results achieved inadequately paid in proportion to the serious risks which they had run in such cases.[291]

Similarly, there is no doubt that, apart from the need to solve this problem (which may be regarded as existing throughout the new law of salvage), the revision of the Convention and the careful working out of a new text also allowed improvements to be made where certain gaps (already mentioned in Chapter 3) had inevitably continued to exist despite the occasional attempts by jurisprudence to give an interpretation more in keeping with the times and situations, now so different from those of the 1910 Brussels Convention.

Apart from the chief innovation, which was the insertion into the Convention of the concepts of environmental damage and of liability salvage (even if with the restrictions discussed below), the aim of the CMI Draft Convention was to give a more complete definition of "salvage operations"; a fuller definition of "vessel"; better qualifications of the duties of the separate parties concerned, introducing the duty for the owner and for the master of the salved ship to take "timely and reasonable action to arrange for salvage operations", to prevent, in certain cases, delay in seeking assistance, which might cause irreparable damage to the environment and to third parties; a more exact and definite exclusion of those cases not governed by the Draft (e.g. removal of wrecks); the express inclusion of the salvor's right to limit his own liability; and, finally, an overall improvement in the norms of jurisdiction. Among the other minor changes to be discussed below were the bringing into line of the Convention's rules with some changes already introduced into the law by LOF 1980, and the regulation of the relations between contractual agreements and law, with definite rules about possible exceptions from the latter.[292]

---

291. See Selvig's *Preliminary Report* to the International Sub-Committee, in *Documentation Montreal*, 1981: *Salvage* 1, II–80, 4 *et seq.*, which correctly pointed out that: "The income of the salvage industry must be sufficient to maintain an internationally adequate salvage capacity. It is probably required that total compensation reach a higher level than at present. Moreover, the risk of incurring expenses without compensation or that of incurring liabilities in connection with salvage operations should not be such that the salvors are discouraged from intervening in particular cases."

292. For a complete examination of the changes to the law of salvage by the CMI Draft Convention, see Nielsen, CMI Report to IMO on the Draft International Convention of Salvage (Montreal, 1891), in CMI News Letter, September 1984. On the relationships between LOF 1980 and the CMI Draft, see Coulthard, *A new cure for salvors?*, 45 *et seq.*

31. ENVIRONMENTAL DAMAGE AND "LIABILITY SALVAGE"

The principal change in international law, as proposed by the 1981 Montreal Convention, consists of the insertion, into the law of salvage at sea, of the concepts of "liability salvage" and "damage to the environment", which are not included among the present provisions of the Convention and which only LOF 1980 took into account, although with the reservations mentioned in the previous chapter.[293]

Even in Selvig's preliminary Report to the International Sub-Committee, the following suggestions were made:

"(a) when revising the law of salvage one should probably distinguish between cases where only the ship and her cargo are at risk and cases where, by the marine accident, there is created a risk of damage to third party interests. The need for revision is particularly clear with respect to the latter cases. However, the need for a coherent legal framework for salvage must also be kept in mind;

(b) the concept of salvage should be extended so as to take account of the fact that damage to third party interests has been prevented. Since the ship, which created the danger, will have a duty to take preventive measures in order to avoid such damage, this will mean that the salvage should refer not only to ship and cargo, but also to the ship's interest in avoiding third party liabilities (liability salvage)."

Those suggestions were to be partially accepted by the Commission and by the Plenary Conference in Montreal, given that the concept of "liability salvage" was included in the text of the Draft in strict relation to the concept of "damage to the environment", with the granting to the salvor of a "special compensation", the maximum limit of which would be double the expenses sustained in the salvage operations and in preventing or minimising damage to the environment.

Thus, during the Conference, a compromise between the opposing viewpoints was reached. One had wished to include in international law the concept of liability salvage, without restrictions, granted that the prevention of any risk to the owners of the salved vessel and her cargo formed an element of

---

293. In Italian jurisprudence two recent but completely contrasting arbitration awards on this point (see Arbitration Award 24 February 1981, published in Dir. Mar. 1981, 264; and Arbitration Award 26 November 1982, cited on various occasions, *ibidem*) dealt with the problem as to whether the so-called "liability salvage" should be admitted *de juro condito*, amongst the elements to be considered in calculating the salvor's remuneration. In fact, whilst the former Award denies that the Convention, like Italian law, allows the admission of this element, the latter, instead, takes that element into consideration, adopting the view that the current Convention, where it reads: "the danger run by the salved vessel," allows the possibility of interpreting it as "risks of a patrimonial nature, run by the Owner of the salved ship," with an extensive interpretation of international uniform law, which reconnects with the theory of third party liability and its evolution towards more modern forms such as liability for company risks. See on this point E. Vincenzini, *Brevi osservazioni in tema di liability salvage*, mentioned in the second Award, and more generally Alpa, *La responsabilità della impresa per i danni all' ambiente e al consumatore* (Milan, 1978), 177.

evaluation for remuneration.[294] The other had wanted the text of the Draft of the new Convention to agree with the wording of LOF 1980, fixing the special compensation as a set percentage in proportion to the costs established as the safety net.

The compromise consisted of the inclusion, in the Draft of the Convention, of the concept of liability salvage. By this, the efforts made by the salvors and the useful results achieved in minimising eventual environmental damage after the marine accident to which the salvage operations related, were to be taken into consideration.

Whilst, on one hand, the concept of liability salvage in its widest sense (that of an action by salvors capable of preventing or minimising damage of any nature of third parties) was not included in the Draft, on the other, with the term "damage to the environment", a widening was made in the concept of damage as it had been qualified in LOF 1980 (where the damage itself was strictly and expressly related to the "escape of oil from the vessel", i.e. to the specific risk of pollution).

The concept of damage to the environment included in the Montreal Draft is somewhat wider than oil pollution damage, and this can be explained by Chapter I, Article 1.1, of the Draft which clarifies that by "damage to the environment," all material damage resulting from pollution, explosion, contamination, fire and other similar accidents of importance occuring in coastal areas or inland waters, is meant.[295]

On this point the intentions of the delegates at the Montreal Conference are even more clearly indicated in the comment to the Draft Convention contained in the CMI Report to IMO:

"Article 1.1.4 refers to physical damage to persons or property, not to the economic consequences thereof. By using the words substantial and major as well as the reference to pollution, explosion, contamination, fire, it is intended to make it clear that the definition does not include damage to any particular person or installation. There must be a risk of damage of a more general nature in the area concerned, and it must be a risk of substantial damage. During the Montreal Conference the words: to human health or to marine life or resources, were added to exclude further from the concept

---

294. Subsequently, as we have seen, at the Montreal Conference English jurisprudence (*The Helenus and The Motaqua* [1982] 2 Lloyd's Rep. 261) also took into consideration, in evaluating the danger, the risk of the salved vessel causing damage to third parties (in that particular case to other vessels moored in the port) referring to somewhat old Italian national cases, opposed in doctrine by various parties; see Trib. Naples 8 June 1963, in Dir. Mar. 1965, 221; Trib. Leghorn 2 February 1971, in Dir. Mar. 1971, 222. In support see Coulthard, *op. cit.*, 31 and Bessemer Clark, *op. cit.*, 299 *et seq.* See also Gold, "Marine Salvage: Towards a New Regime", *op. cit.*, 488; and Brice, *op. cit.*, 33.

295. Selvig's *Report* to the CMI International Sub-Committee represents an improved justification of the concept of environment: "Damage to the environment can in a sense be described as a generic term since, as a rule, it does not refer to damage to any particular person, property or interest, but rather to damage in the area concerned. What is relevant in salvage law is not the damage itself, but rather that there exists a risk of damage emanating from a ship in danger.

cases where there may only be a risk of substantial physical damage to other property e.g. warehouses or other buildings ashore."[296]

It is obvious that the view which prevailed was the one seeking to exclude from damage to the environment, any damage to third party properties (e.g. port shore installations, vessels moored in port, warehouses, etc.)[297] and all such damage to third parties as could be considered as "liability salvage" in a general sense. (As has been fairly noted, there are many case-studies in international law which describe the salvage of vessels on fire or grounded due to the fault of the owner or his employees or servants, where the risk of loss extending to other vessels or properties belonging to third parties, and the risk of damage to the vessel herself, have been taken into consideration when determining the compensation.)[298]

Having so qualified and defined the concepts of liability salvage and the damage to the environment (introduced by the proposals of CMI), it is necessary to examine how the change in the actual fixing of remuneration has led to a substantial benefit for salvors or, at least, to an improvement on the limited remuneration awarded by the introduction of the safety net into the new LOF 1980.

The plan of the Draft which, as we have said, takes into account within certain limits the change effected by LOF 1980, is that of providing that, should the salvage operations be unsuccessful (that is, salvage operations in the traditional sense, of the salvage of vessel and cargo), the salvor would still be entitled to the refund of all the costs incurred, including some remuneration for the craft and personnel used, wherever the salvage services are given to a

296. See Nielsen, CMI Report to IMO on the Draft International Convention on Salvage (Montreal, 1981), 10 *et seq.*; and also Brice, *op. cit.*, 170.

297. For a qualification in jurisprudence after the Montreal Conference, of the concept of damage to the environment as a risk of damage of a more general nature in the area concerned in the casualty, see the case of the *Amoco Cadiz* [1984] 2 Lloyd's Rep. 303 at 304 *et seq.*, where claims for damages were brought by the French government, by the Finisterre administration department, by the general council of the Côtes du Nord, and by a great number of French parties, persons and companies, who suffered loss by the pollution consequent upon the sinking of the vessel.

298. The Arbitration Award of 26 November 1962, *loc. cit.*, 587. We do not approve the solution of a problem, which has merely been touched upon by one other arbitration award (see Arbitration Award, 31 January 1979, in Dir. Mar. 1979, 405) about the relevance which, in certain cases, may be assumed by the elimination, by means of a salvage operation, of possible indirect damage ensuing from the liability risks of the salved vessel when (as was the case in the previous judgment) it hinders, as a result of her grounding position, access to or exit from the port by other vessels, thus allowing the question of the liability of the Port Authorities and of various third party users of the port to be raised. We have already had occasion to point out (see E. Vincenzini, *Brevi osservazioni in tema di liability salvage*, 591) that this interpretation, although marginally expressed by the award, could not be included in the present provisions in *subjecta materia*, in that the extension of "liability salvage" to the risk of indirect damage would, from the point of view of the parties, excessively widen the risk of intrinsic damage to third parties, with implications in abnormal situations which could not easily be qualified or, by cause and effect, lead back to the actual danger run by the salved vessel and/or to the useful result achieved by the salvors.

vessel which threatens serious damage to the environment, plus a reward when the salvor effectively manages to prevent or to minimise the occurrence of such damage.

32. "SPECIAL COMPENSATION"

Two distinct situations, differently regulated by the Draft Convention (Chapter III, Article 3.3: Special Compensation) may arise:

(1) in all cases (whether or not the salvor is successful in preventing or minimising the damage to the environment) the salvor will be entitled to compensation from the owner of the salved vessel for an amount equal to the out-of-pocket expenses incurred;

(2) if, and only if, the salvage operations result in a degree of success in preventing or minimising damage to the environment, the compensation owed by the owner of the salved vessel may be increased to an extent considered fair and reasonable by the court or arbitration tribunal, the ceiling being double the expenses incurred by the salvor.[299]

On special compensation, the Draft Convention follows the same approach as LOF 1980 concerning the debtor of the salvors' special remuneration, when extra salvage is given to prevent or lessen damage to the environment. The owner of the salved vessel is identified as the debtor, and all other parties, even if owners of the salved properties (cargo, freight, bunker, etc.), are excluded.

The *ratio* for this approach is to be found in the comment on the Draft's Articles contained in CMI's Report to IMO, although, it must be admitted, the reasoning leading to this solution seems to be merely pragmatic when relating solely to insurance. In the comment it is acknowledged that:

"In cases where these provisions apply and no or insufficient property has been salved so as to allow adequate recovery under Article 3.2, it is important for the salvor that the person liable is one against whom the claim is easily enforceable. Therefore, it has been provided that the special compensation payable under Articles 3.3.1 and 3.3.2 must be paid by the shipowner. Article 3.3 together with Article 3.2.1(b) must be considered as part of a compromise. The shipowners' willingness to accept the funding of the compensation and to accept the broad definition of salvor's expenses in Article 3.3.3 is clearly connected with the salvor's acceptance of the limit in Article 3.3.2 and his acceptance that he will not insist on any rules in the new convention as to who

---

299. O'May, *op. cit.*, 1431, who points out that the expenses mentioned in the Draft Convention are the actual out-of-pocket expenses sustained by the salvor in the course of the salvage operations with the addition of a certain refund of those general overheads (craft, equipment and personnel) reasonably incurred in relation to the operations. The method used for the calculation of the expenses resembles that established by LOF 1980. On the subject of "special compensation" see also Brice, *op. cit.*, 169 *et seq.*

should be liable for the rewards payable under Article 3.2. Equally, the fact that these provisions should not be made mandatory was an important part of the compromise."

The reasons why the other parties, especially the owner of the polluting cargo, should be excluded from sharing in the salvage's special compensation are not understandable, particulary in those cases where the maritime accident and the consequent pollution do not occur because of the fault of the shipowner, but are fortuitous or an "act of God".

So the Draft Convention again proposes some kind of objective liability for the shipowner, even if the Draft (Article 3.3.6 Chapter III), contrary to LOF, anticipates some chance of recourse, after the maritime venture, against the other parties involved for special compensation paid to the salvor, at least during the general average adjustment.[300]

This possibility must also be regarded as granted because it is accepted that in salvage some operative choices are justified by a series of different but frequently related situations, and in doctrine it is held that, in order either to admit or to exclude the results of some provision from general average, due consideration has to be given to the underlying or primary purpose in relation to the various interests involved.[301]

It cannot be denied that in the lightening or removal of a dangerous or pollutant cargo from a vessel in danger of being lost and of causing serious damage to the environment, the decision taken by the master and put into effect by the salvor may represent a real and proper salvage of cargo carried out with the secondary purpose of performing a preventive anti-pollution measure, or an anti-pollution operation with the intention of preventing or minimising damage to the environment, performed incidentally without salvage of cargo or with, occasionally its partial salvage only.[302]

On the other hand, it cannot be ignored that in some cases the maritime accident capable of producing damage to the environment might not be the outcome of chance or of force majeure or, because of the fault of the vessel, *rectius* of her owner; it may be the responsibility of the cargo owners as a result of defective stowage—obviously so when the stowage is the duty of the shipper.

An example is a cargo of a highly pollutant nature in drums which are badly

300. See the Arbitration Award 26 November 1982, already mentioned on various occasions, *loc. cit.*, 580 *et seq.* This award declared that the expenses and sacrifices voluntarily sustained by the master of the vessel with the primary and prevailing purpose of contributing to the common safety of the properties involved in the maritime venture may be presented in general average provided that such acts may, secondarily, have been instigated by other reasons, such as an attempt to protect the environment. This also applies in a case where the Club, the hull and the cargo underwriters have previously agreed to set up, by equal contributions, a common fund to ensure the prompt refund of the salvor's expenses, costs and disbursements.

301. See Boglione, *Salvataggio, LOF 1980 e misure antinquinamento*, 612.

302. One has only to think of those cases where it is preferred to set fire to the cargo to prevent its spreading over the sea or along the shores, and other cases where the cargo is discharged without measures being taken to preserve its marketable value and quality (e.g., by discharge onto lighters which are dirty with other contaminating products).

stowed. The shifting of the drums in the hold produces the risk of the loss of the carrying vessel, which is obliged to seek assistance for the double purpose of the salvor effecting the salvage of the vessel and her cargo, and also and especially of preventing, by such salvage, serious damage to the environment.

In such a case, it would seem to be unfair for the total cost of the salvage operations (especially if there were no useful result with regard to the properties which are traditionally the object of salvage, i.e. the vessel and her cargo) to be borne by the innocent shipowner under an abnormal principle of objective liability.

De jure condendo, it is hoped that such situations, which are not infrequent, will be taken into consideration on the occasion of the next, inevitable revision of the York-Antwerp Rules. Those Rules need to be adapted to the changed realities of maritime traffic, to the evolution of international law relating to oil pollution, and to the law of salvage at sea (that reform already being under way), with an ever-increasing acceptance of the concept of liability salvage.[303]

33. OTHER INNOVATIONS PROPOSED BY THE CMI DRAFT

In discussing this point we shall follow the order of the CMI Draft, limiting ourselves to mentioning those provisions which are completely new compared with the 1910 Convention, and those which represent a change, or at least an improvement. This will provide a present-day comparison with existing law.[304]

First and foremost it must be noted that the Draft of a new Convention, as distinct from the 1910 Convention, contains various definitions which are extremely useful to the reader. They remove doubts in interpretation which

303. The increasing relevance of the law of salvage at sea in the public interest had already been pointed out by Selvig in the *Preliminary Report* to CMI, in *Documentation—Salvage*, 5–IV–80, which reads: "The public interest in avoiding damage to third party interests is not limited to pollution damage caused by oil escaping from laden tankers. It extends to other types of damage caused by tankers or their cargoes as well as to pollution or other damage caused by ships carrying noxious, hazardous or otherwise dangerous goods. Relevant is actually any risk to third party interests created by international shipping". Moreover, Selvig himself, *op. cit.*, 11, had, with regard to the desirability of introducing the concept of "liability salvage" into the text of the Convention, pointed out that: "The new salvage convention should foresee that a new convention dealing with hazardous substances other than oil may be adopted. To the extent that this convention will impose liabilities for cost of preventive measures beyond the liability of shipowners under the 1976 Limitation Convention, the solution suggested above para. 2 may be used also with respect to such future convention." With regard to the lack of influence of public interest in the salvage, under the 1910 Convention, as an element in calculating the reward, see U.S.D.C., Northern District of California, 18 November 1985, in Dir. Mar., 1986, 748.

304. For a complete examination of the new provisions of the CMI Draft (Montreal 1981) see Nielsen, Report to IMO, in CMI *Newsletter*, September 1984, and the full comment contained in it on the proposed rules and on their *ratio*, and F. Berlingieri, *La XXXII Conferenza del CMI*, 297, *et seq.*; O'May, *op. cit.*, 1425 *et seq.*; Coulthard, *op. cit.*, 45 *et seq.*, and Ferrarini, *Il progetto del CMI*, 401 *et seq.*

used to cause useless doctrinal disputes and conflicting legal decisions. Article 1.1 of the Draft removes once and for all, and buries with it the resulting wasteful and sterile discussions, the two-fold classification of "assistance" and "salvage at sea", and replaces it with the English term "salvage". The general meaning of that term covers not only the salvage of a vessel in distress, but also, as we have seen, the salvage of a wreck.

Consequently a definition of the term "vessel" is given. The Draft for the Convention enlarges this term which in the present Convention is limited to meaning seagoing vessels. Under the new definition of "vessels", all craft and structures capable of navigation are included and vessels which are stranded, abandoned by their crews or sunk represent an object of salvage.

From a combined study of these two provisions, and from the definitions, two important new elements emerge which influence the law:

(1) The Convention does not apply only to seagoing vessels in the traditional sense, but also to all structures capable of navigation, such as oil rigs, floating docks, buoys and fishing gear.[305]

This rule was proposed, with regard to oil rigs, to make it agree with similar proposals relating to the salvage of off-shore rigs as laid down at the CMI Conference of Rio de Janeiro in 1977.

(2) There exists in the Draft Convention a specific and express exclusion regarding the removal of wreck, The Draft leaves it to the national laws to determine the law.

The comment to the Draft Convention states: "The distinction between removal of wreck, which is not governed by the Convention, and salvage services to 'stranded' and 'sunk' ships, to which the Convention applies, may depend on the particular facts of each case. However the criterion may often be that there is some initiative from a public authority."

It is thus clear that the new Convention should, in the process of the unification (which is not merely verbal) of assistance and salvage, towage for salvage purposes and salvage of wreck, include recovery in one law of salvage, the distinction between salvage of wreck and recovery of wreck being the public intervention which normally takes place in the latter.[306]

34. "DAMAGE TO THE ENVIRONMENT"

The Draft also contains a definition of "damage to environment" which deserves study for it expands the concept of oil pollution damage indicated in

305. See Nielsen, CMI Report to IMO, 8, and O'May, op. cit., 1425 et seq. These authors note that: "the definitions encompass offshore mobile craft, such as rigs, which are 'capable' of navigation even though not usually navigated. The intention is expansive rather than restrictive." On the subject of oil rigs, see Summerskill, Oil rigs law and insurance (London, 1979), 12 and 53, as well as the cases mentioned by the latter, op. cit., 58 et seq., in which the English courts have extended the concept of "ship" to other mobile structures capable of navigation.

306. See Nielsen, CMI Report to IMO, 9 et seq. For English doctrine see Brice, op. cit., 105 and 114 and cases cited. Likewise Ferrarini, Il progetto del CMI, 402.

Article 1 of LOF 1980 caused by the escape of oil from the vessel, and it indicates the limits beyond which the damage cannot be considered in the Convention's proposals. Article 1.1.4 of the CMI Draft reads: "Damage to the environment means substantial physical damage to human health or to marine life or resources in coastal or inland waters or areas adjacent thereto, caused by pollution, explosion, contamination, fire or similar major incidents."

Some comments may be made about this provision. There are a similar number of changes in the proposed text:

(1) The intention of the legislators was that the words "substantial" and "major", used in relation to the damage and to the events indicated for purposes of explanation (pollution, explosion, contamination, fire, etc.), make it clear that the definition of damage to the environment does not include damage to a subject or to a particular installation, but refers to a risk of damage of a more general nature in the area affected by the casualty, that is, to a risk of damage of real importance. The rule is not absolutely clear, nor is the comment to it contained in CMI's Report to IMO.[307]

(2) The use of the words "coastal or inland waters" has the intention of fixing the area where the risk of damage to the environment must arise. By these words it is meant to exclude the concept of "environment" from the risk of damage occurring on the high seas. This is to prevent the possibility of speculation and artificially inflated requests for damage based on assertions that the accident has caused damage to the surroundings or to natural resources (e.g. fishing).

In the comment to the Draft, it is stressed that this exclusion must not be considered as mandatory, because damage to the shorelines after an accident on the open sea cannot be excluded. This would appear evident if it is remembered that in the worst accidents, oil pollution, the slick, if not immediately tackled can reach the coast under the effect of wind and currents even if the accident causing the slick occurs in the open sea.

(3) Finally, the fact that among those accidents (apart from pollution) which are capable of causing damage to the environment, other categories of damaging events, such as explosion and fire, are included (even if merely as examples), clearly shows that, despite the precise limits for special compensation, the CMI Draft has

---

307. Nielsen, CMI Report to IMO, 10 et seq. The Report explains that during the Montreal Conference the words "to human health or to marine life or resources" had been added to exclude from the concept those situations in which there arises only a risk of important material damage to other properties, for example to warehouses or to other shore installations. On the nature of damage to the environment, see also Brice, op. cit., 152, et seq. and, finally, Bessemer Clark, op. cit., 59.

introduced to the law of salvage the principle of "liability salvage" in the widest sense of the term.

35. THE NEW CRITERIA PROPOSED BY THE DRAFT CONVENTION

The CMI Draft establishes the standards for the application of the proposed Convention, increasing the number of elements already used by the present Convention. Besides the salved vessel and the salving vessel, both or one or the other being registered in a Contracting State, we find two further criteria which could almost be said to be supplementary, i.e. first, that proceedings to obtain salvage remuneration should be initiated in one of the Contracting States, whether or not either the active or passive subject of the salvage belongs to such States; secondly, that one of these subjects should be a national of one of those States.

Now, if the second assumption appears to be justified by the international requirement of identification of those parties that represent the owners of one of the salved properties, and more often, of the vessel, owing to the lack in many cases of a "genuine link" between the Register of Shipping, the State of the flag and the nationality of the shipowner,[308] the first assumption does not appear to have any satisfactory justification, unless on the Anglo-Saxon principle of *actio in rem*. This principle makes it possible to prove jurisdiction for the State where the action is proposed. This enables the CMI Draft, so far as possible, to identify itself with the principles already laid down in the 1976 Convention on the Limitation of the Shipowner's Liability and, in Article 15.1, with the standard for the fixing of jurisdiction and for the application of the Convention.

However, unlike the present Convention, the new Convention would not apply to vessels used in inland navigation where both the salved and the salvor come under this category; nor to vessels belonging to the same State as that where legal proceedings or an arbitration are brought[309]; nor to ships of war belonging to or operated by a government and used at the time of the salvage, in public, non-commercial services; nor, finally, and as we have seen, to the removal of wrecks.

The most important change is in the fact that, in a certain sense, the CMI

308. See on this point the mentioned work by Carbone, *La disciplina giuridica del traffico marittimo internazionale*, 78 *et seq*.

309. This is in accordance with that established by Art. 1.2.1. insofar as the Convention can be applied to vessels, salved or salving, of the same flag if the claim is brought in a third Contracting State. The rule, in a certain sense, creates a distortion of the general principle that the law applicable to both the salved and the salving vessels, where both belong to the same State, should be in any case the law of the flag. With the rule proposed by the CMI Draft, the subjects are removed from their own natural jurisdiction, *rectius* from their own national law, on the basis of a rule of competence (court of the place where the claim is brought) rather than on a true rule of jurisdiction.

Draft reverts, for warships and government vessels, to the old 1910 Convention, ignoring the amendment to its Article 14 by the 1967 Protocol.

The *ratio* for this change is to be sought in the fact that the Montreal delegates, having noted that there were very few adherences to the 1967 Protocol, chose to return to the original provision. They preferred to leave such cases out of the new Convention, even if this meant, as has been expressly acknowledged, that a special Convention for the purpose will be necessary.[310]

As regards salvage operations performed under the direct control of or directly by a public authority, the proposals for the new Convention leave the Rules of the present Convention virtually unchanged. Article 1.3.2 states that the private salvor who performs the salvage under the direction of the authority will be entitled to carry out all such actions as are provided for by the new Convention against the private interests involved in the operation which have obtained benefit from the operation itself.

The possibility of the salvor exercising his rights against private parties interested in the salvage as the passive subjects of it, depends on whether, in the circumstances, the Convention's requirements for the exercise of those actions have been completely satisfied. Although the 1910 Convention does not prevent the salvor, in such cases, from exercising his rights within the private sector, the provision contained in the Draft is useful in removing all doubts on the point.[311]

36. THE INTERNATIONAL LAW ON SALVAGE AND CONTRACT ACCORDING TO THE DRAFT'S RULES

The Draft Convention also considers and deals with the relationship between international laws and contractual laws of salvage. It resolves in practice the conflict which could arise between the rules of international law (Convention) and the rules adopted by international contractual practice (LOF).

The problem lies in the existing relationship between LOF 1980 and the 1910 Brussels Convention, because the arbitration rulings by Lloyd's can have priority to the Convention's rules each and every time when contract's terms and the decisions of the arbitrators cannot be considered as unfair, and the agreement of the parties to the making of the contract is not rendered void by undue influence, fraud or deceit.[312]

310. As has been seen, only Austria, Brazil, Belgium, Egypt, Great Britain, Yugoslavia, Jersey, Guernsey, the Isle of Man, Papua and Syria have ratified the Protocol.

311. See also O'May, *op. cit.*, 1426.

312. See Coulthard, *op. cit.*, 64 *et seq.*, who points out that the contrast between conventional norms and contractual norms may largely arise in relation to the fixing of remuneration and to the criteria laid down for its calculation, in that, in LOF 1980, the existence of a salvage is presupposed, and the possibility of applying the principles of the Draft Convention would arise in relation to any possible increase or reduction of the remuneration fixed by the arbitrators. This is insofar as a salvor who has performed salvage services in excess of those provided by LOF 1980 could claim increased remuneration on the basis of the Convention.

The problem is approached by the CMI Draft from a different angle. The Draft admits that the Convention's rules cannot be impaired by contractual agreement (Article 1.4.1). It lays down a limit to this possibility of impairment with the combination of the rules in Articles 1.5 "invalid contracts or contractual terms" and 3.6 "services rendered under existing contracts". Those allow for the ineffectiveness of all contracts which have laid down or fixed a remuneration which is "too great or too small for the services actually rendered" or when the salvor's services "exceed what can be reasonably considered as due performance of a contract entered into before the danger arises".[313]

37. THE MASTER OF THE VESSEL AS "AGENT OF NECESSITY"

Another minor problem arose. The 1910 Convention is silent about the point, but it was resolved by the CMI Draft by a special rule. This problem concerns the power of the master of the salved vessel to act, in danger, in the so-called "common venture" (vessel-freight-cargo) as an "agent of necessity" of the individual parties involved in the venture, and consequently to be able to bind the parties to a salvage contract or request for salvage, in the common interests of the properties at risk.

This rule is Article 1.4.2 which, by the term "property" already referred to in the "definitions" of the proposed Convention, expressly provides that the freight should be included within the term.

Obviously the rule refers only to mere agency for the interested parties and therefore it is not binding on them jointly and severally in connection with the payment of remuneration.[314]

313. Whilst preparing the Draft Convention, Selvig, *Documentation-Salvage*, 14, had aired the opinion that: "(1) the new salvage convention should attempt to deal in a generally acceptable manner with the matter presently covered by standard form contracts for salvage; (2) a greatly simplified standard form contract should be prepared; (3) the new salvage convention should contain as the main rule that in cases where there is danger of damage to third party interests outside the ship, a valid contract may only be concluded after the danger is terminated." As to this see O'May, *op. cit.*, 1427 who foretells, should IMO approve the CMI Draft, the adjustment of LOF 1980 to the new provisions of the convention, pointing out that the "Lloyd's Form is not one of the Biblical tablets, engraved on stone. It is a flexible instrument, subject to continuous review, which is able to respond promptly to reflect developments in the infrastructure of international salvage law and practice. Additionally the representatives of international salvors at Montreal were opposed to a mandatory convention. Since one of the primary objects of any new convention is to encourage professional salvors, a stipulation which had a disincentive effect on salvors would be contrary to the best interests of salved property, and third parties generally."

314. See Brice, *op. cit.*, 199, in support. Likewise F. Berlingieri, *La XXXII Conferenza del CMI*, 298, who points out that the absence of joint and several liability between the venture's interests results even more clearly and unequivocally from the text of Art. 4.2–2 of the Draft where, on the question of guarantees for remuneration, it is provided that "the owner of the cargo provide satisfactory security for the claims against them including interest and costs before the cargo is released". The wording of this duty, states Berlingieri, clearly indicates, even if

38. THE DUTY TO CO-OPERATE BETWEEN OWNERS OF SALVED PROPERTIES, SALVORS AND PUBLIC AUTHORITIES

As we have already ascertained, the Draft, based on past experience and especially in view of the events surrounding the notorious case of the *Amoco Cadiz*, provides, under two separate rules, for the duties of the shipowner and of the master to take timely and reasonable measures to ensure the salvage of the vessel in peril and to co-operate with the salvor. There is the corresponding duty of the salvor to use his best endeavours in performing the salvage and, during the operations, to do everything possible to prevent or minimise damage to the environment. Finally, there is the duty of the shipowner and of the master of the salved vessel to accept or to request the co-operation or intervention of other salvors wherever the intervention of the first salvor is obviously inadequate.

As regards co-operation for the success of the salvage operations, the CMI Draft intends to sanction, by a special rule (Article 2.4) if not quite a duty, then at least an exhortation to the Contracting States to co-operate effectively with the salvors, with the parties interested in the salvage and with the public authorities.

We have especially seen that, although the Draft purposes, by Article 2.1.3, to facilitate the salvor's work by compelling the shipowner and the owner of the salved properties to hasten their delivery to a place of safety reasonably requested by the salvors, it plans, with Article 2.4 to make easier the grant to the salvors, by a Contracting State, of a port of refuge when the salvor, having salved a vessel with a dangerous cargo, could be considered as an "international leper".[315]

The rule makes a mere recommendation, and the salvor is not guaranteed against the risk of being refused a port of refuge by the interested coastal State. It must be accepted that, even if it is not essential, it is at least desirable that a more forceful regulation on the matter should be worked out and approved before the new Convention comes into being.[316]

---

impliedly, that no joint and several liability exists between the owner of the vessel and the owner of the cargo with regard to the payment of the salvage remuneration, but that each of these is liable in his respective proportion for remuneration for vessel and cargo. Similarly, also O'May, *op. cit.*, 1428.

315. On the concept of the "international leper or maritime leprosy", see: Bessemer Clark, *op. cit.*, 302; Coulthard, *op. cit.*, 54; O'May, *op. cit.*, 1432. See, more recently, Gold, "Maritime Salvage: Towards a New Regime", 492, and the cases mentioned—*The Christos Bistas, The Andros Patria* and *The Kurdistan*, which had been refused entry into port.

316. Criticisms to this effect have been made by: Bessemer Clark, *op. loc. cit.*: Coulthard, *op. loc. cit.*, and Miller, *op. cit.*, 243.

39. THE NEW CRITERIA FOR CALCULATING REMUNERATION

The changes brought by the CMI Draft to the present regulations of the Convention about the fixing of remuneration are not substantial. Further elements (Article 3.2.1 (b), (g), (h) and (i)) were added to the standards previously put forward by the 1910 Convention in Article 8. These were:

"(b) the skill and efforts of the salvors in preventing or minimising damage to the environment;

(g) the promptness of the service rendered;

(h) the availability and use of vessels or other equipment intended for salvage operations;

(i) the state of readiness and efficiency of the salvor's equipment and its value."

It must be noted that these elements introduced by the Draft are linked (so far as (b) is concerned) to the principal point of the reform of the law (damage to the environment and the concept of liability salvage) whilst (g), (h), and (i) relate to an overall evaluation of the actions and of the organisation of the salvor as well as of the timeliness of his intervention.

The distinction made by the Convention between the so-called primary elements of salvage and the secondary elements has disappeared. The distinction between the two categories no longer exists, i.e. those which were to be considered "firstly" and "secondly" (*en premier lieu*, and *en second lieu* according to the French text of the Convention). The values of the salved properties, although for classification purposes only, now appear under (a) of Article 3.2.1 of the Draft. The present Convention relegates them, alone, to the last place among the factors to be taken into account in fixing remuneration.[317]

When the Draft was being drawn up, there was a discussion about whether it would be better to insert into the proposed Convention the value of the properties based on their insured value. In the end, the view of those delegates who did not wish to introduce elements of uncertainty into the fixing of value prevailed. (Very often, in insurance practice, the real or market value, especially of ships, by no means corresponds with the insured value, since underwriters do not assume, even in the CMI Draft, the position or capacity of the passive subject of the salvage).[318]

---

317. The placing of the value of the property salved at the head of the list of considerations to be taken into account when fixing the reward has, however, no particular significance in the CMI Draft for "it is expressly stated that the order in which the particulars are enumerated is not intended to provide a guidance on such matters". See in support Nielsen, CMI Report to IMO. 19.

318. On the point of valued insurance policies, see in Italian doctrine Ferrarini, *Le assicurazioni marittime*, 174 and 235 *et seq.* and in Anglo-Saxon doctrine Arnould, *The law of Marine Insurance and Average* (London, 1961), 412 *et seq.*, and Colinvaux, *The Law of Insurance* (London, 1984), 9 *et seq.* The latter notes that only in the case of salvage between sister ships may the

Concerning the apportionment of remuneration between co-salvors or between the shipowner, the master and crew of the salving vessel, the Draft follows the present rules. It makes one change in the applicable law which, for salvage services given to the vessel in peril without nautical craft being used, is that of the State where the working contract between the salvor and his employees is made. The link established by the law of the flag is absent in such cases.

The possibility of remuneration for salvage services given with the aim of saving human life in peril remains unchanged in the CMI Draft. There is, however, the necessary adjustment to the new law relating to environmental damage, in all those cases where the salvage services are also given for the salvage of vessel and cargo, and where the result is, at least in part, useful. Of course the Draft allows the salvor of human life to share in the apportionment of the compensation when the salvor has achieved a useful result in preventing or minimising damage to the environment.[319]

40. CONTRACTS OF TOWAGE AND SALVAGE

The rule contained in Article 4 of the 1910 Convention, about salvage services by towage where there is a towage contract in force between the parties made before the event which results in the peril, is not present in the CMI Draft.

underwriters take part in the arbitration procedure on behalf of the salved vessel, while the insured party takes part on behalf of the salving vessel.

319. At the Montreal Conference, the International Sub-Committee headed by Selvig proposed that: "the salvor of human life should have remedies similar to those given to the salvor in Art. 3.3 for avoidance of damage to the environment. Thus it was proposed that the life salvor should in all cases receive compensation for his expenses and in cases of success should be paid a special compensation. The liability for such payments should be imposed on the shipowners or the State of register of the vessel as determined by the law of the State, in which connection it was noted that the law of some countries already had rules on this subject." The Conference did not adopt this proposal, declaring that there was too much emphasis on the commercial interests of the parties involved and, fearing that the new rule proposed would create further problems, it was acknowledged and concluded that the current system, under which the salvage of human life at sea very frequently is not remunerated, had functioned satisfactorily in the past. See Nielsen, CMI Report to IMO, 26. Likewise, Brice, op. cit., 88 for whom: "It may be thought that this is an area of the law requiring the particular attention of maritime nations and their governments; that it is a difficult topic to resolve satisfactorily cannot be doubted for, as in the case of the 'boat people', the magnitude of the problem may be very great and the question of who should pay for the saving of life and on what basis is not an easy one to answer. Statutory provision exists as regards answering distress calls but such may put shipowners to expense. Fortunately mariners and shipowners are habitually prepared to act to save life without any remuneration and at great commercial inconvenience"; and O'May, op. cit., 1435 et seq. Indeed, not only the Anglo-Saxon countries exclude remuneration for the salving of human life. This principle is included in the legislation of countries of different legal traditions. See also Thomas, "Life salvage in Anglo-American law", in Journal of Maritime Law and Commerce (1979), 78. For an argument in favour of the principle of remuneration for the salvage of human life in all cases, see Jarret, "The life salvor problem in admiralty", in Yale Law Journal, 1954, 779.

Although it regulates the situation in the same way, the Draft preferred to tackle the problem from a less limited and more general perspective. Not only is the towage contract included in the law, but also all those contracts to which the evolution of nautical craft and of maritime traffic may give rise. Within the terms of such a contract, an exceptional salvage service for one of the contracting parties may be performed by another party, no longer in terms of a pre-existent duty but rather of a voluntary action, such as is typical of salvage at sea.[320]

For example, with regard to the possibility of salvage services being rendered without the use of nautical craft as allowed by the CMI Draft: let us assume that there is a shore crane, or one mounted on a pontoon, which, under a particular contract, is lightening a cargo which, as a result of shifting in the hold, could cause the vessel to list; let us further assume that listing does occur during the lightening operations, to such an extent that it is probable that the vessel will overturn and sink in port, and that therefore the crane carries out a special service to keep the vessel in good trim, preventing further listing and allowing further lightening of cargo to be effected by other cranes called in. It cannot be denied that such a service represents salvage under Article 3.6 of the Draft and as such must be remunerated.

41. MARITIME LIENS; GUARANTEES; JURISDICTION, ETC. AND LIMITATION OF LIABILITY

The Draft has also introduced a special rule about "maritime liens", related to salvage and salvage remuneration. There is no equivalent to it in the present international regulations, although the rule contains a provision which excepts the rules existing under other international Conventions and under the individual national laws of the Contracting States,[321] and prevents the salvor to whom an adequate guarantee has been offered or given by those interested in the salved properties from bringing a claim for the recognition or preservation of his maritime lien.[322]

Various regulations relating to the issue of a guarantee by those interested in the salved properties govern not only their duty to issue such a guarantee, but also the duty of the shipowner to make all possible efforts for the salvor to

---

320. Thus the case of *The North Goodwin No. 16* [1980] 1 Lloyd's Rep. 71 *et seq.*, which clarifies the precise demarcation line between pre-existing contractual duty and a voluntary action with the purpose of removing the danger.

321. Specific provisions regarding priorities supporting the salvors' claims exist in the 1926 and 1967 Brussels Conventions on maritime liens, and in the 1952 Brussels Convention relating to the arrest of sea-going vessels.

322. See O'May, *op. cit.*, 1433 *et seq.*

be supplied with the necessary guarantees by those interested in the cargo as well, especially when the latter consist of many individuals. There is a corresponding duty on the part of those interested in the salved properties not to remove those properties from their place of arrival, following the salvage, until the guarantees have been issued, as provided by the Draft.[323]

A further change made by the Draft, following the provisions of the 1980 LOF in the respect, is the provision that the competent legal authority may grant the salvor a provisional payment and that the Contracting States should arrange for the publication of those arbitration awards normally reserved for the parties involved in the procedure.[324] There is no doubt that the number of legal precedent cases about salvage at sea made available to the public are few, because the parties often use the standard contract form and the arbitration procedure provided in it, and confidentiality habitually surrounds the decisions.

Moreover, as with the more recent international Conventions, the Draft contains a rule about jurisdiction which allows the parties various alternatives as to forum, indicating that as: the forum of the place where the debtor has his business headquarters; the forum of the place where the salved properties have been brought and redelivered; that of the place where the salved properties have been sequestrated; that where the guarantee has been supplied; or that where the salvage operations were performed.

This rule also leaves the parties free to choose a forum which is not one of those indicated, or to take the dispute to arbitration.[325]

A final and rather important change is the insertion, in the proposed text of the Convention, of a rule governing the possibility, for the Contracting States, of allowing the salvors to limit their own liability in ways and terms similar to those provided by the 1976 Convention on the Limitation of Liability for Maritime Claims.

Originally the Draft imposed a duty on the Contracting States to adopt a set of rules similar to, if not identical with, that of the 1976 Convention. During the Montreal Conference, the argument according to which a duty of the type would have been a hindrance to the ratification of the new Convention on

---

323. O'May, *op. loc. cit.*, 1433 *et seq.*; Ferrarini, *op. ult. cit.*, 406.

324. The mandatory publication of awards is not provided for in the Draft in view of the strong opposition shown towards the introduction of this provision, especially by the larger professional salvage companies which, as supported by O'May, *op. cit.*, 1434, *et seq.*, "are mostly involved in Lloyd's Form arbitrations and are on record as opposing mandatory publication. Other industries, they contend, are not required to disclose their profit figures on particular contracts to competitors and interested observers."

325. Of interest also is the provision of Art. 4.5.2 of the Draft which, reflecting the significance of Arts. 1.3 and 11.2 of the 1969 Convention on Civil Liability of Fuel Oil Pollution Damages, lays down that for vessels belonging to Contracting States, and used in commercial service, the jurisdiction is that generally established by Art. 4.5.1 of the Draft.

Salvage (since such acceptance would have been conditional on the ratification of the 1976 Convention), however, prevailed.[326]

42. APPROVAL OF THE CMI DRAFT AND CONVERSION INTO INTERNATIONAL CONVENTION (LONDON 1989)

Following approval by the CMI Assembly at the Montreal Conference, the CMI Draft was put before IMO's Legal Committee for study before being presented at the Diplomatic Conference, for discussion and approval.

During the procedure required for the Draft's final approval, it underwent further amendments, with the aim—not always achieved—of eliminating those deficiences in the wording of the regulations which this author had himself pointed out. Thus the process of introducing the new law on salvage into uniform international law was finally completed. This is of particular importance, especially if it is remembered that salvage at sea, originally a strictly private law, has taken on, to some extent, the quality of a law of a basically private nature but with public aspects and features, such as to fulfil, internationally, and especially with regard to coastal states, the special and by no means negligible function of an instrument to achieve a uniform policy to protect the environment.[327]

Of course the approval of a new Convention, whose law is based on that proposed by the CMI Draft, demanded the further revision of the standard international contract (Lloyd's Open Form) in order to adapt that to the new principles introduced, and to prevent serious discrepancies between the law and the contract.

As has been correctly noted, the two documents—the CMI Draft and the new LOF 1980—formed the basis for a deeper and more penetrating reform of the institute of salvage at sea, and represented the initial steps in the process of international reform, the conclusion of this process being the

326. See on this topic: Brice, *op. cit.*, 308 *et seq.*; O'May, *op. cit.*, 1433; Coulthard, *op. cit.*, 61 *et seq.*, and Nielsen, CMI Report to IMO, 32, which explains the *ratio* of the new provision: "It was generally recognised that salvors ought to be able to engage fully in difficult salvage operations without fears of subsequently being held liable without limitation. The system of the 1976 London Limitation Convention was considered to provide an adequate solution to this problem which is particularly relevant in cases where the salvage services are not performed from a salvage vessel. The Sub-Committee had proposed to the Montreal Conference that is should be a duty of the parties to the new convention to establish a right equivalent to the 1976 Convention concerning limitation for salvors. This was much debated, and on the strength of the arguments of many national MLA delegations that such a rule might make draft convention unacceptable, it was decided to propose only a recommendation to this effect."

327. See on this point "Revisione della Convenzione di Bruxelles del 1910 in tema di assistenza e salvataggio", in Dir. Mar., 1985, 459. See, more recently, Gold, "A Time for Needed Change, Current Developments in the International Law of Maritime Salvage" in K. D. Troup (ed.), Proceedings of the 9th International Tug Convention; and Gold, "No Cure No Pay? . . . No Way! Towards a New International Regime for Marine Salvage" in *Cinquième Congrès Annuel de la Société Quebecoise de Droit International*, University of Montreal, 1988.

approval of the new LOF 1990 and of the new International Convention on Salvage at Sea 1989, in London. The dual purpose of these documents is now that of achieving increasingly complete co-operation between States and private party interests, there having been established within the law a fair balancing of the public aims of the one, and of the commercial interests of the other.[328]

---

328 Coulthard, *op. cit.*, 67, where he maintains: "should the Draft Convention become widely adopted in its present or similar form, it will surely affect the use of the LOF 1980 and may result in that agreement undergoing a further revision in order to align itself with international practice. On the other hand, there are evident deficiencies in the Draft Convention which may require that its provisions be reviewed as well. Ultimately, one can only consider both documents as initial steps towards the co-operation between sovereign States and commercial interests which is essential to the continued efficiency of ocean transportation." On the subject of marine pollution in the case of accidents, see the recent study by Gaeta, "La difesa del mare nel diritto italiano", in Dir. Mar., 1984, 839, *et seq*.

PART THREE

ACCOMPLISHING THE REFORM OF INTERNATIONAL SALVAGE LAW AND ITS CONSEQUENCES

CHAPTER FIVE

THE LONDON INTERNATIONAL CONVENTION ON SALVAGE 1989 AND ITS SPHERE OF APPLICATION

43. THE SCOPE OF THE NEW CONVENTION AND THE NEW ELEMENTS INTRODUCED

Though differing to some extent from the draft proposed by the IMO Legal Committee, which had revised and elaborated, without altering its philosophy, the CMI 1981 Montreal Draft, the Convention approved in London on 28 April 1989, largely follows the same structure of regulations as drawn up by the afore-mentioned international organs, and represents a decisive and innovatory turning point in international salvage law, introducing once and for all the special consideration of the protection of the environment as an element in evaluating the salvage and the *quantum meruit* of the salvors.[329]

As has been recently and frequently pointed out,[330] the more serious maritime accidents (e.g., that recently involving *The Exxon Valdez* in Alaska),

---

329. See in merit Nielsen, "International Convention on Salvage, report to CMI" in *CMI Newsletter*, December 1989 and Id., "Overview—Improvement and Deficiences from the Legal View Point" in *Salvage, Lloyd's Press Conference papers*, (London, 1990), 53; and in Italy, Caliendo, "Osservazioni sul progetto di Convenzione IMO in materia di assistenza e salvataggio", in *Trasporti* 1988, 153.

330. In merit see the afore-mentioned Gold, "Marine Salvage: Towards a New Regime" in *Journal of Maritime Law and Commerce*, 1989, 407; Allen, "International Convention on Salvage and LOF 90" in *11th International Tug Convention and International Marine Salvage Symposium*, (Halifax 1990, Surrey 1991), 127; Olsen, "The 1989 Salvage Convention, some problems solved and some problems exacerbated" in *IBA Conference*, New York 1990; Brice, "The New Salvage Convention: green seas and grey areas" in [1990] L.M.C.L.Q. 32; Mensah, "Deficiencies found in the regime under the 1910 Convention", in *Salvage*, Lloyd's Press Conference papers (London, 1990), 1; and, in Italy, Gaeta, "La Convenzione di Londra del 1989 sul soccorso in acqua" in Dir. Mar., 1991, 291; and, more recently, Darling and Smith, *LOF 90 and the New Salvage Convention* (London, 1991). The position taken by this very recent book would appear rather strange, as it seems to give more weight and prominence to English contract law than to the uniform international discipline of the new Convention. The title, which places the LOF 1990 in a position of priority and eminence with respect to the Convention, is symptomatic, as is the lack of references relating to the international panorama and the absolute absence of any references to doctrine and jurisprudence other than English. It is worth noting that these authors continue, in our opinion (see Vincenzini, *International Regulation of Salvage at Sea* (London, 1987), 103), to support the erroneous theory according to which a LOF 1990 contract between two non-English subjects (to whom the Convention's rules should apply) is governed by English law, not as the law of the form of the contract and of the arbitration procedure, but as the law of the contract from a substantive point of view.

with their destructive potential no longer limited to the ship and the cargo involved, represent such a threat to the environment and to related interests, such as the fishing industry and tourism, not to mention human health and the preservation of flora and fauna, as to render more stringent measures essential. This encompasses not only the disposition (already existing) of international regulations entitling coastal states to take all those measures necessary to prevent, limit or eliminate heavy environmental damages, but also the formation of an incentive for salvors not to apply themselves merely to the salving of the ship and her cargo, as was the case in the past under the old 1910 Brussels Convention, but to consider the prevention and limitation of environmental damage almost as the principal aim of the salvage operations.[331]

Using as a starting point the so-called "Montreal Compromise", which (apart from the salvage of traditional properties—human life, ship, cargo and freight) had introduced the protection of the environment into the purposes of the salvors, and developing by means of various elaborations prepared by the IMO Legal Committee, the draft of the new Convention finally reached the London Conference. The changes and additions made there did not distort the structure of the original draft, leaving it unaltered and without betraying the fundamental aims of the new law.

Therefore, in the paragraphs which follow we shall examine, point by point, the innovations introduced and the structure of the new international salvage law. We apologise for the sparsity of the bibliography, and the even sparser jurisprudence cited, due both to the brief time between the approval of the new Convention and the date of publication of this work, and because the courts have not yet had time to decide on cases governed by the Convention as it has not yet come into force, the minimum number of required ratifications not yet having been achieved.[332]

331. In this respect Gaeta, "La Convenzione di Londra del 1989 sul soccorso in acqua", *op. cit.*, correctly notes that prior to the safeguards provided by the new Convention on salvage, the protection of the environment was the subject of the international movement for the protection of the marine environment, the basis of which was laid down in the two Brussels Conventions of 29 November 1969, one on the intervention on the high seas by Coastal States in the case of accidents from which oil pollution derives or may derive (integrated by the London Protocol of 2 November 1973 for cases of pollution by substances other than hydrocarbons), and the other on civil liability for damages caused by oil pollution (integrated by the Brussels International Convention of 18 December 1971 on the establishment of an International Fund for the compensation of oil pollution damages). On the concept of international environmental law, see also the 1982 Convention, in Rawakrishna, "Environmental Concerns and the New Law of the Sea", in *Journal of Maritime Law and Commerce*, 1985, 1.

332. Rather sceptical as to the prompt entry into force of the Convention is Allen, "International Convention on Salvage and LOF 90", *op. cit.*, who points out that "despite the noble sentiments expressed at the conference, there has hardly been a rush to adopt the Convention. Indeed only two States have done so to date; Mexico on 20 September 1989 followed by Nigeria on 15 March 1990, neither of which could be regarded as major maritime nations", and Nielsen, "International Convention on Salvage, report to CMI", *op. cit.*, who concludes his report with the following words: " . . . the result was a compromise according to which 15 states should consent to the Convention before it can enter into force, and a minimum of 10 states can call for a

However, as we shall see further ahead, the new Convention has already produced its beneficial effects on international contract law with the publication of the LOF 1990, bringing substantial changes to the LOF 1980 which, though innovatory, contained serious flaws and deficiencies.[333] The Convention, when it comes into force, will have the further, and by no means insignificant, merit of rendering the uniformity of individual national laws on salvage practically useless, by becoming applicable as the *lex fori* every time legal or arbitration proceedings are brought in a Contracting State within the sphere of the material governed by the Convention, thus constituting, finally, a true and proper international salvage law.[334]

The new elements introduced into the wording of the uniform Convention are the fruits of the elaboration of the new concept of salvage, no longer circumscribed by the limits of a purely private nature within which it had been confined by the 1910 Uniform Convention for almost a century, but governed rather by the recognition of the natural and compelling public function which salvage at sea may and does fulfil in preventing, limiting and removing environmental damage. In addition, it is recognised that only a legal incentive to professional salvors will lead them—already in difficulty because of the high running costs of a salvage firm and because of the uncertainties of their interventions—adequately to refurbish their equipment with a view to salvage operations intended at removing or preventing pollution, and to maintain an organisation of highly professional personnel and technologically advanced equipment.[335]

Therefore, it is our opinion that the principal innovatory and basic elements of the new Convention are the following:

(1) The necessity of protecting the environment.
(2) The need to provide the salvage industry with essential and

revision. Consequently one may expect that some time will pass until the Convention enters into force. However, it may be of comfort to the supporters of the Convention that some states may decide to enforce the Convention in their national legislation before the Convention enters into force, and in particular that Lloyd's Forms rather soon may be amended to incorporate the rules of the Convention."

333. See Chapter 3 of this work, "Salvage at sea in international contractual practice", and the bibliography cited in that chapter. See also, Caliendo, "Osservazioni sul progetto di Convenzione", *op. cit.*, 160. Lately, Kovats, "Lloyd's Open Form: Salvors' gain", in *Seatrade* 1990, 75.

334. Thus Gaeta, "La Convenzione di Londra", *op. cit.*, 293 who, moreover, correctly notes that complete national regulations governing salvage will be necessary only if the individual State reserves to itself the right to not apply the Convention in those cases foreseen by Art. 30(1) of the said Convention.

335. Cf. Lacey, "Expansions of salvage industry to meet requirement and the need for substantial rewards to sustain industry" in Salvage, Lloyd's Press Conference papers, (London, 1990), 11; Caliendo, "Osservazioni sul progetto di Convenzione", *op. cit.*, 154; and Allen, "International Convention", *op. cit.*, 127. On this point the last faithfully reproduces the wording of the preamble to the Convention where it states: "conscious of the major contribution which efficient and timely salvage operations can make to the safety of vessels and other property in danger and to the protection of the enviroment, convinced of the need to ensure that adequate incentives are available to persons to undertake salvage operations in respect of vessels and other property in danger". Also see Kerr, "The 1989 Salvage Convention", *op. cit.*, 506.

adequate incentives in order to obtain its prompt and valid intervention in cases of maritime casualties which may cause environmental damage, or, in the case of damage which has already occurred, to limit the extent and the more harmful consequences.

(3) The recognition, even if partial and limited, of so-called "liability salvage" as an element in the determination of the salvor's reward.

(4) The need to extend the law on salvage to other properties at risk, no longer restricting it to the ship and her cargo, i.e., the need to extend the category of properties which may represent the object of salvage.

(5) The need to extend to the utmost the field of application of the Convention's régime, i.e., to render the new Convention a true and proper international salvage law.

(6) The necessity of creating an internationally uniform concept of salvage, avoiding distinctions between assistance, salvage and recovery of wreck.

(7) The necessity of not restricting the application of international salvage law to maritime waters, but extending its provisions to all navigable waters and to all other waters.[336]

44. THE SPHERE AND AREA OF APPLICATION

As we have already mentioned, the intention of new Convention (as is, in fact, declared in its preamble) was to provide an international salvage legislation with as broad a scope as possible with regard to its geographical sphere of application, and, because of the possibility of involving the maximum possible number of parties in the application of the new international uniform regulations, independent of whether the governments of such parties have ratified the Convention or not. Consequently, the wider concept of *lex fori* has been preferred to the restrictive concept of the application of the Convention's regulations to subjects belonging, entirely or in part, to Contracting States, as was (and still is) established by the 1910 Convention.

As the new Convention thus leaves out of consideration any element of internationality of the subjects, it is applied each and every time that legal or arbitration proceedings are brought in a Contracting State; therefore the new regulations are applicable even when the active or passive subject of the salvage operation belongs to a non-Contracting State, and even when both sub-

---

336. For Gaeta, "La Convenzione di Londra", *op. cit.*, 295, one can no longer speak of "salvage at sea", but rather one must speak of "salvage on water". The wording of Art. 1(a) of the Convention will create problems in the United Kingdom where the House of Lords, in *The Goring* [1988] A.C. 831, held that salvage may not be extended beyond tidal waters. See also: Brice, "The New Salvage Convention: green seas and grey areas", in [1990] L.M.C.L.Q. 33.

jects belong to non-Contracting States[337] or to the same State in which the legal or arbitration proceedings are brought (obviously this last State is entitled not to apply the Convention in those cases foreseen by Article 30(1) of the Convention).[338]

Having noted that the Convention's mechanism for extending its application to the highest possible number of subjects, whether or not they belong to Contracting States but based on the concept of *lex fori*, has probably borrowed from Article 15 of the 1976 Convention on limitation of liability for maritime claims, it must also be noted that the new wording of the Convention has brought about extensive innovations even to the geographical sphere of application and to the category of active and passive subjects of salvage.

In fact the new Convention can no longer be qualified, as in the past, as an international law of salvage at sea, but has rather become merely an *international law of salvage*, since Article 1(a) of the Convention extends the application of the new regulations to all navigable waters or to "any other waters whatsoever".

The Convention is thus automatically extended to cover navigable internal waters (rivers, canals, lakes) and any other unnavigable waters; any exclusion of internal waters from the application of the Convention becomes a simple exception to the general rule, given that the Convention grants the right to Contracting States, at the time of signature, ratification, acceptance, approval of or adhesion to the Convention (Article 30 (1)(a) and (b)), not to apply the Convention:

> "(a) when the salvage operation takes place in inland waters and all vessels involved are of inland navigation;
> (b) when the salvage operations take place in inland waters and no vessel is involved;"[339]

The existence of the reservation in Article 30(1)(b) of the Convention implies the introduction to the Convention's wording of salvage without the use of nautical craft, whether the salvage is rendered in maritime or inland waters, in so far as the Convention grants States which have ratified, accepted, approved or adhered to it the right to exclude its application when this particular type of salvage is rendered in inland waters.

337. With regard to the discussion in doctrine and in jurisprudence as to the requirement that only one, or of necessity both, of the subjects of the salvage belong to Contracting States, see Chapter 1, para. 2 of this work. On this point, with reference also to the IMO draft, see Caliendo, "Osservazioni sul progetto di Convenzione", *op. cit.*, 158

338. Thus there is no longer any need for national legislation on salvage, except for the marginal aspects provided for by the Convention under Arts. 5, 10(2), 11, 13(2), 15(2), 16(1), 24. Thus, precisely, Gaeta, "La Convenzione di Londra", *op. cit.*, 296.

339. As already incidentally noted, the introduction of the new Convention into the laws of the United Kingdom will certainly result in the use of the reservation by that State, in compliance with that declared by the House of Lords in the *The Goring*, which held: "The House of Lords, without examining the maritime law of salvage, assumed that tidality was an element of the cause of action and consequently that British courts of admiralty had no jurisdiction to hear claims for

In addition, upon reading Article 1(a), it is clearly indicated, in qualifying the salvage operation, that this must consist of an act or an activity undertaken with the purpose of assisting a ship or any other property which is in peril in waters, without, however, indicating that the salvage must of necessity be rendered using nautical craft.

By co-ordinating these regulations one therefore arrives at the explicit inclusion of salvage without nautical craft, which was totally absent from the text of the 1910 Convention, though the wording of Article 1 of that Convention did lead to the conclusion that salvage without nautical craft was possible, but only at sea.[340]

Likewise, the sphere of application of the new Convention is widened in respect of the objects of the salvage, as, apart from the traditional properties at risk—ship, cargo and freight—Article 1(c) states that "property" means "any property not permanently and intentionally attached to the shoreline and includes freight at risk". Considering the fact that Article 3 explicitly excludes "fixed or floating platforms or . . . mobile offshore drilling units when such platforms or units are on location engaged in the exploration, exploitation or production of sea-bed mineral resources" from the application of the Convention, creating serious problems of interpretation which we shall examine at a later point, it is clear that the sphere of application of the new Convention in respect of the objects is extended not only to the property in peril "on board" the salved vessel ("any things on board", i.e. supplies, bunkers etc.), but to all other property not permanently and intentionally "attached to the shoreline" which may find itself in peril in navigable waters of any type whatsoever or other waters.[341]

With this, in our opinion, it is admitted that the salvage of any property whatsoever which, for one reason or another, may find itself at risk in navigable or other waters, whether or not nautical craft are involved, falls within the sphere of the future application of the 1989 Convention's regulations.

Though granting that a literal interpretation of the new regulations would lead to this extreme conclusion (an absurd example could be that of a caravan which, having fallen into a pond, is salved from the shore without the use of nautical craft, when the suit for remuneration is brought before the courts of a Contracting State), it is clear that, in so far as the objects of the salvage are

non-tidal salvage rewards." See in merit, Hastings, "Non-Tidal Salvage in the United Kingdom: Goring, Goring, Gone", op. cit., 473.

340. In this respect see para. 4 of this book and the CMI Draft, para. 40, which instead explicitly admitted this type of salvage.

341. Nielsen, "Overview—Improvements and Deficiences from the Legal Viewpoint", op. cit., 53, who explicitly indicates the other properties mentioned by the Convention: "Cargo lost from a ship such as a drifting or sunken container; a floating dock in danger, not only on the rare occasions where it is towed in open sea and perhaps lost by the tug, but probably also if it is on fire or sinking at the yard; fishing gears can be subject to salvage; this was expressly excluded by Art. 13 of the 1910 Convention, fishfarms, which are becoming more and more frequent and perhaps also more and more frequently in danger at sea, can of course be the subject of salvage under the new convention." Thus also, Olsen, "The 1989 Salvage Convention", op. cit.

concerned, the purpose of extending the Convention's sphere of application was to include as many properties at risk as possible, creating a general category and indicating the exclusions as exceptions (Article 3), rather than to supply (as in the past) a more or less definite indication of the objects of salvage. This former practice caused not a few problems for the reader, especially when—at a distance from the date of approval and entry into force of the Convention—various substantial technological developments of salved goods rendered it necessary to enlarge the category of objects by means of doctrine or jurisprudence of much wider interpretation.[342]

Moreover, with regard to the object of salvage, the new Convention does not apply to warships or non-merchant vessels belonging to or operated by a State, when such vessels are entitled, after their salvage, to the immunity envisaged by the principles of international law, unless the State in question elects to apply Conventions regulations to such vessels. The matter is, therefore, as has been accepted,[343] left to the national legislation of the individual States.

The wording of the new Convention is innovatory from this point of view too; in fact it completely ignores the 1967 Brussels Protocol which modified Article 14 of the 1910 Convention, having recognised the limited success enjoyed by that Protocol in the international maritime world, which, indeed, had received a very cool reception.

Later we shall see how the Convention has attempted to provide a specific provision for state-owned goods or properties to prevent the afore-mentioned exclusion of military vessels from the sphere of the Convention from causing doubts in respect of any cargoes transported by such vessels, and prevent these cargoes, where they are not of a commercial nature, being erroneously considered as the objects of salvage under the Convention.

45. SALVAGE OPERATIONS CONTROLLED BY PUBLIC AUTHORITIES

Salvage operations may result from private interventions, be they spontaneous or contractual, or from the intervention of public authorities. The new Convention (as in effect did the 1910 Convention) regulates only salvage interventions which fall within the sphere of private initiative, without

---

342. Nielsen, "Report", in *CMI Newsletter*, Autumn 1989, 2, and Gaeta, "Nave", in *Enciclopedia del diritto*, XXVII, 608.

343. Gaeta, "La Convenzione di Londra", *op. cit.*, 294; even if Art. 4(2) of the Convention speaks of warships, which is a more restricted category than that of military vessels, for Gaeta the latter vessels fall within the sphere of the Convention's regulations in accordance with the principle of the regulation itself, asserting that "non-merchant" vessels belonging to and operated by the State are covered by the regulation. With regards to the IMO Draft, with mention of the discussions which led to the exclusion of military vessels from the Convention, see Caliendo, "Osservazioni sul progetto di Convenzione", *op. cit.* 159.

influencing those controlled by public authorities in those specific circumstances in which the latter may or must intervene, thus affording the individual States total liberty to apply their own national laws in the way they find most opportune.

It has, however, been noted that some controversial aspects of salvage operations controlled by public authorities have been treated by Article 5 of the new Convention, by means of a sort of compromise between the right of control existing in the national law of the State involved in the salvage operations and the salvors' right to benefit from the new Convention when the latter render salvage services under the control and by order of the public authority.[344] In effect, under the new Convention, once the organisational phase is at an end, the salvage operations rendered by the public authority or carried out under its control may fall—for the purposes of their regulation—within the Convention's uniform provisions. It therefore follows that all parties carrying out the afore-mentioned operations, whether they be the public authority or a private interest under the control and orders of that authority, may claim the benefit of all rights deriving from the Convention's uniform text and take advantage of all rights (as has been pointed out) foreseen by the Convention in respect of remuneration or special compensation, and so on.[345]

On this subject it must be noted that, with regard to Italian law, the provisions of Articles 69 and 70 of the Navigation Code fall perfectly within the Convention's system, because of the fact that the Convention's international regulations—as we have already pointed out—do not require individual national laws to contain rules of express reference in order for the Convention's regulations to become applicable.[346]

In particular we feel it is worth looking at Article 5(3) of the Convention, which would appear to contain a dual reference to the national law of the State operating the salvage, the article applying primarily to the organisation and control of the salvage operations, leaving it to the Convention to regulate rights and benefits in favour of the salvors, a further reference to the national law of the State involved being made when the salvage is performed directly by public authorities.[347]

---

344. Gold, "Marine Salvage: Towards a New Regime", *op. cit.*, 498.

345. Thus Gaeta, "La Convenzione", *op. cit.*, 296. Of interest in this respect is the case cited by Nielsen, "Overview—Improvements and Deficiences", *op. cit.*, 57, of the Russian submarine which ran aground near a Swedish base. It was first surrounded by vessels of the Swedish Navy and then salved and refloated by a tug which, having acted upon the orders of the Swedish State Navy, asked the latter for salvage remuneration. After three levels of judgment the Swedish Supreme Court rejected the State Navy's argument that the tug's services were not a salvage operation but a military operation, and awarded the tug remuneration for the operation.

346. Thus Vincenzini, "Soccorso per ordine dell'autorità", *op. cit.*, 266 and, more recently, Gaeta, "La Convenzione", *op. cit.*

347. The opinion of Wall, "Overview—Improvements and deficiences from a Government viewpoint" in *Salvage,* Lloyd's Press Conference papers, (London, 1990), 73, is interesting in this respect. He maintains: "as paragraph 2 entitles salvors acting under public authority control to avail themselves of the rights and remedies provided for in this Convention it is possible that this could affect the provisions of national law or other Conventions. Therefore we consider that

46. THE RIGHTS OF COASTAL STATES

One of the primary and most interesting aspects of the new international regulations on salvage is the problem arising from a certain interconnection between the regulations of the institute of salvage, strongly characterised nowadays by the need to bear in mind not only the salvage of the traditional properties of ship and cargo but also the protection of the environment, and the international public and private regulations relating to the struggle against marine and water pollution in general and to the protection of the coasts and connected interests.

Later we shall consider in greater depth the aspects of this interconnection, the problems deriving from it and the solutions which have been or could be proposed.[348] It must also be noted that a specific rule of the new Convention (Article 9) expressly acknowledges the right of coastal States to adopt all those measures held to be necessary, in accordance with general principles of international law, for the purpose of protecting their coastlines and related interests against pollution caused by a maritime accident from which serious environmental damage may result.

Therefore, in this rule it is confirmed that the coastal State is entitled to give orders and instructions in respect of the salvage, even if the rule does not seem to add anything to the current international public law which grants coastal States the right to adopt all measures necessary to protect their coasts from pollution; in this respect the suggestion that the reference to the Brussels Convention of 29 November 1969 (on interventions on the high seas by coastal States in the case of casualties which have caused or may cause environmental pollution) must not be forgotten would seem to be appropriate.[349]

If, on one hand, the new Convention leaves the coastal State the right freely to make arrangements for protection from pollution risks to its coast and environment, on the other hand the Convention takes on the burden (in Article 11) of dealing with the problem of so-called "maritime leprosy", already discussed in this work, obliging coastal States to lend a certain measure of co-operation in order to facilitate the salvors in finding a port of refuge for the properties in distress.

Unfortunately the rule contains less of an obligation and more of a

while the salvor cannot claim double recovery he can avail himself of the Convention's provisions which can override national law. If this is correct we can accept it as the general intent is to encourage salvors whether they are operating voluntarily or under public authority control."

348. On the theme of anti-pollution regulations, see Comenale Pinto, "La responsabilità per inquinamento da idrocarburi fuoriusciti da navi e il regime di norme di diritto uniforme" in *Diritto dei Trasporti*, 1990, I, 11.

349. Thus Gaeta, "La Convenzione", *op. cit*, 292. In this respect see also Gold, "Marine Salvage: Towards a New Regime", *op. cit.* 498 and Nielsen, "Report to CMI", *op. cit.*, 2. For a statistical list of all major cases representing a serious danger of marine pollution see Peet, "Salvage, Hazardous Cargoes and Environmental Protection" in *Salvage,* Lloyd's Press Conference papers (London, 1990), 25.

recommendation to coastal States, and does not therefore provide an adequate solution to this serious and delicate problem for the salvors.

It is, however, to be hoped that the entry into force of the new United Nations Convention on the Law of the Sea 1982 will provide the international community with technical-legal instruments of a general nature for the protection of the marine environment, which, being everyone's property, is a common asset requiring common defensive laws. In this way the co-ordination of the two Conventions—that of the private law now under consideration and that of public law as already mentioned—may give birth to a uniform regime acceptable to both the maritime industry and to the international community.[350]

47. THE COMING INTO FORCE OF THE NEW CONVENTION

While on one hand we must rejoice at the big step ahead taken by international salvage law with the approval of the new Convention, on the other hand we must express our regret that serious difficulties are likely to occur pending its entry into force. There will be substantial differences to be addressed when disputes relating to contract salvage are discussed on the basis of the new LOF 90 (which has accepted and introduced into its text the basic principles of the new Convention), and when the salvage, be it spontaneous, obligatory or contractual, regulated by inadequate and antiquated forms of contract, is governed by the old but still current provisions of the 1910 Convention or by the individual national laws applicable to such cases. National laws which, as in the case of Italian law, take into account neither the environmental factor or the aims which the new type of salvage intends to attain in the prevention, limitation and elimination of the environmental damage, and the consequences which, in respect of salvage remuneration, ensue for the salvors on the basis of the introduction of the new principles.

The courts of the individual States should therefore proceed to the interpretative application of the informative principles of the new Convention, *de jure condendo*, in the hope that the individual national legislations introduce

---

350. See Gold, "Marine Salvage: Towards a New Regime", op. cit. 499 and the suggestions made by Peet, *op. cit.*, 38, who declares: "the present situation may be unsatisfactory, the new salvage convention, once in force, will not help much to solve the problems. Amendments to the new Salvage Convention to improve arrangements with respect to ports of refuge are highly unlikely at a time when the Convention is still brand new and has not even entered into force. One way to develop better guidelines towards the availability of ports of refuge which has been suggested would be to pursue the issue at the Marine Environment Protection Committee of the International Maritime Organization which could, as a minimum, develop such guidelines on the conditions, circumstances and terms under which any port or harbour can be designated and used as a place of shelter."

the Convention's principles even before the Convention itself enters into force.[351]

The problem arises from the fact that a high number of ratifications (15) is required for the new Convention to enter into force, and that on the basis of the experience of the other Conventions, it will certainly take many years to achieve this minimum number.[352]

351. Gold, "Marine Salvage: Towards a New Regime", *op. cit.*, 503 and Rawakrishna, *op. cit.* 1. See also Nielsen, "International Convention on Salvage", *op. cit.*, 6, who hopes that some States may decide to introduce the discipline of the Convention into their national legislation even before the Convention enters into force.

352. All are in agreement on this point, see: Olsen, "The 1989 Salvage Convention", *op. cit.*, 14, Gold, "Marine Salvage: Towards a New Regime", *op. cit.*, 502, Wall, *op. cit.*, 89, Nielsen, "International Convention on Salvage", *op. cit.*, 6 and, most recently, Darling and Smith, *op. cit.* 50.

CHAPTER SIX

THE INNOVATORY PRINCIPLES OF THE NEW INTERNATIONAL REGULATION OF SALVAGE

48. OBJECTS AND ACTIVE AND PASSIVE SUBJECTS OF SALVAGE

In discussing the identification of the objects of salvage under the provisions of the new Convention, it must be repeated that these provisions have brought about a relevant widening of the traditional categories of properties, which were limited to the vessel, cargo, stores, bunker and freight, if at risk, by introducing the new concept of "property", as defined in Article 1(c). Articles 3 and 4 contain exceptions to the general category.

We have already discussed the exception made in Article 4 regarding State-owned vessels and the new provision introduced to support it; we shall not therefore be repeating ourselves in respect of this aspect. We shall limit ourselves to pointing out that the exclusion operated in Article 3 in respect of "fixed or floating platforms or . . . mobile offshore drilling units when such platforms or units are on location engaged in the exploration, exploitation or production of sea-bed mineral resources", would appear to be in contrast to the expansive tendency of the concept of salvage expressed in the new Convention. Platforms and drilling units are, nowadays, somewhat more important than simple properties in danger, to the extent that they represent, on a par with oil tankers, one of the main factors of risk in respect of marine pollution. It does not therefore seem to make sense specifically to include the environmental factor in the purposes of salvage, also introducing elements of so-called "liability salvage" to the concept of salvage, only to exclude from its objects a category of properties which is not only extremely similar to that of ships and their polluting cargoes, but which also, and to an even greater extent, may represent a possible source of damage to the environment.[353]

353. In this respect we prefer to quote a passage from Olsen, "The 1989 Salvage Convention", *op. cit.*, because of its clarity and punctiliousness. This author declares: "That leaves us with the anomalous situation whereby, for example, a drilling rig that breaks adrift becomes an object of salvage as it drifts away from its location, but a drilling rig that catches fire and requires fire-fighting operations by the same salvage tugs would not be an object of salvage. It smacks of casuistry to suggest that the salvor's entitlement to a salvage award would depend in the case of a drilling rig fire on whether the fire was sufficiently serious to cause drilling operations to be suspended, but it is possible, it seems to me, to argue that if operations are suspended as a result of a

153

It must be noted that the exclusion made in Article 3, represents a substantial modification of both the CMI and IMO drafts, both of which, rightly in our opinion, included platforms and drilling units in the category of salvable properties in so far as they are structures capable of navigation.[354] We do not, however, share the opinion that, since pipelines are not mentioned in Article 3, they are not excluded from the category of salvable objects, as, by accepting this theory, a pipeline connected to a fixed platform would represent a salvage object while the platform would not, which would be an absurd situation.[355]

It will be interesting to see, in the near future, the solutions which will be given by arbitrators when they have to adjudicate eventual salvage operations rendered, in a technical sense, to platforms or drilling units for which a LOF 1990 contract has been stipulated, since Clause 2 of the new wording of the LOF contract includes and incorporates the provisions of Article 1(a) to (e) of the new Convention but does not include the exclusion made by Article 3, which could lead the arbitrators to the conclusion that—for LOF 90—platforms and drilling units are properties which may be the object of salvage without any exclusion or restriction whatsoever.[356]

A final observation on the subject of salvable property is that both fishing gear—expressly excluded from salvage by Article 13 of the 1910 Convention—and fishing farms may, under the new uniform international law, represent salvable property.

It could also be argued that the new Convention, by introducing the environmental factor as one of the elements characterising the purposes of salvage, may have extended to the environment itself the attribution of a salvable property, since, in effect, an asset of public dominion, belonging to the inter-

fire, the unit although on location, would no longer be 'engaged in the exploration, exploitation or production of seabed mineral resources'. I suspect, however, that a Tribunal would find that it was necessary to look at its operations in a more general manner, and not link the entitlement of salvors to an award to the question of whether the rig was actually operating at any particular moment."

354. Caliendo, "Osservazioni sul progetto di Convenzione", *op. cit.*, who correctly notes that, under Italian law, there is an explicit equalisation of mobile platforms with ships in Art. 9 of D.P.R., 24 May 1979, No.886. Upon the extension of the institute of salvage to platforms, see also R. Berlingieri, "Salvataggio e assistenza, ricupero e ritrovamento di relitti della navigazione", in *Novissimo Digesto Italiano App.*, vol. VI, 922; Summerskill, *Oil Rigs Law and Insurance* (London, 1979); and Nielsen, "CMI Report to IMO.", *op. cit.*, 8.

355. Thus Gaeta, "La Convenzione", *op. cit.*, 293, who evidently forgets that even pipelines are fixed to the shoreline, or at least to the actual rigs, of which they thus form an extension.

356. Darling and Smith, *op. cit.*, 87, do not seem to have noted this problem, and limit themselves to remarking on the incorporation of the concept of property operated by the new Convention into the wording of the LOF 1990, but make no mention of the fact that the exclusion indicated by Art. 3 of the Convention is not incorporated. In this respect Gold, "Marine Salvage: Towards a New Regime", *op. cit.*, 497, points out: " . . . however, as the IMO is presently developing a new regime for such structures we will have to await its conclusion in the next few years". However, Nielsen, "Improvements and Deficiences", *op. cit.*, 53, thinks that "a floating dock in danger, not only on the rare occasions where it is towed in open sea and perhaps lost by the tug, but probably also if it is on fire or sinking at the yard" can probably be considered as included in the category of objects of salvage.

national Community or to the individual State affected by the casualty, would be involved. This does not seem possible, however, in the light of the definition of property given by Article 1(c) of the new Convention, which definition adheres to the private law concept of asset, and because of the distinct and separate presence, in Article 1(d), of a definition of "damage to the environment" from which it can be directly deduced that the protection of the environment assumes importance in the law of salvage not so much because the environment is a property to be saved by means of salvage operations, but rather because the protection of the environment can be one of the purposes and duties owed by the salvors when they are called in or when they intervene to assist a "property" in danger in navigable or other waters.[357]

With regard to the identification of the active and passive subjects of salvage, the new Convention's text does not appear to have brought about any relevant or significant innovations in respect of that of the old 1910 convention, as, like the latter, it fails to indicate expressly the two categories of subjects which, by implication, derive from the structure of the various regulations.[358]

Until the basic principles of the new Convention are confirmed or given new and original interpretations in future doctrinarian and legal elaborations, let it suffice to point out that the new international law has also enlarged the category of active subjects of salvage. It is no longer restricted to the owner or the master of the salving vessel and her crew, and, to stretch a point, to those such as pilots and mooring-men who, in a technical sense, are connected with the maritime operation by virtue of their specific services, or to those such as the passengers of the salved or salving vessel who have had occasion to take part in the specific salvage operation. Instead the category is extended to all those who, with nautical or other craft, have had occasion to lend assistance to property in danger which belongs to third parties, the new Convention containing no definition of "salvor"; the salvor may therefore be a professional or an occasional maritime salvor equipped with nautical craft, or any other subject who, with nautical or other craft, renders assistance to property in danger, upon condition that such property is afloat, whatever the nature of the waters.

The nature of the active subjects under the new Convention's provisions can also be drawn *a contrariis* from Article 10 of the Convention, under which, with regard to rendering assistance to any person in danger of being lost at sea, the regulation imposes a duty in this respect upon the *master* of the salving vessel, as the active subject of this type of salvage (Article 10(1)).

There is little to add to that already said of the passive subjects of salvage,

---

357. For a full and precise list of all the International Conventions relating to the protection of the environment, see Peet, *op. cit.*, 35.

358. Cf. Part One of this work, paragraphs 9 and 10, and the doctrine and jurisprudence cited therein.

unless to confirm that, just as this category is considerably widened by the increase in salvable properties, so is that of the subjects connected to these properties by virtue of their ties of ownership. Therefore the category of passive subjects of salvage no longer consists only of owners of ships, cargo, bunkers, stores or freight at risk, but is extended to all those who are the owners of property in danger in navigable waters or in any other waters whatsoever, upon condition that the properties at risk are:

(1) ships or craft, or any structure capable of navigation;
(2) any property not permanently or intentionally attached to the shoreline; or
(3) freight, if at risk.

49. THE NOTION OF SALVAGE: OBLIGATORY, SPONTANEOUS AND CONTRACTUAL

Even in the new Convention the notion of salvage does not take into account any of the distinctions between assistance, salvage and recovery; following the Anglo-Saxon concept of salvage, it is defined as "any act or activity undertaken to assist a vessel or any other property in danger in navigable waters or in any other waters whatsoever" (Article (1)(a).[359]

From this definition there immediately arises a series of innovations enlarging the traditional concept of salvage, which, under the provisions of the Convention, is clearly extended to:

(1) salvage without the use of nautical craft;
(2) salvage in any navigable or non-navigable waters, and not limited to the sea;
(3) salvage rendered to any asset or property which is not permanently and intentionally attached to the shoreline;
(4) the environment, which thus clearly and officially becomes one of the indirect objects of salvage, as the protection of the environment from substantial physical damages represents, in some cases, the principal and primary purpose of the salvage.

Therefore, the notion of salvage undergoes a structural transformation, widening the geographical field of the institute's application, amplifying the category of objects which—if salvage services are rendered—fall within the sphere of the Convention's regulations and its legal and financial consequences, and, finally, widening also the scheme of the modalities and func-

---

359. In the new bilingual text of the Convention there is a terminological inaccuracy in the French version, where "salvage" is translated with the word "assistance", which under French law is quite another thing. It would have been better had the term "sauvetage" been used, as has quite correctly been pointed out. See Gaeta, "La Convenzione di Londra", *op. cit.*, 295.

tions of the salvage operations on a technical level, the latter no longer being limited to the intervention of one ship in favour of another, as was restrictively provided by Article 1 of the 1910 Convention.

It is worth noting that Article 30(1) of the new Convention (Reservations) permits any State, at the time of signature, ratification, acceptance, approval or accession, to reserve the right not to apply the Convention's provisions:

"(a) when the salvage operation takes place in inland waters and all vessels involved are of inland navigation;

(b) when the salvage operations take place in inland waters and no vessel is involved;

(c) when all interested parties are nationals of that State;

(d) when the property involved is maritime cultural property of prehistoric archaeological or historic interest and is situated on the sea-bed."[360]

This does not invalidate the new notion of salvage, however, which in general is that of applying the new Convention to all navigable and non-navigable waters, to all subjects independent of their nationality, and to all properties at risk, whether they have been salved by nautical craft or not. This reservation thus represents, as an exception to the general rule, a mere faculty granted to signatory States.[361]

Under the new Convention the notion of salvage substantially differs and distinguishes itself from the traditional notion foreseen by the 1910 Brussels Convention, in so far as it takes into consideration aspects of public law which strongly affect the aims while maintaining the nature of a private law Convention, overturning in some cases the principles of the institute itself in respect of the subjects and objects of salvage, and of the financial consequences to the former when the salvage allows the protection of the environment.[362]

However, upon perusing the new Convention's wording, one can draw the

---

360. In this respect it is interesting to note that in North-American law the problem of the exclusion of discovery of treasures at sea from the concept of salvage has been discussed on several occasions before the US courts with regard to the existence of danger to a wreck of historical relevance or to treasures or archaeological objects. In this respect see Bruce, "Treasure Salvage beyond the Territorial Sea", in *Journal of Maritime Law and Commerce*, 1989, 1, and the copious jurisprudence cited therein. For this author, "it should be presumed that abandoned shipwrecks and treasure are exposed to marine perils for purposes of maritime salvage law".

361. For the problems which could arise in the United Kingdom following the entry into force of the new Convention, apart from the afore-mentioned Hastings, "Non Tidal Salvage", *op. cit.*, 497, see also Gaskell, "Enactment of the 1989 Salvage Convention in English Law: policy issues", in [1990] L.M.C.L.Q. 355. The latter points out that "the Convention will not allow the UK to revert fully to its original tidal/non tidal distinction and it is submitted that the opportunity should be taken to provide a more liberal regime".

362. See in fact the departure from the principle of "no cure no pay" in the case of a salvage where, though no useful results are achieved in respect of the ship and cargo in peril, useful results are instead obtained in the removal or reduction of an environmental damage, which thus qualifies itself as an object of salvage, just as a ship, a cargo or freight.

conclusion that the institute of salvage remains divided into three categories, i.e., obligatory, spontaneous, and contractual.

(a) Obligatory salvage

As we have already seen, Article 10 of the 1989 Convention renders it obligatory for every master to render assistance to persons in danger of being lost at sea, so far as he may do so without seriously endangering his vessel and the persons on her.

This provision evinces that the salvage of life remains a duty, even in the wording of the new Convention, but the wording of Article 10 itself actually causes the first dissonance with the general discipline of the Convention, as here obligatory salvage no longer involves the owner of the salving vessel but is limited subjectively to her master; Article 10(3) in fact expressly stipulates that the "owner of the vessel shall incur no liability for a breach of the duty of the master under paragraph 1".

The second dissonance derives from the fact that the Convention regulates salvage whether it occurs in navigable, marine or other waters, while the duty to assist human life would appear, from a geographical point of view, to be restricted to the sea and, with regard to the salving subjects, to the masters of ships.[363]

Moreover, the Convention specifies (Article 16) that the saving of life gives no entitlement to remuneration, unless provided for by individual domestic laws; it is even left to these laws (Article 10(2)) to adopt measures which will render the saving of life obligatory, and to punish failure to respect this duty.[364]

It is to be noted that, on occasion, the salvage of vessels becomes obligatory when such salvage is the instrument and means of saving persons, passengers and crew on board the ship itself. In this case, if one of the salvors saves the ship and her cargo, and another salvor saves the persons in danger, the latter will be entitled, under Article 16(2) of the Convention, to a "fair share" of the remuneration awarded to the former for salving the vessel and cargo, —and here a new element is introduced with respect to the current norms— for preventing or minimising environmental damage.

As can be seen, both Article 10 and Article 16 contain regulations of a public nature peculiar to the new Convention, inserting the benefits provided for

---

363. In fact, in the example given at p. 146 of the salvage of a caravan which falls into a lake with people inside, it is not obligatory when the recovery is carried out using a crane from the shore as the salvor would not be the master of a ship, and the salvage would not take place at sea.

364. In our national law this sanction is provided by Art. 1158 of the Navigation Code which punishes, penally, failure to lend assistance to a ship or persons in distress. In merit, see also Gaeta, "La Convenzione di Londra", op. cit., 305, who notes that under Italian law such failure (Art. 489 Nav. Code) is mitigated by the fact that an obligation may not exist if the master has received information that others, in more favourable conditions, have hurried to lend assistance.

salvors acting to protect the environment even in the case of the saving of human life, although the latter is in principle held to be gratuitous under the most ancient sea-faring rules.[365]

(b) Spontaneous salvage

Spontaneous, or non-contractual, salvage is foreseen as the general case, given that Article 1(a) defines as a "salvage operation" any act or activity undertaken to assist a vessel or any other property in danger, without qualifying the activity undertaken, and that Article 12(1), which declares that the salvor is entitled to remuneration if the operations have a useful result, makes no distinction between contractual salvage or salvage of another nature.[366]

It can therefore be affirmed that non-contractual salvage is the rule, and contractual salvage the exception specifically provided for and regulated by Articles 6 and 7 of the new Convention, even if, in practice, and as far as statistics go, recourse to contractual salvage will prevail—as in the past—over the non-contractual case.

In fact, if one examines the wording of Article 6(1), it can be seen that the Convention intends to regulate all salvage operations "save to the extent that a contract otherwise provides expressly or by implication", which means that if no specific contract terms are stipulated between the parties derogating from uniform international laws, the Convention governs all cases of spontaneous and contractual salvage when the contracts relating to the latter incorporate the Convention's provisions.[367]

We can by no means express agreement with a certain recent doctrine which asserts that the new Convention does not contain, in the definition of "salvage operation", any "requirement of voluntariness". In effect, speaking of "any act or activity undertaken" by the salvor, the word "undertaken" can refer either to a spontaneous and voluntary activity or to an activity imposed by contract obligations. Similarly, we do not feel that the theory that the absence of the requirement of voluntariness is to be drawn from Article 17 of the new Convention can stand, as this article lays down that no payment is due if the services do not "exceed what can be reasonably considered as due performance of a contract entered into before the danger arose"; in fact, it follows from this article that if a danger is foreseen and a contract is stipulated

---

365. In this respect many discussions arose at the Diplomatic Convention, and many States objected to the insertion of this regulation in a Convention which should have applied solely to private law, but at the end the idea of keeping this regulation in the Convention's text prevailed. See Nielsen, "International Convention on Salvage", *op. cit.*, 3.

366. With Gaeta, "La Convenzione", *op. cit.*, 299.

367. This regulation, contrary to that which would seem to be the case under the current 1910 Convention, would appear to allow a contractual departure from the applicable law on the basis of the Convention's general principles when the parties, for example, stipulate a LOF 1990 which provides that the law governing the contract is English law rather than the Convention.

to eliminate it, the relevant operation does not fall within the sphere of spontaneous salvage as governed by the Convention, nor, equally, does it fall within the sphere of an eventual salvage contract governed by the same Convention, as its wording does not contain, as required by Article 6(1) of the Convention, different or contrary regulations.[368]

Moreover, it must be noted that since, also under the new Convention, the owner and the master of the ship in danger are entitled to reasonably prohibit salvors from rendering services (Article 19), the "voluntariness" of salvage is confirmed as a general rule.

On the subject of spontaneous salvage and of "voluntariness" we must further mention the problem of the institute's legal qualification which, under the new Convention, can no longer be comprised within and limited by an eventual *negotiorum gestio* in favour of the owners of the saved properties, though—as already mentioned—this thesis certainly provokes many doubts and criticisms,[369] as the protection of the environment represents one of the concurrent purposes of salvage, and its defence must be considered as a duty owed in the place of an intervention by the public authority whose duty it is, in general and primarily, to protect and defend the property of the community which it represents.

Whilst any "enhancement of award", i.e., the increase in remuneration to that salvor who has not only obtained a useful result in the traditional salvage of the vessel and her cargo but who, at the same time, has also prevented serious damage to the environment, falls within the concept of "liability salvage" and can therefore be considered within the sphere of a particular form of *negotiorum gestio* in favour of the party who would be liable for the damage, the payment of "special compensation" solely for those operations relating to the protection of the environment in the absence of a traditional useful result would seem rather to fall within the sphere of a service contract, not of an express nature but by "implication".[370]

This is justified not only by the fact that in the former case payment of the reward must be borne by both the passive subjects of the salvage, i.e., by the ship and the cargo interests, but also by the fact that in the latter case the "special compensation", according to Article 14 of the new Convention, is

---

368. See Darling and Smith, *op. cit.*, 54, who declare: "This definition is significant in two respects. First, it contains no requirement of voluntariness. However, this point is dealt with in Art. 17, which provides that no reward is payable if the services do not 'exceed what can reasonably be considered as due performance of a contract entered into before the danger arose'."

369. See p. 53 of this book and the doctrine cited. Upon the interconnection between the two interventions and the diversity of the two types of remuneration, see Caliendo, *op. cit.*, 161.

370. See Dawson, *op. cit.* Contrary to the qualification of spontaneous salvage as *negotiorum gestio* is Gaeta, "La Convenzione", *op. cit.*, 299, who recalls the lack of the "*absentia domini*" as already pointed out by Ripert, *Traité de droit maritime* (Paris 1953). For further investigations into the *negotiorium gestio* of third party interests in common-law systems, see the recent work by Carbone and D'Angelo, *Cooperazione tra imprese e appalto internazionale*, (Milan, 1991), 84.

payable only by the owner of the vessel which caused or threatened damage to the environment and by the underwriter of this specific risk.[371]

In fact the "special compensation" consists of the actual expenses incurred by the salvor and of a "fair rate for equipment and personnel actually and reasonably used", i.e., a reward which is based on elements of tariff rather than on elements determinating a true and proper reward for a useful result achieved within a contractual or non-contractual relationship, which, in either case, would be rather aleatory.

(c) Contractual salvage

Contract salvage (as we have seen) is governed by the Convention, which admits two types:

(1) contracts which do not derogate from the Convention's uniform provisions and which, therefore, fall completely within the sphere of its regulations, even by making express reference to the Convention itself, as does LOF 90 (which entered contractual practice even before the Convention entered into force); and

(2) contracts which regulate—with their terms being valid only as between the stipulating parties—the salvage operations which otherwise would have been governed by the provisions of the Convention (Article 6(1)), in so far as it would be applicable to the subjects of the contract.[372]

It is worth noting here that the new Convention has, once and for all, cleared away the terminological dispute which had, at one time, arisen around the word "owner", which caused no difficulties in the English translation, but which presented problems in the French text of the 1910 Convention which used the word "propriétaire", meaning only the true and proper owner of the ship and not the party operating the ship.[373] In fact, co-ordinating Article 1(c) of the Convention, which speaks of "property" as an object of salvage, and Article 8(1), which speaks of the "owner" in relation to the "property in danger", it is clear that the Convention intends to indicate the passive subjects of salvage as the actual owners of the thing in danger, including amongst these the owner of the ship, but not her operator.[374]

---

371. On the theme of enhancement of awards, see the recent work by Olsen, "The Enhancement of Salvage Awards", in *11th International Tug Convention and International Marine Salvage Symposium* (Halifax 1990, Surrey, 1991), 141.

372. For a panorama of international contract law, see the appendices of the work by Darling and Smith, *op. cit.*, 172 *et seq.* reproducing, apart from the LOF 1990, also the Turkish, Japanese, Chinese, French and Soviet salvage contract forms.

373. See Vincenzini, *International Regulation of Salvage at Sea*, (London, 1987), 34.

374. Thus also Gaeta, "La Convenzione", *op. cit.*, 300, who correctly maintains: "The subjects of the salvage relationship are, under the Convention, the actual owners and not the operators of the ships involved. If one considers that salvage, on one hand, aims to salve the ownership of the property in peril and, on the other, places at risk the ownership of the salving vessels, it is impossible not to share this concept."

Under the 1989 Convention the regulation of contract salvage is covered by three provisions of a general nature (Article 6(1)–(3)). Apart from the afore-mentioned principle admitting the existence of salvage contracts which dero-gate from the international uniform regulations following an express or impli-cit agreement between the parties (Article 6(1)), Article 6(2) authorises the master of the vessel, on the one hand, to conclude salvage contracts on behalf of the owner of the ship, and, on the other, grants the owner of the ship or the master the right to conclude such contracts on behalf of the owner of the property on board the vessel. However, Article 6(3) declares that the pro-vision of the Convention in respect of the annulment and modification of con-tracts (Article 7) must prevail, and, in any case, the duties imposed on the parties by the Convention in respect of the prevention or minimising of damage to the environment cannot be modified (Article 8(1)(b) and 2(b)).

Here, and in a rather evident fashion, the question of the by no means neg-ligible presence of public law provisions within the structure of the new Con-vention—the latter being defined as a private law Convention—is again proposed, these provisions—such as Article 6(1)—being capable of setting impassable limits to the private autonomy of the parties which, in fact, cannot in any case derogate from the regulations relating to the protection of the environment as laid down in the new Convention.

This, in our opinion, confirms the diverse juridical natures of the two oper-ations which may occur in the spontaneous salvage of ship and cargo, as already mentioned, where environmental pollution is occurring or is a threat: one is traditional, the salvage of ship and cargo, falling within the scheme of *negotiorum gestio*, even if with the restrictions and limitations and mitigations brought about by a rather high incidence of risk; the other concerns the pre-vention of environmental damage which, as we have already said, may fall within the juridical scheme of the rendering of a service, and which necess-arily places itself side by side with the completely voluntary service of tra-ditional salvage.[375] We shall see later how the different juridical natures of the two operations represent—as it has recently been defined—the "current dilemma" of salvage, since traditional salvage and the prevention of pollution damages are now so closely intertwined as to represent, for the legal opera-tor, the arbitrator or the judge, a serious problem of interpretation when they must attribute one or the other of the operation's aspects as true and proper salvage activities or as anti-pollution services.[376]

---

375. In this respect it could in fact be argued that a spontaneous salvor who decides to lend assistance to a ship in distress which has a polluting cargo either on board or leaking into the sea, is free, before commencing the operation, to decide whether to lend assistance or not, but is no longer free, after the service has commenced, to decide to refrain from doing everything necess-ary to prevent or to limit environmental damage.

376. Noble, "International Salvage—The current dilemma", in *P. & I. International*, April 1991, 10, who writes: "No doubt arbitrators will be asked to make difficult decisions in discrimi-nating between equipment mobilised that can be considered pure salvage and equipment that

In respect of contract salvage, one of the most discussed problems during the course of the preparation, debate and approval of the wording of the new Convention was that relating to the powers of representation which Article 6(2) confers on the master of the vessel, both in respect of his own operator/owner in situations of *absentia domini* and of the owners of the properties on board the vessel at the time of the salvage, in so far as the *absentia domini* is, in this latter regard, a situation of a general nature.

We do not agree with the authoritative doctrine which places the powers of representation of the master of the salving vessel towards his owner only within the framework of cases of contract salvage, as this type of representation also manifests itself in spontaneous salvage each and every time that the master of a ship decides, without consulting his principal, to render assistance to a ship in distress and his intervention obtains a measure of success.[377]

The principle of the powers of the master, as a subject capable of intervening on behalf of the cargo interests as an "agent of necessity", was, in the past, and in spite of there being no specific provision, generally accepted, and the wording drawn up in this respect by the new Convention attempts to solve, with an appropriate rule, the problems which could arise in such cases, given that no such rule exists in international law.[378]

Now if, on one hand, it is simple to visualise how the "agency" of the masters of both the salved and salving vessels is based on a specific power conferred on them by their respective owners in so far as the latter are not usually present at the place of casualty, it is difficult on the other hand to see how such an "agency" may be expressly conferred, time by time, by the individual cargo interests.[379]

might be designated as pollution threat response. Indeed arbitrators might seek guidance from the test currently used by the IOPC Fund when trying to distinguish between salvage and pollution; the test being one of 'primary purpose'."

377. Gaeta, "La Convenzione", *op. cit.*, 300.

378. On this point see Brice, "The New Salvage Convention", *op. cit.*, 33, who, wondering up to what point Art. 6(2) has changed or improved the current system, notes that: "In answering this and other questions, one must always bear in mind that the Convention will operate in many different and divers legal systems and that the problems of one jurisdiction may not arise in others." He also examines the recent case of *The Choko Star* in [1989] 2 Lloyd's Rep. 42. For a full examination of the agent of necessity, see also Rose, "Restitution for the Rescuer", in 9 O.J.L.S., 1989, 184 *et seq*. In Italian doctrine, for a penetrating investigation into the concept of "agency" in common-law systems, see Carbone and D'Angelo, *op. cit.*, 84 *et seq.*, who point out that "within the sphere of Anglo-Saxon juridical tradition a system of rules has in fact been fashioned, summarized by the formula 'agency', in which importance is assumed by the actual ownership of the interests inherent to the financial operations which are the object of the contract stipulated between the agent and a third party, rather than the contractual declaration of the former to the effect that he is acting on his own behalf or on behalf of a principal".

379. Thus Gaeta, "La Convenzione", *op. cit.*, 301, who seems to identify this type of representation as a sort of implicit mandate to take care of the goods, falling within the scheme of an accessory storage contract and competing with the contract of carriage. On the matter of the extension, to the ship owner, of the power to represent the cargo (Art. 6(2) last sentence), Caliendo, "Osservazioni sul progetto di Convenzione", *op. cit.*, 166, is critical, stating: " . . . however the extension to the owner of the vessel of the power to conclude the contract also on behalf of the cargo interests provokes some perplexity. In fact, on a systematic level the idea that

Competent national doctrine solves this problem by justifying this type of representation with the fact that the cargo owners have entrusted the master and the owner of the ship with their property at the start of the voyage; therefore the master or the owner of the ship, in the absence of the individual cargo owners, are entitled *ab initio* to make all those decisions which may be necessary to intervene usefully in a situation of danger.[380]

Still on the theme of contract salvage, Article 7 of the 1989 Convention dictates some norms from which it is not possible to derogate, decreeing that a salvage contract or any of its clauses may be annulled if:

(a) the contract has been entered into under undue influence or the influence of danger and its terms are inequitable; or

(b) the payment under the contract is in an excessive degree too large or too small for the services actually rendered."

It has recently, and, it is submitted, correctly, been pointed out that the word "inequitable" contained in Article 7(a) will represent a rather arduous interpretative problem for courts and arbitrators, since "danger is a prerequisite of salvage and could not, by itself, therefore, provide a sufficient ground for the annulment of a contract".[381] Therefore, accurate investigations will have to be made in each case into the circumstances under which the salvage became necessary and the contract stipulated, bearing in mind that if danger is a fundamental prerequisite of salvage, it can not have effects of an illicit nature or of coercion on the contractual autonomy of the parties.[382]

---

salvage contract obligations may bind the cargo owners as the result of an agreement stipulated by the operator (or even by the actual owner of the ship, according to the wording of the Article) is rather difficult to figure out, when it would be easier to grant this right only to the Master, given the particular position he holds in respect of the cargo interests in the case of necessity." However, Olsen, "The 1989 Salvage Convention", *op. cit.*, 12, is favourable to the inclusion, in the Convention's regulations, of the owner as a potential representative of the cargo: " . . . the owner of the vessel is for the first time given authority by the Article to conclude contracts on behalf of the property aboard the vessel, and one must anticipate that shipowners will take advantage of that authority. In the past, of course, shipowners had no authority to bind cargo interests, and, even if salvors, they had, ultimately, to leave it to the master to conclude the contract, binding the cargo interests by virtue of his Agency of Necessity." See also Kerr, "The 1989 Salvage Convention", *op. cit.*, 510, who states that Art. 6(2) "removes the 'agent of necessity' test, and vests the master with authority to conclude salvage contracts on behalf of all property on board—an obvious improvement".

380. Worthy of note is the observation made by Gaeta, "La Convenzione", *op. cit.*, 302, who points out that under our national law a contract stipulated under the influence of danger, as referred to in Art. 7 of the new Convention, is not to be identified with a contract stipulated "in a state of danger" as mentioned in Art. 1447 of the Italian Civil Code, since the latter refers only to persons, and not to danger run by things or properties.

381. Darling and Smith, *op. cit.*, 58.

382. This is in spite of the fact that under the Anglo-Saxon contract system the "espousal of the sanctity of contract approach" is accepted; Kerr, "The 1989 Salvage Convention", *op. cit.*, 510.

50. DUTIES OF THE PARTIES

Unlike the 1910 Convention, the 1989 Convention, in Article 8, contains specific regulations in respect of the duties of the parties involved in a salvage operation, whether these parties be the salvors, the owners of the salving craft or of the properties salved, or the master of the ship. With specific regard to the salvor, Article 8(1) prescribes

   (a) that the salvage operations must be carried out with due care;

   (b) that due care must be excercised to prevent or minimise damage to the environment;

   (c) that the assistance of other salvors should be sought each time that it is "reasonably" required by the circumstances;

   (d) that the intervention of other salvors—when reasonably requested by the owners of the properties at risk—be accepted, upon condition that the amount of his reward is not prejudiced should it be ascertained that such request was unreasonable.

Under Article 8(2), the master and the owners of the salved properties owe a duty:

   (a) to co-operate with the salvor during the course of the salvage operations;

   (b) in doing so, to exercise due care to prevent or minimise environmental damage;

   (c) to accept redelivery of the vessel once she has been brought by the salvor to a "place of safety" and when reasonably requested by the salvors to accept such redelivery.

It must immediately be noted that the new wording of the Convention applies, without distinction, both to spontaneous and to contractual salvage, adding new elements, in Article 8(1)(b) and (2)(b), which place the burden of "due care to prevent or minimize damage to the enviroment" on all parties interested in the salvage. And this is the greatest innovation included in this rule, as the other duties expressed therein, though not specifically indicated in the wording of the 1910 Convention, may, upon careful examination of the complex of regulations of the new Convention, be considered as implicitly sanctioned.[383]

But at the same time, though rendering it obligatory for the salvor to prevent or minimise environmental damage, thus substantially reducing the private autonomy of the parties involved in contract salvage, the Convention makes no provisions should this duty be neglected; in fact many are

---

383. Thus, Darling and Smith, *op. cit.*, 60, and Brice, "The New Salvage Convention", *op. cit.*, 39. For Nielsen, in "Improvements and Deficiences", *op. cit.*, 60, "During the work of the CMI and the IMO it was much discussed to what extent the Convention should be mandatory. There was some support for a much more extensive part of the new rules to be mandatory, but luckily it was avoided that e.g. the compensation scheme in Art. 13 and 14 had that fate. What remained was Art. 6.3."

wondering what will be the consequences of a lack of respect of this regulation by the salvor. The duty imposed does not involve a private law obligation towards the salved properties, but rather falls within the sphere of a general respect for public order; therefore the whole thing would come down to the eventual negative effect of such failure when fixing the amount of the reward.[384]

In effect, in the Montreal CMI Draft, other duties of a public nature which would, to some extent, have solved this problem, had been foreseen and included. During the work of the IMO Legal Committee, however, these public law provisions were excluded, in view of the fact that due to their strictly public nature they would have had to be efficacious within the framework of public law Conventions such as the MARPOL Convention 1973–1978.[385]

However, one of the problems which would seem to arise from an interpretation of Article 8(2)(b), is that—as we shall see later—if the salvor, when salving a ship and her cargo, does not obtain a useful result in respect of the salved properties, but due to adequate and timely intervention succeeds in preventing, minimising or removing damage to the environment, he is entitled to "special compensation" under Article 14(1) and (2) of the Convention. This special compensation, as we shall see, no longer represents a debt of the salved traditional properties proportionate to their respective values, but is to be borne only by the owner of the salved ship and his P. & I. Club.

This solution, which is based on insurance practice rather than on the legal qualifications of the operations and of the salvage services rendered by the salvors, would seem to be in contrast with the provision of Article 8(2)(b) of the same Convention which, as we have seen, makes it a duty also of the owner of the salved properties, without distinction, and therefore of the owners of polluting cargo, to prevent or minimise damage to the environment.

Therefore, from a strictly legal point of view, it is difficult to see why the owner of potentially polluting cargo or of a cargo which is causing pollution is exonerated from paying towards the special compensation indicated in Article 14(1) and (2), since this compensation is clearly a reward in respect of

384. Gaeta, "La Convenzione di Londra", *op. cit.*, 303, for whom "the afore-mentioned obligations are not true and proper obligations, the obligations of one party corresponding to the rights of another, but are rather the modalities of the salvage operation which bear influence, positively or negatively depending on the case, in the determination of the measure of remuneration". The problem is posed correctly and penetratingly by Brice, "The New Salvage Convention", *op. cit.*, 38, where he expressly declares: "A question to be addressed is as to the nature in law of these new duties and the means of enforcement. They are not contractual; but do they create, when enacted by national laws, a new statutory duty, the breach of which will sound in damages? Can they be enforced by injunction? Which state will have jurisdiction and be expected to enforce them? Will any new UK statute have effect merely within the realm or within territorial waters? What of breach of duty on the high seas involving foreign ships and salvage *ex contractu*? Can a particular salvage contract dispense with or override them?"

385. Also Nielsen, "Report to CMI", *op. cit.*, 3.

duties owed by all the parties indicated by Article 8(2)(b). This is so especially if one considers that, on the contrary, "the skill and efforts of the salvors in preventing or minimising damage to the environment" indicated by Article 13(1)(b) of the Convention function as an appropriate element in producing an "enhancement of the award" should the results obtained by the salvors be useful in respect of the traditional properties at risk, and at the same time efficacious in respect of the pollution and of the protection of the environment.[386]

As we have seen, the other duties of the salvor include that, whenever circumstances reasonably require, of seeking the assistance of other salvors, and of accepting the intervention of such other salvors when reasonably requested to do so by the owner or master of the vessel or of the other property in danger.

The reason for all these duties is to be sought in the dual purpose set by the new Convention, not only in respect of the successful salvage of ship, cargo and any other property at risk but also in respect of the prevention of that environmental factor which so greatly influences the new international discipline; the intention is clearly to prevent inefficient, unprofessional, poorly equipped or badly organised salvors from intervening—in the hope of obtaining high rewards—and putting into action all their available technical and organisational devices at the place or in the vicinity of the casualty, which could increase the risk of losing the salved properties and of causing serious damage to the environment.[387]

However, the Convention does not appear to establish, clearly and inequivocably, remedies and sanctions in respect of the non-execution of the duties incumbent on the various subjects involved, with the result that the legal practitioner is left with serious doubts as to the legal effectiveness of the duties and their "legal status". In fact, as has recently been declared,[388]

"a further point in relation to the duties imposed by Art. 8 is their legal status. First, it is submitted, compliance with the duties will be a factor in the assessment of the salvage award, but this point is covered by Art. 13. Secondly, failure to comply with the duties might lead to a reduction in the size of the award, but this point is also covered elsewhere (in Art. 18). In cases where the Convention is incorporated into a contract, failure to comply would amount to breach of contract giving rise to a remedy in damages, but only where loss to the innocent party could be shown to have resulted.

386. See Olsen, "The Enhancement of Salvage Awards", *op. cit.*, 6, who points out in this regard that "thus, we have for the first time a general rule that there can be an award in the nature of salvage payable by the owners of property that was lost (although, in practice, in fact payable by the shipowners' P. & I. Club) which represents a marked and revolutionary departure from the basic law of salvage"; and Brice, "The New Salvage Convention", *op. cit.*, 44.

387. The case of *The Pergo* [1987] 1 Lloyd's Rep. 582, cited also by Darling and Smith, *op. cit.*, 61, is symptomatic; the salvor, fearing that the site of the accident may have been identified by other salvors, carried out the salvage at night without lights.

388. Darling and Smith, *op. cit.*, 61, and on the incorporation of the new Convention into English law and the relative problems, see Gaskell, *op. cit.*, 359.

Whether compliance with the duties can be enforced by any other means remains to be seen."

51. NEW CRITERIA FOR DETERMINING REMUNERATION: LIABILITY SALVAGE AND THE ENHANCEMENT OF AWARDS

In setting the criteria for fixing the salvage reward, the new Convention, though maintaining the old principle of "no cure no pay" which remains sanctioned by Article 12 as a general element of the procedure of "assessment of the remuneration",[389] also has regard to "the skill and efforts of salvors in preventing or minimising damage to the environment" (Article 13(1)(b)).

This provision officially introduces the greatly discussed principle of "liability salvage" to uniform international law, even if restricted to environmental damage; thus an intervention on behalf of the liability risks towards the environment, in the sense of damage to the international community, becomes an important element in qualifying the salvage and fixing the reward.[390]

In effect it cannot be said that the general principle of "no cure no pay" with regard to the opportunity for the salvors to earn a reward for the operations carried out, is affected or derogated from by the rule contained in the subsequent Article 14 introducing "special compensation". That article re-establishes the concept of the "safety net" already foreseen by LOF 1980. Since this special compensation makes no reference whatsoever to the salved values, it is proposed more as a true and proper reflection of the salvors' rights, rather than as an exception to the general principle, and is of a different nature and type from the reward made under "no cure no pay" conditions.[391]

For this reason the legal nature of "special compensation" will be dealt with at a later stage, separately from the examination of traditional reward and from the criteria for fixing the same.

Therefore, given that salvage operations which obtain a useful result entitle

389. Thus Gold, "Marine Salvage: Towards a New Regime", op. cit., 499 and Darling and Smith, op. cit., 64.

390. We cannot say that we agree with Gold, "Marine Salvage: Towards a New Regime", op. cit., where he states "It is noteworthy that in order of importance, this environmental criterion is only surpassed by the principal criterion—the salved value of vessel and other property". In fact Art. 13 of the new Convention expressly establishes that in identifying the importance of the new criteria for determining remuneration no regard must be paid to the "order in which they are presented".

391. We perfectly agree with Olsen, "The 1989 Convention", op. cit., 4, when he clearly states that "In the light of those words, it can be seen that the provision for special compensation contained in Article 14 is regarded not so much as a change in the nature of the law of salvage as a kind of 'bolt-on extra'."

the salvor to a reward,[392] even if the result is only partially useful and when these operations have been carried out in the absence of an express and reasonable refusal by the interests of the salved properties, we must identify which are the innovations in the new criteria for fixing salvage rewards listed in Article 13 of the new Convention.

In the first place the order in which the criteria for fixing the reward are placed in the Convention's text would seem to be of no relevance. It must, in fact, be recalled that the 1910 Convention (Article 8), in listing the criteria for fixing the reward, divided them into two distinct categories, one of which was to be taken into consideration before the other, which basically established a certain hierarchy to be acknowledged when considering and evaluating the criteria.

So, having placed "the salved value of the vessel and other property" at the head of the list does not change the order of importance of the elements of salvage with respect to the order in which they were placed in the 1910 Convention, in which the values were inserted in the *second* category of criteria to be taken into account.

A recent decision by an English court confirmed this concept ahead of time, holding that "salvors are not entitled to recover a prescribed proportion of the value of the property salved. Indeed, when the value of the property is very high, the award will be a very low proportion of that value because the Court will not make an award which is out of all proportion to the services rendered. High values make some, but not necessarily a great difference".[393]

Other innovations of note, apart from the major innovation brought about by Article 13(1)(b) discussed above, are those relating to the promptness of the services rendered by the salvors (paragraph (h)), the availability and use of vessels or other equipment intended for salvage operations (paragraph (i)) and, finally, the state of readiness and efficiency of the salvor's equipment and its value (paragraph (j)).

These criteria as listed by the 1989 Convention, linked with the general interpretative principle of the criterion for fixing the reward indicated by Article 13(1) (the reward shall be fixed with a view to encouraging salvage operations) and with that pronounced in the Convention's preamble,[394]

---

392. Rightly Gaeta, "La Convenzione di Londra", *op.cit.* 307, points out that in our Navigation Code (Arts. 491, 492) the principle of "no cure no pay" is in a certain sense ignored, or at least mitigated, as the salvor who has not salved anything may be entitled to claim the refund of costs met and to payment of damages sustained.

393. Thus *The M. Vatan* [1990] 1 Lloyd's Rep. 336, and Olsen, "The Enhancement of Salvage Award", *op. cit.*, 1, who, acutely notes that "Similarly, at the other end of the spectrum it would be equally absurd if a salvor was restricted to a fixed percentage of the value of the property saved in cases where, for example, a vessel is hard aground and severely damaged, and needs underwater patching and repair work, pumping, and other protracted, expensive, and often dangerous services, probably carried out in a bad weather in close proximity to an inhospitable lee shore."

394. The preamble, in fact, contains precise statements of principle in this respect, pointing out that the international agreement between Contracting States was reached in so far as the latter are: "*Conscious* of the major contribution which efficient and timely salvage operations can

confirm, when fixing the salvor's reward, the intention of the international community to supply, with this new law, a more modern legal instrument which reflects the changed technical requirements of salvage, providing an incentive to the salvage industry and adequately rewarding those who, with an increasingly improved technical-logistical organisation and with a high degree of "availability" and "readiness" of vessels and equipment, have, are or will put these efforts into practice.[395]

To conclude, the principle of "enhancement of the awards", takes on the appearance of an innovation, to be included within the sphere of that "environmental factor" which substantially and meaningfully characterises the new regulations.

It must therefore be repeated that this principle has, once and for all, opened the door to the full introduction of "liability salvage" to international law, after both old and recent decisions had allowed its application in different legal systems and jurisdictions to varying degrees.[396]

Clearly and unequivocally admitted by Article 13(1)(b) of the Convention, "liability salvage", though limited to the "skill and efforts" of the salvors in preventing and minimising environmental damage, could also be applied in respect of the merits of the salvors in preventing or minimising damage to third parties, without any express mention of this being made in the uniform international law, basing its application simply on the observation that, as we have already remarked and as has recently been confirmed by others, "the value of the property salved would be adversely affected by 'in rem' claims against it arising from damage to third parties, and there are, therefore, good arguments of principle that awards should be enhanced to reflect the fact that liability to third parties has been avoided".[397]

The introduction of the enhancement of the award for skill and efforts in preventing or minimising damage to the environment as a general principle in

make to the safety of vessels and other property in danger and to the protection of the environment; *Convinced* of the need to ensure that adequate incentives are available to persons who undertake salvage operations in respect of vessels and other property in danger . . . ".

395. Upon this particular aspect of necessity of encouraging the efforts of the salvage industry, see Lacey, "Expansion of the salvage industry to meet modern requirements and the need for substantial rewards to sustain the industry", in *Salvage,* Lloyd's Press Conference papers (London, 1990), 11; see also Noble, *op.cit.*, 10.

396. In English jurisprudence the following, already cited, must again be recalled: *The Buffalo* (1937) 58 Ll.L. Rep. 302; *The Whippingham* (1934) 48 Ll.L. Rep. 49 and *The Gregerso* [1973] 1 Q.B. 247; *The Helenus and The Motagua* [1982] 2 Lloyd's Rep. 261; *The Bertil* [1952] 2 Lloyd's Rep. 176. In US jurisprudence, the case of *The Mimosa* (1987) A.M.C. 2515, and Tribunal of Naples, 8 June 1963, *Rimorchiatori Napoletani* v. *Achille Onorato*, in Riv. Dir. Nav. 221; Trib. Livorno, 2 February 1971, *F.lli Neri* v. *Agemar Shipping G. Ltd.*, in Dir. Mar., 1971, 222, as well as the more recent Arbitration Award of 26 November 1982, *Medit S.p.A.* v. *Petrolmar ed altri*, in Dir. Mar., 1983, 580.

397. Vincenzini, *International Regulation of Salvage at Sea*, 90, and Olsen, "The 1989 Salvage Convention", *op.cit.*, 3. Recently, in the USA, see also the case of *The Mimosa* (1987) A.M.C. 2515, already mentioned, which seems, once and for all, to open the door to liability salvage in the American legal system. See also Brown, "Has the keel been laid for the liability salvage in the Fifth Circuit?", *op. cit.*, 583.

fixing the overall reward due to the salvors, brings to light a new problem in the correct interpretation of the institute of salvage, as it would appear that the sharing out of the payment of this reward amongst the interests of the salved properties should be made according to the similarly general principle of proportionate contribution with respect to the values of the salved properties (Article 13(2)). This would not seem to take into consideration the fact that while the hull and cargo underwriters are usually the debtors in respect of the reward owed by the traditional properties at risk (ship and cargo), the ship's P. & I. Club, which, in effect, covers the shipowners' liability risks but not those of the owners of the cargo, should usually be liable for any enhancement of award resulting from the prevention and minimisation of damage to the environment.

However, we suggest that this problem does not arise in respect of normal rewards under Article 13(1)(b) of the Convention, since, had the Convention wished to eliminate cargo owners from the category of subjects liable to payment of the afore-mentioned enhancement of the award, it would have done so specifically, as in fact is the case with regard to the "special compensation" covered by Article 14(1).[398]

Therefore, should salvage operations obtain the dual useful result of saving a ship and her cargo and of preventing or minimising damage to the environment, both ship and cargo (even so-called "innocent" cargo) must contribute, in proportion to their respective values, to the enhancement of the award.[399] This fact assumes a certain degree of importance if one considers that the new international law, like the new LOF 1990, does not restrict itself to introducing the protection of the environment as a criterion in fixing the reward, linking it to a casualty which may concurrently cause or threaten oil pollution, but extends this risk to all polluting mechanisms which may provoke environmental damage, whatever the cause may be; therefore, not only oil cargoes are to be considered as falling within the category of cargoes at risk, but also chemical cargoes, hazardous substances, whatever their nature, nuclear waste and, last but not least, ship's normal bunker.

A final innovation is contained in Article 13(2) of the new Convention.

---

398. This derives from the application of the concept of the "Montreal Compromise" stipulated on between the Hull Underwriters and the Cargo Underwriters on the one hand, and the P. & I. Clubs on the other. Accordingly the premiums would bear the increased burdens deriving from the enhancement of awards in the presence of anti-pollution services rendered within the sphere of a traditional salvage giving a useful result; in exchange the Clubs would fully bear the burden of payment of the special compensation as indicated in Art. 14 of the Convention.

399. See Shaw, "The insurance arrangements undersigning the payment of salvor's remuneration", in *Salvage*, Lloyd's Press Conference papers (London, 1990), 109. Also see Olsen, "The 1989 Salvage Convention", *op. cit.*, who points out that: "In principle, and, as a consequence of Article 13(2) the owners of an innocent and harmless cargo, and of course the shipowners, would have to bear their pro rata proportion of the enhancement, notwithstanding that their cargo was completely 'environment-friendly' and in the case of the cargo interests, at any rate, they could never have known, and would not have taken into account in assessing insurance risks and rates, the dangers posed by other hazardous cargo that might fortuitously be aboard that vessel."

Though confirming that no solidarity exists between the passive subjects of salvage in respect of the payment of the reward, the paragraph grants individual State Parties the right to derogate from the international general rule by introducing the afore-mentioned principle of solidarity into their own legal systems. This rule allows States which have a rule of this nature in their own national laws to maintain its validity, which is certainly useful to salvors who—especially when container vessels are involved—very often have great difficulty both in obtaining security for the cargo, divided into thousands of bills of lading and with thousands of owners of the various shipments, and in obtaining payment of the countless shares of proportionate reward owed by the latter.[400]

52. ANTI-POLLUTION MEASURES AND SALVAGE

Before passing on to a perusal of the rule containing the other most important and substantial innovation of the new uniform Convention, i.e., the "special compensation" provided for by Article 14, we think it worthwhile to open a parenthesis and examine, within the framework of the problems just discussed regarding the enhancement of awards deriving from Article 13(1)(b), a further problem of interpretation which may originate from the coexistence, in a salvage, of two distinct purposes, that of minimising or preventing pollution and that of assisting and salving the ship causing the pollution within the sphere of a traditional salvage operation, when these purposes may signify different and distinct rewards.

In fact it must be queried and clarified whether a traditional salvage operation to ship and to cargo in which anti-pollution measures are put into effect by the same salvors will entitle the latter to obtain, separately:

(a) an enhancement of the traditional reward from the hull and cargo underwriters should a useful result be obtained;

(b) a refund of the costs incurred and payment of the damages suffered, solely in respect of the anti-pollution operations, payable by the 1969 and 1971 CLC Fund or by reason of the subsequent IOPC Fund.[401]

---

400. For example in Dutch law, which provides, under Art. 564, the principle of solidarity between the ship and the cargo or, rather, the responsibility of the shipowner also for that part of the remuneration owed by the cargo interests. This paragraph was, in fact, introduced to the new Convention thanks to the intervention of the Dutch delegation which wished to preserve this very useful principle in its national legislation.

401. This problem was posed in our legislation with the well-known case of *The Patmos*, in relation to which the Court of Messina, with two separate judgments, first of all allowed the salvors to share in the C.L.C. Fund for the anti-pollution measures taken during the salvage of the ship (Trib. Messina, 30 July 1986, in *Trasporti*, 1987, I, 1817) and subsequently, with another judgment, granted the salvors the traditional 'enhancement' of the salvage award because of the contemporary anti-pollution intervention (Trib. Messina, 12 September 1988, in Dir. Mar. 1989, 1114). On this point see Comenale Pinto, "La responsabilità per inquinamento da idrocarburi provenienti da navi: il regime delle norme di diritto uniforme", in *Trasporti* 1990, I, 63.

This is not an easy problem to solve, even if—as has been pointed out by recent doctrine—it is possible in the Italian legal system for a certain type of behaviour by a subject to be interpreted in two different ways[402] and the formal concurrents of such different aspects of a single operation by the salvor are possible: one falling within the sphere of the institute of salvage, entitling the salvors, once the Convention has entered into force, to receive an enhancement of the award provided for by Article 13(1)(b) of the Convention over and above the traditional reward; the other falling within the sphere of an anti-pollution service and, as such, entitling the salvor to receive the compensation afforded by the 1969 CLC and subsequent modifications.[403]

Such a solution to the problem (which, moreover, was adopted by an Italian court in the only case decided to date[404]) could provoke further interpretative doubts when the new Convention enters into force, and actually does so now within the contractual framework of LOF 1990 if a third hypothesis, or abstract case—as foreseen by Article 14 of the new Convention, to which reference is made by, and which is incorporated into, LOF 1990, Clause 2—is added. In other words, should a salvor not succeed in obtaining a useful result in the traditional salvage, but does prevent, minimise or eliminate damage to the environment, he is entitled, on the one hand, to "special compensation" under Article 14 and, on the other, to present his costs and damages to the CLC Fund for refund.

This might seem to be a duplication of the same claim, in contrast with the principle of *ne bis in idem*. But this is not really the case, because of the different nature of the two "compensations". The first exists in a private law Convention, with the specific purpose of indemnifying the salvor, who, because he prevented or minimised the damage to the environment, giving priority to the anti-pollution operation and not to the traditional salvage, or in any case being strongly influenced by the former operation with respect to the latter, missed the opportunity of obtaining a useful result in the traditional salvage,

---

402. Thus Comenale Pinto, *op. cit.*, 65; we cannot say that we completely agree with Gouillod, "Les mesures de sauvegarde (de quelques difficultés liée à l'indemnisation des frais de lutte contre la pollution)" in D.M.F., 1980, 397 *et seq*, as he proposes, as the criterion of the distinction between salvage and anti-pollution activities, a presumption on a chronological basis according to which all services rendered prior to the commencement of an oil spill should be presumed as having been rendered as salvage services, whilst those rendered subsequent to the leakage should be considered as anti-pollution services. This would seem to ignore the fact that the operations, because of their complex, complementary and contemporaneous nature, must be separated according to the purpose, and that they cannot be divided according to their chronology.

403. It is worth noting that on occasion of *The Patmos* disaster (note 401), the Executive Committee of the C.L.C. Fund, upon being asked for a decision on the possibility of concurrence between anti-pollution measures and salvage, did not propose a clear and unequivocal solution but merely decided to await the decisions of the Italian courts, reserving the right to take a position on this point at a later date. See, in merit, "Raport sur les articles du Fond International d'indemnisation pour le damages dus à la pollution par les hidrocarbures au cours de l'année civile 1985", 19.

404. See Trib. Messina, 30 July 1986, *The Patmos*, *cit.*, and also Abecassis, "The Patmos" [1985] in L.M.C.L.Q. 382.

so that the special compensation interacts as a refund of "all" the expenses incurred by the salvor in either instance; the second exists in a public law Convention, drawn up and enacted in order to remunerate, on a tariff basis, the anti-pollution service, independent of whether it was related to a salvage operation or not.

In fact, as has recently and, it is submitted, accurately been pointed out,[405] in many cases of salvage, salvors who are ordered by State authorities to proceed to the preventive removal of pollutant cargoes from ships in danger lose their chance of earning a salvage reward if, in the course of these operations, the ship is lost because of technical or meteorological reasons.

It cannot be denied that salvage and pollution responses have become closely interlinked, so it is up to the legal practitioner, the judge or the arbitrator to carry out the delicate legal surgery required to separate the two aspects of the same operation by referring these aspects to the norms which, being qualifed within one specific legal institute rather than another, produce separate and different financial consequences for the interested parties.

53. ENVIRONMENTAL DAMAGE AND SPECIAL COMPENSATION

The other substantial innovation introduced by the 1989 Convention to the traditional institute of salvage, in the wake of the reform rudimentarily introduced on a contractual level by LOF 1980 as the so-called "safety net", is the "special compensation" provided for by Article 14.

The introduction of this principle, based—as we have seen—on the new legal·scheme outlined for the new institute of salvage, with particular regard to the environmental factor, results from the need to operate, with all equipment and on every occasion, and especially when a ship and cargo are to be saved and an accident with a high polluting potential is involved, with the purpose of preventing or minimising the damage to the environment. "Damage to the environment" is defined by Article 1(d) of the 1989 Convention as:

" . . . substantial physical damage to human health or to marine life or resources in coastal or inland waters or areas adjacent thereto, caused by pollution, contamination, fire, explosion or similar major incidents."

As we have already pointed out, it is immediately clear from this definition that, objectively speaking, the sphere of application of so-called "damage to the environment" is much wider than that foreseen by LOF 1980, which,

405. See Noble, *op. cit.*, 10, who writes: "The situation envisaged is one where a salvor, having arrived on site, before being permitted to conduct his salvage operation must first deal with a pollution threat under orders of an authority. The author has attended a number of cases where authorities have insisted that all fuel and lubricating oils be removed from a ship before the salvors attempt a re-floating even in circumstances where the salvors have considered it more prudent to move ship and oil together."

inexplicably, had restricted itself to taking into consideration only those cases of "oil pollution" originating from a "laden" tanker, thereby excluding any other type of pollution, and excluding even the bunkers of any ship whatsoever, even of empty tankers.[406]

Likewise, the field of application of the rule is widely extended geographically with respect to the current Convention, as the environmental damage indicated by the 1989 Convention also covers internal waters and areas adjacent to territorial water, and, most importantly, in compliance with the new concept of salvage, which is not only limited to regulating salvage at sea but which extends its rules to any other waters, whether navigable or not.

In paragraph 51 we saw how the 1989 Convention takes the "skill and efforts of the salvors in preventing or minimising damage to the environment" into consideration for the fixing and the eventual enhancement of the award. Now, should the salvors not be successful in the dual purpose of salving ship and cargo and preventing or minimising the damage to the environment, they will still be entitled to a "special compensation". Article 14(1) undertakes to establish the criteria for assessing this compensation:

(1) "If the salvor has carried out salvage operations in respect of a vessel which by itself or its cargo threatened damage to the environment and has failed to earn a reward under article 13 at least equivalent to the special compensation assessable in accordance with this article, he shall be entitled to special compensation from the owner of that vessel equivalent to his expenses as herein defined."

The *ratio* of this rule is, therefore, as follows:
(1) The operations to prevent or minimise damage to the environment must be carried out on the occasion of a salvage of a ship and cargo which gave no useful result (not even partial), so that the salvors failed to earn a reward under Article 13 of the Convention at least equivalent to what would be due under Article 14(1) as "special compensation".
(2) The operations for the prevention or minimising of the damage to the environment were likewise unsuccessful.[407]

With this type of "special compensation" an effort has been made to provide the salvors with an incentive to prevent and minimise the damage to the environment. Its aim is to induce them to attempt difficult operations and to take risks, even in those cases of salvage which, because of the scanty values at stake within the sphere of the traditional salvage and because of the high

---

406. Thus also Brice, "The New Salvage Convention", *op. cit.*, 41, who, amongst other things, makes a precise analysis of the situation of the institute of salvage as it is actually regulated by international law, supplying indications for further future lines of reform tendency.

407. Darling and Smith, *op.cit.* 72, who acknowledge that "under Art. 14(1) there is no requirement that the salvor should actually achieve any success in respect of preventing or minimizing damage to the environment. Cases where such success is achieved are dealt with by Art. 14(2)—which provides for a greater amount of special compensation".

chances of failure, could well discourage salvors who, in the case of failure, would not even recover their costs under the current principle of "no cure no pay".[408]

In such cases the refund of the costs incurred in the operation corresponds to an amount which is established in Article 14(3), which clarifies that in the circumstances set out in Article 14(1) and (2):

"(3) Salvor's expenses for the purpose of paragraphs 1 and 2 means the out-of-pocket expenses reasonably incurred by the salvor in the salvage operation and a fair rate for equipment and personnel actually and reasonably used in the salvage operation, taking into consideration the criteria set out in article 13, paragraph 1(h), (i) and (j)."

The criteria referred to include the promptness, availability, state of readiness and efficiency and the value of the salvor's equipment intended to be used or used in the operation.

Therefore the special compensation clearly corresponds not only to a refund of the actual expenses sustained by the salvor in the operation, but also to a compendium of these and of a fair rate for all tugs, craft, personnel and other equipment used by the salvor; this had been expressly provided for by LOF 1980, too, which had added this criterion of a retributive nature to the "out-of-pocket expenses".[409]

In fact the "fair rate" is not restricted to the expenses incurred by the salvage company in paying its personnel, buying materials and equipment for use by its own craft, etc., but includes a certain measure of profit, which, in such cases, unmistakably assumes the nature of a reward for the risks met in the operation.

We shall now look at the by no means simple mechanism for assessing "special compensation" and its uncertain juridical nature, the fruit of compromises between Contracting States and of influences of a pragamatic and commercial nature rather than of the strict application of the law.

The circumstance set out in Article 14(2), concerns those cases of salvage to a ship and cargo which threaten or are causing damage to the environment, in which the salvors, having failed in their principal purpose of traditional salvage, have obtained a useful result in preventing or minimising damage to the environment. In this case the "special compensation", as defined above, may undergo an enhancement, up to a maximum of 30% of the expenses incurred by the salvor. However, bearing in mind the criteria laid down by Article 13(1), the award may be increased further, to a maximum of 100% of such expenses, if the tribunal "deems it fair and just".

The wording of this rule seems to be rather odd: if, on one hand, a "maxi-

---

408. While LOF 1980 was in force, the exception was obviously limited to the cargo of a "tanker laden with a cargo of oil", and only if the salvage was governed by the said LOF contract.
409. As to the non-remunerative nature of the special compensation, see Gaeta, "La Convenzione di Londra", *op cit.*, 309, compared with Brice, "The New Salvage Convention", *op cit.*, 44.

mum" of 30% is fixed, it is strange, to say the least, that this "maximum" is not really such, as it can be increased in exceptional cases. It would have been better, terminologically, to have said that the "special compensation" of Article 14(2) can, depending on the case and the evaluation of the criteria contained in Article 13(1)(h), (i), (j), be increased to a maximum of 100% of the said expenses, as there is no sense in fixing an intermediate maximum and then granting the judge the authority to exceed it, on the basis of a rather general discretion such as "fair and just".[410]

We have already pointed out the anomalous solution enacted by the Convention, which takes up the Montreal Compromise of the CMI Draft, in rendering only the owner, and consequently the P. & I. Club, of the ship, which by itself or its cargo threatens to damage the environment, liable for payment of the "special compensation" provided for by Article 14(1) and (2). This solution, chosen for reasons pertaining to insurance practice and to related problems of a financial nature (even if it must be admitted that on a practical level answers to these problems, more or less adequate, have been supplied), has certainly exacerbated other problems which, during the discussion of the CMI Draft in Montreal and during the course of the Diplomatic Conference in London, were scarcely considered by the delegates, who were more worried about obtaining the agreement of the more interested categories (hull and cargo underwriters and P. & I. Clubs) to the new legal mechanism proposed.[411]

We shall confine ourselves to mentioning a few of these problems (which have already been noted in doctrine),[412] and to pointing out that one cannot exclude the possibility that others may arise when concrete cases (as opposed to the hypothetical problems envisaged once the Convention enters into force) fall to be examined and evaluated.

One of these problems pertains, for the purposes of obtaining payment of the special compensation, to the lack of any protection of this credit of a

410. Brice, "The New Salvage Convention", op cit., 45, writes: "No guidelines are given as to what may constitute such a case: the matter is left to the discretion of the tribunal. Perhaps (for example) cases will arise when a professional salvor, with a large investment in anti-pollution materials, craft and men, will be entitled in the eyes of the Court to special encouragement to continue providing that service, i.e. by an award in excess of the 30%. Experience will tell how this paragraph is implemented."

411. On this point see Nielsen, "Improvement and Deficiencies", op. cit., 62, who reports the troubled discussion on this point and the US proposal, rejected by the Diplomatic Conference: " . . . according to which a separate and quantified award could be made for the skill and efforts of the salvors in preventing environmental damage. According to the proposal this separate reward should be borne by the property interests in proportion to their value, except when it exceeded a certain percentage of the traditional salvage reward, in which case the excess amount should be borne by the owner of the vessel. The background for this proposal was that it was felt unequitable that the cargo interest in the cases where the environmental enhancement was significant should bear the full proportionate part hereof because often the primary P. & I. responsibilty for pollution damage was exposed. This was felt especially true, where non-pollution cargoes were involved."

412. Thus Brice, "The New Salvage Convention", op.cit., 45, and Gold, "Marine Salvage: Towards a New Regime", op.cit., 501.

special nature within the framework of the Convention; it is obviously not mentioned in the "maritime claims" provided for and listed in the Brussels Convention 1952 on the arrest of sea-going vessels, nor is it amongst the maritime liens covered by the 1967 Convention on maritime liens and mortgages. Therefore, in rewriting the drafts of these Conventions, special compensation must be adequately inserted amongst the maritime claims which grant the possibility of an *actio in rem* against the debtor vessel, and amongst the maritime liens in order to provide special compensation with a satisfactory rank in the gradation of preferred credits against the vessel.[413]

It must be noted that the Convention, thus confirming the torment of the delegates when preparing it, contains two specific Attachments. The first contains a rule of interpretation proposed by the Conference's Working Group:

"It is the common understanding of the Conference that, in fixing a reward under article 13 and assessing special compensation under article 14 of the International Convention on Salvage, 1989 the tribunal is under no duty to fix a reward under article 13 up to the maximum salved value of the vessel and other property before assessing the special compensation to be paid under article 14."

The second Attachment contains a Resolution, in which it is clarified "that payments made pursuant to article 14 are not intended to be allowed in general average," and requesting appropriate steps to be taken in order to amend the York-Antwerp Rules 1974 to reflect this.

The problem relating to this latter aspect will be discussed at a later time and investigated in depth in the last chapter of this work; however, with regard to the regulations and the *ratio* contained in the first Attachment, it must be noted that this resulted from the fact that during the course of the Diplomatic Conference, the CMI representative had commented that the judge or the arbitrator, when fixing within the same context a traditional reward (including the enhancement relating to damage to the environment) of less than the value of the salved properties and a special compensation under Article 14, would have had to take into account the fact that the total payment could not exceed the amount which would have had to be paid if nothing whatsoever had been salved.

In fact, this situation would not have allowed the judge or the arbitrator to pass directly to the calculation of the special compensation whenever the salved properties were of limited value and the expenses and damages sustained by the salvor were considerable as a result of the risk to the environment.[414]

---

413. As mentioned by F. Berlingeri, "Maritime liens and mortgages and related matters", in *CMI Newsletter*, April 1990, 2, it is to be noted that "the reference to general average has been deleted. During the sixth session attention was drawn to the question of whether claims for salvage would include the claims for special compensation pursuant to Article 14 of the new Salvage Convention."

414. Gaeta, "La Convenzione di Londra", *op. cit.*, 312.

The point was taken, and the result was Attachment 1 of the Convention, which represents a rule of interpretation in the new international law.

Thus total compensation is paid only if and to the extent that it exceeds the normal salvage remuneration which, under Article 13, may be obtained by the salvor,[415] but the court or arbitrator is not obliged—when the salved values are clearly inadequate or when the "success" is only partial—to assess the reward before proceeding to calculate the special compensation.

As we have already mentioned several times, special compensation, if due under Article 14(1) and (2) of the Convention, must be borne and paid only by the owner of the ship which, by itself or its cargo, threatened damage to the environment, and consequently by his P. & I. Club, which is, above all, the underwriter of the owner's liabilities. We have indicated the reasons for this more than once; they are founded in areas which are heavily influenced by reasons of financial policy and of the need to maintain a certain balance on the underwriting market. This will not prevent different, and possibly, from a legal point of view, more equitable solutions from being studied and found, since the machinery of the reform of the law of salvage has been set in motion and can no longer free itself of the environmental factor which so strongly influences this institute.[416]

415. Gaeta, "La Convenzione di Londra", op. cit., 311, and Brice, "The New Salvage Convention", op. cit. 44, who, in supplying examples of the method for calculating remuneration as suggested by Attachment 1, finally grants that he cannot "emphasize too strongly that I would be astonished if in practice this type of situation ever arose, but it is theoretically possible".

416. In this respect see Seward, "The Insurance Arrangements Underpinning the Payment of Salvors' Remuneration and P. & I. Insurance", in Salvage, Lloyd's Press Conference papers, (London, 1990), 115, who concludes: "The only good thing that can be said for the Convention from practically every point of view is that it is not worse. The problems were identified but the Convention does not seem to do anything to solve them, with the possible exception of that rare salvage which lies at the margin of viability. Maybe the Clubs and salvors will need to sit down after all and try to find a mutually acceptable contract to deal with the 'failed' salvage situation so as to keep themselves out of the clutches of the dread arbitrators."

CHAPTER SEVEN

OTHER PROVISIONS OF THE NEW CONVENTION

54. APPORTIONMENT BETWEEN SALVORS AND SERVICES RENDERED UNDER EXISTING CONTRACTS

The rule which governs apportionment between the salvors in the 1989 Convention (Article 15), without prejudice to the fact that the apportionment must be effected between the salvors on the basis of the criteria contained in Article 13 of the Convention, defers, for the apportionment between the owners, the master and the other persons in the service of the salvor ship, to the law of the flag of that vessel.

This provision reproduces the final part of Article 6 of the 1910 Convention, but also contains an extension of the norm itself, and this in consideration of the fact that "salvage" in the new Convention is no longer limited to sea-going vessels but may involve non-marine craft, and can even apply in non-navigable waters. Necessary, therefore, for the rule correctly to comply with the general basic principle of the new institute, is the insertion of the words: "If the salvage has not been carried out from a vessel, the apportionment shall be determined by the law governing the contract between the salvor and his servants."

This extension of the law to persons other than the owner, master and crew, clarifies and resolves, once and for all, the problems which had to be dealt with by the 1910 Convention, where discussion was held and a conclusion reached on the possibility of including persons unconnected with the navigating community, such as mooring-men, port pilots and stevedores, in the category of salvors.[417]

A further extension of the range of some of the aspects of salvage governed by the new Convention is to be found in Article 17. Article 4 of the 1910 Convention had established that "A tug has no right to remuneration for assistance to or salvage of the vessel she is towing or of the vessel's cargo, except where she has rendered exceptional services which cannot be considered as rendered in fulfilment of the contract of towage". The new Convention,

---

417. See in this respect Vincenzini, *International Regulations of Salvage at Sea*, 32 et seq., and doctrine and jurisprudence quoted therein.

indeed, does not restrict the range of the rule to the towage contract but generalises it, extends the rule to all contracts existing before the danger arose, acknowledging the salvors' right to remuneration only in the cases where the services rendered go beyond that which "can be reasonably considered as due performance of a contract entered into before the danger arose".

This significant extension of the range of the norm is a direct consequence of the new direction given by international law to the institute of salvage, which is no longer restricted to the marine environment; and by referring to the active and passive subjects, it no longer confines itself to considering as such only the owners, the masters and the crews of vessels involved in the event, or the owners of things which are on board at the time of the accident.[418] These contracts, therefore, can relate to persons on board the salved vessel (enrolment-contract), port pilots, mooring-men, stevedores, port crane operators and, in the event, any person who is connected with the owner of the salved "property" by any type of contractual relationship.[419]

We do not feel we can agree with the statement in a recent doctrine,[420] which peremptorily affirms that "the requirement that any salvor should be a volunteer, and that services are not salvage if performed under a pre-existing contract, is basically preserved by Art. 17". Indeed, Article 17 does not establish that services which are rendered on the basis of a pre-existing contract cannot be "salvage", but rather that if salvage services beyond the limits of the obligations envisaged in a previous contract are rendered should the necessity arise, thus coexisting with and overriding the contractual obligations, these latter services must be considered as "salvage".

Therefore the two relationships which exist between the parties, one of a contractual nature and the other characterised by "voluntariness", are quite distinct; in effect the latter does not exempt the salvor from rendering the services contracted for or from complying with the original contractual obligation, unless the emergency situation makes performance impossible, just as the right to a separate remuneration for the salvage accomplished does not cancel the right to payment for the services rendered on the basis of the previous contract.[421]

418. Gaeta, "La Convenzione di Londra", *op. cit.*, 304, states in this respect that "the generalization of the norm was based on the fact that when interpreting and applying Art. 4 of the previous Convention, it had been maintained that this Article contains a principle which is confined to the towage, an analogical extension being possible, given the *idem ratio*, to all cases in which the salvage operation is rendered by a person (for example, a crew member, a pilot) already bound by contractual relationship with the owner of the ship in danger".

419. To revert to the absurd hypothesis previously formulated in note 363, the driver of a lorry which, during the course of his employment contract, has fallen into a lake and is salved by him, exceeds the contract services due by him to the owner, and is entitled to remuneration for the salvage operation accomplished.

420. Thus Darling and Smith, *op. cit.*, 67. Appropriate and correct, instead, is the subsequent comment that the Convention has not taken into account the fact that in some cases *services rendered pursuant to a statutory rather than a contractual duty* must be dealt with.

421. Also Gaeta, "La Convenzione di Londra", *op. cit.*, 305. On the matter of voluntariness, see also *The Texaco Southampton* [1983] 1 Lloyd's Rep. 94.

55. SALVOR'S MISCONDUCT AND LIMITATION OF LIABILITY

The problem of the salvor's misconduct and of the possibility of the salvor relying upon the limitation of liability was the subject of a lively debate in learned articles, following a by now famous decision in the House of Lords,[422] which had denied the salvors the right to limit their own liability, on the basis of the principle that the salvors do not enjoy a "special status", with the result that "if their efforts produced more harm than good they will be monetarily liable for the difference".

The 1989 Convention deals with and resolves the problem by co-ordinating two specific rules—Article 14(5) and (6), and Article 18:

"Article 14

(5) If the salvor has been negligent and has thereby failed to prevent or minimize damage to the environment, he may be deprived of the whole or part of any special compensation due under this article.

(6) Nothing in this article shall affect any right of recourse on the part of the owner of the vessel.

Article 18
A salvor may be deprived of the whole or part of the payment due under this Convention to the extent that the salvage operations have become necessary or more difficult because of fault or neglect on his part or if the salvor has been guilty of fraud or other dishonest conduct."

The two Articles assert the same principle, but because of the different natures of the special compensation and of the traditional salvage reward, they give separate consideration to the possibility of the two types of remuneration being negatively influenced, reduced or cancelled by culpable or negligent behaviour on the part of the salvor.

It has been pointed out, justly,[423] that Article 18 appears to have a wider range of application than Article 8 of the 1910 Convention, in as much as in the new formulation of the regulation the word "neglect" appears, whereas in Article 8 only the word "fault" was admitted. This leads one to believe that the Brussels Convention 1910 intended to refer only to "grave fault" on the part of the salvors, as negligence (at least with regard to our national law) is

---

422. See *The Tojo Maru* [1971] 1 Lloyd's Rep. 341. This judgment deemed that a diver, working under water and operating from a large tug used in the salvage operation, could not be considered as an extension of the tug, inasmuch as he was no longer "on board" the tug itself; therefore "the prerequisite under the limitation provision of the Merchant Shipping Act" was lacking. For an accurate analysis of the case, see Kerr, "The Salvage Convention, Expediency or Equity", 20 J.L.M.C. 516.

423. Thus Brice, "The New Salvage Convention", *op. cit.*, 45, who justly also points out that both the articles "leave unstated the extent of the liability of a salvor to damages due to his negligence. There can be little doubt that such a liability exists in most and perhaps all jurisdictions: indeed there are special provisions in the London Limitation Convention 1976 as respects a salvor's entitlement to limit his liability to damages."

one of the elements constituting fault in the widest sense, even fault of the lightest nature.[424]

It is necessary to point out right away that, apart from the necessary introduction into the Convention of the provisions contained in Article 14(5) and (6), because of the presence, in the new regulations, of "special compensation" alongside traditional remuneration, the new instrument does not completely solve the problem and does not supply common principles in the matter of liability and "of assessment of damages", leaving the door open to different solutions within the framework of the national jurisdictions of the Contracting States. Also, as things stand, the London Convention 1976 (even though it contains specific provisions in this respect and though it came into force) is binding only on a limited number of States.

In this respect it should be noted that the CMI Montreal Draft had inserted Article 5.1, which expressly established: "A contracting State may give salvors a right of limitation equivalent in manner and extent to the right provided for by the 1976 Convention on the Limitation of Liability for Marine Claims. Lengthy discussion between the delegates had changed "shall" into "may", as the imperative would have caused the States involved to consider respect of the norm to be compulsory.

Having established that many States, as is indeed the case, would not, for various reasons, ratify the 1976 London Convention, the proposed norm was subsequently excluded from the new Convention.[425] It should be noted, however, that the salvor's right to plead limitation of liability still exists, in spite of the absence of any specific inclusion of this right in the uniform text and the lack of any express reference to the 1976 Convention.[426]

It should be pointed out that the Convention does not contain any useful indication regarding the way in which the reward due can be reduced, or as to the systems provided by international law in respect of the setting off of remuneration against damages caused due to fault during salvage operations. The 1989 Convention, in fact, leaves the field completely open to those solutions that arbitrators and courts will actually apply within the sphere of their own national legal systems, but it is certainly to be hoped that, in the near future, the gap will be filled and that uniform international law will establish "a common set of principles on liability and on assessment of damages".[427]

The issues relating to wilful misconduct by the salvor would appear to confine the assessment of damages within the framework and within the limits of

424. The Italian Navigation Code (Art. 275) does not allow the owner to limit his own liability if he is guilty of "gross fault". With regard to the conceptual diversity between "slight and gross" fault in the English and American systems, see Brice, "The New Salvage Convention", *op. cit.*, 52.

425. See Kerr, "The 1989 Salvage Convention, *op. cit.*, 518.

426. See in this respect Brice, "The New Salvage Convention", *op. cit.*, 51, who clearly states, "for better or worse, shipowners, including salvors, can limit their liability and that is a legal right".

427. Thus, textually, Brice, *op. cit.*, 53.

both the special compensation due to the salvor (Article 14) and of the reward for the traditional salvage performed (Article 13). In fact, from a careful perusal of these Articles, it could be argued that the salvor who has acted with fault or negligence, both in attempting to limit damage to the environment and in rendering necessary, or more difficult, the salvage operations provided, may be deprived of the whole or part of what is due to him. This would lead to the conclusion that the special compensation on the one hand, and the traditional reward on the other, already constitute a limit—over and above the general limit existing on the basis of the legal principle of owner's limitation of liability—beyond which the setting off of the damage caused could not operate.

One could therefore say that damage caused by the salvor's wilful misconduct would find an initial obstacle, represented by the salvor's own limit of liability on the basis of the general principles applicable to him; and, in any event, a second and definite obstacle represented by the amount of the special compensation or of the traditional salvage reward earned, as the case may be.[428]

This view does not seem correct to us; instead we consider that the solution to the problem must be found in a formula which is contrary to that mentioned above: if the damage caused by the salvor is greater than what the salvor has earned under the heading of special compensation or of the traditional reward, then he will lose the right to the afore-mentioned remunerations *in toto*, remaining liable for any further damages due within the confines of his own limitation of liability in so far as applicable.

It must not be forgotten that this limitation of liability could fail to find application in those cases where the damage caused is the direct result of a "personal" fault on the part of the owner of the salving vessel.

A final observation must be made in respect of the salvor's limitation of liability, in the light of the fact that the 1989 Convention does not restrict itself to the regulation of salvage at sea.

In effect, the principle of owner's limitation of liability is typical of marine law, and it would not be applied, in our national system, to the salvor who is not an owner, that is to say not even to salvors who have operated at sea without nautical craft, or who have even operated in internal waters, whether navigable or not. The problem of the serious dissonance produced when considering the extension of the field of application, whether subjective or objective, of the Convention, may find a solution within the framework of our own law, as the Italian Code of Navigation also provides for the application of its rules

---

428. For a short and accurate account of the various cases that may be laid before adjudicators, see Brice, *op. cit.*, 47, who after having considered several cases in which numerous difficulties will arise in reaching a correct final decision, concludes by stating that "the problem becomes even more acute if the salvor is allowed to limit his liability to a large amount of damages and then set off the limited damages against an award of salvage made on an inflated notional fund".

by analogy so that to the salvor who is not an owner, one may apply, by analogy, the limit of liability which the Code envisages for the latter.[429]

However, we do not feel that it will be so easy to achieve a solution to the problem which arises out of the new international uniform regulations in matters of salvage. By making no mention whatsoever of the salvor's limitation of liablity in the widest sense, and containing no express references to the 1976 Convention on owners' limitation of liability, nor to analogy, they do not appear to extend to the salvor/non-owner the general principles governing the liability of the owner.[430]

Obviously, once a certain, if only partial, harmonisation has occurred between those States which have ratified the London Convention 1976 on owners' limitation of liability and those States which have ratified the London Convention 1989 on salvage, the problem would be resolved whenever both Conventions would be applicable to the case at hand.[431]

56. LIENS AND SECURITY FOR SALVAGE REMUNERATION

The protection of the payment due to the salvor, be it a reward for services rendered in a traditional salvage or a special compensation under Article 14(1) of the 1989 Convention, would not appear to have been tackled by the new uniform text, and certainly not sufficiently to clear the field of the problems, at times insoluble, which had made it difficult, and sometimes almost impossible, for the salvors to secure suitable security for their own claims.

The problem relating to obtaining security from the saved properties, which was already serious with regard to obtaining security from the interests of cargoes carried by the salved vessel, in the absence—persistent, as we have seen—of any acknowledged principle of solidarity between ship and cargo, appears to be considerably aggravated by the presence in the wording of the new uniform Convention of the so-called "special compensation" which is due to salvors who have attempted to prevent or to minimise damage to the

---

429. In this respect see Gaeta, *Le fonti del diritto della navigazione* (Milan, 1960), 206 *et seq.*

430. It should be noted that if the insertion of the norm of the 1976 Convention had taken place by virtue of the reference proposed by the CMI draft, the salvor who was not an owner would have found a placing among the subjects entitled to invoke limitation of liability, inasmuch as the Convention does not apply solely to shipowners and its extension to "salvors", including "the salvor not operating from a ship", also embraces those who effect the salvage even without nautical craft and those who, by reasons of the performance of the salvage operation, are not on board the salving vessel. In this respect see Dani, *Responsabilità limitata per crediti marittimi* (Milan, 1983), 38.

431. At this stage it is well to remember that the inclusion of salvors among the parties entitled to limitation constitutes the most important of the innovations introduced by the 1976 Convention which, in fact, extended the benefit of the limitation to the "salvor not operating from any ship" and to the "salvor operating solely on the ship, or in respect of which he is rendering salvage services".

environment, even when the salvage services to the ship and cargo in danger have not met with any success.

In fact, the salvor who has not salved anything but who, in any event, has earned the right to a "special compensation" for the above-mentioned reasons, would be without any protection *vis-à-vis* his own debtor, the owner of the salved ship, as the property upon which a maritime lien could be exercised in order to secure the claim no longer exists.

Nor, on the other hand, does the Convention, with Article 21, appear to have solved the problem encountered by the salvor whenever he saves a cargo; the example of a container-ship is typical. This is divided into thousands of bills of lading, cargo in respect of which it is already extremely difficult to effect any arrest because of the considerable and insoluble problems in identifying the individual owners and serving them with the order of arrest; the wording of Article 21 contains nothing more than a simple "recommendation" to the owners of ships to use "their best endeavours to ensure that the owners of the cargo provide satisfactory security".

This norm—as has been pointed out—has not satisfied the salvors' requirements but has effected only a slight improvement in the situation should the shipowners not comply; it remains a mere declaration of principle with no powers of enforcement.[432]

The rule, it is true, finds a certain amount of support in Article 21(3), where the ship and cargo interests are prohibited from removing the saved properties from the port of redelivery until an adequate guarantee has been supplied, but it is just as obvious that the only way of obtaining compliance with this obligation (purely theoretical since it has been left to the voluntary compliance of debtors who could in any event remove their own property) is for the salvor to obtain safeguarding measures on the saved properties to protect his own claims, thus creating a legal obstacle preventing their removal.

Even though the Convention is silent in this respect, one can even theorise, for the salvors, the possibility of taking normal legal steps against the owner of the salved vessel who did not fulfil his duty "to use his best endeavour" in order to obtain adequate security from the cargo interests for the salvor; but the doubts as to which law is applicable to the given case and under which jurisdiction the action can be brought, certainly remain quite strong or persistent in the absence of any specific reference in the text of the Convention.[433]

A recent authoritative doctrine has stated, in this respect, that until the rights of the salvors have been acknowledged by a judge or by an arbitrator by way of a judgment or an award, these remain "pending", which gives absolutely no assurance that they will be granted.[434]

---

432. Thus Darling and Smith, *op. cit.*, 69.

433. Considerable doubts relating to the actual range of the regulations are expressed by Kerr, "The 1989 Salvage Convention", *op. cit.*, 519, who, in this respect, concludes that it only remains to "wait and see" what the courts faced with the problem will decide in such matters.

434. Thus, textually, Gaeta, "La Convenzione di Londra", *op. cit.*, 314.

The remark is pertinent: in the attempt to provide the salvor, pending any decision, with adequate protection for his claims, the 1989 Convention supplies, with Article 20(1) and (2), a regulation of a merely enunciative nature, which, in a certain sense, merely acknowledges existing legal situations either in the national laws of the individual States, or in the current uniform international laws on liens and mortgages (International Conventions for the unification of certain rules relating to Maritime Liens and Mortgages of 1926 and of 1967) or in the uniform discipline which, *de jure condendo*, international organisations are preparing[435] (IMO draft articles for a Convention on Maritime Liens and Morgages).

In fact, in respect of salvage remuneration, the maritime lien exists in all national legislations, though with differing ranks in the gradation of other preferred credits, as is envisaged both by the 1926 and 1967 Conventions and by the above-mentioned IMO Draft, and rules like those of the 1989 Convention do not bring about any improvement to the uniform law, both because of their obviousness (it is superfluous to state that liens cannot be exercised in the event of a suitable guarantee being given) and because they—just as obviously—confirm (not having however in any way arranged anything positive in this respect) that "Nothing in this Convention shall affect the salvor's maritime lien under any international convention or national law".[436]

The doubt remains as to whether the special compensation could (since it does not constitute an actual right on the part of the salvor for salvage in the traditional sense) be protected by any maritime lien; in effect, in drawing up the IMO draft on maritime liens and mortgages it had initially been envisaged that Article 4, in which maritime liens are specifically indicated, would also contain an express inclusion of the claim for special compensation pursuant to Article 14 of the Salvage Convention. In the final text proposed by the IMO, after the sixth session of the Joint Intergovernmental Group of Experts, special compensation does not appear, however, which leads one to the conclusion that as it is a salvor's right, it falls under the generic and general heading of claims for salvage.

In any event, even though the legal nature of the two remunerations—as we have already seen—is quite different, the close interconnection between the two purposes, the salvage of the ship and her cargo and the prevention of damage to the environment, is perfected and falls within the framework of the "salvage" to which Article 4 of the IMO project does in fact make reference.

In the matter of supplying securities, the 1989 Convention does not introduce any new principle into the already existing norms, and even if the 1910 Convention did not make any provisions in this respect, one should consider

---

435. For the text of this IMO Draft and for comment on it, see F. Berlingeri, "Marine Liens and Mortgages and Related Matters", *op. cit.*, 1 et seq., and in Dir. Mar., 1990, 236.4.

436. For a complete examination of salvage liens in various national legislations, see the fundamental study by Tetley, *Maritime Liens and Claims* (London, 1985), 130 et seq., and with regard to the English legal system, Thomas, *Maritime Liens and Claims* (London, 1980), 240.

the responsibility of the salved property interests to issue such security for the purpose of preventing the salvors from seizing the ship and her cargo[437] (in order to guarantee the above-mentioned credits and in order to ensure the maintenance of the maritime lien as prevailing over the salvor's right to obtain adequate security for his own claims).

The Convention, in Articles 25 and 26, takes it upon itself to adopt the policy of excluding from arrest any so-called "State-owned and humanitarian cargoes", not because the salvors are not entitled to claim against them but because the guarantee is in *re ipsa*, since the owing State, rather than "having assumed the obligation to remunerate the salvage operations which concern it"—as has been recently stated[438]—, represents a public body able, from a patrimonial point of view, to supply adequate security to satisfy the salvors' claims, without the need for specific and collateral guarantees.

Still on the subject of protecting the salvor's claim, the new uniform Convention introduces a rule (Article 22) which allows a court or arbitrator to order "interim payments", reverting to the principle of what is "just and fair"—in other words, of equity. This provision is an attempt to meet with the requirements of salvors, particularly of professional salvors, who commonly invest considerable sums of money in the salvage "industry" and then see themselves compelled, due to the slowness of ordinary judgments, and to some extent of arbitration procedures, to wait for years in order to obtain payment of their claims. The rule in question also contains a provision with regard to the reduction of the security issued by debtors of the reward as a consequence of the interim payment, but it does not say anything about the hypothesis envisaged by the wording of the LOF contract, to the effect that the amount of the interim payment may, at the end of the judgment, be greater than the final award.[439]

57. INTEREST, PUBLICATION OF ARBITRATION AWARDS AND LIMITATION PERIODS

In the final provisions of Chapter IV of the 1989 Convention there are some which relate to aspects not expressly envisaged by the old uniform text, such as the fixing of interest due on amounts payable under the heading of salvage reward (Article 24), the publication of arbitral awards (Article 27) and others relating to the limitation of actions (Article 23), which—as we shall see—modify the old conventional text in a singular manner.

---

437. In this respect, our Code of Navigation (Art. 558), in order to safeguard the lien and avoid possible expiry of the legal term of validity, provides for the arrest of the ship and her cargo in Italian territorial waters; in fact the said expiry terms are suspended until it is possible to seize the ship and her cargo.
438. Thus Gaeta, "La Convenzione di Londra", *op. cit.*, 316.
439. Darling and Smith, *op. cit.*, 70.

Interest on amounts due under the new law is determined in accordance with the law of the State where the case is brought, and this is in accordance with Article 2 which provides for recourse to the Convention whenever a legal action or an arbitration is brought in a contracting State, giving absolute prominence to what is known as "forum shopping".

Article 27 contains a simple encouragement to the contracting States to permit the publication of arbitration awards for the purpose of increasing jurisprudence, which, in the matter of salvage, is somewhat scanty, given the tendency of parties, within the framework of this institute, to make frequent recourse to arbitration procedures the decisions of which have always been characterised by confidentiality and circumspection.

The rule in Article 27, as it has been worded, represents merely an invitation to the contracting parties and has no binding effect, particularly if one considers that, in the text drawn up by the CMI in this advanced draft and in that of the IMO Committee, the rule provided that the State parties "shall encourage, as far as possible and if need be with the consent of the parties, the publication of arbitral awards made in salvage cases". The elimination in the course of the Diplomatic Conference of the words "if need be", following a motion by the French delegation, shows that the consent of the parties constitutes a prerequisite in any event, which leads one to believe that as the parties would normally prefer to maintain a certain secrecy about the results of arbitration procedures, the invitation contained in the Article is unlikely to encounter frequent acceptance.[440]

Particularly odd is the Article of the Convention which governs limitation periods for actions by a salvor (Article 23). Though it is of an innovative nature, it is difficult to understand the *ratio* which overturns the basic criterion of all national and international disciplines, whether of common or civil law, relating to limitation periods and the system for interruption or extension.[441] Indeed, without prejudice to the fact that the general limitation period (but perhaps it would be better to speak of the "term of expiry") is two years from the end of the salvage operations (Article 23(1), the owner of the salved property—that is to say the debtor—is permitted, at will, to extend the term. This not only constitutes a novelty but also a solution somewhat open to criticism from a legal point of view, as it allows the party which has an interest in protracting the proceedings as much as possible (particularly in those countries in which statutory interest rates are low) to extend the limitation period or term of expiry to its own liking.

In any event, the Convention, though establishing the new principle, does

---

440. See, in this respect, Nielsen, "Report to CMI", *op. cit.*, 6.
441. This question has been pointedly raised by Gaeta, "La Convenzione di Londra", *op. cit.*, 317, who writes: " . . . this singular extension of the term of prescription by the debtor's decision is an institute which is unheard both in continental law as well as in common law: normally the term of prescription operates in favour of the debtor and the shorter it is, the more it benefits him."

not bother to indicate whether an extension can be called for several times by the debtors of the reward, or by how much the extension, if granted once only, can prolong the term beyond its legal expiry date.[442]

Even if the *ratio* of the provision may have purely practical reasons, if necessary and in some cases, such as allowing debtors of the reward sufficient time to gather all the evidence needed to resist the salvor's claim, it is clear that it makes a substantial modification to the limitation period, particularly with regard to the actual purpose of the time limit, i.e., a punitive measure *vis-à-vis* the party who, though having an interest, remains inactive in claiming his own rights. From being a time limit with the purpose of obtaining greater rapidity in judgments, whether legal or arbitral, the limitation period (so strangely extendible in the wording of the new Convention) becomes an instrument for delaying the decision in cases of salvage brought before judges or arbitrators; and is, in any event, a source of considerable and useless interpretative doubts in the case—as already mentioned—of repeated extensions and in the event of the determination of the duration of any such extension.[443]

58. FINAL CLAUSES

The final clauses of the new Convention (Articles 28 to 34) contain the regulations relating to the entry into force of the Convention, the procedure for putting it into effect, reservations, denunciations and, finally, the means and procedures for its revision or amendment.

In this respect the new Convention does not contain any particular innovations, even if it must be acknowledged that the new discipline *vis-à-vis* that of the 1910 Convention seems to be better structured and more complete; in particular where (Article 30) Contracting States are clearly and unequivocally granted the right to make reservations and not to apply the Convention in the following instances:

"(a) when the salvage operation takes place in inland waters and all vessels involved are of inland navigation;

(b) when the salvage operations take place in inland waters and no vessel is involved;

(c) when all interested parties are nationals of that State;

(d) when the property involved is maritime cultural property of prehistoric archaeological or historic interest and is situated on the sea-bed."

---

442. According to Gaeta, "La Convenzione di Londra", *op. cit.*, 316, the extension should not be granted more than once and for a period of not more than two years, without prejudice to the right on the part of the applicant to extend the limit for a shorter period.

443. It should be noted that when the new Convention comes to form part of our own system, Art. 2936 of our Civil Code which establishes definitely the finality of prescription periods, will undergo a substantial modification, at least for this specific time limit, since a sole party is allowed to extend the duration.

There is, however, an innovation in Article 34, which indicates the official languages on the basis of which the uniform text must be interpreted and applied. Apart from the traditional French and English, Arabic, Chinese, Russian and Spanish are also listed and therefore assume equal dignity and authenticity in this respect.

CHAPTER EIGHT

THE NEW LLOYD'S OPEN FORM (LOF 1990) AND THE AMENDMENT TO THE YORK-ANTWERP RULES (1974)

59. THE ADAPTATION OF INTERNATIONAL CONTRACTUAL PRACTICE TO THE NEW PRINCIPLES INTRODUCED BY THE LONDON CONVENTION

In the early-1980s, at the same time, and on the same basis, as CMI was preparing the groundwork for the draft of new Convention on salvage (a draft which was later approved in Montreal), a new standard wording for the Lloyd's salvage contract was discussed and approved. At the end of the decade—when the new Convention was approved—the new LOF 1990 was unveiled, inspired by this Convention and drawing upon it for its innovative features.

It must be said that while, in 1980, the international contract drawn up by Lloyd's had, by introducing the "safety net", even if with objective limitations (since it applied only to tanker vessels carrying oil fully or partially laden), anticipated to a certain extent what was to be termed the "Montreal Compromise" on special compensation, inserting the environmental factor within the regulations of the institute of salvage at sea, the situation was quite different in respect of the LOF 1990: this contract, while acknowledging the international legislation prepared by the Convention and the presence therein of extremely innovatory elements, sought—in the knowledge and conviction that the high number of ratifications required would considerably delay the entry into force of the Convention—to provide the market and the international salvage industry with a suitable instrument reflecting the proposed innovations, with which to regulate (even if only within the framework of the contractual autonomy of the parties) those contractual commitments which these parties intend to regulate (as is frequently the case in matters of salvage), by resorting to this tried and tested form of contract known throughout the world.[444]

It must therefore be acknowledged that if, on the one hand, the new LOF 1990 represented the activating force in respect of the contractual aspects of

---

444. For a full examination of the evolution and development of the institute of salvage, see Vincenzini, *International Regulation of Salvage at Sea*, 89 *et seq.*, and Darling and Smith, *op. cit.*, 33 *et seq.*

the reform, constituting an awareness of the reform by the insurance market, on the other hand it had the very great merit of actually putting the reform into effect, even if only between those contracting parties which would resort to the use of LOF 1990, permitting the application of the reform's innovatory principles even before these become a legislative reality.[445]

Nevertheless, though LOF 1990 already supplies, and will supply, a useful means of introducing the new basic principles of the institution, this will not prevent a serious dissonance between current uniform international law—still governed by the old regulations—and international contract praxis, anchored as it is to the more modern principles of the new institute of salvage as conceived by the 1989 Convention.

This will also lead to the potential, though limited, risk that the new Convention, should it fail to achieve the minimum number of ratifications, will not enter into force, and that we shall find ourselves faced with the absurd situation in which the new principles of salvage cannot be applied unless mutually agreed by the parties involved, and then only to a specific and restricted number of cases of salvage, or unless applied in those countries which have chosen to incorporate these principles into their own legal systems.[446] This situation, which cannot be entirely ruled out, would result in the coexistence of innovatory national and contractual laws with obsolete uniform international regulations, in what can only be described as an incoherent and confusing legal environment.

It is to be hoped that this will not happen or, if it does, that the situation will not last long, and that it will be mitigated by an enlightened innovatory interpretation of the institute by those courts and arbitration tribunals which will be called upon to hear cases in which the environmental factor and the need to protect the environment cannot be ignored, both in the interests of the international community and of the salvage industry.

The process of preparing and drafting a new standard text for the Lloyd's Open Form Contract was initiated immediately after the adoption at Montreal of the CMI Draft for the new Convention. With the new contractual provisions of the 1980 LOF in force, Lloyd's set up a working group of experts, consisting of representatives from the salvage industry, insurance companies and the legal profession, who were entrusted with the task of keeping abreast of the developments in the reform of the institute of salvage on a year-by-year basis, revising the text of the contract, seeking to adapt it to

445. This situation, however, constitutes a serious problem to uniform law, because contractual and non-contractual relationships governed by out-dated forms which are not in line with the provisions of the new Convention are still regulated by the old 1910 Convention—which is still in force—and contracts which make no provision for the innovatory aspects of the new international regulations.

446. With reference to the problem of the *enactment* of the new Convention in the various national laws, see (with reference to English law) Gaskell, "Enactment of the 1989 Salvage Convention", *op. cit.* 352 *et seq.*

the new principles, assimilating them and, where necessary, absorbing them, with an eye to meeting the latest demands of the international market, ensuring that the contract is workable.

The working group concluded its task in September 1990, around the time the new salvage Convention was due to be approved in London, the preparation and publication of the Convention having been a subject of particular interest to the working group, with considerable time spent on monitoring developments and results achieved by the international legislator in the course of the preparation of the Convention.[447]

As we have already had occasion to point out in the course of this work, the initial impetus, revolutionary and, in a way, devastating with respect to the old regulatory principles, *ab immemorabili*, of salvage, came about in the 1980s with the introduction of the so-called "safety net" into the LOF contract—a principle which constituted the first, and by no means insignificant, retreat from the principle of "no cure no pay", and which admitted, even if only in strictly limited and well defined cases, that an unsuccessful operation was deserving of a certain reward. But for the CMI delegates, the glimmer of light represented by the "safety net" provided an opportunity for the introduction of the principle into the draft of the new Convention, thus broadening its scope, which was dangerously restrictive, and, on the basis of tried and tested contractual procedures, for bringing remuneration more into line with salvors' requirements.

The proposals formulated in the CMI's initial draft—which were incorporated into the IMO Draft and subsequently became part of the new text of the London Convention—opened the door for the entry onto the international scene of the new institute of special compensation, which, included in the text of the LOF 1990, has already been successfully applied.

So, within a single decade we have seen the conclusion of a complex process which has generated these new and revolutionary provisions within the ambit of maritime law, that is to say, within that branch of the law which, with commendable intuition, was once described by an ancient but authoritative doctrine as "the living law" (Scialoia). And the genesis of special compensation clearly supports that assertion, bearing in mind that the principle found application, at the outset and conclusion of this process of reform, in the text of a contract which has made this principle a point both of departure and of arrival, readily and carefully adapting contract praxis and procedure to the demands of a reform which has subsequently become a legislative reality and, finally, to the need for a practical instrument which could be easily applied, if only on a purely voluntary and contractual basis.

---

447. See in this respect the history of the activities of the Working Group as reported by Darling and Smith, *op. cit.*, 83 *et seq.*, with a report on how, within just one month of its publication, the very first LOF 1990 contract had already been stipulated between the parties, thus providing *another indication of the "domination of the LOF in the salvage market"*.

60. JURISDICTION AND THE LAWS APPLYING TO SALVAGE CONTRACTS

Before moving on to an analysis of the new text of the LOF contract and the innovatory principles in that document, we feel it would be helpful if we re-examined one particular aspect of the text which has already been the subject of some discussion in this treatise when dealing with clause 1(d) of LOF 1980.[448]

We have had, in fact, occasion to point out that, though this provision grants English law the right to regulate the form of the contract and of the arbitration procedure, it cannot substantially be considered as the law governing the contract. In fact, when the salvage contract is entered into by parties of different nationalities and belonging to States which adhered to the Brussels Convention 1910, it should fall within the regulatory ambit of that Convention. Indeed, it would have been strange if, having provided the international community with a uniform text, the legislator were to allow the parties wide powers to depart from it and seek a remedy in the national law of just one of the contracting States, and this on the basis of a waiver clause allowing the parties to derogate from international uniform jurisdiction written into the LOF agreement which is issued in England herself.

Since the new LOF 1990 incorporates (clause 2) a number of the Convention's provisions, notably those which contain the "definitions", as well as the new basic principles relating to salvage, in practice the new uniform international law has become, thanks to this incorporation, the law of the contract, and this by reason of the fact that, without such incorporation, this international law would not have been able—since it was not yet in force—to fulfil any sort of regulatory role in respect of the contractual regulations.

Nor does it seem to us that clause 1(g) of the new LOF in any way removes the qualificatory aspects of the new institute from the uniform law, since those aspects are the cornerstones of that discipline, indicating, as that clause clearly states that "This Agreement and Arbitration thereunder shall except as otherwise expressly provided be governed by the law of England, including the English law of salvage".

In fact, the deference to English jurisdiction which, we confirm (in so far as it relates to the law governing the form of the contract and the provisions of a procedural nature regarding arbitration in London) appears to be perfectly in line with the objectives adopted, cannot be interpreted as a departure from the new uniform discipline of the Convention since, the latter, though restricted to Articles 1(a)–(e), 8, 13(1), 13(2) (first sentence), 13(3) and 14, has come to form part of contract law.

Furthermore, clause 1(g) of the LOF 1990, by stating that English law

---

448. See Vincenzini, *International Regulation of Salvage at Sea*, 103.

(including that governing salvage) will regulate the contract "except as other-wise expressly provided", makes it quite clear that English law cannot and is not intended to replace that substantial area of uniform international law which the contract has made its own and which, therefore, falls within those regulations from which area English law has no intention of departing.

In this respect one must also remember that Article 6(1) of the 1989 London Convention—unlike the 1910 Convention, which made no provision for this—specifically allows that salvage contracts can, expressly or implicitly, provide that the Convention's provisions will not apply, though this is not to be interpreted as meaning that those of the Convention's provisions relating to the cancellation or amendment of contracts can be ignored, nor that the principle which requires the salvor to prevent or minimise damage to the environment can be violated.

As we have seen, therefore, the reference to English law, as *lex loci con-tractus*, fulfils a function limiting the application of English law itself (which goes no further than the provisions governing the validity of the contract in respect of its compliance with formal requirements) and the rules governing arbitration, as the provisions of the Convention are substantially safeguarded by Article 6(3) of the Convention itself or are put into effect following their afore-said incorporation into the wording of the LOF 1990.[449]

61. THE ENVIRONMENTAL FACTOR AND THE INCORPORATION OF THE PROVISIONS OF THE 1989 CONVENTION INTO THE LOF 1990

As we have already seen, the greatest merit offered by the new LOF 1990 contract is that it anticipates, for those parties, past and future, availing themselves of the contract, a situation where they may apply the basic prin-ciples of the reformed institute of salvage which, anchored as they are to the future entry into force of the 1989 Convention, are in danger of not being effectively applied for some time to come, and introducing at the same time

---

449. On this point, though, in regard to LOF 1980 and the 1910 Convention, Olsen also har-boured some doubts in his review of "International regulation of salvage at sea" in [1990] L.M.C.L.Q. 1990, foreseeing what was subsequently to occur with the incorporation by LOF 1990 of the uniform Convention's regulations when he wrote: "English lawyers will perhaps be forgiven for not fully appreciating the problem, since, unlike later Conventions, the 1910 Con-vention has not been incorporated, *en bloc*, into English Law (and, indeed, it was effectively the opposite process that occurred, with English Law being incorporated into the Convention). How-ever, it will be fascinating to see how far it will be possible, by means of a new edition of Lloyd's Form to anticipate the provisions of the 1989 Convention in countries that have adopted, and will apply, the 1910 Convention in its entirety."See Darling and Smith, *op. cit.*, 86, who, on the same subject, assert that " . . . should the new Convention be enacted into English law before the next edition of LOF is published, it will be interesting to discover whether all the provisions of the Convention are thereby included into LOF 1990. Clearly, if the whole Convention is enacted, then all of its provisions will form a part of 'the English Law of Salvage'."

essential and long-awaited improvements to the contractual conditions of the LOF 1980, the long-apparent inadequacies and discrepancies of which were hardly compatible with the reformative nature of the new Convention which, for the first time, brought the environmental factor onto the contractual scene.[450]

To correct the distortions which had, in the past, limited the effects of the LOF 1980 (which permitted salvors to avail themselves of the safety net only when the salvage operations involved tankers, laden or partially laden with heavy fuel), and widening the field of application of the new contract conditions to all salvage operations in which the salvors seek to prevent or minimise damage to the environment or where, in pursuing that particular objective, some measure of success is obtained (even if none is achieved in the traditional salvage), irrespective of the type of vessel and the pollutive nature of the cargo, the new LOF incorporates a whole series of articles from the new Convention which, though individually selected, reflect—as we shall see—virtually all the innovatory aspects on which the reform is based.

We shall confine ourselves here to examining the principal changes as they relate to the old contract, there being little point in re-examining those areas of the new discipline which do not constitute any substantial change.

It being given that in the new text the property for which the master of a vessel or other authorised person may enter into a salvage contract has been extended to include—in addition to the ship, her cargo, freight, bunkers and stores—"any other property thereon", with a certain and initial compliance with the provisions of Article 1(c) of the new Convention,[451] we would point out that in the new provisions (clause 1(a)(ii)) the salvor (described, as has always been the custom in LOF, as "the contractor") expressly undertakes also to use his best endeavours "while performing the salvage services to prevent or minimise damage to the environment". It would appear to us that this duty is of a compulsory nature and, so far as the salvor is concerned, it cannot be avoided as is maintained by a recent assertion in Anglo-Saxon doctrine— "... once the new Convention is enacted it may not be possible for the contractor to contract otherwise on the basis of a duty to prevent or minimise damage to the environment"—which suggests that as things stand, since the Convention is not yet in force, such a possibility does exist.

The LOF 1990, which embodies provisions drawn from the 1989 Convention, and with particular regard to Articles 8(1)(b), 13(1)(b) and 14, makes it clear enough that, with the new international rules, the duty incumbent on the salvor to prevent or minimise damage to the environment is not—at present, in so far as the contract incorporating those rules is concerned—a condition which can be waived, nor a rule the imposition of which will be effective on the parties only when the Convention comes into force or, in the

---

450. Again in Darling and Smith, *op. cit.*, 83 *et seq.*
451. Allen, "International Convention on Salvage and LOF 90", *op.cit.*, 1.

case of LOF 1990, with the enactment of the Convention in English law.[452] Indeed, from a contractual viewpoint the important practical effect of the immediate introduction and application of the basic principles of the Convention's reform would fail, since all the regulations relating to the environmental factor (if we were to give credence to this debatable opinion) could be ignored by the contractor in the absence of a specific enactment of the Convention which would have the effect of making them compulsory. It must, therefore, be seen as a contractual obligation assumed by and confined to the parties. But an obligation it is, and adherence to it is incumbent upon the parties in their contractual relationship, irrespective of what might subsequently happen to the new Convention in general, or the incorporation of the latter into the law of one or another individual State.

The incorporation of Article 1(a)–(e) constitutes a perfect alignment of the new LOF with the provisions of the 1989 Convention in respect of the definitions of the terms "salvage operation", "vessel", "property", "damage to the environment", and "payment" of compensation or remuneration.

It is worth noting that the incorporation of paragraphs (a) and (c) of this Article of the Convention may appear to be of limited effect in so far as the LOF 1990 is concerned, since this contract would appear to restrict salvage property other than the ship herself and her cargo, bunkers, stores and freight (if at risk), to "any other property" *on board* the salved vessel ("thereon"), while the Convention, instead, extends this category of property to "any other property in danger in navigable waters or in any other waters whatsoever", specifying (paragraph (c)) that "property means any property not permanently and intentionally attached to the shoreline".

The coexistence in the text of the uniform contract of these two different categories of salvable properties, one limited to presence on board the vessel (clause 1(a) of LOF 1990) and the other not (Article 1(a) and (c) of the incorporated Convention), leads us to conclude that the former of these two provisions would take precedence and would have a limitative effect on the latter, so that the parties would not be able to enter into a LOF 1990 contract which did not relate to the salvage of ships, their cargo, bunkers, stores and freight, if at risk, as is in the new LOF 1990 (unlike LOF 1980), expressly (clause 1(a)(i) of the LOF) or implicitly (Article 1(c) of the Convention) indicated.

The broadening effect that it was intended that the Convention should produce, on any type of salvage of property at risk "in navigable waters or in any other waters whatsoever", even if such property were not actually *on board* a ship, does not appear to have been included in the LOF 1990 which, therefore, remains a typical salvage contract of a ship and "property" carried *on board* her, though one must also consider that, with the incorporation of Article 1(a) of the Convention, the contract would also appear to apply to

452. Again in Darling and Smith, *op. cit.*

vessels navigating in inland waters or vessels such as those under construction in non-navigable docks, which could be interpreted as "any other waters whatsoever".[453]

The incorporation of Article 8 of the Convention certainly produced more important and innovatory effects, since all the reciprocal obligations assumed by the salvors and the owners of the salved property under the provisions of the Convention—with particular and express reference to the duty to exercise "due care to prevent or minimize damage to the environment" (incumbent on both categories of party to the salvage, active and passive, and which, further-more, already constitutes a contractual obligation in that it is confirmed by the provisions of clause 1(a)(ii) of LOF 1990)—form part of the contractual agreement of the new form. This particular obligation also seems to have been strengthened, since—as has been correctly pointed out—the contract clause refers to the use of the salvor's "best endeavours" in preventing or minimising damage to the environment, while Article 8(1)(b) and (2)(b) of the Convention speak of both categories of party exercising "due care".[454]

With the introduction of the new uniform discipline relating to the environment and its protection, it is clear that even in international contract law, freed as it is of the restricted and restrictive effects of the LOF 1980, the environmental factor has forced its way in, finding, by means of the 1990 version of the contract, full, tangible and effective application whenever the parties resort to this instrument to regulate their contractual relationship in compliance with the most up-to-date criteria of the institute.

And the picture is enhanced with the further inclusion in LOF 1990 of the provisions of Articles 13 and 14 of the Convention, particularly the introduction to the contract of the principles of "enhancement of the awards" for the "skill and efforts of the salvors in preventing or minimizing damage to the environment", and of "special compensation" which, as expressly acknowledged in clause 1(b), represents an exceptional departure from the principle of "no cure – no pay".[455]

453. We do not feel that we can share the opinion expressed by Darling and Smith, *op. cit.*, 87, when they state that " . . . by the incorporation of parts of Article 1, the definitions of salvage operation, vessel, property, damage to the environment and payment are included. One consequence of this is that the extension of the classes of property capable of being salved, that we have already discussed in the context of the new Convention, also applies to LOF 90", since the *property* indicated in LOF must be a *property* that is found "*thereon*".

454. In this respect Allen, "International Convention on Salvage and LOF 90", *op. cit.*, 1, wrote that " . . . in performing the services, the Contractor shall use his 'best endeavours'. This is to be compared with Article 8(1)(a) of the Convention which requires the salvor to carry out the salvage operations with due care. It is arguable that the 'best endeavours' obligation of LOF 90 places a greater burden upon the salvor than the Convention, although Article 8 is specifically incorporated by clause 2."

455. A thorough analysis of the subject is to be found in Kerr, "The philosophy of 'no cure no pay', in *11th International Tug Convention and International Marine Salvage Symposium* (Halifax, 1990, Surrey, 1991), 253. The author quite correctly points out that the discrepancy which would arise in practice—in fact, it has already arisen—when courts or arbitration tribunals will have to decide on identical cases, some of which are governed by LOF 90 and others by current

One might well ask whether the incorporation of Article 14 of the London Convention into LOF 1990 (even though no specific mention is made in the contract) might not, by implication, also bring about the incorporation of Attachment 1 of the Convention, bearing in mind that the said Attachment contains a rule of authentic interpretation provided by the international legislator, the purpose of which is to give courts and arbitration tribunals a lead on how to determine salvage payments and special compensation on the basis of the provisions of Articles 13 and 14 of the Convention. In our view the close interconnection and interdependence between Attachment 1 and the two Articles incorporated into the contract, support the theory which calls for the inclusion of the Attachment itself, the contents of which will therefore have to be duly considered by arbitrators.[456]

One problem which arises, for the legal practitioner, with the introduction into contract practice of what is doubtless the most important aspect of the new uniform international discipline, is the need to identify the effects that those new provisions, relating essentially to public law, might have within the context of a strictly private contract where there is no clause providing sanctions in the case of non-fulfilment of conditions which, with reference to the environmental factor, impose specific obligations and rules of conduct upon the salvor. Happily, even if the contract contains no specific provision in this respect, it does provide for a penalty in the event of the salvor's non-fulfilment by fully incorporating Article 14 of the Convention, which has the effect of rendering paragraph (5) of that Article applicable to the contract. Article 14(5) clearly states: "If the salvor has been negligent and has thereby failed to prevent or minimize damage to the environment, he may be deprived of the whole or part of any special compensation due under this Article."

62. DUTIES OWED TO CO-OPERATE, SECURITY FOR CLAIMS AND GENERAL PROVISIONS

One innovation in the new text of the LOF 1990 contract (clause 3), although of minor importance, is that which relates to the obligation incumbent upon the owners of salved properties, their agents or employees, to co-operate to the full with the salvor, thus allowing the latter to make reasonable use of the former's equipment, as well as affording any further and final co-operation

international regulations which take no account of the environmental factor, would lead to " . . . the scandalous result of differing decisions emanating from two Tribunals on the same set of facts".

456. However, Darling and Smith, *op. cit.*, 88, take a different view: " . . . the common understanding contained in Attachment 1 is not incorporated, and this is the only respect in which LOF 90 differs from the Convention in its giving effect to the special compensation provisions." It is to be hoped that Brice, who, before LOF 1990 was published, had already dealt with the specific problem of the correct interpretation of Attachment 1 and the recommended criteria (see "The New Salvage Convention", *op. cit.*, 44), again confronts the problem in the light of the new LOF, providing, as is his wont, a sharp and enlightening opinion on this point.

that might be required to bring the salved property to the location indicated in the contract as the place of redelivery or as a "place of safety", depending on the definition given in clause 1 of the contract.

This duty—as has already been pointed out[457]—constitutes perhaps nothing more than a repetition of the provisions of the Convention (Article 8(2)), but it must be stressed that whereas in the uniform text of the Convention the duty relates to the co-operation of the owner of the salved property by accepting redelivery of the said property in the "place of safety" when reasonably requested to do so by the salvor, clause 3 of LOF 1990 requires the owners of the salved property to co-operate in a far broader sense, that of "obtaining entry to the place named or the place of safety", which is undoubtedly something more than a mere acceptance of redelivery.

With reference to the issue of security, with the exception of a few minor and insubstantial modifications, LOF 1990 adheres to nearly all the provisions of its predecessor though, with the removal of the expression "persons firms or corporations resident in the United Kingdom either satisfactory to the Committee of Lloyd's or agreed by the Contractor" and its replacement by "persons firms or corporations either acceptable to the Contractor or resident in the United Kingdom and acceptable to the Council", the list of subjects accepted by the Council of Lloyd's as guarantors has been slightly increased, and a limit of reasonableness has been introduced with regard to the amount of the security to be assessed on the basis of the information available to the salvors at the time of request.[458]

Other minor modifications, of a remedial nature and of no great significance, are those which affect the "general provisions" and arbitration proceedings at both levels, but we prefer to avoid overburdening this treatise, which is aimed at providing something more than a list of changes.[459] It will suffice if we make mention of just one of these modifications, which has more bearing here than the others, particularly in the light of the fact that there are now two differing aspects to the new institute of salvage—that purely relating to the traditional salvage of a ship and her cargo, and that of public law, concerned with the protection of the environment.

This was taken into consideration when the new Lloyd's Open Form was prepared. Bearing in mind the necessary interconnection between traditional salvage operations and the prevention and limitation of damage to the

---

457. In Darling and Smith, *op. cit.*, 182. This imposition of the new form of co-operation with regard to the property salved falls within the sphere of those measures which, as with LOF 1990, it was intended that the Convention should make with the approval of regulations which, facilitating as they do the redelivery of the salved properties and the reaching of the *place of safety* in order to do so, avoid the phenomenon of *maritime leprosy* which we have had occasion to mention.

458. See Piombino, "Solidarietà tra debitori del compenso di assistenza e salvataggio: orientamenti giurisprudenziali e soluzioni adottate nella pratica (LOF 1990)", in Dir. Mar., 1991, 154.

459. With regard to this aspect of the problem, see the previously quoted Darling and Smith, *op. cit.*, 89 *et seq.*

environment, clause 18 stipulates the requirement which calls for termination of the services of the salvor by the owners of the vessel on notice in writing, in circumstances where such a step is reasonable when "there is no longer any reasonable prospect of a useful result leading to a salvage reward in accordance with Convention Article 13". This clause, in fact, was included for the express purpose of avoiding a situation where operations other than normal salvage services—for instance, operations involving the cleaning up of sea pollution—are prolonged beyond the point at which the salvage could have been positively concluded.

Recent Anglo-Saxon doctrine—already quoted on more than one occasion[460]—has summarised the principal changes brought about by LOF 1990 with respect to the 1980 version:

> "(a) improvement of layout and exclusion of excess verbiage in order to present a clear modern contract, which can be readily understood by all who use it, even though they will necessarily sometimes have a poor understanding of the English language;
>
> (b) the introduction in express terms of obligations to protect the environment so far as possible during the performance of salvage services;
>
> (c) general measures, such as the possibility of interest being awarded from the date of termination, to minimize the financial problems of the contractor without simply increasing the size of awards in general;
>
> (d) the incorporation of procedural rules to speed up the arbitral process; and
>
> (e) the enlargement of the safety net to cover a far wider range of pollutants than heavy fuel oil and with room for more generous treatment of salvors driven back to claiming special compensation."

We agree with this identification of these innovations. In fact, Article 13 of the Convention was, indeed, incorporated into the text of the contract, with particular emphasis on paragraph (1)(b), for which reason LOF is not restricted to the mere introduction of an express invitation to salvors to protect the environment during salvage operations, since it must be remembered that the Convention, and the LOF which incorporates it, indicate a definite duty for which, in the event of a "success", the salvor may obtain an "enhancement of the award", and this very substantial modification and innovation, which LOF 1990 has immediately put into good effect in international contract praxis, should not, indeed must not, be ignored.

63. THE AMENDMENT TO SECTION VI OF THE YORK-ANTWERP RULES 1974 ON GENERAL AVERAGE

The basic principles of the rule of general average—yet another typical institute of maritime law and nonexistent in general law—have been passed down

---

460. See Darling and Smith, *op. cit.*, 94.

to us virtually unchanged from the *lex Rhodia de jactu*, which for the very first time codified the principle that any sacrifice made or cost incurred by one of the parties involved when rendering assistance to the other and their property, had to be proportionally compensated and shared amongst the property which had benefited from or been saved as a result of that sacrifice or expense (a typical example in those times was the jettisoning of all or part of the cargo in order to save an endangered venture).

Until 1974 there had been considerable discussion in doctrine regarding the possibility of including, as a part of general average procedure, the decision of a ship's master to seek the assistance and services of a salvor if his vessel and cargo were at risk. The reply of prevailing doctrine to this problem had been in the negative, in spite of the fact that average adjusters, from a practical point of view, in order to avoid unnecessary problems, had started to deal with cases of salvage as if they were cases of general average, even if their inclusion caused some difficulty because they could not always be dealt with in the same way.[461] Then, in 1974, on the occasion of the CMI's Thirtieth Conference in Hamburg, in order to clear the field of sterile doctrinary diatribes which contributed nothing substantial to average adjustment practice (which, in any event, tended to ignore them), the old Rule VI of the York-Antwerp Rules was repealed and replaced in its entirety by a rule which expressly introduced the concept of spontaneous, obligatory and contractual salvage "expenses", as a compendium of the costs, damages and reward, in general average.

Rule VI, paragraph (a) now reads:

"(a) Expenditure by the parties to the adventure in the nature of salvage, whether under contract or otherwise, shall be allowed in general average provided that the salvage operations were undertaken for the purpose of preserving from peril the property involved in the common maritime adventure . . . "

The introduction of the safety net by LOF 1980 had already posed some problems for average adjusters, because if, on the one hand, there was no doubt that the new principle introduced into the institute of salvage had added a new element to those traditionally held essential when determining the reward (which was now influenced by the efforts of the salvors to protect the environment), on the other hand one could hardly fail to acknowledge that the costs incurred by the salvor for this purpose were, as was quite clearly indicated in LOF 1980, no longer imputable to all those with an interest in the venture, as would normally have been the case, but were chargeable to the owner of the salved vessel, and to her owner alone.

A solution to these problems was provided with the signing of the Funding Agreement in London. Under this agreement the P. & I. Clubs assumed exclusive responsibility for the safety net, while the ordinary underwriters

---

461. There is a recent reference to this problem in Mongrandi, "Modifica della Regola VI delle Regole di York ed Aversa 1974" in Dir. Mar., 1990, 861.

continued to cover salvage reward and the consequent contribution to the general average.[462]

As soon as the stamp of approval had been given to the new 1989 Convention, which introduced two distinct and innovatory principles, the "enhancement of award" and "special compensation", both closely related to the protection of the environment, it had immediately to be made clear whether both were to be excluded from the category of costs foreseen by Rule VI of the York-Antwerp Rules 1974, or whether one or the other could be included.

As we have seen, the Convention contains two Attachments, and Attachment 2 expressly provides, among other things, "that payments made pursuant to Article 14 are not intended to be allowed in general average". Further, it "requests the Secretary-General of the International Maritime Organization to take the appropriate steps in order to ensure speedy amendment of the York-Antwerp Rules, 1974, to ensure that special compensation paid under Article 14 is not subject to general average". In the light of this request—perhaps it would be more accurate to call it a command—the IMO invited the President of the CMI to take the necessary steps to start the procedure for amending Rule VI in compliance with the resolution of the London Diplomatic Conference. Accordingly, the CMI set up a working group which was able to conclude its work before CMI's Paris Conference 1990 opened, recommending the adoption of an amended new text for Rule VI, which was approved by a large majority during the plenary session of the Conference.[463] (The full, revised version of Rule VI is set out in Appendix 9, below.)

This amendment is important. On the one hand, it confirms that the "enhancement of award" provided for by Article 13(1)(b) of the Convention constitutes an integral part of the reward and, as such, must be allowed in general average, even if its legal genesis derives from the prevention of environmental damage (and therefore from something completely extraneous to the principle of the sharing of sacrifices suffered by one of the owners of the saved properties to the benefit of others). On the other hand, by excluding the special compensation from general average in accordance with the recommendations of the Conference as contained in Attachment 2, it is made clear that the incorporation of the Convention's provisions into the LOF 1990 shall be understood as extending also to the *Attachments* themselves and to the concrete results deriving and derived from the recommendations contained in those Attachments. So when it came to approving the amendment to Rule VI, the CMI Conference justified its approval on specific grounds, the third of which we reproduce in its entirety:

462. Mongrandi, *op. cit.*, 865. See recently, and diffusely, N. Geoffrey Hudson, *The York-Antwerp Rules* (London, Lloyd's of London Press Ltd., 1991).

463. A broad and detailed background covering the activities of the CMI Working Group is provided in Taylor, "Revision of the York and Antwerp Rules 1974" in CMI Newsletter, Autumn 1990, January 1991, 1 *et seq.* N. Geoffrey Hudson, *op. cit.*, n. 462.

"It was agreed that any amendment to Rule VI should be given prompt effect, especially since Articles 13 and 14 of the salvage Convention were already, even before ratification of the Convention, being given effect to by reason of those Articles being incorporated into current salvage contracts. Accordingly the Sub-Committee recommended a draft Resolution to the Conference, which was adopted together with the text of Rule VI by 34 votes in favour, none against and three abstentions."

On this basis, notwithstanding some perplexities expressed in recent doctrine, the new text of Rule VI was already operative, to all intents and purposes, by virtue of the incorporation of Attachment 2 into LOF 1990, irrespective of the fact that the London Convention on Salvage has not yet entered into force.[464]

---

464. In Mongrandi, *op. cit.*, 866, which seems to maintain that since the 1989 London Convention has not yet come into effect, " . . . the reference to the Convention, even if we accept that this is solely for the purpose of clarifying the concepts which it had been intended to express, would appear, at the very least, to be somewhat premature, since no Court or Arbitration Tribunal could refer to a Convention until it has actually come into force". N. Geoffrey Hudson, *op. cit.*, n. 462.

APPENDICES

THE 1910 CONVENTION AND 1967 PROTOCOL

CONVENTION FOR THE UNIFICATION OF CERTAIN RULES OF LAW RESPECTING ASSISTANCE AND SALVAGE AT SEA, SIGNED AT BRUSSELS, SEPTEMBER 23, 1910

His Majesty the King of the United Kingdom of Great Britain and Ireland and of the British Dominions beyond the Seas, Emperor of India; His Majesty the German Emperor, King of Prussia, in the name of the German Empire; the President of the Argentine Republic; His Majesty the Emperor of Austria, King of Bohemia, etc., and Apostolic King of Hungary, for Austria and Hungary; His Majesty the King of the Belgians; the President of the United States of Brazil; the President of the Republic of Chile; the President of the Republic of Cuba; His Majesty the King of Denmark; His Majesty the King of Spain; the President of the United States of America; the President of the French Republic; His Majesty the King of the Hellenes; His Majesty the King of Italy; His Majesty the Emperor of Japan; the President of the United States of Mexico; the President of the Republic of Nicaragua; His Majesty the King of Norway; Her Majesty the Queen of the Netherlands; His Majesty the King of Portugal and the Algarves; His Majesty the King of Roumania; His Majesty the Emperor of All the Russias; His Majesty the King of Sweden; the President of the Republic of Uruguay;

Having recognised the desirability of determining by agreement certain uniform rules of law respecting assistance and salvage at sea, have decided to conclude a Convention to that end, and have appointed Plenipotentiaries who, having been duly authorised to that effect, have agreed as follows:

Article 1

Assistance and salvage of seagoing vessels in danger, of any things on board, of freight and passage money and also services of the same nature rendered by seagoing vessels to vessels of inland navigation or vice versa, are subject to the following provisions, without any distinction being drawn between these two kinds of service (*viz.*, assistance and salvage), and in whatever waters the service have been rendered.

Article 2

Every act of assistance or salvage which has had a useful result gives a right to equitable remuneration.

No remuneration is due if the services rendered have no beneficial result.

In no case shall the sum to be paid exceed the value of the property salved.

Article 3

Persons who have taken part in salvage operations notwithstanding the express and reasonable prohibition on the part of the vessel to which the services were rendered, have no right to any remuneration.

Article 4

A tug has no right to remuneration for assistance to or salvage of the vessel she is towing or of the vessel's cargo, except where she has rendered exceptional services which cannot be considered as rendered in fulfilment of the contract of towage.

Article 5

Remuneration is due notwithstanding that the salvage services have been rendered by or to vessels belonging to the same owner.

Article 6

The amount of remuneration is fixed by agreement between the parties and, failing agreement, by the court.

The proportion in which the remuneration is to be distributed amongst the salvors is fixed in the same manner.

The apportionment of the remuneration amongst the owner, master and other persons in the service of each salving vessel shall be determined by the law of the vessel's flag.

Article 7

Every agreement as to assistance or salvage entered into at the moment and under the influence of danger may, at the request of either party, be annulled, or modified by the court, if it considers that the conditions agreed upon are not equitable.

In all cases, when it is proved that the consent of one of the parties is vitiated by fraud or concealment, or when the remuneration is, in proportion to the services rendered, in an excessive degree too large or too small, the agreement may be annulled or modified by the court at the request of the party affected.

Article 8

The remuneration is fixed by the court according to the circumstances of each case, on the basis of the following considerations: (a) firstly, the measure of success obtained, the efforts and deserts of the salvors, the danger run by the salved vessel, by her passengers, crew and cargo, by the salvors, and by the salving vessel; the time expended, the expenses incurred and losses suffered, and the risks of liability and other risks run by the salvors, and also the value of the property exposed to such risks, due regard being had to the special appropriation (if any) of the salvors' vessel for salvage purposes; (b) secondly, the value of the property salved.

The same provisions apply for the purpose of fixing the apportionment provided for by the second paragraph of Article 6.

The court may deprive the salvors of all remuneration, or may award a reduced remuneration, if it appears that the salvors have by their fault rendered the salvage or assistance necessary or have been guilty of theft, fraudulent concealment, or other acts of fraud.

Article 9

No remuneration is due from persons whose lives are saved, but nothing in this article shall affect the provisions of the national laws on this subject.

Salvors of human life, who have taken part in the services rendered on the occasion of the accident giving rise to salvage or assistance, are entitled to a fair share of the remuneration awarded to the salvors of the vessel, her cargo, and accessories.

Article 10

A salvage action is barred after an interval of two years from the day on which the operations of assistance or salvage terminate.

The grounds upon which the said period of limitation may be suspended or interrupted are determined by the law of the court where the case is tried.

The High Contracting Parties reserve to themselves the right to provide, by legislation in their respective countries, that the said period shall be extended in cases where it has not yet been possible to arrest the vessel assisted or salved in the territorial waters of the State in which the plaintiff has his domicile or principal place of business.

Article 11

Every master is bound, so far as he can do so without serious danger to his vessel, her crew and her passengers, to render assistance to everybody, even though an enemy, found at sea in danger of being lost.

The owner of a vessel incurs no liability by reason of contravention of the above provision.

Article 12

The High Contracting Parties, whose legislation does not forbid infringements of the preceding Article, bind themselves to take or to propose to their respective Legislatures the measures necessary for the prevention of such infringements.

The High Contracting Parties will communicate to one another as soon as possible the laws or regulations which have already been or may be hereafter promulgated in their States for giving effect to the above provision.

Article 13

This Convention does not affect the provisions of national laws or international treaties as regards the organisation of services of assistance and salvage by or under the control of public authorities, nor, in particular, does it affect such laws or treaties on the subject of the salvage of fishing gear.

Article 14

This Convention does not apply to ships of war or to Government ships appropriated exclusively to a public service.

Article 15

The provisions of this Convention shall be applied as regards all persons interested when either the assisting or salving vessel or the vessel assisted or salved belongs to a State of the High Contracting Parties, as well as in any other cases for which the national laws provide.

Provided always that:

1. As regards persons interested who belong to a non-contracting State the application of the above provisions may be made by each of the contracting States conditional upon reciprocity.

2. Where all the persons interested belong to the same State as the court trying the case, the provisions of the national law and not of the Convention are applicable.

3. Without prejudice to any wider provisions of any national laws, Article 11 only applies as between vessels belonging to the States of the High Contracting Parties.

Article 16

Any one of the High Contracting Parties shall have the right, three years after this Convention comes into force, to call for a fresh Conference with a view to possible amendments, and particularly with a view to extend, if possible, the sphere of its application.

Any Power exercising this right must notify its intention to the other Powers, through the Belgian Government, which will make arrangements for convening the Conference within six months.

Article 17

States which have not signed the present Convention are allowed to accede to it at their request. Such accession shall be notified through the diplomatic channel to the Belgian Government, and by the latter to each of the Governments of the other Contracting Parties; it shall become effective one month after the despatch of such notification by the Belgian Government.

Article 18

The present Convention shall be ratified.

After an interval of at most one year from the date on which the Convention is signed, the Belgian Government shall place itself in communication with the Governments of the High Contracting Parties which have declared themselves prepared to ratify the Convention, with a view to decide whether it should be put into force.

The ratifications shall, if so decided, be deposited forthwith at Brussels, and the Convention shall come into force a month after such deposit.

The Protocol shall remain open another year in favour of the States represented at the Brussels Conference. After this interval they can only accede to it in conformity with the provisions of Article 17.

Article 19

In the case of one or other of the High Contracting Parties denouncing this Convention, such denunciation shall not take effect until a year after the day on which it has been notified to the Belgian Government, and the Convention shall remain in force as between the other Contracting Parties.

In witness whereof, the Plenipotentiaries of the respective High Contracting Parties have signed this Convention and have affixed thereto their seals.

Done at Brussels, in a single copy, September 23, 1910.

Signatories: Great Britain, Germany, Argentine, Austria/Hungary, Austria, Hungary, Belgium, Brazil, Chile, Cuba, Denmark, Spain, United States of America, France, Greece, Italy, Japan, Mexico, Nicaragua, Norway, Netherlands, Portugal, Roumania, Russia, Sweden, Uruguay.

1967 PROTOCOL

PROTOCOL TO AMEND THE CONVENTION FOR THE UNIFICATION OF
CERTAIN RULES OF LAW RELATING TO ASSISTANCE AND SALVAGE AT
SEA, SIGNED AT BRUSSELS ON SEPTEMBER 23, 1910, DONE AT BRUSSELS
ON MAY 27, 1967

The contracting parties,

Considering that it is desirable to amend the Convention for the unification of certain rules of law relating to assistance and salvage at sea, signed at Brussels on September 23, 1910.

Have agreed as follows:

Article 1

Article 14 of the Convention for the unification of certain rules of law relating to assistance and salvage at sea, signed at Brussels on September 23, 1910, shall be replaced by the following:

"The provisions of this Convention shall also apply to assistance or salvage services rendered by or to a ship of war or any other ship owned, operated or chartered by a State or Public Authority.

A claim against a State for assistance or salvage services rendered to a ship of war or other ship which is, either at the time of the event or when the claim is brought, appropriated exclusively to public non commercial service, shall be brought only before the Courts of such State.

Any High Contracting Party shall have the right to determine whether and to what extent Article 11 shall apply to ships coming within the terms of the second paragraph of this Article."

Article 2

This protocol shall be open for signature by the States which have ratified the Convention or which have adhered thereto before May 17, 1967, and by any State represented at the twelfth session of the Diplomatic Conference on Maritime Law.

Article 3

1. This Protocol shall be ratified.
2. Ratification of this Protocol by any State which is not a Party to the Convention shall have the effect of accession to the Convention.
3. The instruments of ratification shall be deposited with the Belgian Government.

Article 4

1. This Protocol shall come into force one month after the deposit of five instruments of ratification.
2. This Protocol shall come into force, in respect of each signatory State which ratifies it after the deposit of the fifth instrument of ratification, one month after the date of deposit of the instrument of ratification of that State.

Article 5

1. States, Members of the United Nations or Members of the specialized agencies, not represented at the twelfth session of the Diplomatic Conference on Maritime Law, may accede to this Protocol.
2. Accession to this Protocol shall have the effect of accession to the Convention.
3. The instruments of accession shall be deposited with the Belgian Government.
4. The Protocol shall come into force in respect of the acceding State one month after the date of deposit of the instrument of accession of that State, but not before the date of entry into force of the Protocol as established by Article 4.

Article 6

1. Any contracting state may denounce this Protocol by notification to the Belgian Government.
2. This denunciation shall have the effect of denunciation of the Convention.
3. The denunciation shall take effect one year after the date on which the notification has been received by the Belgian Government.

Article 7

1. Any contracting state may at the time of signature, ratification or accession to this Convention or at any time thereafter declare by written notification to the Belgian

Government which among the territories under its sovereignty or for whose international relations it is responsible, are those to which the present Protocol applies. The Protocol shall one month after the date of the receipt of such notification by the Belgian Government extend to the territories named therein, but not before the date of the coming into force of the Protocol in respect of such State.

2. This extension also shall apply to the Convention if the latter is not yet applicable to those territories.

3. Any contracting state which has made a declaration under s. 1 of this Article may at any time thereafter declare by notification given to the Belgian Government that the Protocol shall cease to extend to such territory. This denunciation shall take effect one year after the date on which notification thereof has been received by the Belgian Government; it also shall apply to the Convention.

Article 8

The Belgian Government shall notify the States represented at the twelfth session of the Diplomatic Conference on Maritime Law, the acceding States to this Protocol, and the States parties to the Convention, of the following:

1. The signatures, ratifications and accessions received in accordance with Articles 2, 3 and 5.

2. The date on which the present Protocol will come into force in accordance with Article 4.

3. The notifications with regard to the territorial application in accordance with Article 7.

4. The denunciations received in accordance with Article 6.

In witness whereof the undersigned plenipotentiaries, duly authorized, have signed this Protocol.

Done at Brussels, this 27th Day of May 1967, in the French and English languages, both texts being equally authentic, in a single copy, which shall remain deposited in the archives of the Belgian Government, which shall issue certified copies.

THE 1989 CONVENTION

INTERNATIONAL CONVENTION ON SALVAGE 1989

The States parties to the present Convention,

Recognizing the desirability of determining by agreement uniform international rules regarding salvage operations,

Noting that substantial developments, in particular the increased concern for the protection of the environment, have demonstrated the need to review the international rules presently contained in the Convention for the Unification of Certain Rules of Law relating to Assistance and Salvage at Sea, done at Brussels, 23 September 1910,

Conscious of the major contribution which efficient and timely salvage operations can make to the safety of vessels and other property in danger and to the protection of the environment,

Convinced of the need to ensure that adequate incentives are available to persons who undertake salvage operations in respect of vessels and other property in danger,

Have agreed as follows:

CHAPTER I—GENERAL PROVISIONS

Article 1. Definitions

For the purpose of this Convention:
  (a) *Salvage operation* means any act or activity undertaken to assist a vessel or any other property in danger in navigable waters or in any other waters whatsoever.
  (b) *Vessel* means any ship or craft, or any structure capable of navigation.
  (c) *Property* means any property not permanently and intentionally attached to the shoreline and includes freight at risk.
  (d) *Damage to the environment* means substantial physical damage to human health or to marine life or resources in coastal or inland waters or areas adjacent thereto, caused by pollution, contamination, fire, explosion or similar major incidents.
  (e) *Payment* means any reward, remuneration or compensation due under this Convention.
  (f) *Organization* means the International Maritime Organization.
  (g) *Secretary-General* means the Secretary-General of the Organization.

Article 2. Application of the Convention

This Convention shall apply whenever judicial or arbitral proceedings relating to matters dealt with in this Convention are brought in a State Party.

Article 3. Platforms and drilling units

This Convention shall not apply to fixed or floating platforms or to mobile offshore drilling units when such platforms or units are on location engaged in the exploration, exploitation or production of sea-bed mineral resources.

Article 4. State-owned vessels

(1) Without prejudice to article 5, this Convention shall not apply to warships or other non-commercial vessels owned or operated by a State and entitled, at the time of salvage operations, to sovereign immunity under generally recognized principles of international law unless that State decides otherwise.

(2) Where a State Party decides to apply the Convention to its warships or other vessels described in paragraph 1, it shall notify the Secretary-General thereof specifying the terms and conditions of such application.

Article 5. Salvage operations controlled by public authorities

(1) This Convention shall not affect any provisions of national law or any international convention relating to salvage operations by or under the control of public authorities.

(2) Nevertheless, salvors carrying out such salvage operations shall be entitled to avail themselves of the rights and remedies provided for in this Convention in respect of salvage operations.

(3) The extent to which a public authority under a duty to perform salvage operations may avail itself of the rights and remedies provided for in this Convention shall be determined by the law of the State where such authority is situated.

Article 6. Salvage contracts

(1) This Convention shall apply to any salvage operations save to the extent that a contract otherwise provides expressly or by implication.

(2) The master shall have the authority to conclude contracts for salvage operations on behalf of the owner of the vessel. The master or the owner of the vessel shall have the authority to conclude such contracts on behalf of the owner of the property on board the vessel.

(3) Nothing in this article shall affect the application of article 7 nor duties to prevent or minimize damage to the environment.

Article 7. Annulment and modification of contracts

A contract or any terms thereof may be annulled or modified if:
    (a) the contract has been entered into under undue influence or the influence of danger and its terms are inequitable; or

(b) the payment under the contract is in an excessive degree too large or too small for the services actually rendered.

CHAPTER II—PERFORMANCE OF SALVAGE OPERATIONS

Article 8. Duties of the salvor and of the owner and master

(1) The salvor shall owe a duty to the owner of the vessel or other property in danger:

    (a) to carry out the salvage operations with due care;

    (b) in performing the duty specified in subparagraph (a), to exercise due care to prevent or minimize damage to the environment;

    (c) whenever circumstances reasonably require, to seek assistance from other salvors; and

    (d) to accept the intervention of other salvors when reasonably requested to do so by the owner or master of the vessel or other property in danger; provided however that the amount of his reward shall not be prejudiced should it be found that such a request was unreasonable.

(2) The owner and master of the vessel or the owner of other property in danger shall owe a duty to the salvor:

    (a) to co-operate fully with him during the course of the salvage operations;

    (b) in so doing, to exercise due care to prevent or minimize damage to the environment; and

    (c) when the vessel or other property has been brought to a place of safety, to accept redelivery when reasonably requested by the salvor to do so.

Article 9. Rights of coastal States

Nothing in this Convention shall affect the right of the coastal State concerned to take measures in accordance with generally recognized principles of international law to protect its coastline or related interests from pollution or the threat of pollution following upon a maritime casualty or acts relating to such a casualty which may reasonably be expected to result in major harmful consequences, including the right of a coastal State to give directions in relation to salvage operations.

Article 10. Duty to render assistance

(1) Every master is bound, so far as he can do so without serious danger to his vessel and persons thereon, to render assistance to any person in danger of being lost at sea.

(2) The States Parties shall adopt the measures necessary to enforce the duty set out in paragraph 1.

(3) The owner of the vessel shall incur no liability for a breach of the duty of the master under paragraph 1.

Article 11. Co-operation

A State Party shall, whenever regulating or deciding upon matters relating to salvage operations such as admittance to ports of vessels in distress or the provision of facilities to salvors, take into account the need for co-operation between salvors, other interested parties and public authorities in order to ensure the efficient and successful performance of salvage operations for the purpose of saving life or property in danger as well as preventing damage to the environment in general.

CHAPTER III—RIGHTS OF SALVORS

Article 12. Conditions for reward

(1) Salvage operations which have had a useful result give right to a reward.

(2) Except as otherwise provided, no payment is due under this Convention if the salvage operations have had no useful result.

(3) This chapter shall apply, notwithstanding that the salved vessel and the vessel undertaking the salvage operations belong to the same owner.

Article 13. Criteria for fixing the reward

(1) The reward shall be fixed with a view to encouraging salvage operations, taking into account the following criteria without regard to the order in which they are presented below:
  (a) the salved value of the vessel and other property;
  (b) the skill and efforts of the salvors in preventing or minimizing damage to the environment;
  (c) the measure of success obtained by the salvor;
  (d) the nature and degree of the danger;
  (e) the skill and efforts of the salvors in salving the vessel, other property and life;
  (f) the time used and expenses and losses incurred by the salvors;
  (g) the risk of liability and other risks run by the salvors or their equipment;
  (h) the promptness of the services rendered;
  (i) the availability and use of vessels or other equipment intended for salvage operations;
  (j) the state of readiness and efficiency of the salvor's equipment and the value thereof.

(2) Payment of a reward fixed according to paragraph 1 shall be made by all of the vessel and other property interests in proportion to their respective salved values. However, a State Party may in its national law provide that the payment of a reward has to be made by one of these interests, subject to a right of recourse of this interest against the other interests for their respective shares. Nothing in this article shall prevent any right of defence.

(3) The rewards, exclusive of any interest and recoverable legal costs that may be payable thereon, shall not exceed the salved value of the vessel and other property.

Article 14. Special compensation

(1) If the salvor has carried out salvage operations in respect of a vessel which by itself or its cargo threatened damage to the environment and has failed to earn a reward under article 13 at least equivalent to the special compensation assessable in accordance with this article, he shall be entitled to special compensation from the owner of that vessel equivalent to his expenses as herein defined.

(2) If, in the circumstances set out in paragraph 1, the salvor by his salvage operations has prevented or minimized damage to the environment, the special compensation payable by the owner to the salvor under paragraph 1 may be increased up to a maximum of 30% of the expenses incurred by the salvor. However, the tribunal, if it deems it fair and just to do so and bearing in mind the relevant criteria set out in article 13, paragraph 1, may increase such special compensation further, but in no event shall the total increase be more than 100% of the expenses incurred by the salvor.

(3) Salvor's expenses for the purpose of paragraphs 1 and 2 means the out-of-pocket expenses reasonably incurred by the salvor in the salvage operation and a fair rate for equipment and personnel actually and reasonably used in the salvage operation, taking into consideration the criteria set out in article 13, paragraph 1(h), (i) and (j).

(4) The total special compensation under this article shall be paid only if and to the extent that such compensation is greater than any reward recoverable by the salvor under article 13.

(5) If the salvor has been negligent and has thereby failed to prevent or minimize damage to the environment, he may be deprived of the whole or part of any special compensation due under this article.

(6) Nothing in this article shall affect any right of recourse on the part of the owner of the vessel.

Article 15. Apportionment between salvors

(1) The apportionment of a reward under article 13 betwen salvors shall be made on the basis of the criteria contained in that aticle.

(2) The apportionment between the owner, master and other persons in the service of each salving vessel shall be determined by the law of the flag of that vessel. If the salvage has not been carried out from a vessel, the apportionment shall be determined by the law governing the contract between the salvor and his servants.

Article 16. Salvage of persons

(1) No remuneration is due from persons whose lives are saved, but nothing in this article shall affect the provisions of national law on this subject.

(2) A salvor of human life, who has taken part in the services rendered on the occasion of the accident giving rise to salvage, is entitled to a fair share of the payment awarded to the salvor for salving the vessel or other property or preventing or minimizing damage to the environment.

Article 17. Services rendered under existing contracts

No payment is due under the provisions of this Convention unless the services rendered exceed what can be reasonably considered as due performance of a contract entered into before the danger arose.

Article 18. The effect of salvor's misconduct

A salvor may be deprived of the whole or part of the payment due under this Convention to the extent that the salvage operations have become necessary or more difficult because of fault or neglect on his part or if the salvor has been guilty of fraud or other dishonest conduct.

Article 19. Prohibition of salvage operations

Services rendered notwithstanding the express and reasonable prohibition of the owner or master of the vessel or the owner of any other property in danger which is not and has not been on board the vessel shall not give rise to payment under this Convention.

CHAPTER IV—CLAIMS AND ACTIONS

Article 20. Maritime lien

(1) Nothing in this Convention shall affect the salvor's maritime lien under any international convention or national law.

(2) The salvor may not enforce his maritime lien when satisfactory security for his claim, including interest and costs, has ben duly tendered or provided.

Article 21. Duty to provide security

(1) Upon the request of the salvor a person liable for a payment due under this Convention shall provide satisfactory security for the claim, including interest and costs of the salvor.

(2) Without prejudice to paragraph 1, the owner of the salved vessel shall use his best endeavours to ensure that the owners of the cargo provide satisfactory security for the claims against them including interest and costs before the cargo is released.

(3) The salved vessel and other property shall not, without the consent of the salvor, be removed from the port or place at which they first arrive after the completion of the salvage operations until satisfactory security has been put up for the salvor's claim against the relevant vessel or property.

Article 22. Interim payment

(1) The tribunal having jurisdiction over the claim of the salvor may, by interim decision, order that the salvor shall be paid on account such amount as seems fair and just, and on such terms including terms as to security where appropriate, as may be fair and just according to the circumstances of the case.

(2) In the event of an interim payment under this article the security provided under article 21 shall be reduced accordingly.

Article 23. Limitation of actions

(1) Any action relating to payment under this Convention shall be time-barred if judicial or arbitral proceedings have not been instituted within a period of two years.

The limitation period commences on the day on which the salvage operations are terminated.

(2) The person against whom a claim is made may at any time during the running of the limitation period extend that period by a declaration to the claimant. This period may in the like manner be further extended.

(3) An action for indemnity by a person liable may be instituted even after the expiration of the limitation period provided for in the preceding paragraphs, if brought within the time allowed by the law of the State where proceedings are instituted.

Article 24. Interest

The right of the salvor to interest on any payment due under this Convention shall be determined according to the law of the State in which the tribunal seized of the case is situated.

Article 25. State-owned cargoes

Unless the State owner consents, no provision of this Convention shall be used as a basis for the seizure, arrest or detention by any legal process of, nor for any proceedings *in rem* against, non-commercial cargoes owned by a State and entitled, at the time of the salvage operations, to sovereign immunity under generally recognized principles of international law.

Article 26. Humanitarian cargoes

No provision of this Convention shall be used as a basis for the seizure, arrest or detention of humanitarian cargoes donated by a State, if such State has agreed to pay for salvage services rendered in respect of such humanitarian cargoes.

Article 27. Publication of arbitral awards

States Parties shall encourage, as far as possible and with the consent of the parties, the publication of arbitral awards made in salvage cases.

CHAPTER V—FINAL CLAUSES

Article 28. Signature, ratification, acceptance, approval and accession

(1) This Convention shall be open for signature at the Headquarters of the Organization from 1 July 1989 to 30 June 1990 and shall thereafter remain open for accession.

(2) States may express their consent to be bound by this Convention by:
  (a) signature without reservation as to ratification, acceptance or approval; or
  (b) signature subject to ratification, acceptance or approval, followed by ratification, acceptance or approval; or
  (c) accession.

(3) Ratification, acceptance, approval or accession shall be effected by the deposit of an instrument to that effect with the Secretary-General.

Article 29. Entry into force

(1) This Convention shall enter into force one year after the date on which 15 States have expressed their consent to be bound by it.

(2) For a State which expresses its consent to be bound by this Convention after the conditions for entry into force thereof have been met, such consent shall take effect one year after the date of expression of such consent.

Article 30. Reservations

(1) Any State may, at the time of signature, ratification, acceptance, approval or accession, reserve the right not to apply the provisions of this Convention:

    (a) when the salvage operation takes place in inland waters and all vessels involved are of inland navigation;

    (b) when the salvage operations take place in inland waters and no vessel is involved;

    (c) when all interested parties are nationals of that State;

    (d) when the property involved in maritime cultural property of prehistoric archaeological or historic interest and is situated on the sea-bed.

(2) Reservations made at the time of signature are subject to confirmation upon ratification, acceptance or approval.

(3) Any State which has made a reservation to this Convention may withdraw it at any time by means of a notification addressed to the Secretary-General. Such withdrawal shall take effect on the date the notification is received. If the notification states that the withdrawal of a reservation is to take effect on a date specified therein, and such date is later than the date the notification is received by the Secretary-General, the withdrawal shall take effect on such later date.

Article 31. Denunciation

(1) This Convention may be denounced by any State Party at any time after the expiry of one year from the date on which this Convention enters into force for that State.

(2) Denunciation shall be effected by the deposit of an instrument of denunciation with the Secretary-General.

(3) A denunciation shall take effect one year, or such longer period as may be specified in the instrument of denunciation, after the receipt of the instrument of denunciation by the Secretary-General.

Article 32. Revision and amendment

(1) A conference for the purpose of revising or amending this Convention may be convened by the Organization.

(2) The Secretary-General shall convene a conference of the States Parties to this Convention for revising or amending the Convention, at the request of eight States Parties, or one fourth of the States Parties, whichever is the higher figure.

(3) Any consent to be bound by this Convention expressed after the date of entry into force of an amendment to this Convention shall be deemed to apply to the Convention as amended.

Article 33. Depositary

(1) This Convention shall be deposited with the Secretary-General.
(2) The Secretary-General shall:
  (a) inform all States which have signed this Convention or acceded thereto, and all Members of the Organization, of:
  (i) each new signature or deposit of an instrument of ratification, acceptance, approval or accession together with the date thereof;
  (ii) the date of the entry into force of this Convention;
  (iii) the deposit of any instrument of denunciation of this Convention together with the date on which it is received and the date on which the denunciation takes effect;
  (iv) any amendment adopted in conformity with article 32;
   (v) the receipt of any reservation, declaration or notification made under this Convention;
  (b) transmit certified true copies of this Convention to all States which have signed this Convention or acceded thereto.
(3) As soon as this Convention enters into force, a certified true copy thereof shall be transmitted by the Depositary to the Secretary-General of the United Nations for registration and publication in accordance with Article 102 of the Charter of the United Nations.

Article 34. Languages

This Convention is established in a single original in the Arabic, Chinese, English, French, Russian and Spanish languages, each text being equally authentic.

In witness whereof the undersigned being duly authorized by their respective Governments for that purpose have signed this Convention.

Done at London this twenty-eighth day of April one thousand nine hundred and eighty-nine.

ATTACHMENT I

Common Understanding Concerning Articles 13 and 14 of the International Convention on Salvage, 1989

It is the common understanding of the Conference that, in fixing a reward under article 13 and assessing special compensation under article 14 of the International Convention on Salvage, 1989 the tribunal is under no duty to fix a reward under article 13 up to the maximum salved value of the vessel and other property before assessing the special compensation to be paid under article 14.

ATTACHMENT 2

Resolution Requesting the Amendment of the York-Antwerp Rules, 1974

The International Conference on Salvage, 1989,
  Having adopted the International Convention on Salvage, 1989,

Considering that payments made pursuant to article 14 are not intended to be allowed in general average,

Requests the Secretary-General of the International Maritime Organization to take the appropriate steps in order to ensure speedy amendment of the York-Antwerp Rules, 1974, to ensure that special compensation paid under article 14 is not subject to general average.[1]

1. The relevant rule, rule VI, has now been amended. See Appendix 9, p. 297, *post*.

P. & I. POLLUTION INDEMNITY
CLAUSE—PIOPIC CLAUSE

NOTICE TO SHIPOWNERS

The undersigned, members of the INTERNATIONAL SALVAGE UNION have decided that in view of the claims which may be made against them as a result of pollution which may occur as a consequence of a casualty to a tanker and the salvage operations necessitated by such casualty; they will not be prepared to render salvage services to loaded or partly loaded tankers unless they are given the following indemnity (which shall be countersigned by the P and I Club in which the relevant vessel has been entered) and which shall be known as PIOPIC:

"The Owners shall be responsible for and shall indemnify the Contractor, unless guilty of personal wilful misconduct, in respect of all claims for oil pollution damage, including preventive measures, howsoever arising (including contractual liabilities to sub-contractors) out of the services performed hereunder provided always that the Owners' total liability arising under this indemnity shall in no circumstances exceed:

(AAA) US dollars fifteen million less the aggregate amount of all liabilities, costs and expenses for or in respect of oil pollution damage, including preventive measures, (otherwise than under this indemnity or similar indemnities given to other persons performing salvage operations in connection with the vessel) incurred or to be incurred by the Owners arising out of or in connection with the casualty to the vessel or the consequence thereof or

(BBB) US dollars ten million, whichever is the greater.

Provided always that if the Owners' total liability arising under this and any other similar indemnities given or to be given to other persons performing salvage operations in connection with the vessel exceeds the amount of the applicable limit of liability referred to above such amount shall be distributed rateably among the Contractor and such other persons and the Owners' liability hereunder shall be reduced accordingly.

This clause shall be construed in accordance with English law."

Notwithstanding the foregoing they may require special or general contractual conditions, alternative indemnity arrangements in certain circumstances, or similar or other indemnity arrangements in cases of vessels other than loaded or partly loaded tankers.

227

TOVALOP 1969 AND 1987

TANKER OWNERS VOLUNTARY AGREEMENT CONCERNING LIABILITY FOR OIL POLLUTION (TOVALOP) (1969)

Preamble

The Parties to this Agreement are Tanker Owners and Bareboat Charterers.

By means of the Tanker Owners Voluntary Agreement Concerning Liability for Oil Pollution dated as of January 7, 1969, as amended, (hereinafter called "TOVALOP" the Parties took constructive measures to mitigate and provide compensation for damage by oil pollution from Tankers.

The Parties recognise that the coming into force on June 19, 1975 of the International Convention on Civil Liability for Oil Pollution Damage, 1969 (hereinafter called the "Liability Convention"), and the additional ratifications and accessions to that Convention which have occurred since that date, have established in numerous areas of the world an international legal regime for compensating Persons (including Governments) who sustain Pollution Damage resulting from the discharge of Oil from Tankers. The Parties recognise also that the Liability Convention has remedied in large part deficiencies in traditional maritime law for which TOVALOP offered substantial relief. However, the Parties are aware of the fact that there are still substantial areas of the world where the Liability Convention does not apply and to which its benefits and protection may not be extended for sometime. Therefore, pending the widespread application of the Liability Convention, they have decided to amend TOVALOP, effective as from noon G.M.T. June 1, 1978, so as to provide in these latter areas, in respect of incidents which occur after that date, benefits and protection generally comparable with those available under the Liability Convention, together with certain other benefits and protection.

Accordingly, the Parties, and such other Tanker Owners and Bareboat Charterers as may hereafter become Parties, in consideration of their mutual promises, have agreed with one another and do hereby agree as follows:

I. Definitions

Whenever the following words and phrases appear in the Preamble and other Clauses hereof, they shall have the meaning indicated below:

    (a) "Tanker" means any sea-going vessel and any sea-borne craft of any type whatsoever, designed and constructed for carrying Oil in bulk as cargo, whether or not it is actually so carrying Oil.

(b) "Person" means any individual or partnership or any public or private body, whether corporate or not, including a State or any of its constituent subdivisions.

(c) "Owner" means the Person or Persons registered as the owner of the Tanker or, in the absence of registration, the Person or Persons owning the Tanker. However, in the case of a Tanker owned by a State and operated by a company which in that State is registered as the Tanker's operator, "Owner" shall mean such company. Notwithstanding the foregoing, in the case of a Tanker under bareboat charter, "Owner" means the Bareboat Charterer.

(d) "Bareboat Charterer" means the Person (or Persons) who has chartered a Tanker upon terms which provide, among other things, that the Charterer shall have exclusive possession and control of the Tanker during the life of the charter.

(e) "Party" means a Party to this Agreement.

(f) "Participating Owner" means the Owner of a Tanker who is a Party.

(g) "Oil" means any persistent hydrocarbon mineral oil such as crude oil, fuel oil, heavy diesel oil and lubricating oil whether or not carried as cargo.

(h) "Pollution Damage" means loss or damage caused outside the Tanker by contamination resulting from the escape or discharge of Oil from the Tanker, whatever such escape or discharge may occur, provided that the loss or damage is caused on the territory, including the territorial sea, of any State and includes the costs of Preventive Measures, wherever taken, and further loss or damage caused by Preventive Measures but excludes any loss or damage which is remote or speculative, or which does not result directly from such escape or discharge.

(i) "Preventive Measures" means any reasonable measures taken by any Person after an incident has occurred to prevent or minimise Pollution Damage.

(j) "Incident" means any occurrence, or series of occurrences having the same origin, which causes Pollution Damage, or which creates the Threat of an escape or discharge of Oil.

(k) "Threat of an escape or discharge of Oil" means a grave and imminent danger of the escape or discharge of Oil from a Tanker which, if it occurred, would create a serious danger of Pollution Damage, whether or not an escape or discharge in fact subsequently occurs.

(l) "Threat Removal Measures" means reasonable measures taken by any person after an Incident has occurred for the purposes of removing the Threat of an escape or discharge of Oil.

(m) "Liability Convention" means the International Convention on Civil Liability for Oil Pollution Damage, 1969, which entered into force on June 19, 1975, including legislation and regulations implementing the provisions hereof which are enacted from time to time by any Contracting State thereunder.

(n) A Tanker's "Tonnage" shall be the net tonnage of the Tanker with the addition of the amount deducted from the gross tonnage on account of engine room space for the purpose of ascertaining the net tonnage. In the case of a Tanker for which this Tonnage cannot be ascertained, the Tanker's Tonnage shall be deemed to be 40 per cent. of the weight in tons of 2,240 lbs. of Oil which the Tanker is capable of carrying.

(o) The "Federation" means The International Tanker Owners Pollution Federation Limited, a Company limited by guarantee and formed pursuant to the laws of England for the purpose of administrating this Agreement.

(p) "Cost" or "Costs" means reasonable cost or costs, respectively.

II. General Conditions

(A) Upon acceptance by the Federation of an application in the form annexed hereto as Exhibit "A", any Owner in the world shall become a Party to this Agreement and a member of the Federation.

(B) Each Party shall:

(1) make the terms of this Agreement applicable to all Tankers of which he is or becomes Owner;

(2) establish and maintain his financial capability to fulfil his obligations under this Agreement to the satisfaction of the Federation.

(3) dispose of all valid claims against him arising under this Agreement as promptly as is practicable;

(4) become a member of the Federation and, subject to the Articles of Association of the Federation, remain a member thereof so long as he continues to be a Party hereto;

(5) abide by the Memorandum and Articles of Association of the Federation and all rules and directives of the Federation; and

(6) fulfil all his other obligations under this Agreement.

III. Duration and Coverage

(A) This Agreement may be terminated by Special Resolution adopted at an Extraordinary General Meeting of the Members of the Federation convened and conducted in accordance with the Articles of Association of the Federation upon a poll vote in which at least 75 per cent. of the votes cast are in favour of said Resolution:

(i) upon June 1, 1981 or any successive anniversary of that date, or

(ii) at any time after June 1, 1981 provided that the Board of Directors of the Federation has previously determined that the Liability Convention is sufficiently widespread in application.

(B) A Party may withdraw from this Agreement on June 1, 1981, or on any successive anniversary of that date by giving at least six months prior written notice of withdrawal to the Federation, or in accordance with Clause X.

(C) The withdrawal of a Party from this Agreement under this Clause III, or under Clause X, or termination of this Agreement by the Parties shall not affect any rights and obligations of any Party then accrued under this Agreement.

(D) Upon termination of this Agreement the Federation shall continue in existence for such reasonable period as is necessary to wind up its affairs.

IV. Liability

(A) Subject to the terms and conditions of this Agreement, the Participating Owner of a Tanker involved in an incident agrees to assume liability for Pollution Damage caused by Oil which has escaped or which has been discharged from the Tanker, and the cost of Threat Removal Measures taken as a result of the incident.

(B) No liability for Pollution Damage or for the cost of Threat Removal Measures shall arise if the incident:

    (a) caused Pollution Damage anywhere in the world for any part of which liability is imposed under the terms of the Liability Convention, or

    (b) resulted from an act of war, hostilities, civil war, insurrection or a natural phenomenon of an exceptional, inevitable and irresistible character, or

    (c) was wholly caused by an act or omission done with intent to cause damage, by a third person, or

    (d) was wholly caused by the negligence or other wrongful act of any Government or other authority responsible for the maintenance of lights or other navigational aids in the exercise of that function.

(C) If Pollution Damage or the circumstances which gave rise to Threat Removal Measures resulted wholly or partially from the negligence of the Person who sustained the Pollution Damage or who took the Threat Removal Measures, the Participating Owner shall be exonerated wholly or partially from any liability he would otherwise have to such Person.

V. Liability for Pollution Damage Where Two or More Tankers are Involved

When Oil has escaped or been discharged from two or more Tankers of Participating Owners and causes Pollution Damage, the Participating Owners concerned, except as exonerated by reason of Clause IV, shall be jointly and severally liable for all such Damage which is not reasonably separable.

VI. Preventive Measures and Threat Removal Measures by the Participating Owner

A Participating Owner of a Tanker involved in an incident shall exercise his best efforts to take such Preventive Measures and Threat Removal Measures as are practicable and appropriate under the circumstances. The taking of such Measures shall not constitute an admission of liability.

Each Participating Owner shall, in connection with the establishing and maintaining of financial capability, make appropriate provision for reimbursement of the cost of such Measures.

VII. Limits of Liability

(A) The maximum liability under this Agreement of a Participating Owner in respect of any one incident shall be One Hundred and Sixty U.S. Dollars (U.S. $160.00) per ton of each of his Tankers involved in the Incident, or Sixteen Million, Eight Hundred Thousand U.S. Dollars (U.S. $16,800,000.00), whichever is less.

(B) When the aggregate of the established claims hereunder exceeds the limits specified in Paragraph (A) above, the Participating Owner shall pay that portion of each of the established claims, as the maximum liability calculated in accordance with Paragraph (A) above, bears to the aggregate of established claims.

(C) If before the Participating Owner has satisfied in full his liability under this Agreement, he or any Person providing him insurance or other financial security has as a result of the Incident in question paid compensation for Pollution Damage or the costs of Threat Removal Measures, such Person shall, up to the amount he has paid acquire by subrogation the rights which the Person so compensated would have enjoyed under this Agreement.

(D) When a Participating Owner establishes that he may be compelled to pay at a later date in whole or in part any amount of compensation pursuant to the terms of this Agreement, with regard to which he would have enjoyed a right of subrogation under Paragraph (C) of this Clause, he may set aside a sufficient sum provisionally to enable him at a later date to make appropriate payment, while at the same time satisfying the claims of other Persons having valid claims under this Agreement.

(E) For the purpose of determining the extent of a Participating Owner's liability under this Agreement, claims in respect of Preventive Measures voluntarily taken by the Participating Owner and costs incurred by the Participating Owner in voluntarily taking Threat Removal Measures, shall be treated as if they were claims by Persons other than the Participating Owner in determining Owner's liability up to the limits set forth in Paragraph (A).

VIII. Procedure and Miscellaneous

(A) In the event of the escape or discharge of Oil from the Tanker of a Participating Owner or the Threat thereof, the Participating Owner shall notify the Federation and shall advise the Federation of the Preventive Measures and Threat Removal Measures (if any) he plans to take and whether any claims have been notified under this Agreement.

(B) The Parties hereto authorise the Federation to exercise due diligence to provide Persons concerned with the escape or discharge or the Threat thereof, with a copy of this Agreement and confirmation that the Owner was, at the time of such escape or discharge or Threat, a Participating Owner.

(C) No liability shall arise under this Agreement unless written notice of claim is received by the Participating Owner within two years of the date of the incident.

(D) Persons making claims hereunder may, in the event of a dispute with a Participating Owner concerning same, commence arbitration proceedings, in accordance with Paragraph (I) hereof, within two years of the date of the incident, and these proceedings shall be the exclusive means for enforcing a Participating Owner's liability hereunder. Each Participating Owner by becoming a Party to this Agreement, and so long as he remains bound hereby, shall be deemed irrevocably to have offered to any such Person to submit all such disputes to arbitration as provided in said Paragraph (I).

(E) Unless otherwise agreed in writing, any payment to a Person by or on behalf of a Participating Owner shall be in full settlement of all said Person's claims against the Participating Owner, the Tanker involved, its charterer, their officers, agents, employees and underwriters, which arise out of the incident.

(F) This Agreement does not create any rights against the Federation and the Federation shall have no liability hereunder or otherwise to any Person.

(G) No rights or obligations created hereunder or connected herewith may be assigned or transferred.

(H) Except as provided by Clause V, no Participating Owner shall be liable under this Agreement in respect of an escape or discharge of Oil or the Threat thereof from the Tanker of another Participating Owner.

(I) All claims by any Person or Persons under this Agreement shall, if not otherwise disposed of, finally be settled under the rules of conciliation and arbitration of the

International Chamber of Commerce by one or more arbitrators appointed in accordance with said rules. In any such proceeding the Person allegedly having the claim shall have the burden of proving that Oil discharged from the Tanker caused him Pollution Damage or that the Threat thereof necessitated his taking Threat Removal Measures.

(J) No payment made hereunder shall be deemed (i) an admission of, or evidence of liability on the part of the Participating Owner in any other proceeding or to any other claimant, or (ii) submission to any jurisdiction on the part of the Participating Owner for any purpose whatsoever, other than as provided in this Clause VIII.

(K) Nothing in this Agreement shall prejudice the right of recourse of a Participating Owner against third person or vessels.

IX. Interpretation

The Federation shall have the right to make rules and directives from time to time with respect to the interpretation and administration of this Agreement.

X. Amendments

This Agreement may be amended by Special Resolution adopted at a General Meeting of the members of the Federation convened and conducted in accordance with the Articles of Association of the Federation upon a poll vote in which at least 75 per cent. of the votes cast are in favour of said Resolution. A party who votes against such Resolution shall thereupon have the option, to be exercised by written notice served upon the Federation within sixty days of the date of said Special Resolution, to withdraw from this Agreement, without, however, affecting his rights and liabilities accrued at the time of his withdrawal.

XI. Law Governing

This Agreement shall be governed by the laws of England. However, anything herein to the contrary notwithstanding, a Participating Owner shall not be required:

    (a) To incur any obligation or take any action, with respect to any incident in which his Tanker is involved, which would violate the laws or government regulations of the flag State of the Tanker, or

    (b) To incur any obligation or take any action which would, if a majority of the stock of the Participating Owner is owned, directly or indirectly by another corporation, partnership or individual, violate any laws or government regulations which may apply to said other corporation, partnership or individual.

THE TANKER OWNERS' VOLUNTARY AGREEMENT CONCERNING LIABILITY FOR OIL POLLUTION ("TOVALOP") (1987)

STANDING AGREEMENT

Introduction

The Parties to this Agreement are Tanker Owners and Bareboat Charterers.

    By means of the Tanker Owners' Voluntary Agreement concerning Liability for Oil

Pollution dated January 7th, 1969, as amended, (hereinafter called "TOVALOP") the Parties took constructive measures to mitigate and provide compensation for damage by oil pollution from Tankers.

Pending the widespread application of the International Convention on Civil Liability for Oil Pollution Damage, 1969 ("the Liability Convention") and the Protocol thereto adopted in 1984, the Parties have from time to time amended TOVALOP to enhance the benefits and protection available to persons sustaining Pollution Damage.

Accordingly, the Parties, and such other Tanker Owners and Bareboat Charterers as may hereafter become Parties, in consideration of their mutual promises, have agreed with one another and do hereby agree as follows:

I. Definitions

Whenever the following words and phrases appear in the Introduction and other Clauses hereof, they shall have the meaning indicated below:

(a) "Bareboat Charterer" means the Person(s) who has chartered a Tanker upon terms which provide, among other things, that the Charterer shall have exclusive possession and control of the Tanker during the life of the charter.

(b) "Cost" or "Costs" means reasonable cost or costs, respectively.

(c) The "Federation" means The International Tanker Owners Pollution Federations Limited, a Company limited by guarantee and formed pursuant to the laws of England for the purpose of administering this Agreement.

(d) "Incident" means any occurrence, or series of occurrences having the same origin, which causes Pollution Damage, or which creates the Threat of an escape or discharge of Oil.

(e) "Liability Convention" means the Interventional Convention on Civil Liability for Oil Pollution Damage, 1969, which entered into force on June 19th, 1975, including legislation and regulations implementing the provisions hereof which are enacted from time to time by any Contracting State thereunder.

(f) "Oil" means any persistent hydrocarbon mineral oil such as crude oil, fuel oil, heavy diesel oil and lubricating oil whether or not carried as cargo.

(g) "Owner" means the Person or Persons registered as the owner of the Tanker or, in the absence of registration, the Person or Persons owning the Tanker. However, in the case of a Tanker owned by a State and operated by a company which in that State is registered as the Tanker's operator, "Owner" shall mean such company. Notwithstanding the foregoing, in the case of a Tanker under bareboat charter, "Owner" means the Bareboat Charterer.

(h) "Participating Owner" means the Owner of a Tanker who is a Party.

(i) "Party" means a Party to this Agreement.

(j) "Person" means any individual or partnership or any public or private body, whether corporate or not, including a State or any of its constituent sub-divisions.

(k) "Pollution Damage" means loss or damage caused outside the Tanker by contamination resulting from the escape or discharge of Oil from the Tanker, wherever such escape or discharge may occur, provided that the loss or damage is caused on the territory, including the territorial sea, of any State and includes the costs of Preventive Measures, wherever taken, and further loss or damage caused by Preventive Measures but excludes any loss or damage which is remote or speculative, or which does not result directly from such escape or discharge.

(l) "Preventive Measures" means any reasonable measures taken by any Person after an accident has occurred to prevent or minimise Pollution Damage.

(m) "Tanker" means any sea-going vessel and any sea-borne craft of any type whatsoever, designed and constructed for carrying Oil in bulk as cargo, whether or not it is actually so carrying Oil.

(n) "Threat of an escape or discharge of Oil" means a grave and imminent danger of the escape or discharge of Oil from a Tanker which, if it occurred, would create a serious danger of Pollution Damage, whether or not an escape or discharge in fact subsequently occurs.

(o) "Threat Removal Measures" means reasonable measures taken by any Person after an Incident has occurred for the purposes of removing the Threat of an escape or discharge of Oil.

(p) A Tanker's "Tonnage" shall be the net tonnage of the Tanker with the addition of the amount deducted from the gross tonnage on account of engine room space for the purpose of ascertaining the net tonnage. In the case of a Tanker for which this Tonnage cannot be ascertained, the Tanker's Tonnage shall be deemed to be 40 per cent, of the weight in tons of 2,240 lbs. of Oil which the Tanker is capable of carrying.

(q) "Ton" means a ton of a Tanker's Tonnage.

II. General Conditions

(A) Upon acceptance by the Federation of an application by an Owner in the form annexed hereto as Exhibit "A", that Owner shall become a Party and a member of the Federation.

(B) Each Party shall:

(1) make the terms of this Agreement applicable to all Tankers of which he is or becomes Owner;

(2) at all times be the Owner of a Tanker to which the terms of this Agreement are applied;

(3) establish and maintain his financial capability to fulfil his obligations under this Agreement to the satisfaction of the Federation;

(4) dispose of all valid claims against him arising under this Agreement as promptly as is practicable;

(5) become a member of the Federation and, subject to the Articles of Association of the Federation, remain a member thereof so long as he continues to be a Party hereto;

(6) abide by the Memorandum and Articles of Association of the Federation and all rules and directives of the Federation; and

(7) fulfil all his other obligations under this Agreement.

(C) A Party shall forthwith notify the Federation if he shall fail to perform or observe any of the conditions specified in Clause II(B).

(D) A Party shall forthwith cease to be a Party if he shall fail to perform or observe any of the conditions specified in Clause II(B), but without, however, affecting his rights and obligations accrued at the time of such cessation (including his obligation under Clause II(C)) and without limitation to his right at any time thereafter to become a Party.

(E) Without prejudice to the foregoing provisions of this Clause or to the generality of Clause IX the Federation may at any time by notice in writing require a Party to inform it whether or not that Party has failed to perform or observe any of the conditions specified in Clause II(B) and if that Party shall fail to respond to such request within 28 days after the date of that notice, then that Party shall thereupon forthwith cease to be a Party.

III. Duration

(A) This Agreement may be terminated by Special Resolution adopted at a General Meeting of the Members of the Federation convened and conducted in accordance with the Articles of Association of the Federation upon a poll vote in which at least 75 per cent of the votes cast are in favour of the said Resolution.

(B) A Party may withdraw from this Agreement on any date by giving at least six months prior written notice of withdrawal to the Federation, or in accordance with Clause X.

(C) The withdrawal of a Party from this Agreement under Clause III, or under Clause X, or termination of this Agreement by the Parties shall not affect any rights and obligations of any Party then accrued under this Agreement.

(D) Upon termination of this Agreement the Federation shall continue in existence for such reasonable period as is necessary to wind up its affairs.

IV. Responsibility

(A) Subject to the terms and conditions of this Agreement, the Participating Owner of a Tanker involved in an Incident agrees to assume responsibility hereunder in respect of Pollution Damage caused by Oil which has escaped or which has been discharged from the Tanker, and the Cost of Threat Removal Measures taken as a result of the Incident.

(B) No responsibility for Pollution Damage or for the Cost of Threat Removal Measures shall be assumed if the Incident:
- (a) caused Pollution Damage anywhere in the world for any part of which liability is imposed under the terms of the Liability Convention, or
- (b) resulted from an act of war, hostilities, civil war, insurrection or a natural phenomenon of an exceptional, inevitable and irresistible character, or
- (c) was wholly caused by an act or omission done with intent to cause damage by a third party, or
- (d) was wholly caused by the negligence or other wrongful act of any Government or other authority responsible for the maintenance of lights or other navigation aids in the exercise of that function.

(C) If Pollution Damage or the circumstances which gave rise to Threat Removal Measures resulted wholly or partially from the negligence of the Person who sustained the Pollution Damage or who took the Threat Removal Measures, the Participating Owner shall be exonerated wholly or partially from any responsibility he would otherwise have to such Person under this Agreement.

V. Responsibility for Pollution Damage Where Two or More Tankers are Involved

When Oil has escaped or been discharged from two or more Tankers of Participating Owners and causes Pollution Damage, the Participating Owners concerned, except as exonerated by reason of Clause IV, shall be jointly and severally responsible hereunder in respect of all such Pollution Damage which is not reasonably separable.

VI. Preventive Measures and Threat Removal Measures by the Participating Owner

A Participating Owner of a Tanker involved in an Incident shall exercise his best efforts to take such Preventive Measures and/or Threat Removal Measures as are practicable and appropriate under the circumstances. The taking of such Measures shall not constitute an admission of liability or of responsibility under this Agreement.

Each Participating Owner shall in connection with the establishment and maintenance of financial capability referred to in Clause II(B)(3) make appropriate provision for the reimbursement of the Cost of such Measures.

VII. Limits of Financial Responsibility

(A) The maximum financial responsibility under this Agreement of a Participating Owner in respect of any one Incident shall be One Hundred and Sixty U.S. Dollars (US$160.00) per Ton of each of his Tankers involved in the Incident, or Sixteen Million Eight Hundred Thousand U.S. Dollars (US$16,800,000.00), whichever is less.

(B) When the aggregate of the established claims hereunder exceeds the maximum financial responsibility specified in Clause VII(A), the Participating Owner(s) shall pay that proportion of each of those established claims as the said maximum financial responsibility bears to the total amount of those established claims.

(C) If before the Participating Owner has satisfied in full his financial responsibility under this Agreement, he or any Person providing him insurance or other financial security has, as a result of the Incident in question, paid compensation for Pollution Damage and/or for the Costs of Threat Removal Measures, then

    (a) the amount of that payment shall be taken into account in assessing the aggregate of established claims under this Agreement in respect of that Incident; and

    (b) the Participating Owner or any Person providing him insurance or other financial security shall, to the extent of that payment, be in the same position as the Person to whom that sum of money was paid would have been.

(D) Costs incurred by the Participating Owner or any Person providing him insurance or other financial security as a result of the of the Participating Owner himself taking Preventive Measures and/or Threat Removal Measures shall be treated as if they were claims by Persons other than the Participating Owner and

    (a) the amount of those Costs shall be taken into account in assessing the aggregate of established claims under this Agreement in respect of that Incident; and

    (b) the Participating Owner or any Person providing him insurance or other financial security shall, to the extent of those Costs, be in the same position as if he were any other Person with a claim under this Agreement.

(E) When a Participating Owner extablishes that the aggregate of claims in respect of an Incident may exceed his maximum financial responsibility hereunder, he or any Person providing him insurance or other financial security may in his sole discretion make partial payment to claimants until the full extent of all claims is determined.

VIII. Procedure and Miscellaneous

(A) The Parties hereto authorise the Federation to provide Persons concerned with the escape or discharge of Oil or the Threat thereof with a copy of this Agreement and confirmation that the Owner was, at the time of such escape or discharge or Threat, a Participating Owner.

(B) A participating Owner may require that any payment hereunder to a Person by him, or on his behalf by anyone providing him insurance or other financial security, shall be conditional upon either that Person assigning to that Participating Owner his right of action, or authorising him to proceed in the name of that Person, in each case up to the amounts paid or to be paid to that Person in relation to the Incident in question.

(C) No responsibility shall arise under this Agreement unless written notice of claim is received by the Participating Owner within two years of the date of the Incident.

(D) Unless otherwise agreed in writing, any payment to a Person by or on behalf of a Participating Owner shall be in full settlement of all said Person's claims against the Participating Owner, the Tanker involved, its master, officers and crew, its charterer(s), manager or operator and their respective officers, agents, employees and affiliates and underwriters, which arise out of the Incident.

(E) Persons making claims hereunder may, in the event of a dispute with a Participating Owner concerning same, commence arbitration proceedings, in accordance with Clause VIII(F) hereof, within three years of the date of the Incident, and these proceedings shall be the exclusive means for enforcing a Participating Owner's responsibility hereunder. Each Participating Owner by becoming a Party to this Agreement, and so long as he remains bound hereby, shall be deemed irrevocably to have offered to any such Person to submit all such disputes to arbitration as provided in said Clause VIII(F).

(F) All claims by any Person or Persons under this Agreement shall, if not otherwise disposed of, be finally settled under the rules of conciliation and arbitration of the International Chamber of Commerce by one or more arbitrators appointed in accordance with said rules. In any such proceeding the Person allegedly having the claim shall have the burden of proving that Oil discharged from the Tanker caused him Pollution Damage or that the Threat thereof necessitated his taking Threat Removal Measures.

(G) Except as provided by Clause V, no Participating Owner shall be responsible under this Agreement in respect of an escape of discharge of Oil or the Threat thereof from the Tanker of another Participating Owner.

(H) This Agreement does not create any rights against the Federation and the Federation shall have no liability hereunder or otherwise to any Person.

(I) No rights or obligations created hereunder or connected herewith may be assigned or transferred except as provided in Clause VIII(B).

(J) No payment made hereunder shall be deemed (i) an admission of, or evidence of liability on the part of the Participating Owner in any proceeding or to any Person, or (ii) submission to any jurisdiction on the part of the Participating Owner for any purpose whatsoever.

(K) Nothing in this Agreement shall prejudice the right of recourse of a Participating Owner against third parties or vessels.

IX. Interpretation

The Federation shall have the right to make rules and directives from time to time with respect to the interpretation and administration of this Agreement.

X. Amendments

This Agreement may be amended by Special Resolution adopted at a General Meeting of the members of the Federation convened and conducted in accordance with the Articles of Association of the Federation upon a poll vote in which at least 75 per cent. of the votes cast are in favour of said Resolution. A Party who votes against such Resolution shall thereupon have the option, to be exercised by written notice served upon the Federation within sixty days of the date of said Special Resolution, to withdraw from this Agreement, without, however, affecting his rights and obligations accrued at the time of his withdrawal.

XI. Law Governing

This Agreement shall be governed by the laws of England. However, anything herein to the contrary notwithstanding, a Participating Owner shall not be required:
  (a) to incur any obligation or take any action, with respect of any Incident in which his Tanker is involved, which would violate the laws or government regulations of the flag State of the Tanker; or
  (b) to incur any obligation or take any action which would, if a majority of the stock of the Participating Owner is owned, directly or indirectly by another corporation, partnership or individual, violate any laws or government regulations which may apply to said other corporation, partnership or individual.

SUPPLEMENT

Introduction

The Parties recognise that (i) while the Standing Agreement (as hereinafter defined) has provided constructive measures to mitigate and provide compensation for Pollution Damage, it does not now provide, in all respects, adequate compensation for all legitimate claims for Pollution Damage, (ii) while the Liability Convention has established, in many jurisdictions, a legal system providing for the compensation of persons who sustain Pollution Damage, it does not provide for compensation of Costs incurred to remove a Threat of an escape or discharge of Oil from a Tanker where no pollution occurs, nor does it provide, in all respects, adequate compensation for all legitimate claims for Pollution Damage and (iii) it will require some time before the Protocol to the Liability Convention will come into force in a substantial number of jurisdictions.

Accordingly, the Parties decided to amend TOVALOP pursuant to Clause X thereof effective from February 20th, 1987 by the adoption of this Supplement (as subsequently amended) so as to provide in respect of an Applicable Incident (as herein-after defined) enhanced compensation for Pollution Damage and Costs incurred to remove a Threat of an escape or discharge of Oil, but without affecting the provisions of the Standing Agreement which alone shall continue to apply to any Incident which is not an Applicable Incident.

1. Definitions and Interpretation

(1) Whenever the following words and phrases appear in the Introduction to and other Paragraphs of this Supplement, they shall have the meaning set forth below:

(A) "Applicable Incident" means any occurrence or series of occurrences, having the same origin, which causes Pollution Damage by, or which creates the Threat of an escape or discharge of, Oil when the cargo in the Tanker is "owned", as defined in CRISTAL, by an Oil Company Party to CRISTAL.

(B) "CRISTAL" means the Contract Regarding a Supplement to Tanker Liability for Oil Pollution dated January 14th, 1971, as the same has been and may from time to time be amended.

(C) "Cristal Limited" means Cristal Limited, a company organised and existing under the Laws of Bermuda.

(D) "Fund" means the International Oil Pollution Compensation Fund established under Article 2 of the Fund Convention.

(E) "Fund Convention" means the International Convention on the Establishment of an International Fund for Compensation for Oil Pollution Damage, 1971, as amended from time to time, but excluding amendments set forth in the protocol thereto adopted at an International Conference held in London in 1984.

(F) "Liability Convention" means the International Convention on Civil Liability for Oil Pollution Damage, 1969, as defined in Clause I(e) of the Standing Agreement but excluding amendments set forth in the Protocol thereto.

(G) "Pollution Damage" means (i) physical loss or damage caused outside the Tanker by contamination resulting from the escape or discharge of Oil from the Tanker, wherever such escape or discharge may occur, including such loss or damage caused by Preventive Measures, and/or (ii) proven economic loss actually sustained, irrespective as to accompanying physical damage, as a direct result of contamination as set out in (i) above, including the Costs of Preventive Measures, and/or (iii) Costs actually incurred in taking reasonable and necessary measures to restore or replace natural resources damaged as a direct result of an Applicable Incident, but excluding any other damage to the environment.

(H) "Preventive Measures" means any reasonable measures taken by any Person after an Applicable Incident has occurred to prevent or minimise Pollution Damage.

(I) "Protocol" means the protocol to the Liability Convention adopted at an International Conference held in London in 1984.

(J) "Standing Agreement" means the Tanker Owners Voluntary Agreement concerning Liability for Oil Pollution dated January 7th, 1969, as the same has been and may from time to time be amended, but excluding the provisions of this Supplement thereto.

(K) "Threat Removal Measures" means reasonable measures taken by any Person after an Applicable Incident has occurred for the purposes of removing a Threat of an escape or discharge of Oil.

(L) "Ton" means a ton of a Tanker's gross tonnage as determined in accordance with the provisions of the International Convention on Tonnage Measurement of Ships, 1969, as amended and in force as of the effective date of the Supplement.

(2)(A) Insofar as they are not varied by this Paragraph 1, words and phrases shall have the same meanings as defined in Clause I of the Standing Agreement whenever they appear in this Supplement.

(B) References in this Supplement to Clauses I to XI are references to those Clauses in the Standing Agreement, and references to Paragraphs 1 to 5 are references to those Paragraphs in this Supplement.

(C) References in the Standing Agreement to "this Agreement" shall, where the context permits, apply also to the provisions of this Supplement.

(D) The Standing Agreement alone shall apply to an incident (as defined in Clause I(d) thereof) which is not an Applicable Incident and shall remain in full force and effect in respect of each such Incident. This Supplement shall not apply to any Incident which is not an Applicable Incident.

(E) The provisions of this Supplement shall apply to an Applicable Incident in substitution for and to the exclusion of Clauses IV, V and VII of the Standing Agreement. The provisions of all other Clauses of the Standing Agreement shall apply to an Applicable Incident except where those provisions are inconsistent with this Supplement, in which event this Supplement shall prevail.

2. Duration

(A) This Supplement shall cease to apply to an Applicable Incident occurring after 12.00 hours G.M.T. on February 20th, 1992 (or such later date as may be agreed), it being understood that nothing set forth herein shall affect the obligations of a Participating Owner with respect to an Applicable Incident which shall have occurred prior to 12.00 hours G.M.T. on February 20th, 1992.

(B) Upon termination of this Supplement the existence of the Federation shall not be affected, its continued existence being governed by the terms of the Standing Agreement.

3. Financial Responsibility for an Applicable Incident

(A) If an Applicable Incident occurs which does not cause Pollution Damage in a jurisdiction where the provisions of the Fund Convention are in force (but irrespective as to whether or not the provisions of the Liability Convention or any other applicable domestic laws are in force) the Participating Owner of a Tanker involved in that Applicable Incident shall, subject to the provisions of Paragraph 3(C), take such Preventive Measures and/or Threat Removal Measures as are practical and appropriate under the circumstances and, subject as aforesaid and in the following order of priority—

(1) pay such amount(s) to such Person(s) as may be necessary to fulfil his obli-

gations under the Liability Convention, the Protocol and domestic legislation giving effect thereto or any other law equivalent thereto together with any Costs incurred by the Participating Owner in taking Preventive Measures and/or Threat Removal Measures; and

(2) compensate any Person who would otherwise remain uncompensated and who (i) sustains Pollution Damage and/or (ii) incurs Costs in taking Preventive Measures and/or Threat Removal Measures.

(B) If an Applicable Incident occurs which causes Pollution Damage in a jurisdiction where the provisions of both the Liability Convention and Fund Convention are in force, the Participating Owner of a Tanker involved in that Applicable Incident shall, subject to the provisions of Paragraph 3(C), take such Preventive Measures and/or Threat Removal Measures as are practical and appropriate under the circumstances and, subject as aforesaid and in the following order of priority—

(1) pay such amount(s) to such Person(s) as may be necessary to fulfil his obligations under the Liability Convention, the Protocol and domestic legislation giving effect thereto or any other law equivalent thereto together with any Costs incurred by the Participating Owner in taking Preventive Measures and/or Threat Removal Measures;

(2) compensate Cristal Limited in an amount equal to the amount that the Fund has assessed against Oil Company Parties to CRISTAL as a result of the Applicable Incident; and

(3) compensate any Person who would otherwise remain uncompensated and who (i) sustains Pollution Damage and/or (ii) incurs Costs in taking Preventive Measures and/or Threat Removal Measures.

(C) The responsibilities which a Participating Owner has assumed, pursuant to Paragraphs 3(A) and (B), shall be subject to the following terms and conditions:

(1) A Participating Owner shall not be obligated to take Preventive Measures or Threat Removal Measures or pay Costs or make any compensation to a Person if the Applicable Incident (i) resulted from an act of war, hostilities, civil war, insurrection or a natural phenomenon of an exceptional, inevitable and irresistible character, or (ii) was wholly caused by an act or omission done with intent to cause damage by a third party or (iii) was wholly caused by the negligence or other wrongful act of any Government or other authority responsible for the maintenance of lights or other navigational aids in the exercise of that function. Notwithstanding the foregoing provisions of this sub-paragraph (1), a Participating Owner shall (irrespective as to whether he bears or would bear any liability under the Liability Convention with respect to the Applicable Incident) compensate Cristal Limited pursuant to Paragraph 3(B)(2) except when the Applicable Incident (i) resulted from an act of war, hostilities, civil war or insurrection or (ii) was wholly caused by an act or omission done with intent to cause damage by a third party.

(2) If Pollution Damage or the circumstances which gave rise to Preventive Measures or Threat Removal Measures resulted wholly or partially either from an act or omission done with intent to cause damage by, or from the negligence of, the Person who sustained the Pollution Damage and/or who took the Preventive Measures and/or Threat Removal Measures, the Participating Owner shall be proportionately exonerated from any responsibility he would otherwise have to such Person.

(3) The maximum amount of Costs to be incurred in respect of Preventive Measures and Threat Removal Measures and compensation to be paid by a Participating Owner under Paragraph 3(A) or (B) in respect of any one Applicable Incident, shall not exceed an amount equal, in the case of a Tanker of Five Thousand (5,000) Tons or less, Three Million Five Hundred Thousand United States Dollars (US$3,500,000.00) and for a Tanker in excess of Five Thousand (5,000) Tons, Three Million Five Hundred Thousand United States Dollars (US$3,500,000.00) plus Four Hundred and Ninety-Three United States Dollars (US$493.00) for each Ton in excess of said Five Thousand (5,000) Tons, subject to a maximum of Seventy Million United States Dollars (US$70,000,000.00).

(4) When Oil has escaped or been discharged from two or more Tankers or Participating Owners and/or there is a Threat of an escape or discharge of Oil from two or more Tankers of Participating Owners, the Participating Owners concerned, subject to the other provision of Paragraph 3(C), shall be jointly and severally responsible for all said Costs and compensation under Paragraphs 3(A) and (B) which are not reasonably separable.

(5) If the maximum sum that can be paid by the Participating Owner(s) within the provisions of Paragraph 3(C)(3), after deducting all payments made or to be made together with all Costs incurred under Paragraph 3(A)(1) or, as the case may be, 3(B)(1) and (2), is insufficient to meet all established claims in respect of an Applicable Incident under Paragraphs 3(A)(2) or (B)(3), then the Participating Owner(s) shall pay the proportion of each of those established claims as the available balance of that maximum sum bears to the total amount of those established claims.

4. Special Provisions

(A) If, before the Participating Owner has satisfied in full his financial responsibility under this Supplement, any Person providing him insurance or other financial security has, as a result of the Applicable Incident in question, made payment pursuant to Paragraphs 3(A) or (B), then

(1) the amount of that payment shall be taken into account in assessing the aggregate of established claims under this Supplement in respect of that Applicable Incident; and

(2) that Person shall, to the extent of that payment, be in the same position as the Person to whom that sum was paid would have been.

(B) When a Participating Owner establishes that the aggregate of claims in respect of an Applicable Incident may exceed the available balance of his maximum financial responsibility hereunder, he or any Person providing him insurance or other financial security may in his sole discretion make partial payment to claimants until the full extent of all claims is determined.

(C) For the purpose of determining the extent to which a Participating Owner has discharged his financial responsibility the amount of any payment made by a Participating Owner under this Supplement in a currency or currencies other than United States Dollars shall be converted to United States Dollars at the buy rate of exchange for said currency(ies) to United States Dollars as quoted by the National Westminster Bank Plc in London on the date of payment.

5. Procedure and Miscellaneous

(A) The provisions of Clauses VIII(B), (D) and (E) of the Standing Agreement shall apply to this Supplement as if references in those Clauses to the Incident were to the Applicable Incident.

(B) No financial responsibility shall arise under Paragraph 3(A) or (B) unless written notice of claim is received by the Participating Owner within two years of the date of the Applicable Incident giving rise thereto, it being understood that this provision shall not apply to the Participating Owner's obligation to compensate Cristal Limited under Paragraph 3(B)(2) which obligation shall not arise unless written notice of claim is received by Cristal Limited from an Oil Company Party and notified in writing to the Participating Owner within one year after the date that payment of the contribution under Article 10 of the Fund Convention is to be made.

(C) In the event that during the period of this Supplement there shall be any change to any oil pollution compensation regime, including CRISTAL, which, in the opinion, of the Board of Directors of the Federation, is or may be material to the Parties' obligations hereunder, then the said Board shall further consider the same with a view to making such recommendation to Parties in that regard as it thinks fit.

CRISTAL 1982 AND 1987–1989

CONTRACT REGARDING AN INTERIM SUPPLEMENT TO
TANKER LIABILITY FOR OIL POLLUTION (CRISTAL)
(JANUARY 1, 1982)

Preamble

The Parties to this Contract are various Oil Companies and the Oil Companies Institute for Marine Pollution Compensation Limited, an entity organised and existing under the Laws of Bermuda, hereinafter referred to as the "Institute".

The Parties recognize that marine casualties involving Tankers carrying bulk Oil cargoes can, on occasion, cause substantial Pollution Damage as a result of the escape or discharge of Oil into the sea. They further recognize that in some instances Persons who sustain Pollution Damage may be unable to recover adequate compensation therefor under existing legal and other regimes, including the International Convention on Civil Liability for Pollution Damage, 1969 and the Tanker Owners Voluntary Agreement Concerning Liability For Oil Pollution ("TOVALOP"). Accordingly they have decided by means of this Contract to supplement the compensation currently available to such Persons, at least until the International Convention On The Establishment Of An International Fund For Compensation For Oil Pollution Damage, 1971, comes into force, and to consider continuing this Contract in existence after said Convention comes into force until it is sufficiently widespread in application to provide comparable supplemental compensation throughout major areas of the world. They have also decided by means of this Contract to create financial incentives designed to encourage the Owners of Tankers from which an escape or discharge of Oil or the Threat thereof occurs, and other Persons as well, to take prompt and appropriate measures to prevent or mitigate Pollution Damage which might otherwise result.

In view of the above considerations, the Parties to this Contract and those Oil Companies who later become Parties, have agreed and do hereby agree, that the Institute will provide such supplemental compensation and create such incentives and that the Oil Company Parties will assure the availability of funds to enable the Institute to take such action, upon the following terms and conditions.

Clause 1. Definitions

For the purpose of this Contract, including the Preamble:

(A) "Tanker" means any sea-going vessel and any seaborne craft of any type

247

whatsoever, designed and constructed for carrying Oil in bulk as cargo, and actually so carrying Oil.

(B) "Person" means any individual or partnership or any public or private body, whether corporate or not, including a State or any of its constituent subdivisions.

(C) "Owner" means the Person or Persons registered as the owner of the Tanker or, in the absence of registration, the Person or Persons owning the Tanker. However, in the case of a Tanker owned by a State and operated by a company which in that State is registered as the Tanker's operator, "Owner" shall mean such company. Notwithstanding the foregoing, in the case of a Tanker under bareboat charter, "Owner" as defined above is subject to the Liability Convention.

(D) "Bareboat Charterer" means a Person or Persons who has chartered a Tanker upon terms which provide, among other things, that the Charterer shall have exclusive possession and control of the Tanker during the life of the charter.

(E) "TOVALOP" means the Tanker Owners Voluntary Agreement Concerning Liability for Oil Pollution Damage, as amended from time to time.

(F) "Oil" means any persistent hydrocarbon mineral oil such as crude oil, fuel oil, heavy diesel oil and lubricating oil whether or not carried as cargo.

(G) "Pollution Damage" means loss or damage caused outside the Tanker carrying Oil by contamination resulting from the escape or discharge of Oil from the Tanker, wherever such escape or discharge may occur, provided that said loss or damage is caused on the territory including the territory sea of any State, and includes the costs of Preventive Measures, wherever taken, and further loss or damage caused by such Preventive Measures but excludes any loss or damage which is remote, or speculative, or which does not result directly from such escape or discharge.

(H) "Preventive Measures" means any reasonable measures taken by any Person after an Incident has occurred to prevent or minimize Pollution Damage.

(I) "Incident" means any occurrence, or series of occurrences having the same origin, which causes Pollution Damage or which creates the Threat of an escape or discharge of Oil.

(J) "Threat of an escape or discharge of Oil" means a grave and imminent danger of the escape or discharge of Oil from a Tanker, which, if it occurred, would create a serious danger of Pollution Damage, whether or not an escape or discharge in fact subsequently occurs.

(K) "Threat Removal Measures" means reasonable measures taken by any Person after an Incident has occurred for the purpose of removing the Threat of an escape or discharge of Oil.

(L) "Oil Company" means (i) any Person engaged in the production, refining, marketing, storing or terminaling of Oil, or any one or more of whose affiliates are so engaged and (ii) any Person that receives Oil in bulk for its own consumption or use.

(M) "Oil Company Party" means an Oil Company which is a Party to this Contract.

(N) "Contract Year" means any twelve month period commencing upon the Effective Date (as referred to in Clause III (A) hereof) or any anniversary thereof.

(O) The "Liability Convention" means the International Convention on Civil Liability for Oil Pollution Damage, 1969 which entered into force on June 19, 1975, including legislation and regulations implementing the provisions thereof which are enacted from time to time by any Contracting State thereunder.

(P) "Fund Convention" means the International Convention On the Establishment

Of An International Fund For Compensation For Oil Pollution Damage, 1971, as amended from time to time.

(Q) A Tanker's "Tonnage" means the net tonnage of the Tanker with the addition of the amount deducted from her gross tonnage on account of engine room space for the purpose of ascertaining her net tonnage. In the case of a Tanker for which this Tonnage cannot be ascertained, the Tanker's Tonnage shall be deemed to be 40 per cent. of the weight in tons of 2,240 lbs. of Oil which the Tanker is capable of carrying.

(R) "Cost" or "Costs" means reasonable cost or costs, respectively.

Clause II. General Conditions

(A) Any Oil Company in the world which is willing to be bound by this Contract and to become a shareholder in the Institute and to abide by its By-Laws, Rules and Directives, may become an Oil Company Party to this Contract upon acceptance by the Institute of an application in the form attached hereto as "Exhibit A".

(B) The obligations of an Oil Company Party under this Contract shall extend solely to the Institute and to the other Oil Company Parties hereto.

Clause III. Effective Date and Duration

(A) This Contract came into effect on 1 April 1971, its "Effective Date", except as to various amendments which came into effect thereafter.

(B) This Contract may be terminated at the discretion of the Institute.
  (i) On 1 June 1981, or any successive anniversary of that date, but not before the expiration of the 120 day period after the Fund Convention enters into force in accordance with Article 40, Paragraph 1, thereof, or
  (ii) at any time after 1 June 1981, provided that the Fund Convention has entered into force and that the Institute considers that it is sufficiently widespread in application.

(C) An Oil Company Party may withdraw from this Contract:
  (i) in accordance with Clause X, or
  (ii) on 1 June 1981, or any successive anniversary of that date, provided that it gives at least six months prior written notice of withdrawal to the Institute.
  (iii) at any time after the expiration of the 120 day period following the entry into force of the Fund Convention as referred to in Article 40, Paragraph 1, thereof, provided that the cargo movements of the Oil Company Party desiring to withdraw are entirely within the area to which the Fund Convention applies, and provided further that said party has given six months prior written notice of withdrawal to the Institute.

(D) The withdrawal of an Oil Company Party from this Contract or termination of this Contract shall not affect the rights and obligations already accrued hereunder at the time of said withdrawal or termination.

Clause IV. Compensation and Indemnity

(A) In the event of an Incident the Institute shall:
  (1) compensate any Person who sustains Pollution Damage, including an Owner who takes Preventive Measures, (excluding, however, Pollution Damage in

respect of which the Person is entitled to claim compensation under the Fund Convention), and

(2) compensate a Person who incurs Costs in taking Threat Removal Measures, and

(3) indemnify an Owner in respect of a portion of his liability for Pollution Damage and Threat Removal Measures, (excluding from said portion the amount of any indemnity which the Owner is entitled to claim under the Fund Convention), subject to the conditions and in the amounts set forth in Paragraphs (B) through (L) below.

(B) It shall be a condition precedent to the Institute's obligation to pay such compensation and indemnity that at the time of the Incident:

(1) the Oil involved in the Incident was "owned" by an Oil Company Party, as provided in Clause V, and

(2) the Tanker from which the escape or discharge of Oil occurred, or from which there was a Threat of an escape or discharge of Oil, was owned by or bareboat chartered to a Party to TOVALOP and that said Party had:

(a) made the terms of TOVALOP applicable to the Tanker and

(b) established and maintained his financial capability to fulfil his obligations under TOVALOP.

(C) No compensation or indemnity shall be paid if the Incident:

(1) resulted from an act of war, hostilities, civil war, insurrection or a natural phenomenon of an exceptional, inevitable and irresistible character, or

(2) was wholly caused by an act or omission done with intent to cause damage by the claimant or any other third Person,

(3) was wholly caused by the negligence or other wrongful act of any Government or other authority responsible for the maintenance of lights or other navigational aids in the exercise of that function.

(D) If Pollution Damage or the taking of Threat Removal Measures resulted wholly or partially from the negligence of the Person who sustained the Pollution Damage or who took the Threat Removal Measures, any compensation that would otherwise be payable by the Institute to that Person shall be denied or reduced proportionately; however, this shall not apply to Preventive Measures and Threat Removal Measures taken by the Owner to the extent that they were taken as a result of an Incident caused wholly or partially by the negligence of the Owner.

(E) When an Incident causes Pollution Damage and the Owner of the Tanker from which the escape or discharge of Oil occurred is liable for Pollution Damage under the terms of the Liability Convention, then the Institute shall:

(1) compensate any Person who sustained Pollution Damage (excluding the owner of the Tanker) to the extent that such Person has been unable, after having taken all reasonable steps to pursue the remedies available to him, to obtain full compensation for said Pollution, from:

(a) the Owner of the Tanker, and

(b) any other Person or vessel liable therefor, and

(c) any other source of compensation available under convention, law, or regulation, including but not limited to a fund established and maintained by means of assessments against Oil Companies:

(2) compensate the Owner for the Cost of Preventive Measures taken by him in respect of such escape or discharge to the extent that the Owner has been

unable, after having taken all reasonable steps to pursue the remedies available to him, to obtain full compensation therefor from:

(a) any fund constituted in accordance with the Liability Convention, and

(b) any other Person or vessel liable therefor, and

(c) any other source of compensation available under convention, law, or regulation, including but not limited to a fund established and maintained by means of assessments against Oil Companies.

(F) When an Incident creates a Threat of the escape or discharge of Oil, or causes Pollution Damage and the Owner of the Tanker from which the escape or discharge of Oil occurred is not liable for the Pollution Damage under the terms of the Liability Convention, then the Institute shall:

(1) compensate any Person who sustained Pollution Damage or incurred Costs for taking Threat Removal Measures, or both (excluding the Owner of the Tanker) to the extent that such Person has been unable, after having taken all reasonable steps to pursue the remedies available to him, to obtain full compensation therefor from:

(a) the Owner of the Tanker under the provisions of TOVALOP, or applicable law, and

(b) any other Person or vessel liable therefor, and

(c) any other source of compensation available under convention, law, or regulation, including but not limited to a fund established and maintained by means of assessments against Oil Companies.

(2) compensate the Owner is respect of that portion of Costs incurred by him in taking Preventive Measures or Threat Removal Measures or both, to the extent that he has been unable, after having taken all reasonable steps to pursue the remedies available to him, to obtain full compensation therefor:

(a) under the provisions of TOVALOP, and

(b) from any other Person or vessel liable therefor, and

(c) from any other source of compensation available under convention, law, or regulation, including but not limited to any fund established and maintained by means of assessments against Oil Companies.

(G) The Institute shall, in respect of any Incident, indemnify:

(1) the Owner of the Tanker from which an escape or discharge of Oil occurred for a portion of his liability for Pollution Damage resulting from the Incident when the Owner is liable for the Pollution Damage under the terms of the Liability Convention, or

(2) the Owner of the Tanker for a portion of his liability for Pollution Damage and Threat Removal Measures under TOVALOP, or

(3) the Owner of the Tanker from which an escape or discharge of oil occurred for a portion of his liability for Pollution Damage resulting from the Incident under any applicable law other than the Liability Convention.

The indemnity shall be paid for that amount which:

(a) exceeds One Hundred Twenty U.S. Dollars (U.S. $120.00) per ton of the Tanker's Tonnage or Ten Million U.S. Dollars (U.S. $10,000,000.00), whichever is less, and which

(b) does not exceed One Hundred Sixty U.S. Dollars (U.S. $160.00) per ton of said Tanker's Tonnage, or Sixteen Million Eight Hundred Thousand U.S. Dollars (U.S. $16,800,000.00), whichever is less:

Provided that no such indemnity shall be paid to an Owner whose recklessness or wilful misconduct caused the Incident.

For the purpose of this Paragraph, the Cost of Owner's Preventive Measures shall be included in Owner's liability, in respect of Items 1 and 3 above, and the Cost of Preventive Measures or Threat Removal Measures taken by the Owner shall be included in his liability in respect of Item 2 above.

Notwithstanding the foregoing, the amount of any indemnity otherwise payable under this Paragraph shall be reduced by the amount of any indemnity which the Owner is entitled to claim under the Fund Convention.

(H) In the case of an Incident which does not result from the wilful misconduct of the Owner or from the unseaworthiness of the Tanker where this occurs with the privity of the Owner, the Institute shall indemnify the Owner in respect of his liability for Pollution Damage and Threat Removal Measures to the extent that the aggregate amount of such liability exceeds One Hundred Sixty U.S. Dollars (U.S. $160.00) per ton of the Tanker's Tonnage or Sixteen Million Eight Hundred Thousand U.S. Dollars (U.S. $ 16,800,000.00), whichever is less, by reason of the application to the Incident of a legal regime other than the Liability Convention.

For the purpose of this Paragraph the Cost of Owner's Preventive Measures and Threat Removal Measures taken by an Owner shall be included in Owner's liability.

(I) The aggregate amount payable by the Institute under Paragraphs (E), (F), or (H) of this Clause in respect of any one Incident, regardless of the number of Tankers involved, shall be limited so that the total sum of that amount and the compensation available from all vessels, Persons and sources other than the Institute referred to in such of those Paragraphs as are applicable shall not exceed Thirty Six Million U.S. Dollars (U.S. $36,000,000.00).

Notwithstanding the foregoing, in the case of an Incident which causes Pollution Damage in respect of which a Person is entitled to claim compensation under the Fund Convention as well as Pollution Damage in respect of which a Person is entitled to claim compensation under this Contract, the amount of compensation payable with respect to the latter Pollution Damage shall in no circumstances exceed the amount that would have been payable hereunder with respect to said latter Pollution Damage in the event that all the Pollution Damage resulting from the Incident was compensable hereunder.

If experience indicates that the total amount available hereunder is significantly less than the amount required to satisfy all claims, the Institute shall increase the limit as in its judgment it considers advisable, but not above Seventy Two Million U.S. Dollars (U.S. $72,000,000.00), in respect of Incidents occurring after the effective date of such increase.

(J) If the aggregate amount payable by the Institute pursuant to Paragraph (I) above is insufficient to meet in full all established claims made hereunder, then the Institute shall incorporate the net amount available among the claimants concerned.

(K) The amount to be paid by the Institute as provided in Paragraph (1) above shall be reduced by any amounts paid, or agreed to be paid, by the Institute in settlement of established claims hereunder.

(L) Notwithstanding the foregoing provisions of this Clause IV, the Institute shall not pay compensation or indemnity if the only oil involved in an Incident was transported by Tanker between installations or terminals on the territory or in the territorial sea of a State which at the time of the Incident is a Party to the Fund Convention, and if the Institute, by a determination made prior to said Incident and still in effect at the time thereof, shall have concluded:

(a) that because of the unique geographic position of said State, Oil so transported is highly unlikely to cause Pollution Damage on the territory or in the territorial sea of another State, and

(b) that adequate arrangements exist in said State to compensate the cost of Threat Removal Measures involving Oil so transported.

Clause V. Ownership of Shipments

A particular shipment of Oil shall be considered "owned" by an Oil Company Party for the purpose of Clause IV (B) (1) and Clause VII when:

(i) title to the shipment is in said Oil Company Party, or

(ii) title to the shipment is in a Person not an Oil Company to whom said Oil Company Party has transferred the shipment, provided that prior to any Incident involving said shipment, and in accordance with Rules of the Institute, said Oil Company Party has advised the Institute in writing that it elects to be considered owner thereof, or

(iii) title to the shipment is in a Person not an Oil Company Party but the shipment is being carried by a Tanker owned by or under charter to an Oil Company Party or one of its affiliates, provided that prior to any Incident involving said shipment, and in accordance with Rules of the Institute, said Oil Company Party has advised the Institute in writing that for the purpose of this Contract it elects to be considered owner thereof, or

(iv) title is in a Person not an Oil Company Party who, prior to any Incident involving said shipment, contracted to transfer said shipment to an Oil Company Party.

For the purpose of Clause IV (B) (1) only, bunker oil and lubricating oil of a Tanker carrying any shipment so "owned", and intended for use in the Tanker's operation shall be deemed included in the shipment.

Clause VI. Subrogation

(A) Except with respect to payments made by the Institute under Paragraphs (G) and (H) of Clause IV, the Institute shall, in respect of any amount of compensation for Pollution Damage or of Threat Removal Measures paid in accordance with Clause IV, acquire by subrogation the rights that the Person so compensated may enjoy under the Liability Convention or otherwise against the Owner or his underwriters.

(B) Nothing herein shall prejudice any right of recourse or subrogation of the Institute against Persons other than those referred to in the preceding Paragraph. In any event, the right of the Institute to subrogation against such Person shall not be less favourable than that of an insurer of the Person to whom compensation or indemnity has been paid.

Clause VII. The Fund

(A) (1) The Institute, in order to assure its financial capability to make payments in accordance with Clause IV, shall maintain and administer a Fund, contributions to which shall be made by each Oil Company Party.

(2) Contributions to the Fund shall be calculated on the basis of Crude/Fuel Oil Receipts of the Oil Company Parties.

For the purpose of this Clause, Crude/Fuel Oil Receipts means:

    (i) crude oil and fuel oil received at an installation or terminal by an Oil Company Party which has been transported all or part of the way to such installation or terminal by Tanker (excluding any crude oil which is received solely for transhipment for onward transportation by Tanker to an installation or terminal for receipt by an Oil Company Party) and which at the time of receipt is owned by an Oil Company Party, and

    (ii) crude oil and fuel oil not so received but with respect to which an Oil Company Party has elected to be considered the owner, and

    (iii) crude oil and fuel oil owned by an Oil Company Party but with respect to which title was transferred at destination to a Person not an Oil Company Party, and

    (iv) crude oil and fuel oil at the time when it has been retained on board a Tanker for a period of six months and which at that time is owned by an Oil Company Party, together with any such crude oil and fuel oil retained on board such Tanker on the last day of each ensuing calendar year thereafter which, at that time, is owned by an Oil Company Party.

Notwithstanding the foregoing provisions of this Paragraph (A) (2), in the case of fuel oil as to which a determination under Paragraph (L) of Clause IV applies, the amount of Crude/Fuel Oil Receipts in respect thereof shall be reduced by the amount of said fuel oil reported as "Contributing Oil" under the Fund Convention.

(B) (1) The Fund shall initially be constituted in the amount of Five Million U.S. Dollars (U.S. $5,000,000) (hereinafter referred to as the "Initial Call").

(2) Contributions to the Initial Call shall be calculated by dividing the initial amount of the Fund by the total Crude/Fuel Oil Receipts of all the Oil Company Parties as at the Effective Date during the calendar year preceding that Date, and multiplying the figure so calculated by the Crude/Fuel Oil Receipts of each Oil Company Party received by it during the calendar year preceding the year in which it becomes a Party. For the purpose of these calculations, the Crude/Fuel Oil Receipts of an Oil Company Party shall be the total of the crude oil and fuel oil as defined in paragraph (A) (2) (i).

Notwithstanding the above calculations, the contribution from any Oil Company Party to the Initial Call shall not be less than a minimum sum determined by the Institute to be reasonable under the circumstances.

(C) (1) The Institute shall from time to time estimate any further amount (hereinafter referred to as a "Periodic Call") required to assure the capability of the Fund to make payments in accordance with Clause IV.

(2) Contributions to a Periodic Call shall be calculated by dividing the amount of the Call by the total of the Crude/Fuel Oil Receipts of all the Oil Company Parties as at the date of the Periodic Call during the calendar year preceding the Contract Year in which the Periodic Call is made, and multiplying the figure so calculated by the Crude/Fuel Oil Receipts of each Oil Company Party for such preceding year. For the purpose of these calculations the Crude/Fuel Oil Receipts shall be the total of the crude oil and fuel oil as defined in paragraph (A) (2) (i), (ii), (iii) and (iv).

(3) Notwithstanding the foregoing:

    (i) each such Oil Company Party (whether or not it had any Crude/Fuel Oil

Receipts during such preceding calendar year) shall pay no less than a minimum charge determined by the Institute to be reasonable under the circumstances, and

(ii) no Oil Company Party shall be liable to contribute to any payment of compensation by the Institute in excess of Five Hundred Thousand U.S. Dollars (U.S. $500,000.00) with respect to any incident which occurred before it became a Party to this Contract.

(4) Any Oil Company Party which becomes a Party hereto during a Contract Year shall pay a contribution to any Periodic Call made during that Year, but only in respect of that portion of the Year during which it has been an Oil Company Party, and in no event less than the minimum sum referred to in Paragraph (3) (i) above.

(D) Upon termination of this Contract, any amounts remaining in the Fund after the settlement or other disposition of all claims arising out from Incidents occurring before the date of termination, and the settlement of all costs and expenses relating to the winding up of the Institute, shall be equitably distributed among the Oil Companies that were Parties at the date of termination.

Clause VIII. Notice of Claim

No liability shall arise hereunder unless written notice of claim is received by the Institute within two years of the date of the Incident giving rise thereto.

Clause IX. Rules and Directives

The Institute shall have the right to make rules and directives from time to time with respect to interpretation and administration of this Contract.

Clause X. Amendment

This Contract may be amended by Resolution adopted at any Regular or Special Meeting of the shareholders of the Institute upon a vote in which at least 75 per cent. of the votes cast are in favour of said Resolution. However, an Oil Company Party which votes against said Resolution shall have the option to withdraw herefrom within sixty days of the date of such Resolution by means of written notice to the Institute without, however, affecting its rights and obligations accrued at the time of withdrawal.

Amendments to this Contract shall apply only in respect of Incidents which occur after the time they come into effect and shall not impose upon the Parties any obligation of any kind with respect to an Incident occurring prior to that time. Accordingly the provisions hereof shall apply only as to Incidents which occur after Noon G.M.T. on 1 June, 1981, the effective date of the latest amendments hereto.

Clause XI. Law Governing

(A) This Contract shall be construed and shall take effect in accordance with the laws of England; the Courts of England shall have exclusive jurisdiction over any matter arising therefrom.

(B) This Contract shall not be construed as creating a trust.

(C) A Party hereto shall not be required to incur any obligation to take any action which would violate any laws or Government regulations which apply to it or, in the event its stock or shares are owned by another Person, which would violate any law or Government regulations which apply to said Persons.

CONTRACT REGARDING A SUPPLEMENT TO TANKER LIABILITY FOR OIL POLLUTION (CRISTAL)

(As amended 20 February 1987, and as further amended up to and including 20 February 1989)

Preamble

The Parties to this Contract are various Oil Companies and Cristal Limited (hereinafter referred to as "CRISTAL"), a Company organised and existing under the laws of Bermuda.

The Parties recognize that (i) Tankers carrying bulk Oil cargoes may cause substantial Pollution Damage as a result of the escape or discharge of Oil into the sea, and (ii) Persons who have sustained Pollution Damage are sometimes unable to recover adequate compensation.

Therefore, the Parties have decided by means of this Contract to (i) provide supplemental compensation to such Persons and (ii) reimburse Oil Company Parties their contributions to the Fund, when cargoes are "owned" by Oil Company Parties, all in accordance with the terms and conditions set forth herein.

Clause I. Definitions

For the purpose of this Contract (including the Preamble):

(A) "Bareboat Charterer" means the Person (or Persons) who has chartered a Tanker upon terms which provide, among other things, that the charterer shall have exclusive possession and control of the Tanker during the life of the charter.

(B) "Cost" or "Costs" means reasonable cost or costs, respectively.

(C) "Fund" means the International Oil Pollution Compensation Fund established under Article 2 of the Fund Convention.

(D) "Fund Convention" means the International Convention on the Establishment of an International Fund for Compensation for Oil Pollution Damage, 1971, as amended from time to time, but excluding amendments set forth in the Protocol thereto adopted at an International Conference held in London in 1984.

(E) "Incident" means any occurrence, or series of occurrences having the same origin, which causes Pollution Damage, or which creates the Threat of an escape or discharge of Oil.

(F) "Liability Convention" means the International Convention on Civil Liability for Oil Pollution Damage, 1969, as amended from time to time, but excluding amendments set forth in the Protocol thereto adopted at an International Converence held in London in 1984.

(G) "Oil" means any persistent hydrocarbon mineral oil including, but not limited to, crude oil, fuel oil, heavy diesel oil and lubricating oil whether carried on board a Tanker as cargo or in the bunkers of such a Tanker.

(H) "Oil Company" means any Person (i) engaged in the production, refining, marketing, storing, trading or terminaling of Oil, or any one or more of whose affiliates are so engaged or (ii) that receives Oil in bulk for its own consumption or use.

(I) "Oil Company Party" means an Oil Company which is a Party to this Contract.

(J) "Owner" means the Person or Persons registered as the owner of the Tanker or, in the absence of registration, the Person or Persons owning the Tanker. However, in the case of a Tanker owned by a State and operated by a company which in that State is registered as the Tanker's operator, "Owner" shall mean such company. Notwithstanding the foregoing, in the case of a Tanker under bareboat charter, "Owner" means the Bareboat Charterer or any other Person deemed to be an owner under the laws applicable to the Incident.

(K) "Person" means (i) an Owner and (ii) any individual or partnership or any public or private body, whether corporate or not, including a State or any of its constituent subdivisions.

(L) "Preventive Measures" means any reasonable measures taken by any Person after an Incident has occurred to prevent or minimise Pollution Damage.

*(M) "Pollution Damage" means (i) physical loss or damage caused outside the Tanker by contamination resulting from the escape or discharge of Oil from the Tanker, wherever such escape or discharge may occur, including such loss or damage caused by Preventive Measures, and/or (ii) proven economic loss actually sustained, irrespective as to accompanying physical damage, as a direct result of contamination as set out in (i) above, including the Costs of Preventive Measures, and/or (iii) Costs actually incurred in taking reasonable and necessary measures to restore or replace natural resources damaged as a direct result of an Incident, but excluding any other damage to the environment.

(N) "Tanker" means any seagoing vessel and any seaborne craft of any type whatsoever, designed and constructed for carrying Oil in bulk as cargo, and actually so carrying Oil.

(O) "Threat of an escape or discharge of Oil" means a grave and imminent danger of the escape or discharge of Oil from a Tanker, which, if it occurred, would create a serious danger of Pollution Damage, whether or not an escape or discharge in fact subsequently occurs.

(P) "Threat Removal Measures" means reasonable measures taken by any Person after an Incident has occurred for the purposes of removing the Threat of an escape or discharge of Oil

(Q) "Ton" means a ton of a Tanker's gross tonnage as determined in accordance with the provisions of the International Convention on Tonnage Measurement of Ships, 1969, as amended, and in force at the Effective Date of this Contract.

Clause II. General Conditions

(A) Any Oil Company may become an Oil Company Party to this Contract and a Member of CRISTAL upon acceptance by CRISTAL of an application in the form attached hereto as "Exhibit A".

(B) The obligations of an Oil Company Party under this Contract shall extend solely

---

* Amendment effective October 23, 1989.

to CRISTAL and to the other Oil Company Parties hereto. The obligations of CRISTAL under this Contract shall extend solely to the Oil Company Parties hereto.

Clause III. Effective Date

(A) This Contract shall be applicable to Incidents which shall have occurred after 12.00 hours G.M.T. on February 20, 1987, (the "Effective Date"), and shall no longer be applicable to Incidents occurring at or after 12.00 hours G.M.T. on February 20, 1992, (or such later date as may be agreed); it being understood that nothing set forth herein shall affect the obligations of CRISTAL with respect to an Incident which occurred prior to the Effective Date.

(B) An Oil Company Party may withdraw from this Contract at any time following the Effective Date, provided that it gives at least six (6) months prior written notice of withdrawal to CRISTAL and such withdrawing Oil Company Party shall have no rights hereunder as of the date of withdrawal; however any such withdrawal shall not affect the obligations of the withdrawing Oil Company Party with respect to Incidents which occurred prior to the said date of withdrawal, which obligations shall be satisfied as set forth in Paragraph (C) of this Clause III.

(C) An Oil Company Party shall satisfy its obligations under Paragraph (B) of this Clause III by, either (i) paying a release assessment calculated by CRISTAL in a manner set forth in the Rules to this Contract or (ii) at CRISTAL's option, contributing to Periodic Calls made after the aforesaid date of withdrawal in accordance with terms and conditions set forth in the Rules to this Contract.

Clause IV. Compensation and Payments

(A) If an Incident does not cause Pollution Damage in a jurisdiction where the provisions of the Fund Convention are in force, but irrespective as to whether the provisions of the Liability Convention or any applicable domestic law are in force, CRISTAL shall, subject to the conditions and in the amounts set forth in Paragraphs (D) and (E) of this Clause IV, compensate any Person who, (i) sustains Pollution Damage or (ii) incurs Costs in taking Threat Removal Measures.

(B) If an Incident causes Pollution Damage in a jurisdiction where the provisions of both the Liability Convention and the Fund Convention are in force CRISTAL shall, subject to the conditions and in the amounts set forth in Paragraphs (D) and (E) of this Clause IV:

   (1) pay an Oil Company Party, an amount equal to the contribution assessed by the Fund or made to the Fund by such Oil Company Party under Article 10 of the Fund Convention, with respect to the amount that the Fund intends to pay or did pay as compensation as a result of an Incident; and,

   (2) compensate any Person who (i) sustains Pollution Damage or (ii) incurs Costs in taking Threat Removal Mesures and who would otherwise remain uncompensated.

(C) For the purposes of Paragraphs (A) and (B) of this Clause IV, Pollution Damage shall include amounts paid by a Person to compensate another Person for Pollution Damage.

(D) No Payment or Compensation shall be made under either Paragraphs (A) or

(B) of this Clause IV except subject to and in accordance with the terms and conditions set forth herein.

(1) It shall be a condition precedent to CRISTAL's obligation to make any payment whatsoever that, at the time of the Incident, the Oil involved in the Incident be "owned" by an Oil Company Party, as provided in Clause V.

(2) No compensation shall be paid to a Person, under either Paragraph (A) or (B) (2) of this Clause IV, if the Incident (i) resulted from an act of war, hostilities, civil war, insurrection or a natural phenomenon of an exceptional, inevitable and irresistible character, or (ii) was wholly caused by an act or omission done with intent to cause damage by a third party, or (iii) was wholly caused by the negligence or other wrongful act of any Government or other authority responsible for the maintenance of lights or other navigational aids in the exercise of that function.

Notwithstanding the foregoing provisions of this Subparagraph (2) CRISTAL shall compensate Oil Company Parties under Paragraph B (1) of this Clause IV except when the Incident resulted from an act of war, hostilities, civil war or insurrection, or was wholly caused by an act or omission done with intent to cause damage by a third party.

(3) If Pollution Damage or the taking of Threat Removal Measures resulted wholly or partially either from an act or omission done with intent to cause damage by, or from the negligence of the Person who sustained the Pollution Damage or who took the Threat Removal Measures, any payment or compensation that would otherwise be payable by CRISTAL to that Person, under either Paragraphs (A) or (B) (2) of this Clause IV, shall be denied or reduced proportionately to the extent of that Person's negligence; however nothing set forth in this Subparagraph shall affect CRISTAL's obligations under Paragraph (B) (1) of this Clause IV, or to the Owner in respect of an Incident which does not result from the wilful misconduct of the Owner or from the unseaworthiness of the Tanker where this occurs with the Privity of the Owner.

(4) No payment or compensation shall be made or paid under Paragraphs (A) and (B), of this Clause IV, until evidence, satisfactory to CRISTAL, has been presented demonstrating that claims for Pollution Damage or Costs of Preventive Measures or Threat Removal Measures (including payments made by the Owner to CRISTAL, as agent for Oil Company Party(ies)), and payments or costs incurred by the Owner as a result of the application of the Liability Convention, applicable domestic laws or otherwise have been paid by, or on behalf of, the Owner equal, in the case of a Tanker of Five Thousand (5,000) Tons or less to Three Million Five Hundred Thousand United States Dollars (U.S. $3,500,000.00) and for a Tanker in excess of Five Thousand (5,000) Tons Three Million Five Hundred Thousand United States Dollars (U.S. $3,500,000.00) plus Four Hundred and Ninety Three United States Dollars (U.S. $493.00) for each Ton in excess of said Five Thousand (5,000) Tons, subject to a maximum of Seventy Million United States Dollars (U.S. $70,000,000.00).

(5) (a) The aggregate amount to be paid by CRISTAL, under Paragraph (A), (B) and (D) (8) of this Clause IV, in respect of any one Incident, shall not exceed, after taking into account payments made under Subparagraph (4) of

this Clause IV (D) and amount equal to Thirty Six Million United States Dollars (U.S. $36,000,000.00) for a Tanker of Five Thousand (5,000) Tons or less and for a Tanker in excess of Five Thousand (5,000) Tons Thirty Six Million United States Dollars (U.S. $36,000,000.00) plus Seven Hundred and Thirty Three United States Dollars (U.S. $733.00) for each Ton in excess of said Five Thousand (5,000) Tons, subject to a maximum of One Hundred and Thirty Five Million United States Dollars (U.S. $135,000,000.00).

(b) In the event more than one Tanker discharges Oil or poses a Threat of an excape or discharge of Oil in respect of any one Incident, the aggregate amount to be paid by CRISTAL under Subparagraph (5) (a) of this Clause IV (D) shall be established by reference to the tonnage of the largest of said Tankers. For the purpose of establishing under Subparagraph (4) of this Clause IV (D) whether payment or compensation shall be made or paid, payments or Costs incurred by or on behalf of the Owners of all the said Tankers shall be taken into account.

(6) If the maximum amount that can be paid by CRISTAL, pursuant to Paragraph (D) (5) of this Clause IV, is insufficient to reimburse an Oil Company Party(ies), pursuant to Paragraph (B) (1) of this Clause IV, and meet in full all other claims, approved under Paragraphs (A) and (B) (2) of this Clause IV, then CRISTAL shall prorate the amount available among all claims.

(7) No payment or compensation shall be made or paid to a Person entitled, under Paragraphs (A) and (B) (2) of this Clause IV, to make a claim with respect to an Incident, if that Person prosecutes a claim for Pollution Damage or the Cost of Preventive Measures or Threat Removal Measures against any fund established and/or maintained by means of assessments against Oil Companies, irrespective as to whether any said Person is entitled to either indemnification or compensation under the terms of any such fund; provided that nothing set forth herein shall prevent such a Person from asserting, prosecuting or settling a claim, against any said fund for those amounts not satisfied pursuant to this Contract or, under either (i) the Liability Convention or (ii) against the Fund under the Fund Convention, or both, if or to the extent, they are applicable.

(8) No compensation (except any payment to be made pursuant to Paragraph (B) (1) of this Clause IV) shall be made or paid to a Person until such Person has taken all reasonable steps to obtain full compensation for Pollution Damage or for the Cost of Preventive Measures or Threat Removal Measures or any element thereof from any Person, but not including the Owner unless the Pollution Damage or Costs resulted from the wilful misconduct of the Owner or from the unseaworthiness of the Tanker where this occurs with the privity of the Owner, or ship (which shall include but not be limited to a Tanker or any other vessel or ship) liable therefor, and from any other source of compensation available under convention, law or regulation (except for funds established and maintained by means of assessments against Oil Companies as referred to in Subparagraph (7) of this Clause IV (D)); provided, however, that CRISTAL may, in its sole discretion and to the extent permitted under applicable law, advance monies to said Person to partially or fully compensate for the Costs said Person might incur in taking reasonable steps to obtain full compensation as set forth in this Subparagraph (8).

(9) (a) In the event that CRISTAL should determine that it is unreasonable for a Person to take steps or further steps, pursuant to Subparagraph (8) of this Clause IV (D), CRISTAL may require, prior to compensating said Person under Paragraphs (A) or (B) (2) of this Clause IV, that it receive, in a form acceptable to it, documentation or other instrument(s), executed by said Person (but without prejudice to the rights of the Fund under the Fund Convention if it has made a payment to said Person under the Fund Convention), (i) transferring or assigning to CRISTAL any and all rights of any nature or kind, said Person has or might have to seek compensation from any third party (including a government or governmental agency but excluding the Fund) for the compensation to be paid by CRISTAL to said Person for either Pollution Damage and Costs of Preventive Measures or Threat Removal Measures; or (ii) granting irrevocable authority to CRISTAL to institute, in the name of any said Person, legal, equitable or administrative proceedings in any jurisdiction whatsoever to perfect and exercise the aforesaid rights and if any judgment, award, decision or decree is secured to collect the same, in the name of any said Person, and when collected to endorse and negotiate any cheque, money order, bill of exchange, promissory note, transfer or similar instrument so that the proceeds of any such judgment, award, decision or decree shall be the sole property of CRISTAL; and

(b) no payment shall be made under Paragraph (B) (1) of this Clause IV, until CRISTAL has received, in a form acceptable to it, a document or other instrument evidencing settlement in part or in full, as the case may be, the obligations of CRISTAL pursuant to Paragraph (B) (1) of this Caluse IV.

(10) For the purposes of Paragraph (D) (3) and (8) of this Clause IV the terms "wilful misconduct", "privity" and "unseaworthiness" shall have the same meaning as they have under the Marine Insurance Act 1906 as interpreted by the English Courts under English Law.

(E) For the purposes of determining the amount of any payments or compensation to be paid by CRISTAL hereunder, CRISTAL shall:

(1) Convert any losses or Costs constituting Pollution Damage, Preventive Measures or Threat Removal Measures either incurred or suffered by a Person or any payment made by or on behalf of an Owner, for the purposes of Paragraph (D) (4) and (5) of this Clause IV, if incurred in a currency(ies) other than United States Dollars to United States Dollars at the buy rate of exchange for said currency(ies) as quoted by the National Westminster Bank Plc in London on the date of the payment by or on behalf of the Owner, or by CRISTAL respectively; except when a limitation fund is established under the provisions of the Liability Convention when the said exchange rate shall be that as quoted on the date that the limitation fund is established.

(2) Convert any payments to be made to an Oil Company Party, pursuant to Paragraph (B) (1) of this Clause IV, if incurred in a currency(ies) other than United States Dollars, to United States Dollars at the buy rate of exchange for said currency(ies) to United States Dollars as quoted by the National Westminster Bank Plc in London on the date that the Fund shall have demanded payment by the Oil Company Party.

(3) The amount of all losses or Costs constituting Pollution Damage, Preventive Measures or Threat Removal Measures shall be determined by CRISTAL in

the currency of the jurisdiction where the Incident has occurred or the Costs were incurred by a Person. All payments in compensation therefor made pursuant to Paragraphs (A) or (B) (2) of this Clause VI shall be made by CRISTAL in such currency(ies), if other than United States dollars, by converting the equivalent amount of United States dollars into such currency(ies) at the buy rate of exchange as quoted by the National Westminster Bank Plc in London on the date of payment. If on the date payment of said claim(s) is (are) to be made, an expenditure of United States Dollars (after considering all payments to be made under Paragraph (B) (1) of this Clause IV) is required by CRISTAL in excess of the provisions of Paragraph (D) (5) of this Clause IV, the provisions of Paragraph (D) (6) of this Clause IV shall be applicable.

*Clause V. Ownership of Shipments

(A) A particular shipment of Oil shall be considered "owned" by an Oil Company Party for the purpose of Clause IV (D) (1) and Clause VII if at the time of the Incident title to the shipment is in either:

(1) said Oil Company Party, or
(2) a Person not an Oil Company Party to whom said Oil Company Party has transferred the shipment, or
(3) a Person not an Oil Company Party but the shipment is being carried by a Tanker owned by or under charter to an Oil Company Party or one of its affiliates, or
(4) a Person not an Oil Company party who, prior to any Incident involving said shipment, contracted to trasnfer said shipment to an Oil Company Party, or
(5) a Person not an Oil Company Party who, prior to any Incident involving said shipment, contracted for delivery to, storage, processing or transshipment at or shipment from a terminal or other facility owned, operated, managed, leased, hired or otherwise controlled by an Oil Company Party or in which an Oil Company Party has an interest and an Incident occurs or Pollution Damage is caused in a geographic area within 250 nautical miles in any direction from a point at the geographic centre of said terminal or other facility.

(B) For the purposes of Clause V(A)(2) and (3) such Oil shall be deemed to be so "owned" by an Oil Company Party provided that prior to any Incident involving said shipment of Oil, and in accordance with the Rules of CRISTAL, said Oil Company Party has advised CRISTAL in writing that it elects to be considered the "owner" thereof.

(C) For the purposes of Clause V(A)(5) terminal or other facility shall mean any property, fixed or floating from which Oil can be unloaded from or discharged into a Tanker including, but not limited to oil terminals, tank farms, refineries, single point moorings, floating storage or offshore discharging or loading vessels.

**(D) For the purpose of Clause IV(A) and (B) only, segregated slops of a Tanker carrying any shipment so owned, and bunker oil and lubricating oil intended for use in said Tanker's operation shall be deemed included in such shipment.

* Amendment effective May 16, 1988.
** Amendment effective October 23, 1989.

Clause VI. Subrogation

(A) CRISTAL shall, in respect of any amount of compensation paid in accordance with Clause IV (A) and (B) (2), acquire by subrogation the rights that the Person so compensated may enjoy under applicable legislation, law, convention or otherwise against the Owner or its insurers.

(B) Nothing herein shall prejudice any right of recourse or subrogation of CRISTAL against Persons other than those referred to in the preceding Paragraph. In any event, the right of CRISTAL to subrogation against such Person shall not be less favourable than that of an insurer of the Person to whom compensation has been paid.

*Clause VII. The CRISTAL Fund

(A)(1) CRISTAL, in order to assure its financial capability to make payments in accordance with Clause IV, shall maintain and administer an account, to be known as the "CRISTAL Fund", contributions to which shall be made by each Oil Company Party.

(2) Contributions to the CRISTAL Fund shall be calculated on the basis of the Crude/Fuel Oil Receipts of the Oil Company Parties. For the purpose of this Clause VII, Crude/Fuel Oil Receipts means,

(i) crude oil and fuel oil received at an installation or terminal by an Oil Company Party which has been transported all or part of the way to such installation or terminal by Tanker (excluding any crude oil which is received solely for transshipment for onward transportation by Tanker to an installation or terminal for receipt by an Oil Company Party) and which at the time of receipt is "owned" by an Oil Company Party,

(ii) crude oil and fuel oil not so received but with respect to which an Oil Company Party has elected, pursuant to Clause V, to be considered the "owner",

(iii) crude oil and fuel oil owned by an Oil Company Party but with respect to which title was transferred at destination to a Person not an Oil Company Party,

(iv) crude oil and fuel oil at the time when it has been retained on board a Tanker for a period of six (6) months and which at that time is owned by an Oil Company Party, together with any such crude oil and fuel oil retained on board such Tanker on the last day of each ensuing calendar year thereafter which, at that time, is owned by an Oil Company Party,

(v) that portion of all crude oil and fuel oil received at a terminal or other facility, defined in Clause V(A) (5) and (C), in which an Oil Company Party has an equity interest, equal to that Oil Company Party's proportional equity interest in said terminal or other facility, as compared to the equity interest(s) of all Oil Company Parties in that terminal or other facility and which is not otherwise either reported or to be reported in the crude/Fuel Oil Receipts of the Oil Company Party or any other related or affiliated Oil Company Party, and

(vi) crude oil and fuel oil, transported by Tanker, in which an Oil Company Party had title at some point after loading and prior to discharge from the

---

* Amendment effective October 23, 1989.

Tanker and which (i) is not included in the Crude/Fuel Oil Receipts of that Oil Company Party or any other related or affiliated Oil Company Party by reason of any other provision of this Paragraph, and/or (ii) had not been sold to another Oil Company Party.

(B)(1) CRISTAL shall from time to time estimate amounts (hereinafter referred to as a "Periodic Call") required to assure the capability of the CRISTAL Fund to make payments in accordance with Clause IV.

(2) Contributions to a Periodic Call shall be calculated by dividing the amount of the Call by the total of the Crude/Fuel Oil Receipts of all the Oil Company Parties as at the date of the Periodic Call during the calendar year preceding the year in which the Periodic Call is made, and multiplying the figure so calculated by the Crude/Fuel Oil Receipts of each Oil Company Party for such preceding year. For the purpose of these calculations the Crude/Fuel Oil Receipts shall be the total of the crude oil and fuel oil as defined in Paragraphs (A)(2)(i), (ii), (iii), (iv), (v) and (vi) of this Clause VII.

(3) However, notwithstanding the foregoing provisions of this Paragraph (B) (1) and (2) of this Clause VII:

(i) each such Oil Company Party (whether or not it had any Crude/Fuel Oil Receipts during such preceding calendar year) shall pay no less than a minimum charge determined by CRISTAL to be reasonable under the circumstances, and

(ii) no Oil Company party shall be liable to contribute to any payment of compensation by CRISTAL in respect to any Incident which occurred before it became a Party to this Contract, and

(iii) any Oil Company Party which becomes a Party hereto shall pay a contribution to any Periodic Call made in the calendar year of joining, subject to the provision of Paragraph (B)(3)(ii) of this Clause VII, and in no event less than the minimum sum referred to in Paragraph (B)(3)(i) of this Clause VII.

(C) Upon the Oil Company Parties deciding on a date beyond which claims will not be accepted under this Contract, any amounts remaining in the CRISTAL Fund, after the settlement or other disposition of all claims arising from Incidents occuring before the said date and the settlement of all costs and expenses relating to the winding up of CRISTAL, shall be equitably distributed among the Oil Companies that are Parties at the date when CRISTAL is finally dissolved.

Clause VIII. Notice of Claim

No liability shall arise under Clause IV (A) or (B) (2) unless written notice of claim is received by CRISTAL within two (2) years of the date of the Incident giving rise thereto. In the case of a payment to be made under Clause IV (B) (1) no liability shall arise unless written notice of claim is received by CRISTAL from an Oil Company Party within one year of the date that payment of the Contribution under Article 10 of the Fund Convention is to be made.

Clause IX. Rules and Directives

In fulfilling its obligations, in accordance with the terms of this Contract, CRISTAL shall be the sole judge in accordance with these terms of the validity of any claim made hereunder, except that CRISTAL, for the purposes of Clause IV (B) (1), will accept the validity of any request for a contribution made by the Fund. CRISTAL shall also have the right to make rules and directives from time to time with respect to interpretation and administration of this Contract.

Clause X. Amendment

This Contract may be amended by resolution adopted at any Regular or Special Meeting of the Members of CRISTAL upon a vote in which at least seventy five percent (75%) of the votes cast are in favour of said resolution. Amendments to this Contract shall apply only in respect of Incidents which occur after 12.00 hours G.M.T. on the date on which said amendment is adopted by the Members of CRISTAL.

Clause XI. Law Governing

(A) This Contract shall be construed and shall take effect in accordance with the Laws of England; the Courts of England shall have exclusive jurisdiction over any matter arising therefrom.

(B) This Contract shall not be construed as creating a trust.

(C) A Party hereto shall not be required to incur any obligation or take any action which would violate any laws or government regulations which apply to it or, in the event its stock or shares are owned by another Person, which would violate any laws or government regulations which apply to said Person.

IN WITNESS WHEREOF, the Parties have entered into this Contract upon January 14, 1971, or upon such later date as their applications to become Parties are accepted by CRISTAL.

EXHIBIT "A"

To: Cristal Limited

The undersigned, and such of its affiliates as it may designate in an attachment hereto, hereby applies (apply) to become an Oil Company Party (Parties) to the Contract Regarding a Supplement to Tanker Liability for Oil Pollution, formerly known as the Contract Regarding an Interim Supplement to Tanker Liability for Oil Pollution, dated as of January 14, 1971, as amended from time to time and agrees (agree), if this application is accepted, to fulfil all the obligatins of an Oil Company Party, to become a Member of Cristal Limited, to abide by its Bye-Laws, Rules and Directives and to pay an administrative fee, in an amount of One Thousand Five Hundred United States Dollars (U.S. $1,500.00) or such other amount as may be determined, from time to time, by Cristal Limited.

Company Name ....

Authorised Signature ....

Date of Application ....

Address ....

....

....

Accepted by Cristal Limited..

on the .... date of ....

President ....

CIVIL LIABILITY CONVENTION 1969

INTERNATIONAL CONVENTION ON CIVIL LIABILITY FOR OIL POLLUTION DAMAGE, DONE AT BRUSSELS, NOVEMBER 29, 1969

The States Parties to the present Convention,

Conscious of the dangers of pollution posed by the worldwide maritime carriage of oil in bulk.

Convinced of the need to ensure that adequate compensation is available to persons who suffer damage caused by pollution resulting from the escape or discharge of oil from ships,

Desiring to adopt uniform international rules and procedures for determining questions of liability and providing adequate compensation in such cases,

Have agreed as follows:

Article I

For the purposes of this Convention:

1. "Ship" means any sea-going vessel and sea-borne craft of any type whatsoever, actually carrying oil in bulk as cargo.

2. "Person" means any individual or partnership or any public or private body, whether corporate or not, including a State or any of its constituent subdivisions.

3. "Owner" means the person or persons registered as the owner of the ship or, in the absence of registration, the person owning the ship. However, in the case of a ship owned by a State and operated by a company which in that State is registered as the ship's operator, "owner" shall mean such company.

4. "State of the ship's registry" means in relation to registered ships the State of registration of the ship, and in relation to unregistered ships the State whose flag the ship is flying.

5. "Oil" means any persistent oil such as crude oil, fuel oil, heavy diesel oil, lubricating oil and whale oil, whether carried on board a ship as cargo or in the bunkers of such a ship.

6. "Pollution damage" means loss or damage caused outside the ship carrying oil by contamination resulting from the escape or discharge of oil from the ship, wherever such escape or discharge may occur, and includes the costs of preventive measures and further loss or damage caused by preventive measures.

7. "Preventive measures" means any reasonable measures taken by any person after an incident has occurred to prevent or minimize pollution damage.

8. "Incident" means any occurrence, or series of occurrences having the same origin, which causes pollution damage.

9. "Organization" means the Inter-Governmental Maritime Consultative Organization.

Article II

This Convention shall apply exclusively to pollution damage caused on the territory including the territorial sea of a Contracting State and to preventive measures taken to prevent or minimize such damage.

Article III

1. Except as provided in paragraphs 2 and 3 of this Article, the owner of a ship at the time of an incident, or where the incident consists of a series of occurrences at the time of the first such occurrence, shall be liable for any pollution damage caused by oil which has escaped or been discharged from the ship as a result of the incident.

2. No liability for pollution damage shall attach to the owner if he proves that the damage:
   (a) resulted from an act of war, hostilities, civil war, insurrection or a natural phenomenon of an exceptional, inevitable and irresistible character, or
   (b) was wholly caused by an act or omission done with intent to cause damage by a third party, or
   (c) was wholly caused by the negligence or other wrongful act of any Government or other authority responsible for the maintenance of lights or other navigational aids in the exercise of that function.

3. If the owner proves that the pollution damage resulted wholly or partially either from an act or omission done with intent to cause damage by the person who suffered the damage or from the negligence of that person, the owner may be exonerated wholly or partially from his liability to such person.

4. No claim for compensation for pollution damage shall be made against the owner otherwise than in accordance with this Convention. No claim for pollution damage under this Convention or otherwise may be made against the servants or agents of the owner.

5. Nothing in this Convention shall prejudice any right of recourse of the owner against third parties.

Article IV

When oil has escaped or has been discharged from two or more ships, and pollution damage results therefrom, the owners of all the ships concerned, unless exonerated under Article III, shall be jointly and severally liable for all such damage which is not reasonably separable.

Article V

1. The owner of a ship shall be entitled to limit his liability under this Convention in respect of any one incident to an aggregate amount of 2,000 francs for each ton of the

ship's tonnage. However, this aggregate amount shall not in any event exceed 210 million francs.

2. If the incident occurred as a result of the actual fault or privity of the owner, he shall not be entitled to avail himself of the limitation provided in paragraph 1 of this Article.

3. For the purpose of availing himself of the benefit of limitation provided for in paragraph 1 of this Article the owner shall constitute a fund for the total sum representing the limit of his liability with the Court or other competent authority of any one of the Contracting States in which action is brought under Article IX. The fund can be constituted either by depositing the sum or by producing a bank guarantee or other guarantee, acceptable under the legislation of the Contracting State where the fund is constituted, and considered to be adequate by the Court or another competent authority.

4. The fund shall be distributed among the claimants in proportion to the amounts of their established claims.

5. If before the fund is distributed the owner or any of his servants or agents or any person providing him insurance or other financial security has as a result of the incident in question, paid compensation for pollution damage, such person shall, up to the amount he has paid, acquire by subrogation the rights which the person so compensated would have enjoyed under this Convention.

6. The right of subrogation provided for in paragraph 5 of this Article may also be exercised by a person other than those mentioned therein in respect of any amount of compensation for pollution damage which he may have paid but only to the extent that such subrogation is permitted under the applicable national law.

7. Where the owner or any other person establishes that he may be compelled to pay at a later date in whole or in part any such amount of compensation, with regard to which such person would have enjoyed a right of subrogation under paragraphs 5 or 6 of this Article, had the compensation been paid before the fund was distributed, the Court or other competent authority of the State where the fund has been constituted may order that a sufficient sum shall be provisionally set aside to enable such person at such later date to enforce his claim against the fund.

8. Claims in respect of expenses reasonably incurred or sacrifices reasonably made by the owner voluntarily to prevent or minimize pollution damage shall rank equally with other claims against the fund.

9. The franc mentioned in this Article shall be a unit consisting of sixty-five and a half milligrams of gold or millesimal fineness nine hundred. The amount mentioned in paragraph 1 of this Article shall be converted into the national currency of the State in which the fund is being constituted on the basis of the value of that currency by reference to the unit defined above on the date of the constitution of the fund.

10. For the purpose of this Article the ship's tonnage shall be the net tonnage of the ship with the addition of the amount deducted from the gross tonnage on account of engine room space for the purpose of ascertaining the net tonnage. In the case of a ship which cannot be measured in accordance with the normal rules of tonnage measurement, the ship's tonnage shall be deemed to be 40 per cent. of the weight in tons (of 2240 lbs.) of oil which the ship is capable of carrying.

11. The insurer or other person providing financial security shall be entitled to constitute a fund in accordance with this Article on the same conditions and having the same effect as if it were constituted by the owner. Such a fund may be constituted even

in the event of the actual fault or privity of the owner but its constitution shall in that case not prejudice the rights of any claimant against the owner.

Article VI

1. Where the owner, after an incident, has constituted a fund in accordance with Article V, and is entitled to limit his liability,
    (a) no person having a claim for pollution damage arising out of that incident shall be entitled to exercise any right against any other assets of the owner in respect of such claim;
    (b) the Court or other competent authority of any Contracting State shall order the release of any ship or other property belonging to the owner which has been arrested in respect of a claim for pollution damage arising out of that incident, and shall similarly release any bail or other security furnished to avoid such arrest.
2. The foregoing shall, however, only apply if the claimant has access to the Court administering the fund and the fund is actually available in respect of his claim.

Article VII

1. The owner of a ship registered in a Contracting State and carrying more than 2,000 tons of oil in bulk as cargo shall be required to maintain insurance or other financial security, such as the guarantee of a bank or a certificate delivered by an international compensation fund, in the sums fixed by applying the limits of liability prescribed in Article V, paragraph 1 to cover his liability for pollution damage under this Convention.
2. A certificate attesting that insurance or other financial security is in force in accordance with the provisions of this Convention shall be issued to each ship. It shall be issued or certified by the appropriate authority of the State of the ship's registry after determining that the requirements of paragraph 1 of this Article have been complied with. This certificate shall be in the form of the annexed model and shall contain the following particulars:
    (a) name of ship and port of registration;
    (b) name and principal place of business of owners;
    (c) type of security;
    (d) name and principal place of business of insurer or other person giving security and, where appropriate, place of business where the insurance or security is established;
    (e) period of validity of certificate which shall not be longer than the period of validity of the insurance or other security.
3. The certificate shall be in the official language or languages of the issuing State. If the language used is neither English or French the text shall include a translation into one of these languages.
4. The certificate shall be carried on board the ship and a copy shall be deposited with the authorities who keep the record of the ship's registry.
5. An insurance or other financial security shall not satisfy the requirements of this Article if it can cease, for reasons other than the expiry of the period of validity of the insurance or security specified in the certificate under paragraph 2 of this Article, before three months have elapsed from the date on which notice of its termination is

given to the authorities referred to in paragraph 4 of this Article, unless the certificate has been surrendered to these authorities or a new certificate has been issued within the said period. The foregoing provisions shall similarly apply to any modification which results in the insurance or security no longer satisfying the requirements of this Article.

6. The State of registry shall, subject to the provisions of this Article, determine the conditions of issue and validity of the certificate.

7. Certificates issued or certified under the authority of a Contracting State shall be accepted by other Contracting States for the purposes of this Convention and shall be regarded by other Contracting States as having the same force as certificates issued or certified by them. A Contracting State may at any time request consultation with the State of a ship's registry should it believe that the insurer or guarantor named in the certificate is not financially capable of meeting the obligations imposed by this Convention.

8. Any claim for compensation for pollution damage may be brought directly against the insurer or other person providing financial security for the owner's liability for pollution damage. In such case the defendant may, irrespective of the actual fault or privity of the owner, avail himself of the limits of liability prescribed in Article V, paragraph 1. He may further avail himself of the defences (other than the bankruptcy or winding up of the owner) which the owner himself would have been entitled to invoke. Furthermore, the defendant may avail himself of the defence that the pollution damage resulted from the wilful misconduct of the owner himself, but the defendant shall not avail himself of any other defence which he might have been entitled to invoke in proceedings brought by the owner against him. The defendant shall in any event have the right to require the owner to be joined in the proceedings.

9. Any sums provided by insurance or by other financial security maintained in accordance with paragraph 1 of this Article shall be available exclusively for the satisfaction of claims under this Convention.

10. A Contracting State shall not permit a ship under its flag to which this Article applies to trade unless a certificate has been issued under paragraph 2 or 12 of this Article.

11. Subject to the provisions of this Article, each Contracting State shall ensure, under its national legislation, that insurance or other security to the extent specified in paragraph 1 of this Article is in force in respect of any ship, wherever registered, entering or leaving a port in its territory, or arriving at or leaving an off-shore terminal in its territorial sea, if the ship actually carries more than 2,000 tons of oil in bulk as cargo.

12. If insurance or other financial security is not maintained in respect of a ship owned by a Contracting State, the provisions of this Article relating thereto shall not be applicable to such ship, but the ship shall carry a certificate issued by the appropriate authorities of the State of the ship's registry stating that the ship is owned by the State and that the ship's liability is covered within the limits prescribed by Article V, paragraph 1. Such a certificate shall follow as closely as practicable the model prescribed by paragraph 2 of this Article.

Article VIII

Rights of compensation under this Convention shall be extinguished unless an action is brought thereunder within three years from the date when the damage occurred.

However, in no case shall an action be brought after six years from the date of the incident which caused the damage. Where this incident consists of a series of occurrences, the six years' period shall run from the date of the first such occurrence.

Article IX

1. Where an incident has caused pollution damage in the territory including the territorial sea of one or more Contracting States, or preventive measures have been taken to prevent or minimize pollution damage in such territory including the territorial sea, actions for compensation may only be brought in the Courts of any such Contracting State or States. Reasonable notice of any such action shall be given to the defendant.

2. Each Contracting State shall ensure that its Courts possess the necessary jurisdiction to entertain such actions for compensation.

3. After the fund has constituted in accordance with Article V the Courts of the State in which the fund is constituted shall be exclusively competent to determine all matters relating to the apportionment and distribution of the fund.

Article X

1. Any judgment given by a Court with jurisdiction in accordance with Article IX which is enforceable in the State of origin where it is no longer subject to ordinary forms of review, shall be recognized in any Contracting State, except:
   (a) where the judgment was obtained by fraud; or
   (b) where the defendant was not given reasonable notice and a fair opportunity to present his case.

2. A judgment recognized under paragraph 1 of this Article shall be enforceable in each Contracting State as soon as the formalities required in that State have been complied with. The formalities shall not permit the merits of the case to be re-opened.

Article XI

1. The provisions of this Convention shall not apply to warships or other ships owned or operated by a State and used, for the time being, only on Government non-commercial service.

2. With respect to ships owned by a Contracting State and used for commercial purposes, each State shall be subject to suit in the jurisdictions set forth in Article IX and shall waive all defences based on its status as a sovereign State.

Article XII

This Convention shall supersede any International Conventions in force or open for signature, ratification or accession at the date on which the Convention is opened for signature, but only to the extent that such Conventions would be in conflict with it; however, nothing in this Article shall affect the obligations of Contracting States to non-Contracting States arising under such International Conventions.

Article XIII

1. The present Convention shall remain open for signature until December 31, 1970 and shall thereafter remain open for accession.

2. States Members of the United Nations or any of the Specialized Agencies or of the International Atomic Energy Agency or Parties to the Statute of the International Court of Justice may become Parties to this Convention by:
  (a) signature without reservation as to ratification, acceptance or approval:
  (b) signature subject to ratification, acceptance or approval followed by ratification, acceptance or approval; or
  (c) accession.

Article XIV

1. Ratification, acceptance, approval or accession shall be effected by the deposit of a formal instrument to that effect with the Secretary-General of the Organization.

2. Any instrument of ratification, acceptance, approval or accession deposited after the entry into force of an amendment to the present Convention with respect to all existing Contracting States, or after the completion of all measures required for the entry into force of the amendment with respect to those Contracting States shall be deemed to apply to the Convention as modified by the amendment.

Article XV

1. The present Convention shall enter into force on the ninetieth day following the date on which Governments of eight States including five States each with not less than 1,000,000 gross tons of tanker tonnage have either signed it without reservation as to ratification, acceptance or approval or have deposited instruments of ratification, acceptance, approval or accession with the Secretary-General of the Organization.

2. For each State which subsequently ratifies, accepts, approves or accedes to it the present Convention shall come into force on the ninetieth day after deposit by such State of the appropriate instrument.

Article XVI

1. The present Convention may be denounced by any Contracting State at any time after the date on which the Convention comes into force for that State.

2. Denunciation shall be effected by the deposit of an instrument with the Secretary-General of the Organization.

3. A denunciation shall take effect one year, or such longer period as may be specified in the instrument of denunciation, after its deposit with the Secretary-General of the Organization.

Article XVII

1. The United Nations, where it is the administering authority for a territory, or any Contracting State responsible for the international relations of a territory shall as soon as possible consult with the appropriate authorities of such territory or take such other measures as may be appropriate, in order to extend the present Convention to that territory and may at any time by notification in writing to the Secretary-General of the Organization declare that the present Convention shall extend to such territory.

2. The present Convention shall, from the date of receipt of the notification or from such other date as may be specified in the notification, extend to the territory named therein.

3. The United Nations, or any Contracting State which has made a declaration under paragraph 1 of this Article may at any time after the date on which the Convention has been so extended to any territory declare by notification in writing to the Secretary-General of the Organization that the present Convention shall cease to extend to any such territory named in the notification.

4. The present Convention shall cease to extend to any territory mentioned in such notification one year, or such longer period as may be specified therein, after the date of receipt of the notification by the Secretary-General of the Organization.

Article XVIII

1. A Conference for the purpose of revising or amending the present Convention may be convened by the Organization.

2. The Organization shall convene a Conference of the Contracting States for revising or amending the present Convention at the request of not less than one-third of the Contracting States.

Article XIX

1. The present Convention shall be deposited with the Secretary-General of the Organization.

2. The Secretary-General of the Organization shall:
   (a) inform all States which have signed or acceded to the Convention of
      (i) each new signature or deposit of instrument together with the date thereof;
      (ii) the deposit of any instrument of denunciation of this Convention together with the date of the deposit;
      (iii) the extension of the present Convention to any territory under paragraph 1 of Article XVII and of the termination of any such extension under the provisions of paragraph 4 of that Article stating in each case the date on which the present Convention has been or will cease to be so extended;
   (b) transmit certified true copies of the present Convention to all Signatory States and to all States which accede to the present Convention.

Article XX

As soon as the present Convention comes into force, the text shall be transmitted by the Secretary-General of the Organization to the Secretariat of the United Nations for registration and publication in accordance with Article 102 of the Charter of the United Nations.

Article XXI

The present Convention is established in a single copy in the English and French languages, both texts being equally authentic. Official translations in the Russian and Spanish languages shall be prepared and deposited with the signed original.

In witness whereof the undersigned being duly authorized by their respective Governments for the purpose have signed the present Convention.

Done at Brussels this twenty-ninth day of November, 1969.

LLOYD'S OPEN FORMS (LOF 1980 AND 1990)

LLOYD'S STANDARD FORM OF SALVAGE AGREEMENT: NO CURE—NO PAY (LOF 1980)*

On board the...
Dated................................19.....

IT IS HEREBY AGREED between Captain....................for and on behalf of the Owners of the "...................." her cargo freight bunkers and stores and....................for and on behalf of...................(hereinafter called "the Contractor"):—

1.(a) The Contractor agrees to use his best endeavours to salve the ....and/or her cargo bunkers and stores and take them to....................or other place to be hereafter agreed or if no place is named or agreed to a place of safety. The Contractor further agrees to use his best endeavours to prevent the escape of oil from the vessel while performing the services of salving the subject vessel and/or her cargo bunkers and stores. The services shall be rendered and accepted as salvage services upon the principle of "no cure—no pay" except that where the property being salved is a tanker laden or partly laden with a cargo of oil and without negligence on the part of the Contractor and/or his Servants and/or Agents (1) the services are not successful or (2) are only partially successful or (3) the Contractor is prevented from completing the services the Contractor shall nevertheless be awarded solely against the Owners of such tanker his reasonably incurred expenses and an increment not exceeding 15 per cent of such expenses but only if and to the extent that such expenses together with the increment are greater than any amount otherwise recoverable under this Agreement. Within the meaning of the said exception to the principle of "no cure—no pay" expenses shall in addition to actual out of pocket expenses include a fair rate for all tugs craft personnel and other equipment used by the Contractor in the services and oil shall mean crude oil fuel oil heavy diesel oil and lubricating oil.

(b) The Contractor's remuneration shall be fixed by arbitration in London in the manner herein prescribed and any other difference arising out of this Agreement or the operations thereunder shall be referred to arbitration in the same way. In the event

* Reproduced by kind permission of the Corporation of Lloyd's.

of the services referred to in this Agreement or any part of such services having been already rendered at the date of this Agreement by the Contractor to the said vessel and/or her cargo bunkers and stores the provisions of this Agreement shall apply to such services.

(c) It is hereby further agreed that the security to be provided to the Committee of Lloyd's the Salved Values the Award and/or Interim Award and/or Award on Appeal of the Arbitrator and/or Arbitrator(s) on Appeal shall be in....................currency. If this Clause is not completed then the security to be provided and the Salved Values the Award and/or Interim Award and/or Award on Appeal of the Arbitrator and/or Arbitrator(s) on Appeal shall be in Pounds Sterling.

(d) This Agreement shall be governed by and arbitration thereunder shall be in accordance with English law.

2. The Owners their Servants and Agents shall co-operate fully with the Contractor in and about the salvage including obtaining entry to the place named in Clause 1 of this Agreement or such other place as may be agreed or if applicable the place of safety to which the salved property is taken. The Owners shall promptly accept redelivery of the salved property at such place. The Contractor may make reasonable use of the vessel's machinery gear equipment anchors chains stores and other appurtenances during and for the purpose of the operations free of expense but shall not unnecessarily damage abandon or sacrifice the same or any property the subject of this Agreement.

3. The Master or other person signing this Agreement on behalf of the property to be salved is not authorised to make or give and the Contractor shall not demand or take any payment draft or order as inducement to or remuneration for entering into this Agreement.

PROVISIONS AS TO SECURITY

4. The Contractor shall immediately after the termination of the services or sooner in appropriate cases notify the Committee of Lloyd's and where practicable the Owners of the amount for which he requires security (inclusive of costs expenses and interest). Unless otherwise agreed by the parties such security shall be given to the Committee of Lloyd's and security so given shall be in form approved by the Committee and shall be given by persons firms or corporations resident in the United Kingdom either satisfactory to the Committee of Lloyd's or agreed by the Contractor. The Committee of Lloyd's shall not be responsible for the sufficiency (whether in amount or otherwise of any security which shall be given nor for the default or insolvency of any person firm or corporation giving the same.

5. Pending the completion of the security as aforesaid the Contractor shall have a maritime lien on the property salved for his remuneration. Where the aforementioned exception to the principle of "no cure—no pay" becomes likely to be applicable the Owners of the vessel shall on demand of the Contractor provide security for the Contractor's remuneration under the aforementioned exception in accordance with Clause 4 hereof. The salved property shall not without the consent in writing of the Contractor be removed from the place (within the terms of Clause 1) to which the property is taken by the Contractor on the completion of the salvage services until security has been given as aforesaid. The Owners of the vessel their Servants and Agents shall use

their best endeavours to ensure that the Cargo Owners provide security in accordance with the provisions of Clause 4 of this Agreement before the cargo is released. The Contractor agrees not to arrest or detain the property salved unless (a) the security be not given within 14 days (exclusive of Saturdays and Sundays or other days observed as general holidays at Lloyd's) after the date of the termination of the services (the Committee of Lloyd's not being responsible for the failure of the parties concerned to provide the required security within the said 14 days) or (b) the Contractor has reason to believe that the removal of the property is contemplated contrary to the above agreement. In the event of security not being provided or in the event of (1) any attempt being made to remove the property salved contrary to this agreement or (2) the Contractor having reasonable grounds to suppose that such an attempt will be made the Contractor may take steps to enforce his aforesaid lien. The Arbitrator appointed under Clause 6 or the person(s) appointed under Clause 13 hereof shall have power in their absolute discretion to include in the amount awarded to the Contractor the whole or such part of the expense incurred by the Contractor in enforcing or protecting by insurance or otherwise or in taking reasonable steps to enforce or protect his lien as they shall think fit.

PROVISIONS AS TO ARBITRATION

6.(a) Where security within the provisions of this Agreement is given to the Committee of Lloyd's in whole or in part the said Committee shall appoint an Arbitrator in respect of the interest covered by such security.

(b) Whether security has been given or not the Committee of Lloyd's shall appoint an Arbitrator upon receipt of a written or telex or telegraphic notice of a claim for arbitration from any of the parties entitled or authorised to make such a claim.

7. Where an Arbitrator has been appointed by the Committee of Lloyd's and the parties do not wish to proceed to arbitration the parties shall jointly notify the said Committee in writing or by telex or by telegram and the said Committee may thereupon terminate the appointment of such Arbitrator as they may have appointed in accordance with Clause 6 of this Agreement.

8. Any of the following parties may make a claim for arbitration viz.:— (1) The Owners of the ship. (2) The Owners of the cargo or any part thereof. (3) The Owners of any freight separately at risk or any part thereof. (4) The Contractor. (5) The Owners of the bunkers and/or stores. (6) Any other person who is a party to this Agreement.

9. If the parties to any such Arbitration or any of them desire to be heard or to adduce evidence at the Arbitration they shall give notice to that effect to the Committee of Lloyd's and shall respectively nominate a person in the United Kingdom to represent them for all the purposes of the Arbitration and failing such notice and nomination being given the Arbitrator or Arbitrator(s) on Appeal may proceed as if the parties failing to give the same had renounced their right to be heard or adduce evidence.

10. The remuneration for the services within the meaning of this Agreement shall be fixed by an Arbitrator to be appointed by the Committee of Lloyd's and he shall have power to make an Interim Award ordering such payment on account as may seem fair and just and on such terms as may be fair and just.

CONDUCT OF THE ARBITRATION

11. The Arbitrator shall have power to obtain call for receive and act upon any such oral or documentary evidence or information (whether the same be strictly admissible as evidence or not) as he may think fit and to conduct the Arbitration in such manner in all respects as he may think fit and shall if in his opinion the amount of the security demanded is excessive have power in his absolute discretion to condemn the Contractor in the whole or part of the expense of providing such security and to deduct the amount in which the Contractor is so condemned from the salvage remuneration. Unless the Arbitrator shall otherwise direct the parties shall be a liberty to adduce expert evidence at the Arbitration. Any Award of the Arbitrator shall (subject to appeal as provided in this Agreement) be final and binding on all the parties concerned. The Arbitrator and the Committee of Lloyd's may charge reasonable fees and expenses for their services in connection with the Arbitration whether it proceeds to a hearing or not and all such fees and expenses shall be treated as part of the costs of the Arbitration. Save as aforesaid the statutory provisions as to Arbitration for the time being in force in England shall apply.

12. Interest at a rate per annum to be fixed by the Arbitrator from the expiration of 21 days (exclusive of Saturdays and Sundays or other days observed as general holidays at Lloyd's) after the rate of publication of the Award and/or Interim Award by the Committee of Lloyd's until the date payment is received by the Committee of Lloyd's both dates inclusive shall (subject to appeal as provided in this Agreement) be payable upon any sum awarded after deduction of any sums paid on account.

PROVISIONS AS TO APPEAL

13. Any of the persons named under Clause 8 may appeal from the Award but not without leave of the Arbitrator(s) on Appeal from an Interim Award made pursuant to the provision of Clause 10 hereof by giving written or telegraphic or telex Notice of Appeal to the Committee of Lloyd's within 14 days (exclusive of Saturdays and Sundays or other days observed as general holidays at Lloyd's) after the date of the publication by the Committee of Lloyd's of the Award and may (without prejudice to their right of appeal under the first part of this Clause) within 14 days (exclusive of Saturdays and Sundays or other days observed as general holidays at Lloyd's) after receipt by them from the Committee of Lloyd's of notice of such appeal (such notice if sent by post to be deemed to be received on the day following that on which the said notice was posted) give written or telegraphic or telex Notice of Cross-Appeal to the Committee of Lloyd's. As soon as practicable after receipt of such notice of notices the Committee of Lloyd's shall refer the Appeal to the hearing and determination of a person or persons selected by it. In the event of an Appellant or Cross-Appellant withdrawing his Notice of Appeal or Cross-Appeal the hearing shall nevertheless proceed in respect of such Notice of Appeal of Cross-Appeal as may remain. Any Award on Appeal shall be final and binding on all the parties concerned whether such parties were represented or not at either the Arbitration or at the Arbitration on Appeal.

CONDUCT OF THE APPEAL

14. No evidence other than the documents put in on the Arbitration and the Arbitrator's notes of the proceedings and oral evidence if any at the Arbitration and the

Arbitrator's Reasons for his Award and Interim Award if any and the transcript if any of any evidence given at the Arbitration shall be used on the Appeal unless the Arbitrator(s) on the Appeal shall in his or their discretion call for or allow other evidence. The Arbitrator(s) on Appeal may conduct the Arbitration on Appeal in such manner in all respects as he or they may think fit and may act upon any such evidence or information (whether the same be strictly admissible as evidence or not) as he or they may think fit and may maintain increase or reduce the sum awarded by the Arbitrator with the like power as is conferred by Clause 11 on the Arbitrator to condemn the Contractor in the whole or part of the expense of providing security and to deduct the amount disallowed from the salvage remuneration. And he or they shall also make such order as he or they shall think fit as to the payment of interest on the sum awarded to the Contractor. The Arbitrator(s) on the Appeal may direct in what manner the costs of the Arbitration and of the Arbitration on Appeal shall be borne and paid and he or they and the Committee of Lloyd's may charge reasonable fees and expenses for their services in connection with the Arbitration on Appeal whether it proceeds to a hearing or not and all such fees and expenses shall be treated as part of the costs of the Arbitration on Appeal. Save as aforesaid the statutory provision as to Arbitration for the time being in force in England shall apply.

PROVISIONS AS TO PAYMENT

15.(a) In case of Arbitration if no Notice of Appeal be received by the Committee of Lloyd's within 14 days (exclusive of Saturdays and Sundays or other days observed as general holidays at Lloyd's) after the date of the publication by the committee of the Award and/or Interim Award the Committee shall call upon the party or parties concerned to pay the amount awarded and in the event of non-payment shall realize or enforce the security and pay therefrom to the Contractor (whose receipt shall be a good discharge to it) the amount awarded to him together with interest as hereinbefore provided but the Contractor shall reimburse the parties concerned to such extent as the final Award is less than the Interim Award.

(b) If Notice of Appeal be received by the Committee of Lloyd's in accordance with the provisions of Clause 13 hereof it shall as soon as but not until the Award on Appeal has been published by it call upon the party or parties concerned to pay the amount awarded and in the event of non-payment shall realize or enforce the security and pay therefrom to the Contractor (whose receipt shall be a good discharge to it) the amount awarded to him together with interest if any in such manner as shall comply with provisions of the Award on Appeal.

(c) If the Award and/or Interim Award and/or Award on Appeal provides or provide that the costs of the Arbitration and/or of the Arbitration on Appeal or any part of such costs shall be borne by the Contractor such costs may be deducted from the amount awarded before payment is made to the Contractor by the Committee of Lloyd's unless satisfactory security is provided by the Contractor for the payment of such costs.

(d) If any sum shall become payable to the Contractor as remuneration for his services and/or interest and/or costs as the result of an agreement made between the Contractor and the parties interested in the property salved or any of them the Committee of Lloyd's in the event of non-payment shall realize or enforce the security and pay therefrom to the Contractor (whose receipt shall be a good discharge to it) the amount agreed upon between the parties.

(e) Without prejudice to the provisions of Clause 4 hereof the liability of the Committee of Lloyd's shall be limited in any event to the amount of security held by it.

GENERAL PROVISIONS

16. Notwithstanding anything hereinbefore contained should the operations be only partially successful without any negligence or want of ordinary skill and care on the part of the Contractor his Servants or Agents and any portion of the vessel her appurtenances bunkers stores and cargo be salved by the Contractor he shall be entitled to reasonable remuneration and such reasonable remuneration shall be fixed in case of difference by Arbitration in manner hereinbefore prescribed.

17. The Master or other person signing this Agreement on behalf of the property to be salved enters into this Agreement as Agent for the vessel her cargo freight bunkers and stores and the respective owners thereof and binds each (but not the one for the other or himself personally) to the due performance thereof.

18. In considering what sums of money have been expended by the Contractor in rendering the services and/or in fixing the amount of the Award and/or Interim Award and/or Award on Appeal the Arbitrator or Arbitrator(s) on Appeal shall to such an extent and in so far as it may be fair and just in all the circumstances give effect to the consequences of any change or changes in the value of money or rates of exchange which may have occurred between the completion of the services and the date on which the Award and/or Interim Award and/or Award on Appeal is made.

19. Any Award notice authority order or other document signed by the Chairman of Lloyd's or any person authorised by the Committee of Lloyd's for the purpose shall be deemed to have been duly made or given by the Committee of Lloyd's and shall have the same force and effect in all respects as if it had been signed by every member of the Committee of Lloyd's.

20. The Contractor may claim salvage and enforce any Award or agreement made between the Contractor and the parties interested in the property salved against security provided under this Agreement if any in the name and on behalf of any Sub-Contractors Servants or Agents including Masters and members of the Crews of vessels employed by him in the services rendered hereunder provided that he first indemnifies and holds harmless the Owners of the property salved against all claims by or liabilities incurred to the said persons. Any such indemnity shall be provided in a form satisfactory to such Owners.

21. The Contractor shall be entitled to limit any liability to the Owners of the subject vessel and/or her cargo bunkers and stores which he and/or his Servants and/or Agents may incur in and about the services in the manner and to the extent provided by English law and as if the provisions of the Convention on Limitation of Liability for Maritime Claims 1976 were part of the law of England.

For and on behalf of the Contractor.

(To be signed either by the Contractor personally or by the Master of the salving vessel or other person whose name is inserted in line 3 of this Agreement).

For and on behalf of the owners of property to be salved.

(To be signed by the Master or other person whose name is inserted in line 1 of this Agreement).

LLOYD'S STANDARD FORM OF SALVAGE AGREEMENT: NO CURE—NO PAY (LOF 1990)*

Notes

1. Insert name of person signing on behalf of Owners of property to be salved. The Master should sign wherever possible.

2. The Contractor's name should always be inserted in line 4 and whenever the Agreement is signed by the Master of the Salving vessel or other person on behalf of the Contractor the name of the Master or other person must also be inserted in line 4 before the words "for and on behalf of." The words "for and on behalf of" should be deleted where a Contractor signs personally.

3. Insert place if agreed in clause 1(a)(i) and currency if agreed in clause 1(e).

On board the..

Dated...

IT IS HEREBY AGREED between Captain†...for and on behalf of the owners of the ".." her cargo freight bunkers stores and any other property thereon (hereinafter collectively called "the Owners") and..for and on behalf of.......................................(hereinafter called "the Contractor"*) that:

   1.(a) The Contractor shall use his best endeavours:

      (i) to salve the "..." and/or her cargo freight bunkers stores and any other property thereon and take them to‡.......................................or to such other place as may hereafter be agreed either place to deemed a place of safety or if no such place is named or agreed to a place of safety and

      (ii) while performing the salvage services to prevent or minimize damage to the environment.

    (b) Subject to clause 2 incorporating Convention Article 14 the services shall be rendered and accepted as salvage services upon the principle of "no cure—no pay".

    (c) The Contractor's remunderation shall be fixed by Arbitration in London in the manner hereinafter prescribed and any other difference arising out of this Agreement or the operations thereunder shall be referred to the Artibtration in the same way.

    (d) In the event of the services referred to in this Agreement or any part of such services having been already rendered at the date of this Agreement by the Contractor to the said vessel and/or her cargo freight bunkers stores and any other property thereon the provisions of this Agreement shall apply to such services.

    (e) The security to be provided to the Council of Lloyd's (hereinafter called "the Council") the Salved Value(s) the Award and/or any Interim Award(s) and/

---

* Reproduced by kind permission of the Corporation of Lloyd's.
† See Note 1 above.
* See Note 2 above.
‡ See Note 3 above.

or any Award on Appeal shall be in‡...cur-
rency.

(f) If clause 1(e) is not completed then the security to be provided and the Salved
Value(s) the Award and/or Interim Award(s) and/or Award on Appeal shall
be in Pounds Sterling.

(g) This Agreement and Arbitration thereunder shall except as otherwise
expressly provided be governed by the law of England, including the English
law of salvage.

PROVISIONS AS TO THE SERVICES

2. Articles 1(a) to (e), 8, 13.1, 13.2 first sentence, 13.3 and 14 of the International
Convention on Salvage 1989 ("the Convention Articles") set out hereafter are hereby
incorporated into this Agreement. The terms "Contractor" and "services"/"salvage
services" in this Agreement shall have the same meaning as the terms "salvor(s)" and
"salvage operation(s)" in the Convention Articles.

3. The Owners their Servants and Agents shall co-operate fully with the Contractor
in and about the salvage including obtaining entry to the place named or the place of
safety as defined in clause 1. The Contractor may make reasonable use of the vessel's
machinery gear equipment anchors chains stores and other appurtenances during and
for the purpose of the salvage services free of expense but shall not unnecessarily
damage abandon or sacrifice the same or any property the subject of this Agreement.

PROVISIONS AS TO SECURITY

4. (a) The Contractor shall immediately after the termination of the services or
sooner notify the Council and where practicable the Owners of the amount for which
he demands security (inclusive of costs expenses and interest) from each of the
respective Owners.

(b) Where the exception to the principle of "no cure—no pay" under Convention
Article 14 becomes likely to be applicable the owners of the vessel shall on the demand
of the Contractor provided security for the Contractor's special compensation.

(c) The amount of any such security shall be reasonable in the light of the knowledge available to the Contractor at the time when the demand is made. Unless otherwise agreed such security shall be provided (i) to the Council (ii) in a form approved by
the Council and (iii) by persons firms or corporations either acceptable to the Contractor or resident in the United Kingdom and acceptable to the Council. The Council
shall not be responsible for the sufficiency (whether in amount or otherwise) of any
security which shall be provided nor for the default or insolvency of any person firm or
corporation providing the same.

(d) The owners of the vessel their Servants and Agents shall use their best endeavours to ensure that the cargo owners provide their proportion of security before the
cargo is released.

5. (a) Until security has been provided as aforesaid the Contractor shall have a
maritime lien on the property salved for his remuneration. The property salved shall
not without the consent in writing of the Contractor (which shall not be unreasonably

withheld) be removed from the place to which it has been taken by the Contractor under clause 1(a).

(b) The Contractor shall not arrest or detain the property salved unless:

    (i) security is not provided within 14 days (exclusive of Saturdays and Sundays or other days observed as general holidays at Lloyd's) after the date of the termination of the services or

    (ii) he has reason to believe that the removal of the property salved is contemplated contrary to clause 5(a) or

    (iii) any attempt is made to remove the property salved contrary to clause 5(a).

(c) The Arbitrator appointed under clause 6 or the Appeal Arbitrator(s) appointed under clause 11(d) shall have power in their absolute discretion to include in the amount awarded to the Contractor the whole or part of any expenses reasonably incurred by the Contractor in:

    (i) ascertaining demanding and obtaining the amount of security reasonably required in accordance with clause 4.

    (ii) enforcing and/or protecting by insurance or otherwise or taking reasonable steps to enforce and/or protect his lien.

PROVISIONS AS TO ARBITRATION

6. (a) Where security is provided to the Council in whole or in part the Council shall appoint an Arbitrator in respect of the property covered by such security.

(b) Whether security has been provided or not the Council shall appoint an Arbitrator upon receipt of a written request made by letter telex facsimile or in any other permanent form provided that any party requesting such appointment shall if required by the Council undertake to pay the reasonable fees and expenses of the Council and/or any Arbitrator or Appeal Arbitrator(s).

(c) Where an Arbitrator has been appointed and the parties do not proceed to arbitration the Council may recover any fees costs and/or expenses which are outstanding and thereupon terminate the appointment of such Arbitrator.

7. The Contractor's remuneration shall be fixed by the Arbitrator appointed under clause 6. Such remuneration shall not be diminished by reason of the exception to the principle of "no cure—no pay" under Convention Article 14.

REPRESENTATION

8. Any party to this Agreement who wishes to be heard or to adduce evidence shall nominate a person in the United Kingdom to represent him failing which the Arbitrator or Appeal Arbitrator(s) may proceed as if such party had renounced his right to be heard or adduce evidence.

CONDUCT OF THE ARBITRATION

9. (a) The Arbitrator shall have power to:

    (i) admit such oral or documentary evidence or information as he may think fit

    (ii) conduct the Arbitration in such manner in all respects as he may think fit subject to such procedural rules as the Council may approve

    (iii) condemn the Contractor in his absolute discretion in the whole or part of the expense of providing excessive security and deduct the amount in which the Contractor is so condemned from the salvage remuneration and/or special compensation

    (iv) make Interim Award(s) on such terms as may be fair and just

    (v) make such orders as to costs fees and expenses including those of the Council charged under clauses 9(b) and 12(b) as may be fair and just.

  (b) The Arbitrator and the Council may charge reasonable fees and expenses for their services whether the Arbitration proceeds to a hearing or not and all such fees and expenses shall be treated as part of the costs of the Arbitration.

  (c) Any Award shall (subject to Appeal as provided in this Agreement) be final and binding on all the parties concerned whether they were represented at the Arbitration or not.

INTEREST

10. Interest at rates per annum to be fixed by the Arbitrator shall (subject to Appeal as provided in this Agreement) be payable on any sum awarded taking into account any sums already paid:

    (i) from the date of termination of the services unless the Arbitrator shall in his absolute discretion otherwise decide until the date of publication by the Council of the Award and/or Interim Award(s) and

    (ii) from the expiration of 21 days (exclusive of Saturdays and Sundays or other days observed as general holidays at Lloyd's) after the date of publication by the Council of the Award and/or Interim Award(s) until the date payment is received by the Contractor or the Council both dates inclusive.

PROVISIONS AS TO APPEAL

11. (a) Notice of Appeal if any shall be given to the Council within 14 days (exclusive of Saturdays and Sundays or other days observed as general holidays at Lloyd's) after the date of the publication by the Council of the Award and/or Interim Award(s).

  (b) Notice of Cross-Appeal if any shall be given to the Council within 14 days (exclusive of Saturdays and Sundays or other days observed as general holidays at Lloyd's) after notification by the Council to the parties of any Notice of Appeal. Such notification if sent by post shall be deemed received on the working day following the day of posting.

  (c) Notice of Appeal or Cross-Appeal shall be given to the Council by letter telex facsimile or in any other permanent form.

  (d) Upon receipt of Notice of Appeal the Council shall refer the Appeal to the hearing and determination of the Appeal Arbitrator(s) selected by it.

  (e) If any Notice of Appeal or Cross-Appeal is withdrawn the Appeal hearing shall nevertheless proceed in respect of such Notice of Appeal or Cross-Appeal as may remain.

  (f) Any Award on Appeal shall be final and binding on all the parties to that Appeal Arbitration whether they were represented either at the Arbitration or at the Appeal Arbitration or not.

CONDUCT OF THE APPEAL

12. (a) The Appeal Arbitrator(s) in addition to the powers of the Arbitrator under clauses 9(a) and 10 shall have power to:

  (i) admit the evidence which was before the Arbitrator together with the Arbitrator's notes and reasons for his Award and/or Interim Award(s) and any transcript of evidence and such additional evidence as he or they may think fit.

  (ii) confirm increase or reduce the sum awarded by the Arbitrator and to make such order as to the payment of interest on such sum as he or they may think fit.

  (iii) confirm revoke or vary any order and/or Declaratory Award made by the Arbitrator.

(b) The Appeal Arbitrator(s) and the Council may charge reasonable fees and expenses for their services in connection with the Appeal Arbitration whether it proceeds to a hearing or not and all such fees and expenses shall be treated as part of the costs of the Appeal Arbitration.

PROVISIONS AS TO PAYMENT

13. (a) In case of Arbitration if no Notice of Appeal be received by the Council in accordance with clause 11(a) the Council shall call upon the party or parties concerned to pay the amount awarded and in the event of non-payment shall subject to the Contractor first providing to the Council a satisfactory Undertaking to pay all the costs thereof realize or enforce the security and pay therefrom to the Contractor (whose receipt shall be a good discharge to it) the amount awarded to him together with interest if any. The Contractor shall reimburse the parties concerned to such extent as the Award is less than any sums paid on account or in respect of Interim Award(s).

(b) If Notice of Appeal be received by the Council in accordance with clause 11 it shall as soon as the Award on Appeal has been published by it call upon the party or parties concerned to pay the amount awarded and in the event of non-payment shall subject to the Contractor first providing to the Council a satisfactory Undertaking to pay all the costs thereof realize or enforce the security and pay therefrom to the Contractor (whose receipt shall be a good discharge to it) the amount awarded to him together with interest if any. The Contractor shall reimburse the parties concerned to such extent as the Award on Appeal is less than any sums paid on account or in respect of the Award or Interim Award(s).

(c) If any sum shall become payable to the Contractor as remuneration for his services and/or interest and/or costs as the result of an agreement made between the Contractor and the Owners or any of them the Council in the event of non-payment shall subject to the Contractor first providing to the Council a satisfactory Undertaking to pay all the costs thereof realize or enforce the security and pay therefrom to the Contractor (whose receipt shall be a good discharge to it) the said sum.

(d) If the Award and/or Interim Award(s) and/or Award on Appeal provides or provide that the costs of the Arbitration and/or of the Appeal Arbitration or any part of such costs shall be borne by the Contractor such costs may be deducted from the amount awarded or agreed before payment is made to the Contractor unless satisfactory security is provided by the Contractor for the payment of such costs.

(e) Without prejudice to the provisions of clause 4(c) the liability of the Council shall be limited in any event to the amount of security provided to it.

GENERAL PROVISIONS

14. The Master or other person signing this Agreement on behalf of the property to be salved enters into this Agreement as agent for the vessel her cargo freight bunkers stores and any other property thereon and the respective Owners thereof and binds each (but not the one for the other or himself personally) to the due performance thereof.

15. In considering what sums of money have been expended by the Contractor in rendering the services and/or in fixing the amount of the Award and/or Interim Award(s) and/or Award on Appeal the Arbitrator or Appeal Arbitrator(s) shall to such an extent and in so far as it may be fair and just in all the circumstances give effect to the consequences of any change or changes in the relevant rates of exchange which may have occurred between the date of termination of the services and the date on which the Award and/or Interim Award(s) and/or Award on Appeal is made.

16. Any Award notice authority order or other document signed by the Chairman of Lloyd's or any person authorised by the Council for the purpose shall be deemed to have been duly made or given by the Council and shall have the same force and effect in all respects as if it had been signed by every member of the Council.

17. The Contractor may claim salvage and enforce any Award or agreement made between the Contractor and the Owners against security provided under clause 4 if any in the name and on behalf of any Sub-Contractors Servants or Agents including Masters and members of the crews of vessels employed by him or by any Sub-Contractors in the services provided that he first provides a reasonably satisfactory indemnity to the Owners against all claims by or liabilities to the said persons.

18. When there is no longer any reasonable prospect of a useful result leading to a salvage reward in accordance with Convention Article 13 the owners of the vessel shall be entitled to terminate the services of the Contractor by giving notice to the Contractor in writing.

19. No person signing this Agreement or any party on whose behalf it is signed shall at any time or in any manner whatsoever offer provide make give or promise to provide demand or take any form of inducement for entering into this Agreement.

THE CONVENTION ARTICLES

Article 1. Definitions

(a) *Salvage operation* means any act or activity undertaken to assist a vessel or any other property in danger in navigable waters or in any other waters whatsoever

(b) *Vessel* means any ship or craft, or any structure capable of navigation

(c) *Property* means any property not permanently and intentionally attached to the shoreline and includes freight at risk

(d) *Damage to the environment* means substantial physical damage to human health or to marine life or resources in coastal or inland waters or areas ajacent thereto, caused by pollution, contamination, fire, explosion or similar major incidents

(e) *Payment* means any reward, remuneration or compensation due under this Convention

Article 8. Duties of the Salvor and of the Owner and Master

1. The salvor shall owe a duty to the owner of the vessel or other property in danger:

(a) to carry out the salvage operations with due care;

(b) in performing the duty specified in subparagraph (a), to exercise due care to prevent or minimize damage to the environment;

(c) whenever circumstances reasonably require, to seek assistance from other salvors; and

(d) to accept the intervention of other salvors when reasonably requested to do so by the owner or master of the vessel or other property in danger; provided however that the amount of his reward shall not be prejudiced should it be found that such a request was unreasonable

2. The owner and master of the vessel or the owner of other property in danger shall owe a duty to the salvor:

(a) to co-operate fully with him during the course of the salve operations;

(b) in so doing, to exercise due care to prevent or minimize damage to the environment; and

(c) when the vessel or other property has been brought to a place of safety, to accept redelivery when reasonably requested by the salvor to do so

Article 13. Criteria for fixing the reward

1. The reward shall be fixed with a view to encouraging salvage operations, taking into account the following criteria without regard to the order in which they are presented below:

(a) the salved value of the vessel and other property;

(b) the skill and efforts of the salvors in preventing or minimizing damage to the environment;

(c) the measure of success obtained by the salvor;

(d) the nature and degree of the danger;

(e) the skill and efforts of the salvors in salving the vessel, other property and life,

(f) the time used and expenses and losses incurred by the salvors;

(g) the risk of liability and other risks run by the salvors or their equipment;

(h) the promptness of the services rendered;

(i) the availability and use of vessels or other equipment intended for salvage operations;

(j) the state of readiness and efficiency of the salvor's equipment and the value thereof.

(2) Payment of a reward fixed according to paragraph 1 shall be made by all of the vessel and other property interests in proportion to their respective salved values

(3) The rewards, exclusive of any interest and recoverable legal costs that may be payable thereon, shall not exceed the salved value of the vessel and other property

Article 14. Special compensation

1. If the salvor has carried out salvage operations in respect of a vessel which by itself or its cargo threatened damage to the environment and has failed to earn a reward under Article 13 at least equivalent to the special compensation assessable in accordance with this Article, he shall be entitled to special compensation from the owner of that vessel equivalent to his expenses as herein defined

2. If, in the circumstances set out in paragraph 1, the salvor by his salvage operations has prevented or minimized damage to the environment, the special compensation payable by the owner to the salvor under paragraph 1 may be increased up to a maximum of 30% of the expenses incurred by the salvor. However, the Tribunal, if it deems it fair and just to do so and bearing in mind the relevant criteria set out in Article 13, paragraph 1, may increase such special compensation further, but in no event shall the total increase be more than 100% of the expenses incurred by the salvor

3. Salvor's expenses for the purpose of paragraphs 1 and 2 means the out-of-pocket expenses reasonably incurred by the salvor in the salvage operation and a fair rate for eqipment and personnel actually and reasonably used in the salvage operation, taking into consideration the criteria set out in Article 13, paragraph 1(h), (i) and (j)

4. The total special compensation under this article shall be paid only if and to the extent that such compensation is greater than any reward recoverable by the salvor under article 13

5. If the salvor has been negligent and has thereby failed to prevent or minimize damage to the environment, he may be deprived of the whole or part of any special compensation due under this Article

6. Nothing in this Article shall affect any right of recourse on the part of the owner of the vessel

For and on behalf of the Contractor	**For and on behalf of the Owners of property to be salved**
.... (To be signed either by the Contractor personally or by the Master of the salving vessel or other person whose name is inserted in line 4 of this Agreement.)	.... (To be signed by the Master or other person whose name is inserted in line 1 of this Agreement.)

CMI DRAFT INTERNATIONAL CONVENTION ON SALVAGE (MONTREAL 1981)

CHAPTER I. GENERAL PROVISIONS

Article 1.1. Definitions

1. *Salvage operations* means any act or activity undertaken to assist a vessel or any property in danger in whatever waters the act or activity takes place.

2. *Vessel* means any ship, craft or structure capable of navigation, including any vessel which is stranded, left by its crew or sunk.

3. *Property* includes freight for the carriage of the cargo, whether such freight be at the risk of the owner of the goods, the shipowner or the charterer.

4. *Damage to the environment* means substantial physical damage to human health or to marine life or resources in coastal or inland waters or areas adjacent thereto, caused by pollution, explosion, contamination, fire or similar major incidents.

5. *Payment* means any reward, remuneration, compensation or reimbursement due under the provisions of this Convention.

Article 1.2. Scope of Application

1. This Convention shall apply whenever judicial or arbitral proceedings relating to matters dealt with in this Convention are brought in a contracting State, as well as when the salvor belongs to, or the salving vessel or the vessel salved is registered in a contracting State.

2. However, the Convention does not apply:
   (a) when all vessels involved are vessels of inland navigation,
   (b) when all interested parties are nationals of the State where the proceedings are brought,
   (c) to warships or to other vessels owned or operated by a State and being used at the time of the salvage operations exclusively on governmental non-commercial services,
   (d) to removal of wrecks.

Article 1.3. Salvage operations controlled by Public Authorities

1. This Convention shall not affect any provisions of national law or international convention relating to salvage operations by or under the control of public authorities.

2. Nevertheless, salvors carrying out such salvage operations shall be entitled to avail themselves of the rights and remedies provided for in this Convention in respect of salvage operations.

3. The extent of which a public authority under a duty to perform salvage operations may avail itself of the rights and remedies provided for in this Convention shall be determined by the law of the State where such authority is situated.

Article 1.4. Salvage contracts

1. This Convention shall apply to any salvage operations save to the extent that the contract otherwise provides expressly or by implication.

2. The master shall have authority to conclude contracts for salvage operations on behalf of the owner of the vessel and of property thereon.

3. Nothing in this article shall affect the application of the provisions of article 1.5.

Article 1.5. Invalid contracts or contractual terms

A contract or any terms thereof may be annulled or modified if:

    (a) the contract has been entered into under undue influence or the influence of danger and its terms are inequitable, or,

    (b) the payment under the contract is in an excessive degree too large or too small for the services actually rendered.

CHAPTER II. PERFORMANCE OF SALVAGE OPERATIONS

Article 2.1. Duty of the owner and master

1. The owner and master of a vessel in danger shall take timely and reasonable action to arrange for salvage operations during which they shall co-operate fully with the salvor and shall use their best endeavours to prevent or minimize danger to the environment.

2. The owner and master of a vessel in danger shall require or accept other salvor's salvage services whenever it reasonably appears that the salvor already effecting salvage operations cannot complete them alone within a reasonable time or his capabilities are inadequate.

3. The owners of vessel or property salved and brought to a place of safety shall accept redelivery when reasonably requested by the salvors.

Article 2.2. Duties of the salvor

1. The salvor shall use his best endeavours to salve the vessel and property and shall carry out the salvage operations with due care. In so doing the salvor shall also use his best endeavours to prevent or minimize damage to the environment.

2. The salvor shall, whenever the circumstances reasonably require, obtain assistance from other available salvors and shall accept the intervention of other salvors when requested so to do or the owners or master pursuant to paragraph 2 of Article

2.1; provided, however, that the amount of this reward shall not be prejudiced should it be found that such intervention was not necessary.

Article 2.3. Duty to render assistance

1. Every master is bound, so far as he can do so without serious danger to his vessel and persons thereon, to render assistance to any person in danger of being lost at sea.

2. The contracting States shall adopt the measures necessary to enforce the duty set out in the preceding paragraph.

3. The owner of the vessel shall incur no liability for a breach of the duty of the master under paragraph 1.

Article 2.4. Co-operation of contracting States

A contracting State shall, whenever regulating or deciding upon matters relating to salvage operations such as admittance to ports of vessels in distress or the provision of facilities to salvors, take into account the need for co-operation between salvors, other interested parties and public authorities in order to ensure the efficient and successful performance of salvage operations for the purpose of saving life or property in danger as well as preventing damage to the environment in general.

CHAPTER III. RIGHTS OF SALVORS

Article 3.1. Conditions for reward

1. Salvage operations which have had a useful result give right to a reward.

2. Except as otherwise provided, no payment is due under this Convention if the salvage operations have no useful result.

3. This chapter shall apply, notwithstanding that the salved vessel and the vessel undertaking the salvage operations belong to the same owners.

Article 3.2. The amount of the reward

1. The reward shall be fixed with a view to encouraging salvage operations, taking into account the following considerations without regard to the order in which presented below:

    (a) the value of the property salved,

    (b) the skill and efforts of the salvors in preventing or minimizing damage to the environment,

    (c) the measure of success obtained by the salvor,

    (d) the nature and degree of the danger,

    (e) the efforts of the salvors, including the time used and expenses and losses incurred by the salvors,

    (f) the risk of liability and other risks run by the salvors or their equipment,

    (g) the promptness of the service rendered,

    (h) the availability and use of vessels or other equipment intended for salvage operations,

    (i) the state of readiness and efficiency of the salvor's equipment and the value thereof.

2. The reward under paragraph 1 of this Article shall not exceed the value of the property salved at the time of the completion of the salvage operation.

Article 3.3. Special compensation

1. If the salvor has carried out salvage operations in respect of a vessel which by itself or its cargo threatened damage to the environment and failed to earn a reward under Article 3.2 at least equivalent to the compensation assessable in accordance with Article 3.3, he shall be entitled to compensation from the owner of the vessel equivalent to his expenses as herein defined.

2. If, in the circumstances set out in paragraph 1 of Article 3.3 hereof, the salvor by his salvage operations has prevented or minimized damage to the environment, the compensation payable by the owner to the salvor thereunder may be increased, if and to the extent that the tribunal considers it fair and just to do so, bearing in mind the relevant criteria set out in paragraph 1 of Article 3.2 above, but in no event shall it be more than doubled.

3. "Salvor's expenses" for the purpose of paragraphs 1 and 2 of this Article means the out of pocket expenses reasonably incurred by the salvor in the salvage operation and a fair rate for equipment and personnel actually and reasonably used in the salvage operations, taking into consideration the criteria set out in paragraph 1 (g), (h) and (*i*) of Article 3.2.

4. Provided always that the total compensation under this Article shall be paid only if and to the extent that such compensation is greater than any reward recoverable by the salvor under Article 3.2.

5. If the salvor has been negligent and has thereby failed to prevent or minimize damage to the environment, he may be deprived of the whole or part of any payment due under this Article.

6. Nothing in the Article shall affect any rights of recourse on the part of the owner of the vessel.

Article 3.4. Apportionment between salvors

1. The apportionment of a reward between salvors shall be made on the basis of a criteria contained in Article 3.2.

2. The apportionment between the owner, master and other persons in the service of each salving vessel shall be determined by the law of the flag of that vessel. If the salvage has not been carried out from a vessel the apportionment shall be determined by the law governing the contract between the salvor and his employees.

Article 3.5. Salvage of persons

1. No remuneration is due from the persons whose lives are saved, but nothing in this Article shall affect the provisions of national law on this subject.

2. A salvor of human life, who has taken part in the services rendered on the occasion of the accident giving rise to salvage, is entitled to a fair share of the remuneration awarded to the salvor for salving the vessel or other property or preventing or minimizing damage to the environment.

Article 3.6 Services rendered under existing contracts

No payment is due under the provisions of this Convention unless the services rendered exceed what can be reasonably considered as due performance of a contract entered into before the danger arose.

Article 3.7 The effect of salvor's misconduct

A salvor may be deprived of the whole or part of the payment due under the provisions of this Convention to the extent that the salvage operations have become necessary or more difficult because of fault or neglect on his part or if the salvor has been guilty of fraud or other dishonest conduct.

Article 3.8 Prohibition by the owners or master

Services rendered notwithstanding the express and reasonable prohibition of the owner or the master shall not give rise to payment under the provisions of this Convention.

CHAPTER IV. CLAIMS AND ACTIONS

Article 4.1. Maritime lien

1. Nothing in this Convention shall affect the salvor's maritime lien under any international convention or national law.

2. The salvor may not enforce his maritime lien when satisfactory security for his claim, including interest and costs, has been duly tendered or provided.

3. The salved property shall not without the consent of the salvor be removed from the port or place at which the property first arrives after the completion of the salvage operations until satisfactory security has been put up for the salvor's claim.

Article 4.2. Duty to provide security

1. Upon the request of the salvor a person liable for a payment due under the provisions of this Convention shall provide satisfactory security for the claim, including interests and costs of the salvor.

2. Without prejudice to paragraph 1 of this Article, the owner of the salved vessel shall use his best endeavours to ensure that the owners of the cargo provide satisfactory security for the claims against them including interest and costs before the cargo is released.

Article 4.3. Interim payment

The court or arbitral tribunal having jurisdiction over the claim of the salvor may by interim decision order that the salvor shall be paid such amount on account as seems fair and just and on such terms including terms as to security where appropriate as may be fair and just according to the circumstances of the case. In the event of an interim payment the security provided under Article 4.2 shall be reduced accordingly.

Article 4.4. Limitation of actions

1. Any action relating to payment under the provisions of this Convention shall be time-barred if judicial or arbitral proceedings have not been instituted within a period of two years. The limitation period commences on the day on which the salvage operations are terminated.

2. The person against whom a claim is made at any time during the running of the limitation period may extend that period by a declaration to the claimant. This period may in the like manner be further extended.

3. An action for indemnity by a person liable may be instituted even after the expiration of the limitation period provided for in the preceding paragraphs, if brought within the time allowed by the law of the State where proceedings are instituted. However, the time allowed shall not be less than 90 days commencing from the day when the person instituting such action for indemnity has settled the claim or has been first adjudged liable in the action against himself.

4. Without prejudice to the preceding paragraphs all matters relating to limitation of action under this Article are governed by the law of the State where the action is brought.

Article 4.5. Jurisdiction

1. Unless the parties have agreed to the jurisdiction of another court or to arbitration, an action for payment under the provisions of this Convention may, at the option of the plaintiff, be brought in a court which, according to the law of the State where the court is situated, is competent and within the jurisdiction of which is situated one of the following places:
  (a) the principal place of business of the defandant,
  (b) the port to which the property salved has been brought,
  (c) the place where the property salved has been arrested,
  (d) the place where security for the payment has been given,
  (e) the place where the salvage operations took place.

2. With respect to vessels owned by a contracting State and used for commercial purposes, each State shall be subject to suit in the jurisdiction set forth in paragraph 1 of this article and shall waive all defences based on its status as a sovereign State. In the case of a vessel owned by a State and operated by a company which in that State is registered as the ship's operator, owner shall for the purpose of this paragraph mean such company.

3. Nothing in this article constitutes an obstacle to the jurisdiction of a contracting State for provisional or protective measures. The exercise by the salvor of his maritime lien whether by arrest or otherwise against the property salved shall not be treated as a waiver by the salvor of his rights, including the right to have claim for salvage remuneration adjudicated by court or arbitral proceedings in another jurisdiction.

Article 4.6. Interest

1. The right of the salvor to interest of any payment due under this Convention shall be determined according to the law of the State in which the court or arbitral tribunal seized of the case is situated.

Article 4.7. Publication of arbitral awards

1. Contracting States shall encourage, as far as possible and if need be with the consent of the parties, the publication of arbitral awards made in salvage cases.

CHAPTER V. LIABILITY OF SALVORS

Article 5.1. Limitation of liability

1. A contracting State may give salvors a right of limitation equivalent in manner and extent to the right provided for by the 1976 Convention on the Limitation for Maritime Claims.

MODIFICATION OF THE YORK— ANTWERP RULES 1974

YORK ANTWERP RULES RESOLUTION

The delegates representing the National Associations of Maritime Law of the States listed hereunder:
  1. Having noted with approval the amendments which have been made to Rule VI of the York-Antwerp Rules, 1974,
  2. Propose that the new text be referred to as the York-Antwerp Rules, 1974 as amended,
  3. Recommend that the York-Antwerp Rules, 1974 as amended 1990 should be applied in the adjustment of claims in General Average as soon as practicable after 1st October 1990.

RULE VI—SALVAGE

(a) Expenditure by the parties to the adventure in the nature of salvage, whether under contract or otherwise, shall be allowed in general average provided that the salvage operations were carried out for the purpose of preserving from peril the property involved in the common maritime adventure.

Expenditure allowed in general average shall include any salvage remuneration in which the skill and efforts of the salvors in preventing or minimizing damage to the environment such as is referred to in Art. 13 paragraph 1(b) of the International Convention on Salvage, 1989 have been taken into account.

(b) Special compensation payable to a salvor by the shipowner under Art. 14 of the said Convention to the extent specified in paragraph 4 of that Article or under any other provision similar in substance shall not be allowed in general average.

INDEX